FRAMING CANADIAN FEDERALISM

Historical Essays in Honour of John T. Saywell

Framing Canadian Federalism assembles an impressive range of scholars to consider many important issues that relate to federalism and the history of Canada's legal, political, and social evolution. Covering topics such as the Supreme Court of Canada, changing policies towards human rights, First Nations, as well as the legendary battles between Mitchell Hepburn and W.L. Mackenzie King, this collection illustrates the central role that federalism continues to play in the Canadian polity.

Editors Dimitry Anastakis and P.E. Bryden and the volume's contributors demonstrate the pervasive effects that federalism has on Canadian politics, economics, culture, and history, and provide a detailed framework in which to understand contemporary federalism. Written in honour of John T. Saywell's half-century of accomplished and influential scholarly work and teaching, *Framing Canadian Federalism* is a timely and fitting tribute to one of the discipline's foremost thinkers.

DIMITRY ANASTAKIS is an associate professor in the Department of History at Trent University.

P.E. BRYDEN is an associate professor in the Department of History at the University of Victoria.

John T. Saywell

EDITED BY DIMITRY ANASTAKIS AND
P.E. BRYDEN

Framing Canadian Federalism

Historical Essays in Honour of
John T. Saywell

UNIVERSITY OF TORONTO PRESS
Toronto Buffalo London

© University of Toronto Press Incorporated 2009
Toronto Buffalo London
www.utppublishing.com
Printed in Canada

ISBN 978-0-8020-9193-2 (cloth)
ISBN 978-0-8020-9436-0 (paper)

Printed on acid-free paper

Library and Archives Canada Cataloguing in Publication

Framing Canadian federalism : historical essays in honour of
  John T. Saywell / edited by Dimitry Anastakis and P.E. Bryden.

  Includes bibliographical references and index.
  ISBN 978-0-8020-9193-2 (bound)   ISBN 978-0-8020-9436-0 (pbk.)

  1. Federal government – Canada.   2. Canada – Politics and government.
  I. Anastakis, Dimitry, 1970–   II. Bryden, Penny   III. Saywell, John, 1929–

  JL27.F72 2009   320.471   C2008-907727-X

University of Toronto Press acknowledges the financial assistance to its
publishing program of the Canada Council for the Arts and the Ontario
Arts Council.

University of Toronto Press acknowledges the financial support for its
publishing activities of the Government of Canada through the Book
Publishing Industry Development Program (BPIDP).

This book has been published with the help of a grant from the Canadian
Federation for the Humanities and Social Sciences, through the Aid to
Scholarly Publications Program, using funds provided by the Social
Sciences and Humanities Research Council of Canada.

Contents

Acknowledgments

Our thanks fo to the T.H.B. Symons Trust Fund at Trent University for supporting the publication of this collection. At the University of Toronto Press, we would like to thank Len Husband, Frances Mundy, and our two anonymous reviewers for their helpful suggestions.

FRAMING CANADIAN FEDERALISM

Historical Essays in Honour of John T. Saywell

Introduction

DIMITRY ANASTAKIS AND P.E. BRYDEN

To a very great degree, the story of Canada is the story of federalism. There is an implied dichotomy to our national tale, a bifurcation of narratives, a form of federalism in the way we understand ourselves. In order to understand Canada, one must not only acknowledge the federal structure of our constitutional institutions, but also the federal tone of our story. All historians of Canada have dealt, in one way or another, with this federal reality. They have explored, in a multiplicity of ways, Canada's 'historic unwillingness to choose either "the one" or "the many" [which] has produced a complex sense of community and has facilitated the realization of values that require the multiplication (rather than the unification) of community.'[1] Our federal structure has produced not only complexities in our government institutions, but also an expectation of complexity in our community. The result has been fertile ground for the historian, lover of complication and conflict.

Few historians have engaged so directly in the analysis of federalism as John T. Saywell. Others have built their works on the foundation of our federal structure, or have written in the environment of our strangely divided sense of community, but rarely has there been a scholar who has deepened our knowledge of the actual functioning of the federal system so consistently over such a long career. In many ways, his approach to the historical study of federalism has mirrored the evolution of the field of federal study in Canada, and in many cases has pointed directly toward new and important areas of further inquiry for other scholars. This collection is, therefore, an attempt to take up the challenge that Saywell has been issuing now for more than half a century: look at the structure upon which this country was built, the ways that conflict has been institutionalized, the multiple manifestations of our federal design, and you will understand Canada (better).

The study of federalism in Canada began, as did Saywell himself, with an understanding of its most basic institutional structures. His *Office of the Lieutenant Governor* was an exploration of the role of the Crown, and the ways in which the federally appointed lieutenant-governors executed their peculiarly Canadian brand of power. In exploring this particular office, Saywell was contributing to a growing literature, as Canadianists explored the ways that their political and constitutional bodies functioned.[2] Studies of this kind were important in establishing the parameters of Canada's polity and identifying what was unique in the Canadian experience. While this type of scholarship was instrumental in establishing a solid foundation upon which to study Canadian development, such structural work continues still; a recent ten-volume 'democratic audit' explored the functioning of such components of the Canadian system as political parties, the courts, advocacy groups, and, of course, federalism.[3]

More recently, scholars have begun to ask probing questions about how institutions have changed as the nation evolves. The very meaning of federalism has recently come under review. Building on the example of the European Community and other quasi-federal combinations, as well as on an expanding understanding of First Nations in Canada, scholars such as Thomas Hueglin have broadened our definition of federalism by exploring it in its *treaty* variant.[4] This has proven to be a very useful concept in working out the relationship between constitutionally established national and provincial governments in Canada, and the treaty-established authority of First Nations governments.[5] Not only has work on the institutions that comprise the very framework of Canadian federalism continued well into the twenty-first century, but in expanding the meaning of federalism itself, scholars are opening up whole new avenues of inquiry. The institutional work that began with monographs like *The Office of the Lieutenant Governor* continues to inform our understanding of federalism.

But offices are filled with people, however, and while *The Office of the Lieutenant Governor* had its share of fascinating characters, it was, at heart, the study of an office rather than of the individuals who filled it. An important component of the body of work on federalism extends the analysis beyond the structures of federalism and into an examination of the people who have played the game. Few have been as intemperate in their approach to the federal system in Canada as Ontario's Depression premier, Mitch Hepburn. The subject of Saywell's sweeping biography, *'Just Call Me Mitch,'* Hepburn fought with the federal government during the 1930s to assume greater control over national finances, and during the 1940s to exert more effort on the battlefields. The biography makes it clear that Canada's federal landscape is populated with very political characters, whose actions often shake the assumptions and expectations of federalism to its very core.

First ministers, whether of the federal or the provincial variety, have always been popular areas for historical inquiry into the ways in which federalism shapes the political environment. Intergovernmental relations is therefore one of the most enduring areas of inquiry in the field of federalism. Whether examinations of the legendary battles of the past, like Christopher Armstrong's *Politics of Federalism* and Garth Stevenson's *Ex Uno Plures*, or exposés of more recent constitutional wrangling, like Patrick Monahan's *Inside Meech Lake*, these sorts of intergovernmental studies have been, and no doubt will continue to be, a mainstay of Canadian academic output. It is surely a commentary on the Canadian identity that our national gossip revolves upon how premiers have bested prime ministers – and the reverse – around the constitutional negotiating table. *'Just Call Me Mitch'* was an important addition to that literature.

One of the most popular figures in the battles over our federal structure, and hence the subject of a huge number of both scholarly and popular studies, is Pierre Elliott Trudeau. Out of all the first ministers, Trudeau is probably the one most closely associated with the federal system: a trenchant commentator on federalism and the place of French Canadians within its structure, as well as the perpetrator of a more centralist vision of Canada through the constitutional battles of 1982, Meech Lake, and the Charlottetown Accord, Trudeau has personified the federal system in Canada. Any scholar who tackles him as a subject of biography must necessarily deal with his vision of federalism.[6] Saywell recognized the significance of this vision early on, long before Trudeau had imposed it on the Constitution Act, 1982. In writing the introduction to what is perhaps the best known document on federalism in Canada, Trudeau's *Federalism and the French Canadians*, Saywell brought the politician's ideas to the attention of English Canadians. This was an individual who was larger than life, and whose impact on Canadian federalism would, in Saywell's words, 'bear watching.'[7]

But just as individuals are important characters in these tales, so too have the events, issues, and policies become important players in the story of federalism in Canada. As our understanding of the nature of intergovernmental conflict has increased, scholars have become increasingly interested in examining the points of contact between the two levels of government. Certain policies have engendered more debate than others because of their constitutional ambiguity. Medicare, for example, that most quintessential Canadian program, has been the subject of a number of studies that add to our understanding of federalism.[8] Similarly, pensions and education have occasioned intergovernmental squabbling, and therefore attracted academic attention to the policies themselves.[9] New areas of policy interest in government almost automatically have implications for federalism, so pervasive are the structural dynamics in Canada. Climate change and serious concerns over global warming have prompted policy makers and scholars alike to pay more attention to the environment. How our bifurcated system will deal with environmental regulation and related topics has been the subject of a growing number of studies.[10] In mapping the ways in which governments have struggled for control of these policy areas, we gain a better understanding of the way the federal system works in practice.

Similarly, a focus on the actual strategies of federalism has also proven to be fertile territory for scholars. The spending power, which has been the tool most effectively used to establish social security programs, has attracted some interest, but the broader question of how tax money has been shared is of enduring fascination. Economists are particularly drawn to examine questions of fiscal federalism and issues such as equalization, but their interest has been infectious and students of other disciplines are beginning to jump on this bandwagon.[11]

Each of these types of studies focuses on a issue in the field of federalism rather than on an institution. Building on the earlier work on the structures of federalism, these procedural inquiries invariably stem from an interest in relationships: how do governments interact, under what circumstances do they collide, and what are the outcomes of such contests? Saywell provided a very useful look inside one very dysfunctional intergovernmental relationship – the one between Mackenzie King and Mitch Hepburn – and in the process illuminated the human nature of the federal-provincial clash. But he has also made a significant contribution to one of the most recent frontiers in the study of federalism in Canada, marrying the original structural studies with an examination of the relationships – both human and governmental – that resulted. *The Lawmakers* extends our understanding of federalism by illuminating the structural realities that the Constitution imposes with an understanding of the process of 'making' the law that the judiciary undertakes.

Our understanding of Canadian federalism has benefited a great deal from the insights of scholars working on the courts in Canada. Although the Charter of Rights and Freedoms has, to a certain degree, drawn scholarly attention away from federalism as the Supreme Court itself has become preoccupied with Charter cases, the effect of the judiciary on our current political environment ensures that there will continue to be assessments of the role it plays in determining the balance of power. Some are overtly political, like Rainer Knopf and F.L. Morton's *Charter Revolution and the Court Party* and James B. Kelly's *Governing with the Charter: Legislative and Judicial Activism and Framers' Intent*; others try to trace the evolution of federalism in the context of court decisions, like Katherine Swinton's *Supreme Court and Canadian Federalism* and Gerald Baier's *Courts and Federalism*.[12] Regardless, though, they add to an understanding of the way Canada's most pervasive institutional framework functions and the myriad ways that scholars have developed to investigate the inner workings of federalism.

As a historian, John Saywell has played a key role in mining the archives for material to better understand the structure of federalism. In *Office of the Lieutenant Governor, 'Just Call Me Mitch,'* and *The Lawmakers*, as well as in twenty years of the *Canadian Annual Review* and countless other projects, he has demonstrated the ways in which we must examine the institution of federalism in order to fully understand it.[13] In doing this, he has also inspired a generation of scholars who have taken the study of federalism in new directions, adding new chapters to our national story.

The role of lawmakers in shaping Canadian history provides a useful entry into this collection's first trio of articles, all of which address the narratives of federalism that remain a central feature of Saywell's work. Blake Brown's article, 'One Version of History: The Supreme Court of Canada's Use of History in the *Quebec Secession Reference*,' begins the collection and is perhaps the first assessment of how Canada's chief lawmakers, the justices of the Supreme Court, (mis)used history to explain their reasoning in one of the most contentious and important decisions in recent Canadian history. Brown shows that the Court created a version of Canada's constitutional past that was 'positive, bland, and seemingly uncontroversial' and missed an opportunity to educate a generation of Canadians, law students, and legal scholars.

Instead, the Court's narrative was designed to reflect current-day assumptions about Canada and its history and to deflect the question of secession back upon the politicians. In doing so, Brown effectively argues that the lawmakers need to pay better attention to the professional historians, and to the history itself, in making their decisions. Blake's work reminds us also that the historical truism 'What is past is prologue' remains profound: battles over Canada's constitutional past are really fights over the future direction of the Canadian polity.

Propagating competing narratives of Canada's past to create imagined communities is not just a judicial or national prerogative. Politicians, of course, are famous for doing so. In a federal state such as Canada's, regional politicians are particularly well versed in building entire movements upon the alleged injustices or misinterpretations of history. Thus, another narrative of federalism comes to us from Stephen Henderson, who explores the aspirations of Nova Scotia politicians in the wake of one of Canada's most important royal commissions in '"A New Federal Vision": Nova Scotia and the Rowell-Sirois Report, 1938–1948.' Henderson's article shows, from a Nova Scotia perspective, that the nitty-gritty of federal-provincial diplomacy surrounding the Rowell-Sirois Commission was not the usual arcane constitutional minutiae. It was a vision of how Confederation should work, one that was based upon a classical conception of the federation, and one that ultimately allowed strong provinces within a united, strong, and sharing Canada. In the views of Angus L. Macdonald and his fellow Nova Scotians, provincialism was nationalism.

Similarly, Penny Bryden examines another narrative of federalism in her article, 'The Obligations of Federalism: Ontario and the Origins of Equalization.' Bryden explains how Ontario articulated its own vision of how the federation should function when it came to sharing the wealth of the nation. Tracing the discourse surrounding federal-provincial taxing arrangements that emerged from the Second World War and into the post-war period, Bryden shows how Ontario politicians sought to protect the province's advantageous financial position from the machinations of a centralizing federal government. In doing so, Ontario Premier Leslie Frost, like Nova Scotia's Angus L. Macdonald, articulated a unique vision of his province within the federation. Frost ultimately ended up supporting a version of equalization that was designed to ensure Ontario's pre-eminent position, yet at the same time was an important step in establishing a key, yet often contentious, aspect of Canadian federalism.

These three articles examine different narratives of federalism: how judges, or provinces, or politicians have conceived of the federation, and how they wanted their views to shape the future of federal-provincial relations. All three articles reflect the salience of historic federalist conceptions of nation and region upon contemporary Canadian narratives of space and place: from the ongoing battles over resources and equalization between the federal government and new/old provincial oil sheikdoms in Newfoundland, Nova Scotia, and Alberta, to Ontario's (and all the provinces') complaints about a fiscal imbalance. Clearly, if there is a lesson to be learned here, it is that when it comes to using the past to shape the narratives of the future, the more things change, the more they stay the same.

Exploring and exposing grand narratives, however, was only one segment of Saywell's work. People were just as important as abstract legal theories, or conceptions of state and society. In detailing the battles over the office of lieutenant-governor, or the federal-provincial struggles between Ontario Premier Mitch Hepburn and Prime Minister William Lyon Mackenzie King, Saywell was equally at ease addressing the conflicting personalities of the day, and contending with the legal and political ramifications upon society. The evolving federal condition has had unintended consequences and has had unexpected impact upon groups of people, be they First Nations or the unemployed. Indeed, as the next two chapters illustrate, these two groups became, in their own ways, both actors and victims in the never-ending tension between federal and provincial governments.

Mark Kuhlberg's '"As the Indians were wards of the Dominion Government": The Anishinabe of McIntyre Bay in the Hepburn-King Constitutional Battle' utilizes Saywell's expansive biography of Hepburn to bring to light more carefully the sometimes less well-known consequences of federal-provincial conflict. The Anishinabe of Northwestern Ontario acutely felt the chill between Parliament Hill and Queen's Park in the Second World War era as the two levels of government squared off over First Nations and natural resources. In Kuhlberg's tale, 'Ontario seemed to delight in using the aboriginals as pawns in its game of one-upmanship with the dominion government,' a consequence of the poor intergovernmental relations and sometimes worse interpersonal relations between federal and Ontario politicians.

Poor intergovernmental relations during the administration of Liberal Prime Minister William Lyon Mackenzie King is well known to historians and observers of federalism. The depth of conflict over responsibilities to the unemployed in British Columbia during the Depression years is examined by Richard Rajala in his 'From "On-to-Ottawa" to "Bloody Sunday": Unemployment Relief and British Columbia Forests, 1935–1939.' Echoing Saywell's understanding of King's conflict with

Mitch Hepburn's Ontario during this difficult period, Rajala provides a detailed examination of the battles between King and Premier Duff Patullo over the plight of the unemployed and indigent in the 1930s. Rajala explains both the nature and events surrounding this federal-provincial battle over providing (or not providing, in King's case) some sort of relief for thousands of unemployed men in this volatile period, and the agency that these people exhibited in demanding some form of support from either, and both levels of government.

The Kuhlberg and Rajala articles both illustrate how federalism affects groups of people, in contradistinction to, yet in conjunction with, the important discourse of narratives and themes in federalism yesterday and today. We can see how the federal-provincial battles over the Anishinabe of the mid-twentieth century echo the political sparring over the Kesheshewan in the early twenty-first century, or how the politics of the unemployed during the Great Depression can inform our understanding of recent federal-provincial battles over changes to the employment insurance system, or manpower training. These people – First Nations or the unemployed – have played and continue to play a role in their own stories. Sometimes there are casualties in the federal-provincial arena, while there are also heroes who use federalism's sometimes undefined edges to empower themselves and display an agency that historians often overlook.

Canadian federalism has not remained static and over the broad sweep of time has had to project itself into an untested and unknown milieu. In his examination of institutions, people, and power, Saywell's work has shown that federalism has evolved. Government responsibilities, jurisdictions, and political, social, and economic change have all ensured that Canadian federalism has adapted to changing realities. In 1867 there was no notion of 'human rights' as a government responsibility; no one could have imagined the vast impact of the automobile on all aspects of life, nor could anyone have predicted that provinces would one day play a role in international and trade relations, or that the federal government would one day play a role in education, or research and development.

But all of these things did indeed happen, and all of them underscore the projections of federalism into new circumstances. An excellent example comes from Michael Behiels and his examination of 'Canada and the Implementation of International Instruments of Human Rights: A Federalist Conundrum, 1919–1982.' After the Second World War, the federal government sought to resolve a longstanding question in Canadian federalism: were provinces bound by federally ratified international treaties within their spheres of jurisdiction? This was a particular issue for human rights, which had come to the forefront of international discourse after 1945. Behiels examines the efforts of Pierre Trudeau to bind all Canadian governments to a new notion of individual rights that would sever the Gordian knot of this human rights conundrum once and for all, and forge a 'mutually reinforcing interplay between Canada's international human rights commitments and the Canadian Charter of Rights and Freedoms.' This projection of federalism onto a new area of conflict reflects perfectly the ever-shifting parameters and limits of jurisdictions and spheres that have bedevilled policy makers and academics alike for generations.

Another new projection of Canadian life that collided with federalism that emerged in the twentieth century was the impact of the automobile. Dimitry Anastakis's 'Cars, Conflict and Cooperation: The Federalism of the Canadian Auto Industry,' further illustrates the adaptability of federalism, in this case in addressing the vast economic changes engendered by this paradigm-shifting technology, and illustrates the two-way street that battles over jurisdiction became over time. Indeed, as Anastakis shows, federal-provincial relations over the automobile industry shifted from one in which the provincial governments (chiefly Ontario's) played virtually no role, to one in which a new-found cooperative federalism emerged as both Ontario and the federal government sought to ensure the ongoing success of what emerged as Canada's most important economic sector.

As with the automobile, the emergence of international trade became a benchmark of twentieth-century Canadian economic development, one that, like human rights, had implications for federal-provincial relations on the international scene. Bruce Muirhead's 'Ottawa, the Provinces, and the Evolution of Canadian Trade Policy since 1963' shows how provincial governments became active players on the trade file after the Second World War, particularly in matters relating to the General Agreement on Tariffs and Trade (GATT) and the 1989 Free Trade Agreement (FTA), to the point where 'in 2006, one could almost speak of co-responsibility' between the two levels of government. Again, as with human rights, economic issues in the twentieth century became a two-way street, where federal and provincial spheres of jurisdiction increasingly overlapped, or whose boundaries blurred beyond recognition.

Provinces, however, were not the only governments crossing jurisdictional boundaries. As Paul Axelrod shows in his 'Implementing the "In-

novation" Strategy: Post-secondary Education in the Chrétien Years,'
in the 1990s the federal government projected itself onto post-secondary education, a traditional provincial responsibility, during a period in
which the federal government's influence receded in many other areas
of Canadian life. The vast array of federal educational initiatives, from
the Canada Research Chairs to the Millennium Scholarships to the Canadian Foundation for Innovation, essentially all intruded upon provincial jurisdiction – with little if any criticism. Provincial governments,
including that of Quebec, were not averse to this particular use of the
federal spending power, it seems. But, as Axelrod remarks at the end of
his paper, this 'paradigm shift' towards federal support for universities
and their people may not last forever.

The new territories embraced by both levels of government in the
twentieth and twenty-first centuries capture the projection of federalism
in different and new directions. Changing circumstances have prompted adaptation by federal and provincial governments and actors – when
provinces penetrate the national sphere in the need to adapt to changing
economic patterns or free trade, or when national governments move
into education, research, and development to adapt to the realities of a
knowledge-based, global economy. Clearly, the articles illustrate that
understanding these developments is not just about the traditions of
jurisdictional blurring, but that these are new departures, not just for the
study of federalism, but in Canadian federalism's actual functioning.

The last article in this collection acts as a coda to Blake Brown's head-
note, and a reminder of Saywell's main intellectual concern – the role of
judges and courts in Canadian federalism. Peter Russell's 'The Unreal-
ized Benefits of Canada's Unfederal Judicial System' also reminds us of
the salience of federalism in contemporary Canadian life. In assessing
the evolution and current state of Canada's courts, Russell examines
how the unitary court system established in the British North America
Act could frame a new approach to solving the administratively dysfunctional operation of the confusing federal/provincial court system.
As such, Russell delves deep into Canada's constitutional past to recon-
nect readers with what seems to be a sensible remedy to what he calls a
'dysfunctional and illogical two-tier system of provincial trial courts.'

As with all of the other articles in this Festschrift, this is perhaps the
collection's most important lesson: that federalism's past frames its
future, and that one cannot understand how Canada may evolve in
the twenty-first century, without understanding how it evolved in the
nineteenth and twentieth centuries. Saywell's work, whether it dealt

with people, provinces, or power, was always in some way connected to Canada's 'federal condition,' and illustrates the centrality of federalism in understanding so many issues, both past and present.

NOTES

1 Samuel LaSelva, *The Moral Foundations of Canadian Federalism: Paradoxes, Achievements, and Tragedies of Nationhood* (Montreal and Kingston: McGill-Queen's University Press, 1996), 9.
2 See, for example, Norman Ward, *The Canadian House of Commons: Representation* (Toronto: University of Toronto Press, 1950).
3 William Cross, *Political Parties* (Vancouver: UBC Press, 2004); Joanna Everitt and Lisa Young, *Advocacy Groups* (Vancouver: UBC Press, 2004); Ian Greene, *The Courts* (Vancouver: UBC Press, 2006); Jennifer Smith, *Federalism* (Vancouver: UBC Press, 2004).
4 Thomas O. Hueglin, 'From Constitutional to Treaty Federalism: A Comparative Perspective,' *Publius* 30, no. 4 (2000): 137–53; Thomas Hueglin and Alan Fenna, *Comparative Federalism: A Systematic Inquiry* (Peterborough: Broadview, 2006).
5 See, for example, Graham White, 'Treaty Federalism in Northern Canada: Aboriginal-government land claims boards,' *Publius* 32, no. 2 (2002): 89–114.
6 Stephen Clarkson and Christina McCall, *Trudeau and Our Times*, vol. 1, *The Magnificent Obsession* (Toronto: McClelland and Stewart, 1990); John English, *Citizen of the World: The Life of Pierre Elliott Trudeau*, vol. 1, *1919–1968* (Toronto: Knopf, 2006).
7 John T. Saywell, introduction to *Federalism and the French Canadians*, by P.E. Trudeau (Toronto: McClelland and Stewart, 1968).
8 See, for example, Keith Banting and Stan Corbett, eds., *Health Policy and Federalism: A Comparative Perspective on Multi-Level Governance* (Montreal and Kingston: McGill-Queen's University Press, 2001); P.E. Bryden, *Planners and Politicians: The Liberal Party and Social Policy, 1957–1968* (Montreal and Kingston: McGill-Queen's University Press, 1997); Gwendolyn Gray, *Federalism and Health Policy: The Development of Health Systems in Canada and Australia* (Toronto: University of Toronto Press, 1991); Carolyn Tuohy, *Policy and Politics in Canada: Institutionalized Ambivalence* (Philadelphia: Temple University Press, 1992).
9 Matthew Hayday, *Bilingual Today, United Tomorrow: Official Languages in Education and Canadian Federalism* (Montreal and Kingston: McGill-Queen's University Press, 2006).

10 Kathryn Harrison, *Passing the Buck: Federalism and Canadian Environmental Policy* (Vancouver: UBC Press, 1996).
11 See, for example, Robin W. Boadway and Paul A.R. Hobson, eds., *Equalization: Its Contribution to Canada's Fiscal and Economic Progress* (Toronto: University of Toronto Press, 1998); Keith Banting, Douglas Brown, and Thomas Courchene, eds., *The Future of Fiscal Federalism* (Kingston: School of Policy Studies, Queen's University, 1994).
12 Gerald Baier, *Courts and Federalism: Judicial Doctrine in the United States, Australia and Canada* (Vancouver: UBC Press, 2006); Rainer Knopf and F.L. Morton, *Charter Revolution and the Court Party* (Peterborough: Broadview, 2000); James B. Kelly, *Governing with the Charter: Legislative and Judicial Activism and Framers' Intent* (Vancouver: UBC Press, 2005); Katherine Swinton, *Supreme Court and Canadian Federalism: The Laskin-Dickson Years* (Toronto: Carswell, 1990).
13 Saywell's career has spanned six decades and the amount of material he produced over that time that has implications for our understanding of federalism is vast. In addition to the works discussed above, interested readers should also be aware of his indispensable textbook, edited with George Vegh, *Making the Law: The Courts and the Constitution* (Toronto: Copp Clarke Pitman, 1991); 'The Cabinet of 1896,' in *Cabinet Formation and Bicultural Relations* (Ottawa: Studies of the Royal Commission on Bilingualism and Biculturalism, 1965), 37–46; 'The Crown and the Politicians: The Canadian Succession Question, 1891–1896,' *Canadian Historical Review* 37, no. 4 (1956): 309–37; 'Reservation Revisited: Alberta, 1937,' *Canadian Journal of Economics and Political Science* 28, no. 7 (1961): 367–72; 'Sir Joseph Trutch, British Columbia's First Lieutenant-Governor,' *British Columbia Historical Quarterly* 19, no. 12 (1955): 71–92.

1 One Version of History: The Supreme Court of Canada's Use of History in the *Quebec Secession Reference*

R. BLAKE BROWN

This article considers and critiques the vision of Canadian constitutional history presented by the Supreme Court of Canada in its 1998 Secession Reference decision.[1] The Supreme Court held that while Quebec does not have the right to unilaterally secede, the rest of Canada would have a constitutional obligation to negotiate Quebec's withdrawal from the federation after a clear majority of Quebec citizens voted yes on a clear question of sovereignty. As part of its decision, the Court offered (after many years of avoiding the topic) an extended consideration of the history of Canadian federalism.

This article demonstrates that the Court crafted a historical narrative that supported its judgment, and, more broadly, imagined Canada as a nation founded upon principles to which many Canadians now aspire. Drawing upon Benedict Anderson's definition of a nation as an 'imagined political community,'[2] Daniel Francis reminds us that historical narratives explain 'where our institutions and values came from,' and that 'out of this shared experience of the past is supposed to emerge a "national identity."' The Court concluded that the evolution of the nation's constitutional arrangements has been characterized historically by 'adherence to the rule of law, respect for democratic institutions, the accommodation of minorities, insistence that governments adhere to constitutional conduct and a desire for continuity and stability.'[3] From this history, the Court drew four unwritten but 'foundational constitutional principles' said to underlie the constitution, which the Court then used to help resolve the reference: federalism, democracy, constitutionalism and the rule of law, and respect for minority rights.[4]

In drawing out these principles, the Court carefully crafted a narrative that omitted more troublesome historical developments. This selectivity is not surprising. 'Memory implies its opposite – forgetting,' Francis tells us, since 'we forget as much as we remember, and what we choose to forget tells us as much about us as what we choose to remember.'[5] By carefully selecting what to remember and what to forget of Canada's constitutional story, the Court contributed to Canadian nation building in the course of, ironically, laying out a legal framework for the dissolution of Canada.[6]

In its efforts to support current national myths, and to deflect the secession issue back upon Canadian politicians, the Court entered clumsily into numerous debates about the history of Confederation and federalism. Surprisingly, the Supreme Court did not cite a single professional historian in writing its history of Confederation. As a result, the Court offered a vision of Confederation that was positive, bland, and seemingly uncontroversial. How Canadian. But also how inaccurate. The Court's carefully written history was designed to support its legal conclusions, but, in so doing, it missed an opportunity to educate a generation of Canadian lawyers and law students about the debate, argument, and protest that marked the creation and evolution of the Canadian federation.

This article begins by briefly outlining the political background of the Secession Reference and summarizing the Court's judgment. The bulk of the article then analyses three aspects of the decision. It first identifies the Court's historical methodology and queries whether the Court should have considered alternative interpretations of Canada's constitutional development. It demonstrates that the Court used a poorly supported 'progressive evolutionary functionalist' approach to Canadian constitutional history at the expense of employing alternative, and potentially fruitful, interpretations. Second, it then interrogates the validity of the constitutional principles said to support the rest of the judgment by assessing the Court's claims regarding the causes and goals of Confederation. It demonstrates that the Court appears to have omitted mention of a number of factors that led to Confederation because of the Court's desire to support its unstated principles. Finally, this article evaluates the Court's adoption of a 'compact' theory of federalism. It lays bare the difficulty of applying the compact idea to the entrance of Nova Scotia and New Brunswick into Confederation, and reveals the inconsistencies of this theory in relation to the Court's own comments concerning the Nova Scotia secession movement of the nineteenth century and the patriation of Canadian constitution in the early 1980s. In sum, this article demonstrates that the Court used history to identify unwritten principles to support its judgment by offering a poorly substantiated progressive evolutionary functionalist analysis, in which it did not consider factors inconsistent with its interpretation of Confederation or post-1867 developments in Canadian federalism.

The Political Background

Only a brief summary of the political events immediately preceding the Secession case can be offered here.[7] In 1994, the Parti Québécois, led by Jacques Parizeau, defeated the Liberals in a provincial election. Premier Parizeau tabled a draft bill in the National Assembly in December 1994, An Act Respecting the Sovereignty of Québec, which set out six steps for Quebec independence, including the passage of a sovereignty bill by the National Assembly, a successful referendum, and the drafting of a Quebec constitution during negotiations with Canada to settle debts and property issues. In June 1995, Parizeau agreed with Lucien Bouchard, the leader of the Bloc Québécois, and Mario Dumont, the leader of the Action démocratique du Québec, on a 'tripartite agreement.' The three leaders asserted that after a yes vote in a referendum, the National Assembly would proclaim Quebec's sovereignty and begin negotiations with Canada on a new economic and political partnership. In the 30 October 1995 referendum, a tiny majority of Quebecers – 50.58 per cent – rejected secession.[8]

The Liberal government of Prime Minister Jean Chrétien, startled by how close the separatists had come to winning the referendum, pursued simultaneously two plans to prevent Quebec from separating in the future. First, it sought reconciliation with Quebec by, for example, tabling motions in the House of Commons and Senate to recognize that Quebec was a distinct society. Second, it sought to clarify if Quebec could legally separate, and, if so, what this process would look like. The 1995 referendum had exposed a vacuum in Canadian law with respect to the right of any province or territory to leave the federation.[9] The federal government thus sought to establish a legal framework, preferably on federalist terms, to guide future attempts at secession. To this end, in September 1996 it submitted reference questions to the Supreme Court of Canada regarding the legality of unilateral secession by Quebec.[10]

The Supreme Court of Canada's Secession Reference Decision

The Quebec government refused to participate in the reference; as a result, the Supreme Court appointed an amicus curiae to put forward legal arguments in opposition to the federal position. Lawyers for the federal government, the amicus curiae, and a number of interveners, argued the Secession Reference before the Supreme Court over four days in February 1998. A unanimous Court handed down its decision on 20 August.

The federal government had referred three questions to the Court pursuant to section 53 of the Supreme Court Act:[11]

1 Under the Constitution of Canada, can the National Assembly, legislature, or government of Quebec effect the secession of Quebec from Canada unilaterally?
2 Does international law give the National Assembly, legislature, or government of Quebec the right to effect the secession of Quebec from Canada unilaterally? In this regard, is there a right to self-determination under international law that would give the National Assembly, legislature, or government of Quebec the right to effect the secession of Quebec from Canada unilaterally?
3 In the event of a conflict between domestic and international law on the right of the National Assembly, legislature, or government of Quebec to effect the secession of Quebec from Canada unilaterally, which would take precedence in Canada?[12]

In answering the first question, the Court said that the constitution is more than a written text. Rather, it includes the entire system of unwritten principles that underlie the structure of the constitution and govern the exercise of constitutional authority. These principles, the Court said, inform the constitutional rights and obligations if a clear majority of Quebecers voted on a clear question in favour of secession. The arguments in favour of unilateral secession relied on the principle of democracy – that is, that the people of Quebec should have the right to secede if that was the will of the National Assembly or as expressed in a referendum. Democracy, however, means more than simple majority rule. According to the Court, democracy exists in the larger context of other constitutional values that must be balanced with the democratic principle. To identify these values, the Court considered the history of Confederation. History thus played a key role in the reference, as the Court used its historical interpretation of Canadian federalism to select the unwritten principles that then informed the rest of its judgment. The Court concluded that the provinces and territories had created close economic, social, political, and cultural ties based on the shared principles of 'federalism; democracy; constitutionalism and the rule of law; and respect for minorities.'[13] A democratic decision of Quebecers in favour of secession would create tensions between these principles. The Court held that a clear majority vote in Quebec on a clear question in favour of secession would confer democratic legitimacy on the secession initiative, but Quebec could not invoke a right of self-determination to dictate the terms of a proposed secession. The democratic vote could not push aside the principles of federalism and the rule of law, the rights of individuals and minorities, or the operation of democracy in the rest of Canada.

In its response to question number two – that is, whether international law gave Quebec the right to secede from Canada unilaterally – the Court considered the claim that international law supports a right to self-determination belonging to all 'peoples.' The Court said that a right to secession arises only under the principle of self-determination of a people where 'a people' was governed as part of a colonial empire, in which 'a people' was subject to alien subjugation, domination, or exploitation. If these conditions do not exist, then peoples are expected to achieve self-determination within the framework of their existing state. According to the Court, a state whose government represents the whole of the people on a basis of equality and without discrimination, and respects the principles of self-determination in its internal arrangements, is entitled (under international law) to maintain its territorial integrity and to have that territorial integrity recognized by other states. Quebec, the Court decided, did not meet the threshold of a colonial people or an oppressed people, nor could it claim that Quebecers had been denied meaningful access to government to pursue their political, economic, cultural, and social development. Quebec, therefore, had no right under international law to secede from Canada unilaterally. Finally, the Court held in response to the third question that, in view of its answers to questions one and two, there was no conflict between domestic and international law.

Academic Treatment of the *Secession Reference*

The *Secession Reference* generated a veritable cottage industry of commentary. Politically, both Ottawa and Quebec declared victory.[14]

Political scientists and legal scholars have been intrigued by several aspects of the case. Political scientist Daniel Drache and law professor Patrick Monahan speculate on the Court's concern for itself. They suggest that the Secession decision indicates that the 'justices were not distinguished actors but together formed a court that wanted to guarantee its own survival and integrity as Canada's primary legal institution.'[15] Political scientist Stephen Clarkson is also interested in the 'message' the Court's judgment sends: he finds that the Court successfully 'pulled off a coup,' by, among other things, denying separatists a provocation to ground further referendums.[16] Other political scientists and legal experts have commented upon the importance of the decision for the constitution's amending formula,[17] and for Aboriginal law in Canada.[18] Others have criticized the Court for writing a judgment that had more than a few loose ends. For example, the Court chose not to define what a 'clear question' would be for a referendum or what a 'clear majority' meant.[19]

Despite the extensive commentary on the case by politicians, legal experts, and political scientists, little attention has been paid to the Court's historical claims in the judgment that identified and supported the principles said to underlie Canada's constitution. Unfortunately, John Saywell devotes only a few paragraphs to the case in the conclusion of his history of the Canadian constitution. Saywell calls the Supreme Court's judgment a 'long and sometimes elegant essay, blending law and political culture.' He does not, however, analyse the Court's historical claims.[20] Other commentators simply note and accept the historical discussion.[21] A few have expressed concern with the Court's decision to rest much of its Secession judgment on unwritten principles,[22] but only Dale Gibson and Mark Walters have offered some sustained historical criticism of the Court's decision to draw upon unwritten constitutional principles.

Gibson questions the Court's assertion that 'the protection of minority rights' is a fundamental organizing principle in Canadian constitutional history. The Court wrote that 'the protection of minority rights had a long history before the enactment of the *Charter*,' and that 'the protection of minority rights was clearly an essential consideration in the design of the constitutional structure even at the time of Confederation.' The Court noted that Canada's 'record of upholding the rights of minorities is not a spotless one,' but that the goal was 'one towards which Canadians have been striving since Confederation,' and that the 'process has not been without some successes.'[23] These statements lead Gibson to conclude that if 'one were to lay bare Canada's historical foundations with utter candour and thoroughness ... some darker roots would be exposed: racism, political patronage, profiteering and so on.' Further, Gibson asks, rightly, 'How can they be avoided without distorting history?'[24] The Court, however, chose not to mention the long history of cases in which Canada's minorities sought in vain constitutional protections from Canada's courts, including the Supreme Court.[25]

Walters, a law professor and legal historian at Queen's University, has offered an especially nuanced critique of the Court's use of underlying principles. He evaluates the Supreme Court's claim that unwritten laws – *lex non scripta* – were exported from England into the Canadian constitution as unwritten principles through the preamble of the BNA Act, which refers to Canada having a constitution 'similar in Principle to that of the United Kingdom.'[26] After a careful analysis of common law thought over several centuries, colonial legislation, and Confederation debates, Walters concludes that it 'simply cannot be maintained seriously that the framers of the BNA Act intended the preamble's reference to the UK constitution to mean that judges thereafter were to regard certain unwritten British constitutional norms as justiciable constraints upon Canadian legislative authority.'[27]

Several factors possibly explain the general lack of academic interest in the Court's historical analysis in the Secession Reference. First, most of today's Canadian constitutional law scholars have shown little interest in the history of the constitution generally, in part because the courts have traditionally dissuaded litigants from offering evidence concerning the 'true' meaning of constitutional provisions as discernible from sources that could shed light on legislative intent.[28] Second, Sujit Choudhry and Robert Howse point out that academics have focused on the outcome of the case, rather than carefully analysing the Court's reasoning, including its claims regarding Canada's constitutional history.[29] Third, the BNA Act, long a key topic in Canadian political history, was for a time deemed passé by many Canadian academic historians. This view is lamentable since a historian's perspective on the history of Canadian federalism exposes weaknesses in the Court's reasoning, casts light on some of the implications of the Court's judgment, and helps discern the vision of Canada the Court attempted to promote.

The Supreme Court's History of the Canadian Constitution

The Supreme Court introduced its historical context section with the claim that Canada's 'constitutional history demonstrates that our governing institutions have adapted and changed to reflect changing social and political values.'[30] Since the Reference dealt with questions 'fundamental to the nature of Canada,' the Court suggested that it 'should not be surprising that it is necessary to review the context in which the Canadian union has evolved.' The Court excused itself from future critique by admitting that its purpose was 'not to be exhaustive,' but instead 'to highlight the features most relevant in the context of this Reference.'[31]

The ensuing summary of Canadian constitutional history began in 1864 in the United Province of Canada. In 1864, the Court wrote, George Brown chaired a select committee of the colony's Legislative Assembly that recommended the formation of a federal union between Canada East and Canada West, and perhaps the other British North American colonies. The Province of Canada then sent a delegation to a meeting of the Maritime colonies at Charlottetown in September 1864 meant to discuss Maritime union. The meeting resulted in a plan for federal union, which, the Supreme Court believed, was designed to secure the agreement of Quebec and the Maritime colonies to the proposal.

Because several matters still had to be resolved, the Charlottetown delegates met again at Quebec in October. The delegates considered each aspect of the proposed federal structure, ultimately approving seventy-two resolutions that would shape the final text of the BNA Act. These resolutions included guarantees to protect French language and culture. According to the Court, this meant that the 'protection of minorities was thus reaffirmed.'[32] The Court pointed out that the only legal hurdle remaining was for the Quebec Resolutions to be put into proper form and passed by the British Parliament. However, 'politically, it was thought that more was required.'[33] As a result, each colony had to approve the proposed union before joining. Confirmation of the Quebec Resolutions was 'achieved more smoothly in central Canada than in the Maritimes.'[34] Thus, while the Canadian Legislative Assembly approved the Quebec Resolutions, the governments of Prince Edward Island and Newfoundland chose not to enter Confederation. New Brunswick and Nova Scotia, after considerable debate, decided to join with the Canadas.

Delegates from New Brunswick, Nova Scotia, and the Province of Canada met in London in December 1866 to finalize the plans for Confederation. They slightly modified the Quebec Resolutions, including changes to the distribution of powers, the appointment of extra senators in the event of a deadlock between the House of Commons and the Senate, and a provision for certain religious minorities of a right to appeal to the federal government when their denominational school rights were adversely affected by provincial legislation. The BNA Act received royal assent on 29 March 1867. Its proclamation on 1 July 1867 made the nation of Canada a reality.

The Supreme Court then related the attempt of Nova Scotia to secede from the new union. According to this account, in the federal and provincial elections held in September 1867, opponents of Confederation won eighteen of Nova Scotia's nineteen federal seats, and thirty-six of thirty-eight seats in the provincial legislature. The new premier, Joseph Howe, led a delegation to the Imperial Parliament in London in an effort to undo the new constitutional arrangements, but, noted the Supreme Court, 'it was too late,' for too many obligations had already been undertaken between the colonies.[35]

The Court next offered several comments concerning what it took to be the realities reflected in the design of the new federation. It noted that federalism 'was a legal response to the underlying political and cultural realities that existed at Confederation and continue to exist today.' Federalism and the division of powers was 'a legal recognition of the diversity that existed among the initial members of Confederation, and manifested a concern to accommodate that diversity within a single nation by granting significant powers to provincial governments.'[36]

The BNA Act was, the Court suggested, 'the first step in the transition from colonies separately dependent on the Imperial Parliament for their governance to a unified and independent political state in which different peoples could resolve their disagreements and work together toward common goals and a common interest.'[37] The Confederation agreement emphasized the 'continuity of constitutional principles, including democratic institutions and the rule of law; and the continuity of the exercise of sovereign power transferred from Westminster to the federal and provincial capitals of Canada.'[38] After 1867, the federation continued to evolve with the addition of new provinces and territories. Canada's independence from Britain was 'achieved through legal and political evolution with an adherence to the rule of law and stability,' culminating in the proclamation of the Constitution Act, 1982, which removed the last vestige of British authority over the Canadian Constitution and 're-affirmed Canada's commitment to the protection of its minority, aboriginal, equality, legal and language rights, and fundamental freedoms as set out in the *Canadian Charter of Rights and Freedoms.*'[39]

In addressing the implementation of the 1982 constitutional amendments, the Supreme Court noted that while legally the amendments needed to be made only by the British Parliament, 'the legitimacy as distinguished from the formal legality of the amendments derived from political decisions taken in Canada' within a legal framework that the Supreme Court set out in the Patriation Reference.[40] The Court commented, parenthetically, that while Quebec had refused to approve the new constitution, the 1982 amendments had not altered the basic division of powers in sections 91 and 92, though it did bind Quebec to constitutional terms different from those agreed to in 1867, particularly with the inclusion of new amendment procedures and the Charter of Rights.

In concluding its historical discussion in the Secession Reference, the Court wrote that it thought it 'apparent from even this brief historical review' that the 'evolution of our constitutional arrangements has been characterized by adherence to the rule of law, respect for democratic institutions, the accommodation of minorities, insistence that governments adhere to constitutional conduct and a desire for continuity and stability.'[41] These commitments, drawn from the Supreme Court's vision of Canadian constitutional history, ground the unwritten principles that then supported the Court's judgment: federalism, democracy, constitutionalism and the rule of law, and respect for minorities.

Analysis

What should Canadian legal scholars and historians make of the Supreme Court's use of history in the Secession Reference? What did the Court say, and what did it omit, and can we speculate why the Court made those choices? In answering these questions, the remainder of this article will address three aspects of the Court's decision. It first identifies the historical methodology employed by the Court, considers whether the Court provided adequate support for its chosen methodology, and queries whether other historical approaches might have been more appropriate. Analysis then turns to the substantive historical claims of the Court. The second aspect of the decision to be interrogated is the Court's limited discussion of the causes and goals of Confederation. This article then turns to examining a third aspect of Court's analysis: the acceptance of a compact theory of federalism, and whether the Nova Scotia secession movement and the patriation of the constitution in 1982 can be reconciled with the Court's vision of Canadian federalism.

The Supreme Court's Historical Methodology

What historical methodology should the Court have employed in writing about the history of Confederation? One suspects that the justices did not consider this issue when drafting the judgment, despite the importance the question has for, among other things, explaining historical causation. It seems clear that the Court offered a 'progressive evolutionary functionalist' interpretation of Canada's constitutional history.[42] Traditionally, this is perhaps the most common way that legal historians have understood the past. The core idea is that law develops with society. As society changes, the law and legal institutions reflect those developments. A close reading of the historical context section shows that the 'progressive' aspect of this approach is also prominent in the judgment. Not only does law reshape itself as society shifts, legal change is teleological – that is, it embodies a story of progress.

The Court made clear its methodological approach (probably unintentionally) at the beginning of the historical context section. The Court claimed that Canada's constitutional history 'demonstrates that our governing institutions have adapted and changed to reflect changing social and political values.'[43] Legal structures, according to the Court, reflected broader social forces. Thus, federalism was 'a legal response to the underlying political and cultural realities that existed at Confederation.'[44] The division of powers was a 'legal recognition of the diversity that existed among the initial members of Confederation, and manifested a concern to accommodate that diversity within a single nation by granting significant powers to provincial governments.'[45]

The teleological aspect is also apparent, as the Court asserted that the development of Canada's constitutional arrangement 'has generally been accomplished by methods that have ensured continuity, stability and legal order.'[46] Further evidence of the Court's teleological assumptions came later. When quoting one of its own previous decisions, it said that the Canadian tradition was 'one of evolutionary democracy moving in uneven steps toward the goal of universal suffrage and more effective representation.'[47] The country's 'evolution from colony to fully independent state was gradual,'[48] wrote the justices, who noted that the Canadian constitution was 'the product of 131 years of evolution,' and that behind the written words of the constitution is 'an historical lineage stretching back through the ages.'[49]

What emerges, then, from the Supreme Court's historical discussion, is a story of gradual constitutional evolution and improvement shaped by changing societal circumstances. The Court, however, does not explicate the circumstances driving constitutional change, and, in failing to do so, provides a poor functionalist analysis. The strength of a good functionalist analysis is the ability to connect legal change to specific social, cultural, or economic contexts. I have written elsewhere that functionalist interpretations 'at their worst ... provide generalized explanations to address historical causation while leaving unexplored the specific details of why and how change occurred in a particular way in a particular place.'[50] In retrospect, perhaps I was overly optimistic, since what the Supreme Court offers in the Secession Reference is worse. The Supreme Court says that the constitution has developed with society, but offers almost no contextual information, whether specific or general, to support this assertion.

It is important to consider historical methodology because employing one methodology often precludes, or at least limits, opportunities to ask questions that flow naturally from other approaches. For example, the Court might have considered two other approaches employed commonly in legal history: 'dialectical materialism' and 'styles of legal thought.' The dialectical materialism approach has several subcategories, but all consider the relationship between class and legal change. For example, some historians using this approach perceive law as a blunt instrument used in class struggles. Others offer more nuanced analyses that examine the role of law as a vehicle of legitimation and class hegemony. A dialectical materialism approach has of course been applied in examining the creation of the American constitution. Almost a century ago, the American progressive Charles Beard argued that the drafters of the United States constitution sought to benefit the ruling economic oligarchy of American society through the terms of the constitution.[51] While Canadian historians have not explored the framing of the BNA Act in quite these terms, it is possible that the development and interpretation of the Canadian constitution has had much to do with creating economic advantages for some citizens at the expense of others. For example, most of the Maritime delegates at the Quebec Conference wanted to ensure that men with substantial stakes in society governed the new country and thus, as Phillip Buckner concludes, these delegates shared 'anti-democratic and anti-majoritarian objectives.'[52] Most of the framers of the BNA Act, in fact, wished to protect property and prevent democratic excesses.[53] At the least, this alternative approach undermines the Supreme Court's claim in the Secession Reference that the democracy principle is best 'understood as a sort of baseline against which the framers of our Constitution' operated. The Court speculates, without offering evidence of what 'democracy' meant in 1867, that 'perhaps for this reason ... the principle was not explicitly identified in the text of the *Constitution Act, 1867*, itself. To have done so might have appeared redundant, even silly, to the framers.'[54]

The Court might also have considered Canada's constitutional development through the lens of the 'styles of legal thought' methodology. This approach suggests that legal developments are affected by the particular ways in which legal professionals think about the law. Thus, in this view, the adherence of many lawyers, judges, and academics to the style of thought known as 'legal formalism' in the late nineteenth and early twentieth centuries shaped the constitution's development as much as, if not more than, economic or social change. The Court might have investigated the role that lawyers' thinking played in the restrictive approach used to interpret the BNA Act in the late nineteenth century and for much of the twentieth century, and how this legacy affects modern views of the constitution. This article will later tease out the important questions raised by the styles of legal thought approach for the Court's understanding of Canadian federalism.

The Causes and Goals of Confederation

With an appreciation that the Court employed a poorly supported evolutionary functionalist analysis, it is important to now interrogate how the Court crafted a historical narrative to find the four unwritten constitutional principles that supported the rest of the judgment. This can be done by assessing the Court's claims regarding the causes and goals of Confederation. This section will demonstrate that the Court appears to have omitted mention of a number of factors that led to Confederation because of the Court's desire to identify a certain set of principles. In limiting its comments on the reasons for Confederation, the Court completely avoided the academic discussions that have long swirled around the multiple and complex factors that led to the union of northern North America.[55]

There is only one possible factor that led to Confederation that can be gleaned from the decision. The Court wrote that British North Americans before 1867 were 'living in the colonies scattered across part of what is now Canada.'[56] This statement suggests that the formation of Canada was a natural result of dispersion – that the scattered colonials needed a union to connect themselves to each other. It is possible that the Court was here referring to several factors historians often suggest were important in the creation of Canada (some of which will be discussed in a moment), but the Court remains silent on why dispersion led to union.

The Court may have been intent on avoiding the issue of the causes of Confederation for the reason that such a survey would have seriously undermined some of the unwritten principles the Court identified. This section will discuss briefly two causes of Confederation (ethnic tensions in the Canadas, and the role of imperial authorities in encouraging union) and suggest why the Supreme Court avoided mentioning them. It also problematizes the Court's assertions regarding the appropriate balance between the legislative jurisdictions of the federal and provincial governments, and suggests that the Court adopted a model of federalism that continues to be affected by the formalist period of Anglo-Canadian law, with the result that the Court asserts, not uncontroversially, that both levels of government were intended to possess equal legislative jurisdictions.

ETHNIC CONFLICT

The Court might have discussed several important reasons for Confederation, even though these additional factors would have undermined the foundations of the Court's unstated principles. One such factor was the ethnic tensions rampant in the Canadas. The Court noted that the experience of Lower and Upper Canada in the United Province of Canada 'had not been satisfactory,'[57] and that there were fears that, without a new union, minorities in Lower Canada and Upper Canada 'would be submerged and assimilated.'[58]

These comments understate the incredibly difficult problems facing the Canadas before Confederation. The 1837 and 1838 rebellions had spurred significant political reform. In his famous report on the political problems of British North America, Lord Durham proposed combining the two colonies to help assimilate the French-speaking citizens of Lower Canada, a proposal that was implemented in 1841.[59] The new arrangement ensured that both Upper Canada (which became 'Canada West') and Lower Canada ('Canada East') had the same number of seats in the United Province of Canada's Assembly. By the 1850s, however, large levels of immigration into Upper Canada meant that it had a greater population than Lower Canada. Many reformers soon began calling for representation by population for the Assembly. This would have made Upper Canada the more powerful partner in the United

Province. Among the strongest proponents of the 'rep by pop' idea was George Brown, the editor of the *Globe*. Brown had long chafed at the power of francophone Lower Canadians in the United Province and he proposed a federation that would have divided legislative jurisdiction, with Lower and Upper Canada each taking responsibility for local matters like schools, but leaving matters important to the whole colony to a central government. Brown makes an appearance in the Supreme Court's historical context section, a fact that is not without some irony, given the overarching themes of peaceable ethnic cooperation in which the Supreme Court seems to root Confederation. The Court wants to ensure that Confederation be seen as a means of protecting minorities. Brown, however, saw it as a way of freeing Upper Canada from the francophone encumbrance of Lower Canada after the failure of Durham's assimilationist experiment.[60]

Ethnic conflict in the Canadas was accentuated by severe economic troubles. By the early 1860s, the Grand Trunk Railway, the colony's biggest corporation, was almost bankrupt, causing fears that its failure might prevent future investment in the colony. In addition, much of the good agricultural land in Upper Canada was under till by the 1860s, and Upper Canadian proponents of a new nation saw Confederation as a means of allowing expansion in what is now western Canada. Lower Canadian politicians, who saw little need for western expansion, when it would primarily benefit Upper Canada, frustrated Brown, among many others.

Upper Canada's complaints about its union with Lower Canada thus resulted in a constitutional crisis in which Upper Canada sought to destroy the existing arrangement and negotiate a new constitutional order that would provide a greater benefit to its citizens. This lesson – that existing political arrangements can be destroyed and renegotiated because of ethnic and economic conflict and jealousies – obviously does not sit well with the Court's vision of a Canadian past marked by a desire to protect minority rights.[61]

ROLE OF IMPERIAL AUTHORITIES

While the Court offers little discussion of the reasons for Confederation, it makes the effort to point out that Confederation 'was not initiated by Imperial *fiat*.'[62] In making this claim, the Court has intentionally or unintentionally omitted several important factors that led to the creation of Canada. First, Confederation *was*, in part, an effort at imperial administrative restructuring. In the mid-1860s, the British government was keen to limit the costs of administering its empire. A federation of the colonies in the eastern half of northern North America seemed to offer a cost-savings opportunity. For example, the meeting at Charlottetown was partly the response of Maritime politicians to the pressure from the imperial capital to consider a union to reduce the substantial costs born by the British treasury. The lieutenant governor of New Brunswick, Arthur Gordon, had pressed his fellow governors and colonial politicians into the meeting at Charlottetown.[63]

Second, British authorities also wanted the colonies to consider a union so that British North America could defend itself from potential American attacks. The American Civil War had resulted in a massive militarization of the United States. Relations between Britain and the United States had deteriorated badly during the Civil War, as Americans accused Britain and its North American colonies of supporting the breakaway southern Confederacy. The rapid industrialization and militarization of the United States meant that British North America would be almost impossible to defend if the Americans marched north. In 1864, a British military report concluded that the Americans could not be stopped if they made a sustained attack, and thus spending money on defending Canada was throwing good money after bad. This report helped motivate British support for Confederation, though the British did not tell the framers of Confederation of their dire military assessment. Instead, they asserted that a union of the colonies would go a considerable way towards allowing the colonies to fend for their own defence.[64]

The British also encouraged a federation to protect against Fenian attacks. The Fenians consisted of many Irish-American veterans of the Civil War who sought to invade and capture Canada, then trade British North America for the freedom of Ireland from Britain. In 1866, Fenians launched several small attacks in Lower Canada, Upper Canada, and New Brunswick. Colonial militia and British regulars repulsed these assaults, but British officials and many Canadian advocates of Confederation believed that a formal union of the British North American colonies would provide better protection against further Fenian incursions.[65]

Why, then, did the Court incorrectly assert that Confederation was not initiated by imperial authorities? To be fair, the Court was *partly* right – it was not *just* imperial fiat – though clearly the concerns of politicians and officials in London had more of a role than the Court admits. As this article will later demonstrate, the refutation of the imperial role is important for the Court's interpretation of Confederation as a 'compact' between the colonies. For now, however, it is sufficient to suggest that a consideration of the role of Fenianism and American militarism would have done little to support the Court's argument that the 'evolution of our constitutional arrangements has been character-ized by adherence to the rule of law, respect for democratic institutions, the accommodation of minorities, insistence that governments adhere to constitutional conduct and a desire for continuity and stability.'[66]

A CENTRALIZED UNION?

The Court was thus reluctant to consider the fullness of the reasons for Confederation; it was also rather hesitant to use its rare foray into constitutional history to comment on the intended design of the new nation put in place by the BNA Act. The balance of legislative responsi-bilities between the provinces and the government in Ottawa has long intrigued Canadian legal scholars and historians. It became an especial-ly heated topic of academic legal debate in the 1930s, when many Ca-nadian law professors became dissatisfied with the 'formalist' judicial interpretation of the BNA Act. This interpretation had, federalist legal scholars asserted, weakened the power of the federal government at the expense of the provinces. In the late nineteenth century, a formalist approach dominated the thinking of many common law lawyers. Le-gal professionals came to see the law as apolitical; judges and lawyers instead sought to identify scientific legal rules from larger principles. This way of thinking also emphasized that most legal documents spoke for themselves, such that extrinsic evidence was unnecessary to deter-mine the 'plain meaning' of texts. Moreover, judges claimed to avoid policy considerations in reaching decisions, and tended to draw sharp lines that the law would enforce between, for example, individuals and state actors.[67]

Legal scholars in the 1930s charged that these tendencies in formalist thinking had reshaped Confederation for the worse. The spheres of leg-islative responsibility were judicially interpreted as separate, and the courts struck down as ultra vires any law that encroached upon the jurisdictions of the federal government, or, more typically, the provinc-es.[68] In addition, since the BNA Act was said to speak for itself, like any other legal document, judges refused to investigate the intention of the framers of the 1867 constitution.[69] In the 1930s, numerous writers be-gan to question whether the courts were intent on freezing the meaning of the BNA Act by refusing to examine extrinsic material, particularly the Confederation debates, which, they claimed, demonstrated that the original design of the constitution was for a powerful central government, not for legislative responsibilities equally split between the Dominion and the provinces.[70]

Despite the pleas of Canadian legal academics that the courts use a more historically informed contextual analysis, in its constitutional jurisprudence the Supreme Court remained remarkably silent on the origins of Canada's constitution, even after new appeals to the Judicial Committee of the Privy Council (JCPC) were ended in 1949. Not until the mid-1970s and early 1980s did the Supreme Court take a more permissive approach to statutory interpretation in constitutional cases, but even then the contextual material allowed concerned statutes whose constitutionality was under question, not the constitution itself.[71] Despite this loosening, the Supreme Court is still reluctant to enter into discussions of the intentions of the framers of the BNA Act.[72]

It was not of course just legal academics who suggested that Confederation was meant to create a centralized nation. English Canadian historians such as Donald Creighton and W.L. Morton were also motivated by the ineffectual federal government during the Great Depression to argue that the courts had destroyed the original meaning of the BNA Act. They believed that the 'Fathers of Confederation' desired to prevent the type of national disintegration that had occurred in the United States in its Civil War.[73] Many contemporary proponents of Confederation warned that federalism would result in internal divisions, and, even those who came to accept the federal principle (to encourage the success of the Confederation project), believed that a powerful central government had been negotiated that could and would prevent provinces from seeking independence. As proof, historians asserting that Confederation was meant to create a relatively centralized state could point to, among other examples, the fact that the BNA Act dictated that any area of legislative authority not specifically granted to the provinces or the federal government would become Ottawa's responsibility, the federal power to disallow provincial legislation, and the federal Cabinet's role in recommending the appointment of provincial lieutenant governors to the governor general.[74]

Not everyone who participated in the negotiations over Confederation shared this centralized vision. As political scientist Robert Vipond correctly notes, there were competing views of the new federation, and 'for a significant number of Confederationists – drawn especially from the ranks of the Reform party of Upper Canada (Ontario) and the conservative Bleus of Lower Canada (Quebec) – the [American] Civil War did not discredit the federal principle so much as it issued a challenge to place federalism on a more secure constitutional footing.'[75] Thus, George-Étienne Cartier, the leader of the Bleus in Lower Canada, for example, had done his best to ensure that the potentially broad legislative head of 'property and civil rights' was included in the list of enumerated heads of provincial jurisdiction in order to blunt the power of the new central government.[76]

The diversity of contemporary viewpoints at Confederation on the proper meaning of the BNA Act has allowed historians to argue various positions.[77] In its historical context section of the Secession Reference, however, the Court chose to leave unacknowledged this diversity of professional opinion. The result was a selective examination of Canada's past. The Court briefly mentioned that the BNA Act may have been designed to subordinate the provincial governments to federal authority. This, the Court suggested, meant that 'on paper, the federal government retained sweeping powers which threatened to undermine the autonomy of the provinces.' The Court concludes, however, that just looking at the BNA Act 'does not provide the entire picture,'[78] since the underlying principle of federalism meant that the constitution was eventually interpreted to limit Ottawa's legislative jurisdiction. In making this leap in reasoning, the Court pointed out that the federal power to disallow provincial legislation was included in the BNA Act, but that 'the underlying principles of federalism triumphed early' and the practice of disallowing provincial laws fell into disuse.[79] The Canadian legal scholars and historians who have argued for a centralized interpretation of the BNA Act would be aghast at the Court's reasoning – amazed that the Court could use the provision of a strong power to the federal government at Confederation as evidence that the provinces were intended to be autonomous.

They also would have complained vociferously that one of the main pieces of evidence used by the Court to substantiate its interpretation of the relative disposition of legislative jurisdictions at Confederation was a 1919 JCPC decision. In 1919, the JCPC had said that the BNA Act was not meant 'to subordinate Provincial Governments to a central authority, but to establish a central government in which these Provinces should be represented, entrusted with exclusive authority only in affairs in which they had a common interest. Subject to this each Province was to retain its independence and autonomy.'[80] The Supreme Court thus uses evidence from 1919 to substantiate its conclusions about the design of Confederation five decades earlier. Moreover, the Supreme

Court quoted a JCPC decision written at the height of the formalist period, when the Privy Council refused to examine the Confederation debates in interpreting the BNA Act. This position is historically unconvincing at best, or, at worst, intellectually dishonest, and should cast doubt on the probity of the Court's claims regarding the appropriate division of legislative jurisdictions at Confederation.

Federalism and the 'Compact Theory'

Like its comments concerning the causes and goals of the Canadian constitution, the Court's assertions regarding the development of Canadian federalism since Confederation are also notable for a failure to consider alternative interpretations. This weakness is illustrated by examining the Court's adoption of a 'compact' (or 'contract') theory of federalism, and the inconsistency of applying this theory to the Court's analysis of the Nova Scotia secession movement of the nineteenth century and to the patriation of the Canadian constitution in the early 1980s.

Proponents of the compact theory argue that Confederation was a treaty, or 'contract,' between the colonies.[81] They perceive that Confederation occurred as a result of the unanimous consent of the constituent colonies, and thus presume that the provinces should continue to have a prominent voice vis-à-vis the federal government in the creation of national policies. The compact theory fit well with the assumptions of legal formalism, for which a contractual arrangement was the paradigmatic legal relationship. Formalist contract doctrine was marked by an assumption of equality of bargaining positions between parties, while legal principles were abstract, non-political, and unconcerned with policy outcomes.[82] Many legal relationships were conceptualized as contractual in the nineteenth century, and the BNA Act failed to escape this trend. Formalists claimed that the BNA Act (i.e., the 'contract') was formed by equal parties, and alterations to the constitution could occur only with the consent of the provinces. The federal and provincial governments possessed roughly equal powers, and interpretations of the BNA Act were not to weigh the practical results of potential legal decisions.[83]

Critics have long attacked the compact theory. The progressive Canadian legal scholars of the 1930s attempted to re-imagine Canada by returning the constitution to what they believed to be its original, centralist orientation.[84] The compact theory, however, continues to have supporters. Paul Romney, for example, asserts that the critique of the compact theory simply reflected the wishful thinking of Canadian academic nationalists in the 1930s, and that, in fact, the compact theory may be found in the thought of several Upper Canadian political leaders.[85] Romney's scholarship has not silenced critics of the contract theory. In *The Lawmakers*, John Saywell recognizes the importance of the powers granted to the provinces and that the meaning of some sections of the BNA Act were unclear, but also concludes that the 'federal government was endowed with the capacity, the institutions, and the resources to develop and manage a national economy and ensure the expansion and viability of the new state.'[86] To substantiate his assertions, Saywell offers new research into the early interpretation of the BNA Act by judges who had been involved in its drafting to demonstrate that the intention of Confederation was to create a relatively centralized union.

While the scholarly debate over the historical foundations of the compact theory continues, it is true that by the early twentieth century a number of scholars, politicians, and judges had begun to perceive of Canada as a compact. The Secession Reference demonstrates that this conception still plays an important role in the Supreme Court's understanding of Confederation. So natural, in fact, is this interpretation that the Court did not even make reference to the historical debate over the compact theory. Instead, it offered a history of Canadian federalism that simply reflected today's jurisprudence and political realities. The idea of Canada as a compact can be seen in several aspects of the Court's Secession decision. It is most obviously apparent in its acceptance of the idea of a decentralized federal structure. The Court, for example, provides a long quotation from George-Étienne Cartier in which Cartier suggests that Canada would always comprise a 'diversity of "races."'[87] According to the Court, this diversity meant that Confederation was intended to grant 'significant powers to provincial governments.'[88] On the other hand, the Court makes no mention of the provision in the 'peace, order, and good government' clause of the BNA Act that the government in Ottawa would legislate in areas not enumerated by the BNA Act. The Court's compact interpretation is also discernible in its discussion of how Canada formed. By underplaying the imperial role, the Court emphasizes the independence of the colonies to negotiate and enter into a 'deal.' Lastly, the Court's conclusion that Quebec and the rest of Canada would be required to negotiate after a yes vote in a referendum reflects the Court's acceptance of the view that Canada was not created as a perpetual union, but was instead formed by an agreement that allows contracting parties to opt out, negotiate obligations, and mitigate damages.[89]

There are complications in using a compact theory to understand the history of Confederation and Canadian federalism in light of the unwritten principles the Court wished to draw from the past. The first complication is that it begs an analysis of whether each contracting party to Confederation freely made the bargain. The compact theory assumes that, like contracting parties, each colony that entered Confederation was self-interested and aware of its situation, and entered the 'bargain' without undue influence from any other party. This view is especially problematic in understanding Nova Scotia's and New Brunswick's entry into Confederation. In discussing the Atlantic provinces' decision whether to join Confederation, the Supreme Court notes, 'Confirmation of the Quebec Resolutions was achieved more smoothly in central Canada than in the Maritimes.'[90] In regards to New Brunswick, the Court simply notes that 'a general election was required before Premier Tilley's pro-Confederation party prevailed,' while in Nova Scotia Premier Charles Tupper 'ultimately obtained a resolution from the House of Assembly favouring Confederation.'[91] These are grand understatements, which gloss over the political skulduggery and arm-twisting that ensured that New Brunswick and Nova Scotia would enter the Confederation deal. Not incidentally, a fuller narrative of the challenges that Confederation faced in the Maritimes would have made it more difficult to argue that Canada's constitutional history has been defined by the principles of democracy and the rule of law.

Confederation might have offered promises of an intercolonial railway and better defence, but in the Maritime colonies it lacked many of the perceived benefits appreciated by Upper and Lower Canadians. The Canadas were debt ridden, more exposed to American attack (the British Navy helped defend the Maritimes), and ripe with ethnic and linguistic disputes that had made them almost ungovernable. Many Maritime critics of the Quebec resolutions believed that the provincial governments would have insufficient resources to administer local affairs.[92] In Nova Scotia, Joseph Howe led a fierce anti-Confederation campaign against Premier Charles Tupper, appealing to Nova Scotians' pride and sense of independence. Fearing defeat, Tupper refused to hold an election on Confederation, or even let the topic be debated in the Assembly. Tupper found the resolve to move forward only when the Nova Scotia lieutenant governor, Sir William Fenwick Williams, made clear that Britain did not want Nova Scotia to pursue alternative arrangements, such as Maritime union. Tupper finally pushed a weakly worded resolution through the legislature that called for the continuance of talks regarding a British North American union with the promise of the construction of an intercolonial railway.[93] This resolution constituted Nova Scotia's acceptance of the Confederation bargain.

In New Brunswick, the pro-Confederation premier, Leonard Tilley, was badly beaten in the March 1865 election. With New Brunswick leaning away from Confederation, the British government again played a role in assisting in the creation of Canada. Lieutenant Governor Arthur Gordon ordered the colony's legislature to debate Confederation. The anti-Confederation premier, Albert James Smith, resigned in the face of this order. An especially fierce election campaign followed, and proponents of union drummed up fears of Fenian attacks by casting suspicion upon the Catholic population of the colony. Moreover, John A. Macdonald sent as much as $40,000 to Tilley to help wage the campaign, which Tilley won.[94] The events that led to the entrance of New Brunswick and Nova Scotia into Confederation therefore cast doubt on the extent to which each party made choices freely. As Peter Waite concludes, 'New Brunswick was pushed into Union, Nova Scotia was dragooned into it, and Newfoundland and Prince Edward Island were subjected to all the pressure that could be brought to bear – short of force – and still refused.'[95]

The Court's discussion of the Nova Scotia anti-Confederation movement and the patriation of the constitution in 1982 also reveal the Court's tendency to gloss over the problems of adopting the compact theory as a way of understanding Canada's constitutional history. In its discussion of the Nova Scotia secession movement, the Court noted that after Confederation there was 'an early attempt at secession.' In September 1867, Premier Charles Tupper's government was badly defeated by opponents of Confederation. Premier Joseph Howe led a delegation to the British Parliament in an effort to undo Nova Scotia's place in Confederation, but, according to the Court, 'it was too late.'[96] The Colonial Office rejected Howe's plea. The Court then quoted the British Colonial Secretary, who in 1868 wrote that the

neighbouring province of New Brunswick has entered into the union in reliance on having with it the sister province of Nova Scotia; and vast obligations, political and commercial, have already been contracted on the faith of a measure so long discussed and so solemnly adopted ... I trust that the Assembly and the people of Nova Scotia will not be surprised that the Queen's government feel that they would not be warranted in advising the reversal of a great measure of state, attended by so many extensive consequences already in operation.[97]

The Supreme Court downplays Nova Scotians' sense that they had been forced undemocratically into Confederation. The 1867 election in Nova Scotia resulted in an anti-Confederation victory, according to Phillip Buckner, because many Nova Scotians felt 'they had been forced into the union and by the fact that the Nova Scotia election took place after it had become certain that there would be no substantial alterations in the Quebec plan.'[98]

The Court has difficulty dealing with the Nova Scotia secession movement for two reasons. First, although the people of Nova Scotia elected, by a huge majority, a government desirous of taking Nova Scotia out of Confederation, there was no evidence that this clear vote meant that the rest of Canada had to negotiate with Nova Scotia over the withdrawal of the colony from Confederation. It runs counter to the Court's claim that Canada's democratic institutions accommodate 'a continuous process of discussion and evolution, which is reflected in the constitutional right of each participant in the federation to initiate constitutional change.'[99] Second, the response of the colonial secretary suggested that Confederation was not, in fact, a compact from which parties could walk away. Rather, it hints at the extent to which imperial fiat was important in deciding the continuation of the country, and, more importantly, indicates that the bond created at Confederation was to be very difficult to break.[100]

The Supreme Court's discussion of the patriation of the Canadian constitution constitutes another aspect of the historical context section of the Secession Reference that is difficult to reconcile with the Court's compact theory. After noting that 'Canada's independence from Britain was achieved through legal and political evolution with an adherence to the rule of law and stability,' the Court suggests that the 1982 constitution 'removed the last vestige of British authority over the Canadian Constitution and re-affirmed Canada's commitment to the protection of its minority, aboriginal, equality, legal and language rights, and fundamental freedoms as set out in the Canadian Charter of Rights and Freedoms.'[101]

Then, suddenly, the compact story of Canada's constitutional development breaks down. The Court avoids the implication that Pierre Trudeau's decision to force a new constitution on Canada was a substantial deviation from the compact theory's principle that all parties had to agree in order to alter the constitution. Trudeau sought to flex the federal government's power, and the Supreme Court allowed him to do so in the 1981 Patriation Reference by declaring that there was no legal requirement that the federal government attain provincial assent before asking the British Parliament to alter the Canadian constitution.[102] In the Secession Reference, the Supreme Court wrote that it had ruled in the Patriation Reference that Trudeau's amendments were passed 'in accordance with our Constitution.' As if to excuse the Court's Patriation decision, the Court also noted, 'parenthetically, that the 1982 amendments did not alter the basic division of powers in ss. 91 and 92 of the *Constitution Act, 1867.'*[103] The Court also defended its previous decision on the ground that section 33 of the Charter, the 'notwithstanding clause,' allows provincial governments to legislate on matters within their jurisdiction in derogation of the fundamental freedoms (section 2), legal rights (sections 7 to 14), and equality rights (section 15) provisions of the Charter. The problem for the Court in interpreting the Patriation judgment is obvious. The principles enunciated in the Secession Reference, including respect for democratic institutions, and the value of federalism were undermined, not strengthened, by the Court's own Patriation decision.[104]

Conclusion

A steady stream of decisions emanating from the Supreme Court on the rights of Aboriginal peoples has been replete with historical considerations of treaties. Many historians, including some who have been involved in these cases, have written critically about courts' use of history. John Reid, for example, warns that while academic historians enjoy 'no monopoly of the past,' they 'have techniques for examining it that cannot be ignored by others without serious risk of misunderstanding.'[105] The trial judgment of Justice Allan McEachern in *Delgamuukw v. B.C.*, in particular, resulted in extensive historical commentary, because McEachern portrayed historians as antiquarians who were useful for finding historical 'facts' with 'minimal editorial comment.'[106] His comments led several historians to express serious concerns about the extent to which the courts appreciated the complexity of historical analysis, including the very role of interpretation of documents and the difficulties of determining historical causation.[107]

The Supreme Court has not always appreciated such criticism. In

1999, Justice Ian Binnie struck back at historians who judged the Supreme Court's Aboriginal law jurisprudence. 'The courts have attracted a certain amount of criticism from professional historians for what these historians see as an occasional tendency on the part of judges to assemble a "cut and paste" version of history,' wrote Binnie testily, who noted that the 'tone of some of this criticism strikes the non-professional historian as intemperate.'[108] Binnie understood the basic objection to be that

> the judicial selection of facts and quotations is not always up to the standard demanded of the professional historian, which is said to be more nuanced. Experts, it is argued, are trained to read the various historical records together with the benefit of a protracted study of the period, and an appreciation of the frailties of the various sources. The law sees a finality of interpretation of historical events where finality, according to the professional historian, is not possible.[109]

In recognizing these issues, Binnie reminded academic historians that 'the courts are handed disputes that require for their resolution the finding of certain historical facts.' Litigating parties 'cannot await the possibility of a stable academic consensus,' and instead the 'judicial process must do as best it can.'[110]

Despite Binnie's reprimand, it seems fair to say that any Canadian court offering a historical narrative to support a legal decision should be aware that its conclusions are as open to debate and analysis as any legal argument it sets out. In the future, the Supreme Court might avoid criticism by doing the work that historians ask of their students, namely, to canvass the existing literature, to consider alternative interpretations, to use evidence to support conclusions, and to avoid overdrawn and broad assertions. The role of historians vis-à-vis the courts is to hold a light to their historical interpretations, and, when called for, recognize the Court's misuse of history. The role of courts is not to wait for historical consensus on an issue, but to at least recognize the historiographical debates. No one asks for historian-judges; one can only expect as much from judges as one expects from students of history.

While legal scholars have interrogated the legal inconsistencies of the Secession Reference judgment, this article demonstrates the benefits of critically considering the historical claims in the ruling upon which much of the Supreme Court's analysis rests. The Court constructed several key constitutional principles upon a rather rickety narrative of the country's constitutional development. Using a progressive evolutionary functionalist methodology, the Court indicated that Canada's constitutional development has been gradual and progressive, driven by social forces that the Court itself does not identify. The Court avoided the complex set of social, economic, political, and cultural forces at play in the formation and interpretation of Confederation, providing a watered down version of the debate, negotiation, and, sometimes, vicious argument, that has resulted in Canada's constitutional design. To do so, the Court ignored the extensive historiography on Confederation and Canadian federalism, a literature in which, for example, fierce debates have taken place between historians arguing over the relative level of centralization the BNA Act was meant to enshrine. Instead of engaging these debates, the Court simply adopted the decentralized compact theory of Confederation – an idea that formed during a period of intense legal formalism in Canada in the late nineteenth and early twentieth century, and which sits uneasily with even the Court's own descriptions of the Nova Scotia secession movement and the patriation of the constitution.

The Secession judgment's historical content also provides insights into the type of nation the Court hopes Canada to be. The Court offered a view of history that imagines Canada as devoted to decentralized federalism, democracy, constitutionalism and the rule of law, and respect of minorities. These are perhaps values to which many Canadians aspire, but as underlying principles of our history they draw attention away from the strong centralist impulses, the elitism, the racism, the anglophilism, and the dismissal of inconvenient constitutional protections, that marked, and often stained, Canada's constitutional past.

NOTES

1 *Reference re Secession of Quebec* [1998] 2 S.C.R. 217.
2 Benedict Anderson, *Imagined Communities: Reflections on the Origin and Spread of Nationalism*, rev. ed. (New York: Verso, 1991), 6.
3 *Reference re Secession of Quebec*, para. 48.
4 *Reference re Secession of Quebec*, para. 49.
5 Daniel Francis, *National Dreams: Myth, Memory, and Canadian History* (Vancouver: Arsenal Pulp, 1997), 11.
6 For recent studies of the use of history to support or contradict Canadian national myths see, for example, Colin M. Coates and Cecilia Morgan,

Heroines and History: Representations of Madeleine de Verchères and Laura Secord (Toronto: University of Toronto, 2002); Norman Knowles, *Inventing the Loyalists: The Ontario Loyalist Tradition and the Creation of Usable Pasts* (Toronto: University of Toronto Press, 1999); H.V. Nelles, *The Art of Nation Building: Pageantry and Spectacle at Quebec's Tercentenary* (Toronto: University of Toronto Press, 1999); Jonathan F. Vance, *Death So Noble: Memory, Meaning, and the First World War* (Vancouver: UBC Press, 1997).

7 The irony of offering a necessarily brief history of the political events leading to the *Secession Reference*, then critiquing the Supreme Court for its partial account of the development of federalism, is not lost on me.

8 Robert A. Young, *The Secession of Quebec and the Future of Canada*, rev. ed. (Montreal and Kingston: McGill-Queen's University Press, 1998), 225–90; Young, *The Struggle for Quebec: From Referendum to Referendum?* (Montreal and Kingston: McGill-Queen's University Press, 1999), 13–38.

9 Peter W. Hogg, *Constitutional Law of Canada, 2004*, student ed. (Toronto: Carswell, 2004), 136.

10 Prior to the 1995 referendum, a private citizen, Guy Bertrand, had obtained a declaration from the Quebec Superior Court that Quebec could not disregard the amending procedures of the Canadian constitution in declaring itself independent. However, the Superior Court refused to stop the referendum by issuing an injunction. *Bertrand v. Quebec* (1995), 127 D.L.R. (4th) 408 (Que. SC); Warren J. Newman, *The Quebec Secession Reference: The Rule of Law and the Position of the Attorney General of Canada* (Toronto: York University, Centre for Public Law and Public Policy), 10–15.

11 *Supreme Court Act*, R.S.C., 1985, c. S-26, s. 53.

12 *Reference re Secession of Quebec*, para. 2.

13 Ibid., para. 32.

14 Patrick J. Monahan, 'The Public Policy Role of the Supreme Court of Canada in the Secession Reference,' *National Journal of Constitutional Law*, 11 (2000): 66; Kenneth McRoberts, 'In the Best Canadian Tradition,' *Canada Watch* 7, nos. 1–2 (1999): 11–13. For examples of the federalist and separatist interpretations of the judgment, see David Schneiderman, ed., *The Quebec Decision: Perspectives on the Supreme Court Ruling on Secession* (Toronto: Lorimer, 1999).

15 Daniel Drache and Patrick J. Monahan, 'In Search of Plan A,' *Canada Watch* 7, nos. 1–2 (1999): 29. Similarly, Robert A. Young compliments the Court's ability to 'preserve its own legitimacy.' Robert A. Young, 'A Most Political Judgement,' *Constitutional Forum* 10 (1998): 14–18.

16 Stephen Clarkson, 'Anglophone Media and the Court's Opinion,' *Canada Watch* 7, nos. 1–2 (1999): 26.

17 Donna Greschner, 'The Quebec Secession Reference: Goodbye to Part V?' *Constitutional Forum* 10 (1998): 19–25.

18 Paul Joffe, 'Quebec's Sovereignty Project and Aboriginal Rights,' *Canada Watch* 7, nos. 1–2 (1999): 6–7, 13.

19 Jacques-Yvan Morin, 'A Balanced Judgement?' *Canada Watch* 7, no. 1–2 (1999): 3, 5; McRoberts, 'In the Best Canadian Tradition,' 11–13; Peter McCormick, 'The Political Jurisprudence of Hot Potatoes: A Comparison of the Secession Reference and Bush v. Gore,' *National Journal of Constitutional Law* 13 (2002): 271–305.

20 John T. Saywell, *The Lawmakers: Judicial Power and the Shaping of Canadian Federalism* (Toronto: University of Toronto Press, 2002), 306.

21 See, for example, Mary Dawson, 'Reflections on the Opinion of the Supreme Court of Canada in the Quebec Secession Reference,' *National Journal of Constitutional Law* 11 (2000): 28; Jean Leclair, 'The Secession Reference: A Ruling in Search of a Nation,' *Revue juridique Thémis* 34 (2000): 887; Gregory Millard, 'The Secession Reference and National Reconciliation: A Critical Note,' *Canadian Journal of Law & Society* 14 (1999): 12; Monahan, 'The Public Policy Role of the Supreme Court of Canada,' 74; Newman, *The Quebec Secession Reference*, 43.

22 See, for example, Alan C. Cairns, 'The Constitutional Obligation to Negotiate,' *Constitutional Forum* 10 (1998): 26–30; Peter W. Hogg, 'The Duty to Negotiate,' *Canada Watch* 7, nos. 1–2 (1999): 1, 33–5; W.H. Hurlburt, 'Fairy Tales and Living Trees: Observations on Some Recent Constitutional Decisions of the Supreme Court of Canada,' *Manitoba Law Journal* 26 (1999): 181–202; Jean Leclair, 'Canada's Unfathomable Unwritten Constitutional Principles,' *Queen's Law Journal* 27 (2002): 441; John D. Whyte, 'Constitutionalism and Nation,' *Canada Watch* 7, nos. 1–2 (1999): 16–17, 21–2.

23 *Reference re Secession of Quebec*, para. 81.

24 Dale Gibson, 'Constitutional Vibes: Reflections on the Secession Reference and the Unwritten Constitution,' *National Journal of Constitutional Law* 11 (2000): 63.

25 In a particular bit of irony, the Court cites with approval Chief Justice Lyman Duff's application of unwritten constitutional principles in the 1938 *Reference re Alberta Legislation* case, in which the Supreme Court struck down legislation passed by William Aberhart's Social Credit government in Alberta that placed limits on freedom of the press. *Reference re Alberta Legislation* [1938] S.C.R. 100. However, the Court does not mention the string of cases in which Duff refused to assist minorities. See references to Duff in Constance Backhouse, *Colour-Coded: A Legal History of Racism in Canada, 1900–1950* (Toronto: University of Toronto Press and the Osgoode

Society, 1999); James W. St G. Walker, '*Race*,' *Rights and the Law in the Supreme Court of Canada: Historical Case Studies* (Waterloo: Wilfrid Laurier University and the Osgoode Society, 1997).
26 *Constitution Act, 1867*, preamble.
27 Mark D. Walters, 'The Common Law Constitution in Canada: Return of Lex Non Scripta as Fundamental Law,' *University of Toronto Law Journal* 51 (2001): 137.
28 See Stéphane Beaulac, 'Parliamentary Debates in Statutory Interpretation: A Question of Admissibility or of Weight?' *McGill Law Journal* 43 (1998): 300–8; William H. Charles, Thomas A. Cromwell, and Keith B. Jobson, *Evidence and the Charter of Rights and Freedoms* (Toronto: Butterworths, 1989), 75–84; Peter W. Hogg, 'Legislative History in Constitutional Cases,' in *Charter Litigation*, ed. Robert J. Sharpe, 131–58 (Toronto: Butterworths, 1987); Ruth Sullivan, *Sullivan and Driedger on the Construction of Statutes*, 4th ed. (Markham, ON: Butterworths, 2002), 480–500.
29 Sujit Choudhry and Robert Howse, 'Constitutional Theory and the Quebec Secession Reference,' *Canadian Journal of Law and Jurisprudence* 13 (2000): 143–4.
30 *Reference re Secession of Quebec*, para. 33.
31 Ibid., para. 34.
32 Ibid., para. 38.
33 Ibid., para. 39.
34 Ibid., para. 40.
35 Ibid., para. 42.
36 Ibid., para. 43.
37 Ibid.
38 Ibid., para. 44.
39 Ibid., para. 46.
40 Ibid., para. 47, discussing *Reference re Resolution to Amend the Constitution*, [1981] 1 S.C.R. 753.
41 *Reference re Secession of Quebec*, para. 48.
42 I have briefly discussed several methodologies employed in Canadian legal history. See R. Blake Brown, 'A Taxonomy of Methodological Approaches in Recent Canadian Legal History,' *Acadiensis* 34 (2004): 145–55.
43 *Reference re Secession of Quebec*, para. 33.
44 Ibid., para. 43.
45 Ibid.
46 Ibid., para. 33.
47 Ibid., para. 63, quoting *Reference re Provincial Electoral Boundaries* (Sask.), [1991] 2 S.C.R. 158, p. 186.

48 Ibid., para. 46.

49 Ibid., para. 49. The Court invokes the Judicial Committee of the Privy's reference to the *BNA Act* as a 'living tree' in *Edwards v. Attorney General for Canada*, [1930] A.C. 124 (P.C.), at p. 136. The Supreme Court wrote that the identification of the underlying principles of the constitution was important 'to the ongoing process of constitutional development and evolution of our Constitution as a "living tree".' *Reference re Secession of Quebec*, para. 52.

50 Brown, 'A Taxonomy of Methodological Approaches,' 147.

51 Charles A. Beard, *An Economic Interpretation of the Constitution of the United States* (New York: Macmillan, 1913).

52 Phillip Buckner, 'The Maritimes and Confederation: A Reassessment,' *Canadian Historical Review* 71 (1990): 24. Also, Del Muise demonstrates that residents of areas of the Maritimes that could benefit from the industrialization promised by Confederation were more often in support of the union. Delphin A. Muise, 'The Federal Election of 1867 in Nova Scotia: An Economic Interpretation,' *Collections of the Nova Scotia Historical Society* 36 (1968): 327–51.

53 Bruce Hodgins, 'The Canadian Political Elite's Attitudes towards the Nature of the Plan of Union,' in *Federalism in Canada and Australia: The Early Years*, ed. Bruce W. Hodgins, Don Wright, and W.H. Heick, 43–59 (Waterloo: Wilfrid Laurier Press, 1978).

54 *Reference re Secession of Quebec*, para. 62.

55 The Court also avoids detailing the development of the idea of Confederation before 1864. For discussions of the issue before 1864, see, for example, John Heisler, 'The Halifax Press and British North American Union, 1856–1864,' *Dalhousie Review* 30 (1950), 188–95; L.F.S. Upton, 'The Idea of Confederation, 1754–1858,' in *The Shield of Achilles: Aspects of Canada in the Victorian Age*, ed. W.L. Morton, 184–204 (Toronto: McClelland & Stewart, 1968).

56 *Reference re Secession of Quebec*, para. 35.

57 Ibid., para. 59.

58 Ibid., para. 79.

59 Janet Ajzenstat, *The Political Thought of Lord Durham* (Montreal and Kingston: McGill-Queen's University Press, 1988).

60 J.M.S. Careless, *Brown of the Globe*, vol. 2, *Statesman of Confederation, 1860–1880* (Toronto: Dundurn, 1989); Christopher Moore, *1867: How the Fathers Made a Deal* (Toronto: McClelland & Stewart, 1997), 1–31.

61 While the Supreme Court glosses over the reasons that Upper and Lower Canada sought a new arrangement, it offers no discussion for why the Maritime provinces sought to enter the union.

62 *Reference re Secession of Quebec*, para. 35.

63 Ged Martin, *Britain and the Origins of Canadian Confederation, 1837–67* (Vancouver: UBC Press, 1995); P.B. Waite, *The Life and Times of Confederation, 1864–1867: Politics, Newspapers and the Union of British North America* (Toronto: Robin Brass Studio, 2001), 17–28; Bruce A. Knox, 'The Rise of Colonial Federation as an Object of British Policy, 1850–1870,' *Journal of British Studies* 11 (1971): 91–112; Ged Martin, 'An Imperial Idea and Its Friends: Canadian Confederation and the British,' in *Studies in British Imperial History: Essays in Honour of A.P. Thornton*, ed. Gordon Martel, 49–94 (New York: St Martin's, 1985). .

64 Desmond Morton, *Shaping a Nation: The History of Canada's Constitution* (Toronto: Umbrella, 1996), 34.

65 Hereward Senior, *The Fenians and Canada* (Toronto: Macmillan, 1978); Senior, *The Last Invasion of Canada: The Fenian Raids, 1866–1870* (Toronto: Dundurn, 1991); W.S. Neidhardt, *Fenianism in North America* (University Park: Pennsylvania State University Press, 1975).

66 *Reference re Secession of Quebec*, para. 48.

67 R. Blake Brown, 'The Canadian Legal Realists and Administrative Law Scholarship, 1930–1941,' *Dalhousie Journal of Legal Studies* 9 (2000): 36–72; Brown, 'Realism, Federalism, and Statutory Interpretation during the 1930s: The Significance of Home Oil Distributors v. A.G. (B.C.),' *University of Toronto Faculty of Law Review* 59 (2001): 1–23; R.C.B. Risk, 'The Many Minds of W.P.M. Kennedy,' *University of Toronto Law Journal* 48 (1998): 353–86; Risk, 'The Scholars and the Constitution: P.O.G.G. and the Privy Council,' *Manitoba Law Journal* 23 (1996): 496–523..

68 R.C.B. Risk, 'Canadian Courts under the Influence,' *University of Toronto Law Journal* 40 (1990): 687–737; Risk, 'Constitutional Thought in the Late Nineteenth Century,' *Manitoba Law Journal* 20 (1991): 196–203.

69 In 1887, the JCPC determined that the provisions of the *BNA Act* had to be treated with the same methods of construction applied to other statutes. *Bank of Toronto v. Lambe*, (1887) 12 A.C. 575, p. 579. For criticism of this approach, see, for example, Vincent MacDonald, 'Judicial Interpretation of the Canadian Constitution,' *University of Toronto Law Journal* 1 (1935–6): 278.

70 Criticisms of literal interpretation increased following the 'New Deal' references when the Supreme Court of Canada and the JCPC struck down most of the social reform legislation initiated by Prime Minister R.B. Bennett. See, for example, W.P.M. Kennedy, 'The British North America Act: Past and Future,' *Canadian Bar Review* 15 (1937): 394; Vincent C. Macdonald, 'Constitutional Interpretation and Extrinsic Evidence,' *Canadian Bar Review*, 17 (1939): 77–93.

71 See, for example, *Re Anti-Inflation Act* [1976] 2 S.C.R. 373, pp. 387–91.

72 This contrasts sharply with judicial analysis in the United States, where 'originalism' is a method of constitutional interpretation that seeks to determine the meaning of the American Constitution by analysing the original intent of the men who wrote the Constitution. See, for example, Dennis J. Goldford, *The American Constitution and the Debate over Originalism* (New York: Cambridge University Press, 2005).

73 Donald Creighton's argument that the design of Confederation was a centralized one was undermined by his vociferous attack on biculturalism. D.G. Creighton, *Canada's First Century, 1867–1967* (Toronto: Macmillan, 1970); Creighton, 'Confederation: The Use and Abuse of History,' *Journal of Canadian Studies* 1, no. 1 (1966): 3–24; Creighton, *The Road to Confederation: The Emergence of Canada, 1863–1867* (Toronto: Macmillan, 1964). In a scathing 1971 article, Ralph Heintzman attacked Creighton's view of the historical foundations of biculturalism. Ralph Heintzman, 'The Spirit of Confederation: Professor Creighton, Biculturalism, and the Use of History,' *Canadian Historical Review* 52 (1971): 245–75.

It is important to note that Heintzman did not attack Creighton's underlying theory that Confederation was designed to create a strong central government; instead, Heintzman focused on Creighton's fear of biculturalism. The arguments regarding biculturalism and the division of powers, can, and should, be separated. W.L. Morton's approach to Confederation avoids this problem of conflating cultural dualism and the design of the division of powers. Morton recognizes the acceptance at Confederation of a cultural duality, but the rejection of political duality. See, for example, W.L. Morton, 'British North America and a Continent in Dissolution, 1861–71,' in *Contexts of Canada's Past: Selected Essays of W.L. Morton*, ed. A.B. Mckillop, 186–207 (Toronto: Macmillan, 1980); Morton, 'Confederation, 1870–1896,' in *Contexts of Canada's Past*, 208–28; Morton, *The Critical Years: The Union of British North America, 1857–1873* (Toronto: McClelland and Stewart, 1964).

74 Morton, *Shaping a Nation*, 29–30.

75 Robert Vipond, *Liberty & Community: Canadian Federalism and the Failure of the Constitution* (Albany, NY: University of New York Press, 1991), 16.

76 See A.I. Silver, *The French-Canadian Idea of Confederation, 1864–1900*, 2nd ed. (Toronto: University of Toronto Press, 1997), 33–50.

77 Ramsay Cook, *Provincial Autonomy, Minority Rights and the Compact Theory, 1867–1921* (Ottawa: Royal Commission on Bilingualism and Biculturalism, 1969), 2; Richard Simeon and Ian Robinson, *State, Society, and the Development of Canadian Federalism* (Toronto: University of Toronto Press, 1990), 21–7.

48   R. Blake Brown

78 *Reference re Secession of Quebec*, para. 55.
79 Ibid., para. 55.
80 Ibid., para. 58, quoting *Re the Initiative and Referendum Act*, [1919] A.C. 935 (P.C.), p. 942.
81 Cook, *Provincial Autonomy*.
82 For a discussion of formalist contract doctrine, see, for example, P.S. Atiyah, *The Rise and Fall of Freedom of Contract* (Oxford: Clarendon, 1984); Morton J. Horwitz, *The Transformation of American Law, 1780–1860* (Cambridge, MA: Harvard University Press, 1977), 168–210.
83 Risk, 'Canadian Courts under the Influence,' 687–737; Risk, 'Constitutional Thought in the Late Nineteenth Century,' 196–203; R.C.B. Risk, 'Constitutional Scholarship in the Late-Nineteenth Century: Making Federalism Work,' *University of Toronto Law Journal* 46 (1996), 427–57.
84 See Norman McL. Rogers, 'The Compact Theory of Confederation,' *Canadian Bar Review* 9 (1931): 395; Rogers, 'The Compact Theory of Confederation,' *Papers of Proceedings of the Annual Meeting of the Canadian Political Science Association*, 3 (1931): 205–30; Rogers, 'The Dominion and the Provinces,' *Canadian Bar Review* 11 (1933): 338; Vincent C. MacDonald, 'Canadian Constitution Seventy Years After,' *Canadian Bar Review* 15 (1937): 423.
85 Paul Romney, *Getting It Wrong: How Canadians Forgot Their Past and Imperilled Confederation* (Toronto: University of Toronto Press, 1999), 6. Also see Paul Romney, 'The Nature and Scope of Provincial Autonomy: Oliver Mowat, the Quebec Resolutions and the Construction of the British North America Act,' *Canadian Journal of Political Science* 25 (1992): 3–28. Alan Cairns argues that the constitutional interpretation of the *BNA Act* by the JCPC reflected accurately the political and cultural diversity of Canada. Alan Cairns, 'The Judicial Committee and Its Critics,' *Canadian Journal of Political Science* 4 (1971): 301–45. Also see G.P. Browne, *The Judicial Committee and the British North America Act: An Analysis of the Interpretive Scheme for the Distribution of Legislative Powers* (Toronto: University of Toronto Press, 1967); Frederick Vaughan, 'Critics of the Judicial Committee of the Privy Council: The New Orthodoxy and an Alternative Explanation,' *Canadian Journal of Political Science* 19 (1986): 495–519.
86 Saywell, *The Lawmakers*, 12.
87 *Reference re Secession of Quebec*, para. 43.
88 Ibid.
89 John Whyte has also identified the compact theory strain in the Court's Secession judgment. See Whyte, 'Constitutionalism and Nation,' 21; John D. Whyte, 'The Secession Reference and Constitutional Paradox,' in *The Quebec Decision*, ed. Schneiderman, 135.

The Supreme Court does say that Confederation was meant to create 'a unified country, not a loose alliance of autonomous provinces,' but makes this statement in the context of mentioning the myriad and complex economic and social issues that would need to be negotiated if and when Quebec decided to leave Canada. *Reference re Secession of Quebec*, para. 96.

90 *Reference re Secession of Quebec*, para. 40.

91 Ibid.

92 Buckner, 'The Maritimes and Confederation,' 29.

93 Kenneth E. Pryke, *Nova Scotia and Confederation, 1864–74* (Toronto: University of Toronto Press, 1979); Delphin A. Muise, 'The Federal Election of 1867 in Nova Scotia: An Economic Interpretation,' *Collections of the Nova Scotia Historical Society* 36 (1968): 327–51; James L. Sturgis, 'The Opposition to Confederation in Nova Scotia, 1864–1868,' in *The Causes of Confederation*, ed. Ged Martin, 141–29 (Fredericton: Acadiensis, 1990).

94 A.G. Bailey, 'The Basis and Persistence of Opposition to Confederation in New Brunswick,' *Canadian Historical Review* 23 (1942): 374–97; W.S. MacNutt, *New Brunswick: A History* (Toronto: Macmillan, 1963), 414–61; Morton, *Shaping a Nation*, 37–8; George E. Wilson, 'New Brunswick's Entrance into Confederation,' *Canadian Historical Review* 9 (1928): 4–24; Carl Wallace, 'Albert Smith, Confederation and Reaction in New Brunswick: 1852–1882,' *Canadian Historical Review* 44 (1963): 285–312.

95 Waite, *The Life and Times of Confederation*, 3.

96 *Reference re Secession of Quebec*, para. 42.

97 Ibid., quoting the colonial secretary to Lord Monck, in H. Wade MacLauchlan, 'Accounting for Democracy and the Rule of Law in the Quebec Secession Reference,' *Canadian Bar Review* 76 (1997): 168.

98 Buckner, 'The Maritimes and Confederation,' 16.

99 *Reference re Secession of Quebec*, para. 150.

100 Peter Hogg also identifies this inconsistency, in 'The Duty to Negotiate,' 34.

101 *Reference re Secession of Quebec*, para. 46.

102 A majority of the Court did say, however, that there was a legally non-enforceable 'constitutional convention' that the federal government get the agreement of the provinces. *Reference re Resolution to Amend the Constitution*, [1981] 1 S.C.R. 753. On the Patriation Reference, see Edward McWhinney, *Canada and the Constitution, 1979–1982: Patriation and the Charter of Rights* (Toronto: University of Toronto Press, 1982), 80–9; David Milne, *The Canadian Constitution: From Patriation to Meech Lake* (Toronto: Lorimer, 1989), 106–36; Robert Sheppard and Michael Valpy, *The National Deal: The Fight for a Canadian Constitution* (Toronto: Macmillan, 1982), 224–44; Roy Romanow, John Whyte, and Howard Leeson, *Canada ... Not-*

withstanding: The Making of the Constitution, 1976–1982 (Toronto: Carswell, 1984), 155–87; Peter Russell, 'Bold Statecraft, Questionable Jurisprudence,' in *And No One Cheered: Federalism, Democracy and the Constitution Act*, ed. Keith Banting and Richard Simeon, 210–38 (Toronto: Methuen, 1983).

103 *Reference re Secession of Quebec*, para. 47.

104 Political scientists and legal scholars have been quick to note this contradiction. See Jean Leclair, 'A Ruling in Search of a Nation,' *Canada Watch* 7, nos. 1–2 (1999): 22; McRoberts, 'In the Best Canadian Tradition,' 12; José Woehrling, 'Unexpected Consequences of Constitutional First Principles,' *Canada Watch* 7, nos. 1–2 (1999): 19.

105 John G. Reid, 'History, Native Issues and the Courts: A Forum,' *Acadiensis* 28 (1998): 7. Stephen Patterson is more dismissive of judges' ability to analyse historical developments on their own: 'Historians do not practice law, and in my view, jurists should not practice the historian's craft.' Stephen E. Patterson, 'Historians and the Courts,' *Acadiensis* 28 (1998): 21. Also see, for example, D.G. Bell, 'Historians and the Culture of the Courts,' *Acadiensis* 28 (1998): 23–26; Lori Ann Roness and Kent McNeil, 'Legalizing Oral History: Proving Aboriginal Claims in Canadian Courts,' *Journal of the West* 39, no. 3 (2000): 66–74; William C. Wicken, 'The Mi'kmaq and Wuastukwiuk Treaties,' *University of New Brunswick Law Journal* 43 (1994): 241–53; Wicken, 'R. v. Donald Marshall Jr, 1993–1996,' *Acadiensis* 28 (1998): 8–17.

106 *Delgamuukw v. British Columbia* (1991), 79 D.L.R. (4th) 185 (B.C.S.C.), p. 251.

107 Robin Brownlie and Mary Ellen-Kelm, 'Desperately Seeking Absolution: Native Agency as Colonialist Alibi?' *Canadian Historical Review* 75 (1994): 543–56; Robin Fisher, 'Judging History: Reflections on the Reasons for Judgment in Delgamuukw v. B.C.,' *BC Studies* 95 (1992): 43–54. Also see Donald J. Bourgeois, 'The Role of the Historian in the Litigation Process,' *Canadian Historical Review* 67 (1986): 195–205; G.M. Dickinson and R.D. Gidney, 'History and Advocacy: Some Reflections on the Historian's Role in Litigation,' *Canadian Historical Review* 68 (1987): 576–85.

108 *R. v. Marshall* [1999] 3 S.C.R. 456, para. 37.

109 Ibid.

110 Ibid.

2 'A New Federal Vision': Nova Scotia and the Rowell-Sirois Report, 1938–1948

T. STEPHEN HENDERSON

In the decade after the Second World War, the federal government of Canada expanded its reach into areas of taxation and spending that had traditionally belonged to the provinces. The trend of centralization of powers and resources had begun in earnest during the war and was bolstered by a series of tax rental agreements negotiated by Ottawa with most provincial governments. Many students of Canadian history assume that these developments were perfectly in line with the recommendations of the Royal Commission on Dominion-Provincial Relations, better known the Rowell-Sirois Commission. Indeed, some draw a straight line between the Rowell-Sirois Report and the tax rental agreements.[1]

The government of Nova Scotia carefully distinguished between the Rowell-Sirois Report and the tax rental agreements, hailing the former as the salvation of provincial autonomy and damning the latter as a trampling of provincial rights. Nova Scotia had long concerned itself with matters of federalism,[2] and in 1934 it conducted an inquiry into the province's economy and its place in the federation. The Jones Commission, as it became known, represented the latest in constitutional and liberal thinking in Canada and closely foreshadowed the Rowell-Sirois Report.[3] Nova Scotia also had a consistency in government, with the Liberals in power from 1933 to 1956, under Angus L. Macdonald from 1933 to 1940 and 1945 to 1954. Thus an examination of Nova Scotia's position on Rowell-Sirois and the tax rental agreements reveals subtle yet important differences in the two approaches to federalism at mid-century.

Was the Rowell-Sirois Report a blueprint for Dominion control or provincial autonomy? Much of the confusion certainly lies in the language historians have used – many routinely contrast 'centralization' with 'provincialism,' failing to define clearly either term; the former is often taken to mean 'national unity' while the latter term is used almost exclusively in a negative fashion.[4] According to the Rowell-Sirois Report, it was necessary to *centralize* many powers of taxation to better redistribute resources and ensure *provincial autonomy*. As the Report argues, 'National unity and provincial autonomy must not be thought of as competitors for the citizens' allegiance, for, in Canada at least, they are but two facets of the same thing … a sane federal system.'[5] Thus, upon closer examination, 'centralization' – as used in the Report – and 'provincialism' are not necessarily polar opposites; they may very well complement each other.

Political scientists have paid closer attention than historians to the subtleties of Dominion–provincial relations, often praising elements of 'classical federalism' in the constitution. Most studies of provincial autonomy, however, focus on the late nineteenth century or the period after Quebec's 1980 referendum on sovereignty. The first eight decades of the last century are disregarded, and even the monumental Rowell-Sirois Report often is viewed as irrelevant to contemporary federal discussions.[6] Donald V. Smiley made a very good beginning,[7] and Paul Romney – who makes a valiant defence of the compact theory of Confederation – accurately links a healthy federal balance to the liberal concept of responsible government, but misreads the Rowell-Sirois Report and is silent on post-war federalism.[8]

The recent work of historians Barry Ferguson and Robert Wardhaugh reclaims the Report's classical federalism, as envisioned by one of its central authors, Commissioner John W. Dafoe. The authors show that Dafoe's traditional liberalism had been undermined by the economic plight of the Prairie provinces; this rekindled his 'feisty regionalism' and 'led him to embrace positive government and to insist on the redistribution of wealth on a systematic basis not only from richer to poorer regions but also from richer to poorer individuals.' Dafoe believed that the Report's recommendations would enable provinces to meet their constitutional obligations and provide them with a greater measure of self-determination through a rational redistribution of wealth.[9]

Angus Macdonald and his political compatriots, certainly, saw Rowell-Sirois as the culmination of the 'new liberalism' – which embraced a 'positive' role for the state in building infrastructure and establishing social insurance programs – that had developed between the wars.[10] The Report proposed a standard quality of social services for Canadians, provided by whatever level of government could deliver them most effectively, and a system of resource-redistribution to ensure that financial hardship did not compromise a province's ability to meet its responsibilities. For Macdonald, Rowell-Sirois became the last best chance for the economically weaker provinces to direct their own affairs while providing modern services to their citizens.

Rowell-Sirois was born of economic and constitutional chaos. Seven years of depression had destroyed the faith that Dafoe and most Canadians had in laissez-faire capitalism and exposed serious flaws in the federal division of powers. The economic relapse of 1937 left most provincial governments either tremendously upset with W.L. Mackenzie King's Liberal government in Ottawa or willing to embrace unorthodox theories to deal with crushing poverty.[11] King faced simultaneously the looming bankruptcy of Manitoba and Saskatchewan, rumblings of revolt in British Columbia, Alberta, and Ontario, and a National Employment Commission proposal for an expensive, constitutionally questionable Dominion program of unemployment insurance. He breathed an immense sigh of relief when his Cabinet agreed to a commission to investigate matters between Ottawa and the provinces.[12] King selected five commissioners to represent the major regions of Canada: Newton Rowell, chief justice of the Supreme Court of Ontario; Joseph Sirois, professor of law at Laval University; Dafoe, editor of the *Winnipeg Free Press*; Henry Angus, professor of economics at the University of British Columbia, and R.A. MacKay, professor of political science at Dalhousie University.[13]

The province of Nova Scotia emerged as Rowell-Sirois's foremost champion. The provincial government cooperated fully with the commission at its 1938 hearings and supported its proposals at the 1941 Dominion-Provincial Conference called to consider the Report. At the conferences on Reconstruction in 1945 and 1946 Nova Scotia continued to urge the adoption of the key Rowell-Sirois recommendations. The provincial government publicly pined for the principles of federalism expressed in the Report, even as it signed a tax rental agreement with the Dominion in 1947. Finally, at the 1948 Liberal leadership convention, Premier Macdonald decried the federal government for ignoring the recommendations of the Rowell-Sirois Report.

Nova Scotia's affinity for constitutional review and reform was the result both of frustration and careful study. The province was well known for seeking 'better terms' to address its dissatisfaction with the British North American Act.[14] Previous royal commissions investigating the state of affairs in Nova Scotia had found merit in the case the province put forward. In 1926, the Royal Commission on the Claims of the Maritime provinces – chaired by Sir Andrew Rae Duncan – investigated the grievances of the Maritime provinces and recommended a significant increase in subsidies, changes to federal transportation policies, and several other measures intended to revive the economies of the three eastern provinces. In 1935, the Royal Commission of Inquiry into the Readjustment of the Financial Arrangements between the Maritime provinces and the Dominion of Canada, chaired by Sir Thomas White, again found in favour of the Maritimes and recommended another increase in subsidies.[15] More importantly, the provincial Jones Commission concluded in 1934 that 'constitutional changes are essential to the maintenance of national standards.'[16]

Shortly after the Macdonald Liberals took power in 1933, they appointed a royal commission of inquiry into the province's economy. J.H. Jones, a professor of economics at the University of Leeds, chaired the commission and was joined by H.A. Innis, a political economist from the University of Toronto, and Alexander Johnston, former deputy minister of marine and fisheries. Queen's professor Norman McLeod Rogers prepared Nova Scotia's brief, and R.A. MacKay, R. MacGregor Dawson, and S.A. Saunders contributed research studies. The Jones Commission drew on the same academic circles and reached many of the same conclusions as the Rowell-Sirois Commission four years later.[17] In particular the Jones Report argued that it was Ottawa's task to 'establish equity' among the provinces because federal economic policies differently affected the several regions of the country.[18] It called for the Dominion to assume responsibility for some services currently provided by provincial governments and for 'other services, such as health and employment insurance, that may be established in the future.' Ottawa could also create 'a fund for allocation among the different Provinces in accordance with their needs ... [calculated by] impartial study.'[19]

Macdonald warmly received the Rowell-Sirois Commission in Halifax in February 1938. For their part, the commissioners must have relished a trip to the East Coast, especially considering the unpleasant receptions it had received and anticipated elsewhere. In British Columbia, a hostile representative of the provincial government confronted the commissioners, and in Alberta, the provincial government refused even to appear at the public hearings.[20] New Brunswick had recently been hostile to any constitutional discussions and repeatedly asked to postpone its presentation to the commission to the last.[21] Finally, most observers were not surprised by the cool welcome later shown by both of the central provinces. Ontario Premier Mitchell Hepburn lectured the commission on his version of provincial rights: the protection of wealth in Ontario from outside tax collectors. Quebec's Maurice Duplessis, steadfast in his resistance to any federal incursion into the provincial sphere, refused to appear at the hearings but did host a dinner where his colleagues' crude jokes offended most of the commissioners.[22]

Most of the Nova Scotian brief was written by the premier himself and was thus a well-crafted legal argument rather than a statistical analysis of Nova Scotia's place in Confederation.[23] Trained in law at Dalhousie and Harvard, Macdonald adroitly presented the brief to the commission, proposing that constitutional powers and responsibilities be adjusted to meet the needs of an industrialized nation:

> For the economic and social welfare of the people, there should be a significant redistribution of financial powers and responsibilities. Responsibility for paying for and administering old age pensions and mothers' allowances should be shifted to Ottawa, as well as exclusive jurisdiction over marketing, unemployment insurance, employment service, maximum hours of labour, weekly rest, and related matters. In return for the assumption of these responsibilities, as well as for reasons of efficiency and economy, Ottawa should have exclusive access to income taxes and succession duties.
>
> Secondly, for the welfare of the provincial governments themselves, they should be given access to such indirect taxes as gasoline and sales taxes. More importantly, however, a Federal Grants Commission should be established, along the lines of the Australian Commonwealth Grants Commission, to respond to provincial applications for special grants or subsidies. The appointment of such a commission, argued Macdonald, would be an explicit recognition of what had always been the case: federal subsidies to the provinces ... were based on fiscal need.[24]

Macdonald's familiarity with his subject struck one observer: 'He is the first witness to testify with utter self-confidence, no fumbling for words or ideas, and something like a prose style.'[25]

Newton Rowell was cool to the idea of a grants commission and asked Macdonald if it were possible that such a commission would reduce a province's subsidy, hinting that Nova Scotia might not like what it was asking for. Macdonald agreed that a province might get no subsidy at all; its fiscal need would be gauged annually. The Dominion need not go further into debt to assist the poorer provinces, according to Macdonald. 'Instead, Ottawa could serve as the distributing agent for the wealth of other provinces ... it was only reasonable that some of that wealth [enhanced by certain national policies] should be distributed on what we think is a more equitable basis.'[26]

In Macdonald, the Rowell-Sirois Commission had found a very cooperative premier. He was willing to participate in fundamentally redrafting the BNA Act, which he saw as piece of imperial legislation badly in need of modernizing.[27] He favoured centralizing the most important progressive taxes and key areas of social responsibility to enable the Dominion to mitigate the disparities between rich and poor provinces. While his proposals might have been less possible politically than even the Rowell-Sirois Report proved to be, Macdonald believed strongly that discussion and negotiation could lead to some improvements in Canadian federalism.

When finally written, the Report's basic scheme, known as Plan One, echoed most of the main points of Nova Scotia's presentation. It suggested that the Dominion assume responsibility for 'unemployed employables' and Old Age Pensions, leaving the provinces all 'residuary responsibility for social welfare expenditures.' In the interests of rationalizing taxation and equitably distributing national wealth, the Report recommended that Ottawa assume exclusive control of income and corporate taxes and succession duties, giving the provinces 'adjustment grants' based on fiscal need, rather than 'subsidies' based on a per capita rate. To sweeten the deal and entice the provinces to support the Report, Plan One also recommended that the Dominion assume the 'deadweight' debts of the provinces.[28]

The Report was tabled in the House of Commons in May 1940 shortly after the King government won a sizeable majority and an apparent mandate to conduct a limited war effort.[29] Germany's march through Western Europe that spring pushed Canadian constitutional questions aside for a time, but eventually a Dominion-provincial conference was called for early in 1941, with the Rowell-Sirois Report as the only item on the agenda.

Nine premiers gathered in Ottawa on 14 January to hear Ottawa's proposals and to voice their differing views on the Report. Provinces that were in dire financial situations throughout the 1930s and provinces whose economies had not been rosy in decades welcomed the idea of redistributing wealth. After all, the argument ran, most large corporations were based in Toronto and Montreal and paid taxes to Ontario and Quebec, even though their profits were earned across Canada. All provinces had a right to share in the nation's wealth. Furthermore, as the Report noted, 'The general effect of national policies has been to accelerate the natural shift of industry and finance, and of concentration of wealth and income, to Central Canada.'[30] If something were not done to halt the concentration of capital, provincial autonomy would wither.[31]

The provinces that held the lion's share of the national wealth, however, found little to admire in the Report. Duff Pattullo, premier of British Columbia, told his legislature that he disagreed with the conclusions of the commission and 'the very bases' upon which these conclusions were drawn.[32] At the conference, Ontario's Premier Hepburn referred derisively to the 'five hundred thousand dollar report – the product of the minds of three professors and a Winnipeg newspaper man.' He went on to compare its proponents to 'the enemies of civilization' currently afoot in Europe.[33] Alberta's Social Credit Premier William Aberhart recognized that change was necessary in Canada, but doubted very much that the Report was the best option.[34] Of course the Liberal premier of Quebec, Adelard Godbout, was politely reserved in his discussion.[35]

Nova Scotia was represented at the conference by Premier A.S. MacMillan, Macdonald having taken a post in the Dominion Cabinet for the war. MacMillan was relatively uneducated, but years of experience in government had made him an effective administrator. He believed in 'tangible' politics; his most common boast was of how many miles of Nova Scotian roads the Liberal government had paved.[36] MacMillan said that if he were forced to accept or reject Plan One as it stood, he would have to reject it. Yet he went on to say that the recommendations offered 'no insurmountable difficulty to our province,' and that he intended to rely on the Report in negotiating a new plan for Confederation.[37] Clearly, MacMillan was taking a cautious-but-congenial approach in the plenary session.

Sitting on the Dominion's side of the table, Macdonald worked to mend fences and get negotiations moving after Hepburn's opening tirade. He passed a note to the prime minister, urging King to show some flexibility as a sign of goodwill. 'Mr Aberhart is willing to consider the Sirois Report, along with other matters. Hepburn is willing to talk about the war. If we accepted the idea of discussing *something*, could we by degrees get to a consideration of the Report?'[38] MacMillan warned that the public would think those in attendance were 'afraid to tackle the situation.'[39] The conference, however, broke up in failure on the second day.

It has been argued that the Dominion government not only expected but also hoped that the conference would collapse quickly.[40] Christopher Armstrong writes, 'Gradually, prime ministers like R.B. Bennett and Mackenzie King also recognized that the holding of such conferences might be either a substitute for action or a means of legitimizing actions already planned to which the provinces would not consent. A skilfully orchestrated meeting which broke up in disagreement could provide an excuse for the prime minister to act unilaterally to deal with pressing national problems. Thus, ceremony served a useful purpose, and in the course of time it began to be accepted that a conference of first ministers was the proper forum for discussions of the highest constitutional significance.'[41] Armstrong and others might be reading too much method into King's madness – he later blamed the report itself for the failure of the conference[42] – but the Dominion did move quickly to centralize control of most of Canada's taxation system.

In his April 1941 budget speech, Finance Minister J.L. Ilsley announced that Ottawa would be raising income and corporate taxes significantly, in effect forcing the provinces from these fields. The Dominion then negotiated agreements with the provinces to 'rent' tax fields from them in exchange for a subsidy representing what the fields had been worth. These agreements preserved the inequalities between provinces, as those who had large tax bases to give up got more revenue back from Ottawa. Provinces such as Nova Scotia, which in 1939 had no income tax and low corporate tax rates, got little from the Dominion treasury. MacMillan was not pleased with the deal Nova Scotia signed but, like most premiers, felt obliged to 'support the war effort.' Rowell-Sirois was a better plan, and perhaps it would be introduced after the war.[43]

David Fransen argues that the collapse of the conference was the end of the Rowell-Sirois Report, though most people did not notice. Certainly commissioners Dafoe, Angus, and MacKay all assumed that the logic of their Report would make it indispensable to the nation in the Reconstruction period.[44] The economic trauma of the 1930s had eased but was near enough in memory to compel Dominion and provincial leaders to seriously consider reforming the BNA Act.

In the summer of 1945, with the European war won and the Pacific war winding down, the Dominion presented its plan for reconstruction to the provinces. Essentially, Ottawa proposed to entrench centralized taxation powers and assume responsibility for some social welfare programs but to leave constitutional questions aside. Keynesian monetary policy obviously influenced the Dominion's proposals, as it promised to develop a depression-resistant economy through a centralized fiscal policy. To entice the provinces to sign the new tax rental agreements, the Dominion tacked on a substantial social welfare package – which would add universal Health Insurance to existing Old Age Pension, Unemployment Insurance, and Family Allowances programs – along with generous subsidies to the provinces based on population and previous taxation levels. Ottawa's proposals for reconstruction became known as 'the Green Book.' As Janine Brodie points out, this plan was a significant divergence from the Rowell-Sirois Report: 'In the heady days of economic growth immediately following the war, the federal government chose to ignore, largely because of the opposition of the richer provinces, the recommendations of the Rowell-Sirois Commission for unconditional grants targeted to the poorer regions of the country. Instead, emphasis was placed on promoting aggregate economic growth and stability, and on creating the outlines of the modern welfare state.'[45] Dominion officials accepted the formula that national economic growth, combined with a social welfare net, would raise the standard of living of all provinces.[46] Rather than moving toward a clearer division of constitutional powers, the Green Book proposed extending Ottawa's reach even further into provincial spheres in the interest of managing the economy.

Ottawa's shift from Rowell-Sirois to the Green Book lay almost entirely with its senior civil servants and might be attributed both to fear and mental exhaustion. Queen's professor J.A. Corry conducted research for Rowell-Sirois and worked on the final draft of the Report; he returned to Ottawa in 1943–4 to advise on the shift to peace. Corry later wrote that those in Ottawa feared a post-war economic collapse without aggressive action: 'Almost all the attention during the discussions was focused on finding ways to extend the federal government's reach ... In the circumstances we were then facing, the federal government, the one with the longest reach, was, of course, best equipped to take the lead in moving us from a war to a peace-time footing. But in later less critical circumstances, even strong nationalists are learning now that centralization of power and activity isn't automatically the best arrangement.'[47] Journalist Grant Dexter found a level of weariness in the planners at the end of the war. W.A. Mackintosh, who was just leaving the Department of Finance to return to Queen's, told Dexter that he had been playing 'an intellectual form of volleyball – bouncing ideas off Mr [C.D.] Howe's battleship steel headpiece. Some of 'em bounce pretty far … He finds that Howe agrees but does not know what he is agreeing with.'[48]

The August 1945 Dominion-Provincial Conference proved much more amiable than the 1941 version. Some of the more 'difficult' personalities were gone, and the provincial representatives were in Ottawa only to hear the Dominion's proposals, not to come to any immediate decisions.[49] Mackenzie King opened the proceedings on 6 August 1945 in a cordial manner: 'We believe that the sure road of Dominion-Provincial cooperation lies in the achievement in their own spheres of genuine autonomy for the provinces. By genuine autonomy, I mean effective financial independence, not only for the wealthier provinces but also for those less favourably situated.'[50] Premiers Drew and Duplessis followed King, both voicing the expected distaste for further centralization of revenue and responsibilities. Nova Scotia's MacMillan stood and said he welcomed their comments opposing centralization and hoped that they would participate in reversing the centralization of Maritime industries to Ontario and Quebec.[51]

MacMillan's general approach at the August conference, however, was reserved to say the least. Though he had told no one, he had decided to retire in two weeks and either would not or could not get into a detailed discussion of the Dominion's proposals. Rather, he explained with folksy humour that he had no brief to present and that it would take him several months to read and understand the Dominion's offer. The tax rental agreement would be left to the next Nova Scotian premier to negotiate.[52]

Angus L. Macdonald returned to the premiership of Nova Scotia unopposed at the Liberal leadership convention held on 31 August 1945; he solidified his position with an electoral landslide on 23 October 1945.[53] Macdonald was welcomed home by the *Halifax Chronicle* as the man needed to 'hammer into the federal mind that we are against further centralization … that we want nothing to do with any proposal to exchange what remains of our birthright for a slightly increased mess of federal pottage.'[54] Indeed, in his acceptance speech at the convention, Macdonald said his government's task was to 'secure equality of opportunity for Nova Scotians' and 'to guard Nova Scotia's rights.'[55] Certainly, Macdonald appeared as Achilles finally come out of his tent, but his position was consistent over the next twenty months and very close to the Rowell-Sirois Report.

Macdonald quickly prepared a reply to the Dominion's proposals,

which he presented at the November Dominion-provincial conference.[56] He argued that 'the road to genuine provincial autonomy' was
not necessarily 'the road of financial independence.' A clear division of
responsibilities and resources was necessary to ensure balance in the
federal system; the Dominion was premature in its proposals of fiscal
reform

> To be strictly logical, it seems to me that we should make constitutional
> changes first and taxation arrangements afterward. This is indeed more
> than a matter of logic. It is the essence, for it is basic to a Federal system
> that the Constitution shall divide the responsibilities of a government first,
> and arm the responsible units with the legal power and sources of revenue
> appropriate to that division ...
> When the Sirois Commission sat, the Nova Scotia Government of that
> day intimated its willingness to have the British North America Act
> amended so that the Provinces could delegate powers to the Dominion,
> and the Dominion could delegate powers to the Provinces. The Govern-
> ment of Nova Scotia still adheres to that view, and we are prepared to
> enter into discussion with the Dominion along that line.

Macdonald said that the Report was clearly acceptable to the Dominion when it was presented, even if the 1941 conference failed. The
tax rental proposals were something new. 'I should like to know why
the principles and conclusion of the Sirois Report, framed after such
careful study, framed by a Commission appointed by the Dominion
Government, approved by the Dominion Government, should now be
disregarded and abandoned by that Government.'[57]
    Macdonald then posed thirteen questions to the Dominion, essen-
tially seeking to determine if it was planning further invasions of provincial tax fields, or if it would offer guarantees against doing so. He
specifically asked if the Dominion would vacate the fields of gasoline,
electricity, and amusement/pari-mutuel taxes – fields that Ottawa had
entered during the war – and recognize them as fields belonging exclusively to the provinces.[58] The Dominion responded on 5 December
1945, refusing to commit itself to anything: 'The Dominion is not willing to give general commitments which might hamper, in unexpected
ways, future budgetary policy.'[59] It would abandon the minor tax fields
only if compensated by the provinces for its losses.
    Macdonald received encouragement in his stand from several sourc-
es. Wishart Robertson, an old friend and now the government leader in

the Senate, wrote that he had 'heard several complimentary references to your representation of Nova Scotia's case, in Cabinet circles. They seem to think that you are one of the few who seem to know exactly what they wanted.'[60] Sir James Dunn urged Macdonald to 'hold on to the essentials of democracy. I wish to be saved from the slavery of bureaucracy, particularly centralized bureaucracy.'[61]

In January 1946, as he was preparing his province's next submission, Macdonald sought advice from two leading scholars, J.A. Corry and H.A. Innis. Macdonald knew Corry's work for Rowell-Sirois and also had sought advice from Corry while he was a member of Parliament for Kingston. Innis, of course, had been recruited for the Jones Commission. In a telegram, Macdonald asked, 'Will centralization of taxing authority in these fields tend to promote employment and prosperity throughout Canada?'[62]

Corry replied that he had been considering this question for three or fours years and still was not sure of the answer. The economists he most respected were Keynesians, but he was not sold on the appropriateness of the theory to a federal state such as Canada. Corry doubted whether Dominion officials had the political will to follow the dictates of Keynesianism and suspected that they would repeatedly opt for politically expedient solutions. He also warned that the Dominion's corps of civil servants was dangerously more adept than the provinces'; capable Dominion bureaucrats could 'out-talk provincial civil servants and confuse them with massive statistics and recondite theoretical arguments.'[63]

Innis responded that Ottawa's faith in monetary policy was misplaced. This approach, he argued, would do nothing to achieve parity between the Maritimes and the St Lawrence.[64] Innis implored Macdonald to stand firm: 'It seems to me that the federal principle disappears unless you continue to insist on your position in Nova Scotia.' The problems of the Maritime provinces 'can only be met by piecemeal *ad hoc* considerations and not by overall blank checks.'[65]

Macdonald held his position as he laid out Nova Scotia's proposals to the Dominion in late January. Though he would prefer constitutional discussions to precede any financial arrangements, Macdonald insisted on a few key principles if financial talks were to continue.[66] Provinces must have guaranteed and exclusive sources of revenue; thus, the Dominion would have to vacate the minor tax fields – gasoline, electricity, and amusement/pari-mutuel taxes – and pledge not to expand further into other provincial fields, in exchange for exclusive Dominion control of income and corporate taxes and succession duties. Fiscal need must be the basis of determining provincial subsidies rather than the fixed, per capita formulae; the Duncan Commission recognized this principle in 1926, and the Rowell-Sirois Commission, in 1940. Finally, Macdonald called for fixed, annual Dominion-provincial conferences.

The Dominion, for its part, repeated that it would not vacate the minor fields without compensation, but it was willing to discuss the matter. It was open to seeking a constitutional amendment allowing provinces to collect a sales tax, but made no further mention of constitutional discussions.[67] The Dominion argued that the per capita grant system was virtually the same as the fiscal need basis. Finally, the Dominion stated that it felt fixed, annual conferences would be too rigid for Canada's parliamentary system.[68]

At the Dominion-provincial conference held in April and May 1946, Macdonald went back to his theme that the fiscal negotiations were premature until constitutional responsibilities had been properly divided. He suggested discussions to revise the BNA Act within three years, the life of the proposed tax rental agreements. He also repeated his demand that the minor fields be provincially controlled, as they had been first implemented and administered by the provinces. Furthermore, these revenues were used for provincial purposes: gasoline taxes went toward road construction and maintenance, electricity taxes supported rural electrification programs, and amusement taxes paid for censor boards.[69]

Overlapping responsibilities and resources, Macdonald maintained, threatened federalism in Canada. As it stood, the Dominion could continue to enter provincial fields, gradually weakening a province's position. The provinces would end up either helping to fund programs about which they were not consulted or surrendering resources to the Dominion so that it could fund the programs alone. The results would be catastrophic for the provinces: 'Provincial autonomy will be gone. Provincial independence will vanish. Provincial dignity will disappear. Provincial governments will become mere annuitants of Ottawa. Provincial public life ... will be debased and degraded.' Finance minister and fellow Nova Scotian J.L. Ilsley could not accept his long-time colleague's assessment. Fixed subsidies, he argued, were more dignified than fiscal need subsidies that would require a province to prove its penury.[70]

As a conciliatory gesture, Macdonald said that he was willing to compensate the Dominion if it would vacate the minor fields.[71] He also recommended that the conference be adjourned for a time to enable all parties to consider the proposals and their positions. He noted that the Confederation talks took more than two years and hinted that the representatives need not be hasty now.[72]

The conference did adjourn, but the adjournment became permanent. The Dominion appeared once again to use a Dominion-provincial conference's failure to justify taking unilateral action. In his June budget, Ilsley announced the Dominion's intention to obtain agreements on its tax rental proposals on a province-by-province basis, rather than in a general conference. Macdonald criticized this approach as 'undignified' and apt to promote jealousy, as each province would have to seek better terms than those who signed before.[73]

Macdonald's vocal opposition to the Dominion's tactics and his continued refusal to sign a tax rental agreement made him rather notorious in national political circles. In the national press, he was linked with Drew and Duplessis as one of the 'Trio of Malcontents.'[74] Macdonald met with Drew and Duplessis in Montreal in November 1946 to discuss Dominion-provincial relations, but their goal was to find common ground in pursuit of a deal rather than to conspire against Ottawa. Macdonald had earlier complimented Drew on his attempts to find a solution,[75] and in Montreal's Windsor Hotel he found that the sides were not as far apart as Ottawa seemed to think. Duplessis said that Quebec would give up income and most corporate taxes, but not succession duties. Drew said he was willing to surrender income and corporate taxes and succession duties but not the minor fields, especially electricity. The three premiers also talked about the possibility of Macdonald's hosting a provincial conference in Halifax to develop a united proposal for the Dominion.[76]

Some observers attributed Macdonald's intransigence to his hostility toward King, stemming from their wartime break over conscription.[77] King, however, provided virtually no leadership to the government on the tax rental question and was inclined to agree with his former naval minister on the subject of Dominion-provincial relations. After meeting with Macdonald for an afternoon in January 1947, King wrote that 'the Finance Dept. had in its original programme gone too far in what appeared to be taking from the provinces certain fiscal rights and leading to centralization in expenditure.' Yet the prime minister would not consent to calling another Dominion-provincial conference, though his reason was one of indignation, rather than strategy. 'I told [Macdonald] there were times and seasons for all things – he could hardly expect, recalling the way Duplessis had behaved at the last conference and the way he talked, and of Drew speaking about the government being incompetent, etc., that men like St Laurent, Ilsley, Abbott, and myself could be expected to want to have annual conferences with them.'[78]

By the end of 1946, New Brunswick, Prince Edward Island, Manitoba, Saskatchewan, and British Columbia had agreed tentatively on tax rental issues with the Dominion.[79] Liberals across Canada were increasingly displeased with Macdonald for his standoff with Ottawa. As Macdonald's former executive assistant at Naval Affairs informed him, 'The great secrecy surrounding your position on Dominion-Provincial relations has always caused considerable speculations here. [Senator] Rupert Davies was complaining about the damage being done to the Party in Ontario because of the fact that the Globe and Mail speaks of Drew and Duplessis and yourself in the same sense.'[80] Macdonald was getting frustrated with those who misunderstood his position: 'I thought that Drew was a Christian and believed in God. Was it therefore to be expected that I should renounce my belief in a Deity? I cannot help it if on this point of Dominion-Provincial relations Drew's stand in several respects agrees with mine. I feel definitely sure that I am right – that is, it is impossible to talk of a federal state, unless the Provinces have some tax fields of their own.'[81]

Macdonald had his supporters at the national level, but they tended to be 'on the outs' with the King government. Writing from the Senate, T.A. Crerar advised Macdonald that he was on 'solid ground' in his stand.[82] Macdonald told Crerar he thought that the Rowell-Sirois Report was 'pretty profound' and that the Dominion officials were too optimistic about their plan to manage the economy with monetary measures.[83] Crerar, a Manitoban, wrote that Stuart Garson would have preferred a deal based on Rowell-Sirois, but that he took the current offer, as it put Manitoba in good fiscal shape.[84]

Another wanderer from King's Cabinet, C.G. 'Chubby' Power, thought Macdonald was correct in his principles on this point. He chided Macdonald for his increasing infamy in Ottawa: 'I note with some interest that the practice of black-mail which legend hath said originated in the Highlands of Scotland is now being practiced with great success by one Rob Roy McDonald with a poor unfortunate Southron Abbot as the victim and as usual the peasantry and commonalty suffer.'[85]

In the end, Nova Scotia negotiated a deal with the Dominion. The province was given almost $11 million in annual subsidies – about one-third of its total revenues for 1947–8 – in exchange for vacating the income tax, corporate tax, and succession fields. The Dominion agreed to withdraw from the gasoline tax field, but not from electricity, and as for the other minor fields, 'The Dominion recognizes the desire of the Provinces to have taxation fields of their own. We are prepared, therefore, to say that in view of the nature of amusement and pari-mutuel fields, and of the special interest of the Provinces in respect thereto, it will be our policy to vacate these fields as soon as circumstances permit.'[86] Ottawa also agreed to hold a Dominion-provincial conference *at least* one year before the expiry of the tax rental agreement.

Macdonald won some victories in the agreement, including the Duncan and White subsidies, the Dominion's vacating the field of gasoline taxes, and especially its recognition that having exclusive sources of revenue for provinces was a desirable thing. He did not win other important points, however. The Dominion did not agree to hold regular conferences; its statement about exclusive tax fields was equivocal, and the subsidies, though generous, did not establish fiscal need as a basis for the redistribution of national wealth. Nova Scotia signed because its wartime budget surpluses were dwindling and because it had no allies left among the poorer provinces.[87]

Macdonald did not give up hope. He continued to sing the praises of the Rowell-Sirois Report, always implying that its recommendations should be used as a guide in the *next* round of negotiations. Shortly after the Nova Scotia legislature ratified the tax rental agreement, Macdonald explained his position once more to a delegate to the upcoming Young Liberal convention in Hamilton:

> While the Dominion proposals give us much more money than we could get by ourselves, the same result could have been obtained in other ways without infringing so much on provincial autonomy ... If the Sirois plan had been adopted, we would be getting more money, and while the Sirois Report recommended that we should give up income taxes, corporation tax and succession duties, it stated very definitely that if the Dominion got these fields of taxation they should be very careful to respect the provinces' rights in the remaining fields.
>
> In this instance, the Dominion started out by trying to take a great deal more than the Sirois Commission suggested and it was only after a very long struggle that we were able to beat them down to the present position.[88]

Macdonald's references to Rowell-Sirois became less frequent after he signed the tax rental agreement, but he still brought it up and drew some important lessons from it.[89]

The Rowell-Sirois Commission did recommend a transfer of powers from the provinces to the Dominion, but it is inaccurate to view the Report as an instrument of centralization. The centralization of taxation powers was intended to rationalize the tax system, to lower the costs of collection, and to make the system more progressive. Fundamental to the Report was the assumption that the new taxation system would be used to redistribute national wealth and support provincial autonomy by shrinking the gap between rich and poor provinces. In other words, *centralization* would assist the achievement of *equalization*.

Some historians have contemptuously referred to the 'provincialism' of any critic of Rowell-Sirois or the tax rental agreements, lumping together a wide range of arguments and ignoring the fact that Ottawa ultimately killed the Report. This prejudice masks the subtleties of the criticisms and the constructive ideas put forward in defence of provincial autonomy. The same observers often assume that the 1945 tax rental agreements were merely Rowell-Sirois by a different name. Thus, Angus L. Macdonald, who supported the first and resisted the second, appears initially as a 'centralizer' when he supported Rowell-Sirois[90] and as someone who 'held strong views on provincial rights' when he refused to sign a tax rental agreement.[91]

In fact, Macdonald was consistent in his stand from 1938 to 1948 on the question of Dominion-provincial relations. He agreed with the Rowell-Sirois Report that a healthy federal system necessitated that all levels of government be able to perform their assigned functions. This required the adoption of two new constitutional principles. First, provinces must be relatively equal in their powers to serve their citizens, lest the weaker provinces atrophy while the stronger ones grow to compete directly with the Dominion. To achieve this equality, some measure of revenue redistribution would be necessary, and that redistribution would be best managed by the central power: the Dominion. Second, provinces must be assured independence of action in areas that were their own. This meant that responsibilities must be clearly divided and that revenues allocated must be appropriate to the responsibilities. For Macdonald, the Rowell-Sirois Report articulated both of these principles, and thus he worked – unsuccessfully – to give life to its recommendations.

NOTES

1 See, for example, J.M. Bumsted, *The Peoples of Canada: A Post-Confederation History*, 2nd ed. (Toronto: Oxford University Press, 2004), 229–30.

2 See, for example, Colin D. Howell, 'W.S. Fielding and the Repeal Elections of 1886 and 1887 in Nova Scotia,' *Acadiensis* 8, no. 2 (1979): 28–46; and E.R. Forbes, *The Maritime Rights Movement, 1919–1927: A Study in Canadian Regionalism* (Montreal and Kingston: McGill-Queen's University Press, 1979).

3 Nova Scotia, *Report of the Royal Commission of Provincial Economic Inquiry* (Halifax: King's Printer, 1934).

4 See, for example, Robert Bothwell, Ian Drummond, and John English, *Canada 1900–1945* (Toronto: University of Toronto Press, 1987), 276; and Bothwell, Drummond, and English, *Canada since 1945: Power, Politics and Provincialism* (Toronto: University of Toronto Press, 1981), 73.

5 Canada, *Report of the Royal Commission on Dominion-Provincial Relations,* book 2, *Recommendations* (Ottawa: King's Printer, 1940), 269, quoted in Angus L. Macdonald's 'Federalism in Canada,' a speech given to the Canada Club of Toronto, 1 December 1947, file 31-3(a), vol. 920, MG2, Angus L. Macdonald Papers (hereafter ALM Papers), Nova Scotia Archives and Records Management.

6 On the contributions and shortfalls of political science's discussion of the development of Canada's federal system, see Barry Ferguson and Robert Wardhaugh, '"Impossible Conditions of Inequality": John Dafoe, the Rowell-Sirois Commission, and the Interpretation of Canadian Federalism,' *Canadian Historical Review* 84, no. 4 (2003): 552–3.

7 See, especially, Donald V. Smiley, 'The Rowell-Sirois Report, Provincial Autonomy, and Postwar Canadian Federalism,' *Canadian Journal of Economics and Political Science* 28, no. 1 (1962): 54–69.

8 Paul Romney, *Getting It Wrong: How Canadians Forgot Their Past and Imperilled Confederation* (Toronto: University of Toronto Press, 1999). See also Romney, 'Provincial Equality, Special Status and the Compact Theory of Canadian Confederation,' *Canadian Journal of Political Science* 32, no. 1 (1999): 21–39.

9 Ferguson and Wardhaugh, '"Impossible Conditions of Inequality,"' 576–7, 581.

10 On the shift from classical to new liberalism, see Barry Ferguson, *Remaking Liberalism: The Intellectual Legacy of Adam Shortt, O.D. Skelton, W.C. Clark, and W.A. Mackintosh, 1890–1925* (Montreal and Kingston: McGill-Queen's University Press, 1993); and Doug Owram, *The Government Generation: Canadian Intellectuals and the State, 1900–1945* (Toronto: University of Toronto Press, 1986).

11 Blair Neatby, *William Lyon Mackenzie King, 1932–1939: The Prism of Unity* (Toronto: University of Toronto Press, 1976), 186–7.

12 Ibid., 195–201. On the creation of the Rowell-Sirois Commission, see Ferguson and Wardhaugh, '"Impossible Conditions of Inequality,"' 556–9; David

W. Fransen, '"Unscrewing the Unscrutable": The Rowell-Sirois Commission, the Ottawa Bureaucracy and Public Finance Reform, 1935–1941' (PhD dissertation, University of Toronto, 1984), 58–81; and James Struthers, *No Fault of Their Own: Unemployment and the Canadian Welfare State, 1914–1941* (Toronto: University of Toronto Press, 1983), 175–84.

13 Sirois replaced Supreme Court Justice Thibaudeau Rinfret, who resigned as a result of ill health, as Quebec's representative late in 1937.

14 See, for example, J. Murray Beck, *Joseph Howe*, vol. 1, *The Briton Becomes Canadian, 1848–1873* (Montreal and Kingston: McGill-Queen's University Press, 1983), 197–250; Howell, 'Fielding and the Repeal Elections'; and Forbes, *Maritime Rights.*

15 Canada, *Report of the Royal Commission on Maritime Claims* (Ottawa: King's Printer, 1927); and Canada, *Report of the Royal Commission on Financial Arrangements between the Dominion and the Maritime Provinces* (Ottawa: King's Printer, 1935).

16 Norman McL. Rogers, 'The Constitutional Impasse,' *Queen's Quarterly* 46, no. 4 (1934): 475–86.

17 See T. Stephen Henderson, *Angus L. Macdonald: A Provincial Liberal* (Toronto: University of Toronto Press, 2007), 61–5; Nova Scotia, *Provincial Economic Inquiry*; and John Richard Rowell, 'An Intellectual in Politics: Norman Rogers as an Intellectual and Minister of Labour, 1929–1939' (MA thesis, Queen's University, 1978), 59–66. By 1937, Rogers had become the federal minister of labour and strongly supported the creation and work of the Rowell-Sirois Commission.

18 Rogers presented the Jones Commission with figures that indicated that the national tariff structure worked to the detriment of Nova Scotia and to the clear benefit of Quebec and Ontario. His methods and statistics were quickly challenged; see D.C. MacGregor, 'The Provincial Incidence of the Canadian Tariff,' *Canadian Journal of Economics and Political Science* 1 (1935): 384–95.

19 Nova Scotia, *Provincial Economic Inquiry*, 71–7. The report did not go into detail on how 'fiscal need' might be determined but suggested that the decennial census could be used to calculate population change, taxation capacity, and economic conditions.

20 See Fransen, "Unscrewing the Unscrutable," 180–200. British Columbia had employed Senator J.W. deB. Farris, a private lawyer, to act as its counsel.

21 Since 1935, New Brunswick's constitutional policies had been shaped by the unorthodox ideas of A.P. Paterson, a self-taught 'expert' on the *BNA Act* and minister without portfolio in the Alison Dysart government. Paterson argued that no constitutional changes were necessary; if only Ottawa

would fulfil its contractual obligations under the *BNA Act*, New Brunswick
would become a land of plenty. See Paterson, *The True Story of Confederation* (Saint John: Saint John Board of Trade, 1926); and Kenneth H. LeBlanc,
'A.P. Paterson and New Brunswick's Response to Constitutional Change,
1935–1939' (MA thesis, University of New Brunswick, 1989), 31.

22 Fransen, '"Unscrewing the Unscrutable,"' 212–31, 243–6.

23 Ibid., 161; Macdonald to Sister Veronica (Mairi Macdonald), 12 February
1940, file 414, vol. 1506, ALM Papers; and Macdonald to Alex Johnston,
10 January 1938, file 398, vol. 1504, ALM Papers. Macdonald noted that he
wrote the first and third sections, while the Attorney-General's office
wrote the second. He worried that the brief had been imperfect, for he
had not had sufficient time to work on it, as a result of other government
business.

24 Fransen, '"Unscrewing the Unscrutable,"' 162–3. See also Nova Scotia, *Submission of the Government of the Province of Nova Scotia to the Royal Commission on Dominion-Provincial Relations, February 1938* (Halifax: King's Printer,
1938); and Nova Scotia, 'Submission by the Government of Nova Scotia
to the Dominion-Provincial Conference, 1945–1946,' 26 January 1946, in
*Dominion-Provincial Conference (1945): Dominion and Provincial Submissions
and Plenary Conference Discussions*, Canada, 315–17 (Ottawa: King's Printer,
1946).

25 J.B. McGeachy, 'Confederation Clinic, 1867–1937,' *Winnipeg Free Press*, 4
February 1938. McGeachy added that Macdonald appears as if he 'knows
Confederation was a mistake but accepts it as a man accepts having a
wooden leg.'

26 Fransen, '"Unscrewing the Unscrutable,"' 164–6.

27 Macdonald to J.D. MacKenna, *St John Telegraph Journal*, 17 May 1938.

28 See especially *Report*, 2:81–130.

29 For the 1940 election and the development of Canada's war effort, see J.L.
Granatstein, *Canada's War: The Politics of the Mackenzie King Government,
1939–1945* (Toronto: University of Toronto Press, 1975), 77–91.

30 *Report*, 2:111, quoted by J.B. McNair, premier of New Brunswick, 'Plenary
Session: Dominion-Provincial Conference on Reconstruction,' 6 August
1945, in *Dominion-Provincial Conference (1945)*, 24.

31 J.A. Corry, 'Some Aspects of the Sirois Report,' speech to the Canadian
Club of Ottawa, 17 December 1940, quoted in Fransen, '"Unscrewing the
Unscrutable,"' 421–4.

32 'Statement by Premier T.D. Pattullo in Legislature,' 7 November 1940,
quoted in Canada, *Dominion-Provincial Conference, 1941* (Ottawa: King's
Printer, 1941), ix.

33 'Plenary Session,' 14 January 1941, Canada, *Dominion-Provincial Conference, 1941*, 11–12.

34 Ibid., 54–61.

35 Ibid. 16–17. Maurice Duplessis, an ardent Quebec nationalist, had been defeated in October 1939.

36 For a brief account of MacMillan's career as premier (1940–5), see J. Murray Beck, *The Politics of Nova Scotia*, vol. 2, *Murray to Buchanan, 1896–1988* (Tantallon: Four East, 1988), 187–203. Macdonald had accepted the appointment as minister of national defence for naval affairs and sat for the riding of Kingston, Ontario.

37 'Plenary Session,' 14 January 1941, 18.

38 Quoted in John T. Saywell, *Just Call Me Mitch: The Life of Mitchell F. Hepburn* (Toronto: University of Toronto Press, 1991), 461.

39 'Plenary Session,' 15 January 1941, 83.

40 See, for example, Fransen, '"Unscrewing the Unscrutable,"' 408–9; and Christopher Armstrong, 'Ceremonial Politics: Federal-Provincial Meetings before the Second World War,' *National Politics and Community in Canada*, ed. R. Kenneth Carty and W. Peter Ward (Vancouver: University of British Columbia Press, 1986), 139.

41 Armstrong, 'Ceremonial Politics,' 114.

42 In his diary, the fickle King alternated between praise for the omniscience of the commission and scorn for its attempt to manipulate the nation's leaders. On 6 January 1941 he referred to sections by Dafoe as 'excellent,' by Bob Fowler as 'even better.' After the conference, King blamed the Finance Department and its allies in the Bank of Canada. He also derided Plan One as 'largely a Dafoe report ... too highly coloured by the needs of the Prairies.' Quoted in Fransen, '"Unscrewing the Unscrutable,"' 439–40.

43 Beck, *Politics*, 2:193.

44 Fransen, '"Unscrewing the Unscrutable,"' 448. Rowell had been incapacitated by a stroke in May 1938 and died in 1941; Sirois suffered a heart attack and died two days after the 1941 conference ended. On Dafoe's faith that the *Report* would provide the basis for post-war constitutional talks, see Ferguson and Wardhaugh, '"Impossible Conditions of Inequality,"' 579.

45 Janine Brodie, *The Political Economy of Canadian Regionalism* (Toronto: Harcourt Brace Jovanovich, 1990), 29.

46 Ibid. 155–6.

47 J.A. Corry, *My Life and Work: A Happy Partnership* (Montreal and Kingston: McGill-Queen's University Press, 1981), 111–12. On Corry's work for Rowell-Sirois, see his *Difficulties of Divided Jurisdiction: A Study Prepared for the*

Royal Commission on Dominion-Provincial Relations (Ottawa: King's Printer, 1939).

48 F.W. Gibson and Barbara Robertson, eds., *Ottawa at War: The Grant Dexter Memoranda, 1939–1945* (Winnipeg: Manitoba Record Society, 1994), 498, Dexter memo to G.V. Ferguson, 1 March 1945.

49 Ontario's Hepburn was replaced by George Drew; Alberta's Aberhart had been succeeded by Ernest Manning, and British Columbia's Pattullo had given way to John Hart. In a more ominous vein, Maurice Duplessis had returned, unseating Godbout as premier of Quebec. An unknown factor was Saskatchewan's Tommy Douglas, who succeeded W.J. Patterson. Prince Edward Island (Walter Jones instead of Thane Campbell) and Manitoba (Stuart Garson in lieu of John Bracken) also changed leaders since 1941, but these new premiers were believed to be cut from the same cloth as their predecessors.

50 Canada, *Dominion-Provincial Conference (1945): Dominion and Provincial Submissions and Plenary Conference Discussions* (Ottawa: King's Printer, 1946), 5.

51 Ibid., 21–2.

52 Ibid., 124–8.

53 Macdonald's Liberals took twenty-eight of the thirty seats, and the CCF two, while the Conservatives were shut out.

54 'Angus L's Back,' *Halifax Chronicle*, 10 September 1945.

55 A.L. Macdonald, 'Diary,' 31 August 1945, file 389, vol. 1503, ALM Papers.

56 See 'Preliminary Statement of Province of Nova Scotia,' 28 November 1945, in *Dominion-Provincial Conference (1945)*, 215–18.

57 Canada, *Dominion-Provincial Conference (1945)*, 216–17. Grant Dexter also believed the Dominion had abandoned the recommendations of the *Report*, especially as they pertained to the principle of fiscal need in subsidy allocation. See Dexter to Macdonald, 28 October 1945, Macdonald to Dexter, 1 November 1945, file 28(a)-3, vol. 900, ALM Papers; and Ferguson and Wardhaugh, '"Impossible Conditions of Inequality,"' 580–1.

58 Canada, *Dominion-Provincial Conference (1945)*, 217–18.

59 'Reply by Dominion Government to Questions Raised in the Preliminary Statement of Province of Nova Scotia,' 5 December 1945, in *Dominion-Provincial Conference (1945)*, 219.

60 Robertson to Macdonald, 10 December 1945, file 28(a)-2, vol. 903, ALM Papers.

61 Dunn to Macdonald, 17 December 1945, file 28(a), vol. 899, ALM Papers.

62 Macdonald to Corry, and Macdonald to Innis, 16 January 1946, file 19½(d), vol. 898, ALM Papers.

63 Corry to Macdonald, 17 January 1946, file 19½(d), vol. 898, ALM Papers.

64 Innis to Macdonald, 17 January 1946, file 19½(d), vol. 898, ALM Papers. Innis was not impressed with Keynesianism, at least as it applied to Canada. Economic management along these lines, he maintained, was necessarily centralized and could not be adapted to the regional patterns of Canada's economy. See Brodie, *Political Economy*, 155–6.

65 Innis to Macdonald, 23 January 1946, file 19½(d), vol. 898, ALM Papers.

66 See 'Submissions by the Government of Nova Scotia to the Dominion-Provincial Conference, 1945–46,' 26 January 1946, in *Dominion-Provincial Conference (1945)*, 315–17.

67 By section 92 of the *BNA Act*, the provinces were allowed to impose direct taxes; a sales tax was considered an indirect tax, and therefore, ultra vires of the provinces.

68 'Replies by the Dominion Government to the Questions Put by the Provincial Premiers, January 1946,' 25 April 1946, *Dominion-Provincial Conference (1945)*, 333–8.

69 'Dominion-Provincial Conference, 29 April 1946,' *Dominion-Provincial Conference (1945)*, 416–17.

70 Canada, *Dominion-Provincial Conference (1945)*, 418–19, 510–11.

71 'Dominion-Provincial Conference, 1 May 1946,' *Dominion-Provincial Conference (1945)*, 603–4. Macdonald later announced that if the Dominion would vacate certain minor fields, his government would pledge not to increase taxes in those fields for several years, demonstrating that, for Nova Scotia, this was a matter of principle rather than finance. See Macdonald to Douglas Abbott, 26 March 1947 (telegram), file 14, vol. 913, ALM Papers.

72 Canada, *Dominion-Provincial Conference (1945)*, 604.

73 Beck, *Politics*, 209. In the autumn of 1946, both Alex Skelton and Ilsley went to Nova Scotia to negotiate with Macdonald's government. Macdonald asked Skelton, 'Why was [the] Sirois report thrown out?' Ilsley asked Macdonald not to press for the conference to be reconvened. He also said that the Dominion would announce its withdrawal from the gasoline tax field if Nova Scotia would sign. See 'Notes for 1 October 1946,' 'Notes for 26 November 1946,' and 'Notes for 30 November 1946,' file 19½(d), vol. 898, ALM Papers.

74 See *Ottawa Citizen*, 4 December 1946.

75 See Macdonald to Alex Johnston, 18 January 1946, file 28(a)-2, vol. 903, ALM Papers. Macdonald thought Drew's proposals – which included the provinces' retaining the major taxes but paying into an 'equalization' fund – had 'one or two things' to recommend them, but were unrealistic as they assumed all provinces had equal wealth to tax.

76 Macdonald, 'Diary,' 17 November 1946, file 394, vol. 1503, ALM Papers.

The premiers agreed that a successful conference of the provinces would prove 'overwhelming' to the Dominion, but an unsuccessful one would hurt the provinces' position more than it might help. By early December, the plan was abandoned.

77 On this confrontation, see T. Stephen Henderson, 'Angus L. Macdonald and the Conscription Crisis of 1944,' *Acadiensis* 27, no. 1 (Autumn 1997): 84–104. On his post-war relationship with King, Macdonald wrote, 'I have no bitterness there, but on the other hand it was, for some time before I left his company, impossible to have anything like friendship for him. I simply resolved to try to do my work in my own job as best I could, and avoid any rupture. This I succeeded in doing, but of course it is foolish to say that we are warm friends.' Macdonald to John J. Connolly, 9 April 1947, file 31-1(b), vol. 918, ALM Papers.

78 W.L.M. King, *Diaries* (Toronto: University of Toronto Press, 1980), microfiche, 16 January 1947 and 28 July 1948.

79 Alberta signed early in 1947.

80 John Connolly to Macdonald, 26 March 1947, file 31-1(b), vol. 918, ALM Papers.

81 Macdonald to Connolly, 9 April 1947, file 31-1(b), vol. 918, ALM Papers.

82 Crerar to Macdonald, 21 December 1946, file 31-1(b), vol. 918, ALM Papers.

83 Macdonald to Crerar, 13 January 1946, file 31-1(b), vol. 918, ALM Papers.

84 Crerar to Macdonald, 30 April 1946, file 31-1(b), vol. 918, ALM Papers.

85 Power to Macdonald, 27 January 1947, file 31-2, vol. 920, ALM Papers. Douglas Abbott replaced Ilsley as minister of finance late in 1946.

86 Douglas Abbott to Macdonald, 21 April 1947, file 11, vol. 911, ALM Papers.

87 Macdonald to W.A. Macdonald, 25 February 1947, file 31-2, vol. 920, ALM Papers.

88 Macdonald to Ralph M. Kelley, 29 August 1947, file 31-1(c), vol. 919, ALM Papers.

89 See, for example, Macdonald's speech 'Federalism in Canada,' delivered to the Canada Club of Toronto, 1 December 1947, file 31-3(a), vol. 920, ALM Papers.

90 Bothwell, Drummond, and English, *Canada 1900–1945*, 276.

91 Bothwell, Drummond, and English, *Canada since 1945*, 75.

3 The Obligations of Federalism: Ontario and the Origins of Equalization

P.E. BRYDEN

In the aftermath of a relatively recent failed attempt to amend Canada's constitution, Robert Vipond noted that the idea of provincial equality had slipped into political discourse quietly but had nevertheless become a powerful concept in constitutional battles. The Meech Lake Accord could be criticized for entrenching Quebec's demands in a manner that 'could not be reconciled with the constitutional equality of the provinces' and the subsequent Charlottetown Accord could somewhat ahistorically depict provincial equality as 'one of the foundational principles upon which the Canadian nation is built.'[1] But just as we have moved towards an expectation of constitutional equality, we have also, somewhat paradoxically, moved toward a constitutional *recognition* of inequality. Differences and the inequalities they implied were what drove most of the debate in the years prior to Confederation: how would each province continue to be able to protect that which was unique about it in the context of participation in a new nation? How would the differing debt levels be financed upon entry into Confederation? How would the very unequal populations of each colony be represented within the new polity? There have been innumerable examples of the recognition of inequalities since those years of the Confederation debates, and there have been just as many examples of efforts to redress those imbalances. The federal government's equalization scheme of 1957 is only the most obvious example of these attempts to address the problem of the fundamental inequality across provincial lines. Inequality was constitutionally recognized with the entrenchment of equalization in section 36(2) of the Constitution Act, 1982, as the requirement to 'ensure that provincial governments have sufficient revenues to provide reasonably comparable levels of public services at reasonably comparable levels of taxation.'

This is only the most formal way of recognizing the inherent inequality of, for example, Prince Edward Island and Ontario, and attempting to limit the effects of that inequality as much as possible. The roots of the equalization program can be found in formal and informal arrangements in the ninety years prior to its implementation. Throughout it all, though, one thing is clear: in order to establish a system that compensated the poorer provinces, the richer provinces would inevitably end up being net contributors to the program. Without the agreement of the largest, wealthiest province of Ontario, either tacit or otherwise, there was no way that any system of equalization could have come into being. Early wartime and post-war efforts to provide a coherent system of equalization were destined for failure until two preconditions were met: the federal government began to tap into Ontario's rich fiscal capacity, and Ontario agreed on a political level to this form of redistribution. When these two prerequisites had been fulfilled, in the late 1950s, Canada was able to embark on a course of development that would leave commentators at century's end heralding equalization as 'the glue that holds the federation together' and 'one of the most tangible manifestations of Canadian solidarity.'[2]

The first and still the most impressive evaluation of the workings of the federal system in Canada was the Royal Commission on Dominion-Provincial Relations, known as the Rowell-Sirois Commission, which issued its final report in 1940.[3] Struck in the depths of the Depression when provinces found themselves without the financial capacity to begin to deal with a crisis of this magnitude, the commission was designed to investigate the workability of the existing division of powers, and propose solutions when that division no longer seemed to work. In addition to suggesting that the federal government should take control of unemployment insurance and pensions, and that the provinces should cease collecting direct taxes, the Report also recommended that a 'National Adjustment Grant' be established. This payout to provinces was designed to replace the "illogical' subsidies that had developed over the years,' and was the first proposal for a coordinated, coherent system of equalization. These grants would be by far the biggest source of revenue for the provinces after they relinquished any jurisdiction over direct taxation fields, and were therefore regarded as yet another centralizing feature of the recommendations, as provincial budgets would be almost entirely federally determined.[4] The two levels of government could not reach agreement on the recommendations, and the Report was shelved indefinitely. Not surprisingly, few provincial premiers were more vehement in their rejection than Ontario's Mitch Hepburn.[5]

While war occupied the attentions of players at both levels of government immediately following the rejection of the Rowell-Sirois recommendations, the contents of the Report was not completely forgotten. In preparation for the demands of peacetime, federal officials devised their blueprint for reconstruction. In addition to calling for government to ensure full employment in the White Paper on Employment and Income, the proposals for post-war rebuilding contained in the popularly named Green Book repeated many of the recommendations of the Rowell-Sirois Report. Calling for the continuation of the Wartime Tax Rental Agreements, which had delivered the direct tax fields into Ottawa's hands in return for a 'rental' payment, the Green Book also described a vastly expanded federal social security state. The rental scheme, implemented with the federal budget of 1941, advised in the Green Book and continued on an ad hoc basis in 1947, contained an element of equalization. Because it was up to provincial discretion as to how the rental value would be calculated, 'it is possible to argue that ... [the scheme] embodied some consideration of fiscal need and, hence, some aspects of equalization.' The possibility of electing to receive as payment for the vacation of income, corporate, and succession tax fields the value of the tax collected within the provincial boundaries, however, suggests that the scheme was, in fact, 'the antithesis of equalization.'[6] From the Ontario perspective, the Green Book proposals were also unacceptable within the current framework of Confederation.

Containing as many features of the hated Rowell-Sirois Report as it did meant that it was no surprise that the provincial premiers, or at least some of them, were disinclined to accept the Green Book proposals. This time, however, rather than outright and vocal rejection, Ontario's new Conservative premier George Drew opted to offer an alternative scheme for post-war reconstruction. Ultimately, he hoped to persuade the first ministers of the utility of his plan rather than the one espoused by the federal government. His proposals, prepared by the Ontario Bureau of Statistics and Research, made a number of points clear. First, provincial jurisdiction was sacrosanct, and the provincial governments should remain free to legislate in any way they saw fit in areas that were clearly their constitutional responsibility. Second, economic stability had to be maintained at all costs. Within this framework, however, Drew and his officials sought to address some of the concerns of the poorer provinces and hopefully bring them on side. The odious Wartime Tax Rental Agreements had to be terminated; this would provide the opportunity for the provinces to cover the costs associated with post-war reconstruction costs. Provincial spending on such things as school and hospital construction, as well as on mothers' allowances and old age pensions, would inject money into the economy and thereby jump-start economic recovery.[7] The Ontario plan also included an as-yet undecided formula for equalization. The one thing that was clear, however, was that it would not be based purely on population, as it was in the federal proposal.[8] Ontario officials had objected to this method of determining fiscal-need subsidies as unfair, but even centralist commentators such as Grant Dexter of the Winnipeg *Free Press* considered the federal proposal 'old stuff' and unable to solve the problem.[9]

The Ontario position held enormous appeal for a large province, rich in both resources and corporate tax bases, but Drew's government was attempting to do more than merely outline an alternative to the anticipated federal position that would serve their purely provincialist goals. Instead, it was clear from the Ontario brief that it was designed to appeal to a much broader spectrum of the country. For example, despite acknowledging 'a strong conviction in Ontario ... that when a provincial government got into financial difficulties it should find its own solution by resorting to direct taxation or curtailing expenditure,' the brief nevertheless proposed a system of subsidies for have-not provinces.[10] The complaints about the current fiscal situation were moderate, at least in contrast to the traditional Ontario strategy of detailing at length the costs of Confederation it bore, and the document was able to end on a much more positive note than was common: 'We consider that Ontario now has a splendid opportunity as the "keystone" province to give leadership in establishing subsidies on a sound basis and to improve Dominion-Provincial and interprovincial relations generally.'[11] Ontario did not really propose a comprehensive system of equalization, but it recognized the absence of uniformity in the financial capacity of the provinces, and the need to address the problem.

In offering an alternative to the federal Green Book, the Ontario officials responsible for drafting the document, and the politicians responsible for selling it to the public, were careful to ensure the broadest possible appeal. Drew attempted in an informal way to win over the support of his fellow premiers, but it was most important to construct the alternative plan for reconstruction in a way that was 'not unattractive to the "have not" provinces.'[12] Drew was careful to address his public comments not simply to the audience at hand, but also to a potentially wider national group. While he generally spoke on the need to establish a solid basis for the sharing of tax revenue, arguing in favour of 'a high measure of uniformity of legislation and simplification of tax collection,'[13] his remarks suggested that the Ontario premier had warmed to the idea of some form of equalization. Nothing he said, he claimed, should 'be interpreted as an objection to the pooling of our resources for the welfare of Canada as a whole. I believe that Ontario should take her full share in building the strength and security of every part of Canada.'[14]

The actual text of Ontario's counter-proposals was not ready until early January 1946, when Drew sent it to the other first ministers. The initial response was 'a flood of comment across the Dominion, largely favourable.'[15] According to the Ontario government's own survey, eleven newspapers contained favourable accounts of the alternative submission, eight had negative articles, and thirty-eight had comments that were regarded as 'neutral' but, according to Conservative organizer Harry Robbins, tended to praise Drew for 'producing a highly constructive brief' and demonstrating 'statesmanlike' behaviour.[16] Sentiment in provincial capitals was more muted. In New Brunswick, for example, the provincial treasurer was sure that others would not find Ontario's proposal a 'satisfactory alternative' to the Green Book, but thought himself that the former were 'advantageous to N.B.'[17]

But like the federal proposals, which failed to win the acceptance of either Ontario or Quebec, the Ontario proposals were also insufficiently attractive to generate enough provincial support to be adopted. Canada thus entered the post-war period without a blueprint for action. Instead of coordinated activity, ad hoc arrangements governed the sharing of tax fields and the responsibility for expensive social policies, and the uncoordinated statutory subsidies remained the only way in which provincial inequalities were balanced. It was still possible for the finance minister to argue that, with the tax rental payment to the Maritime and Prairie provinces, the federal government was 'going very far to meet the test of fiscal need,' but by basing payment on population rather than revenue, the provinces were moving toward equality of taxes rather than equalization.[18] True equalization depended upon the participation of Ontario, which, along with Quebec, had refused to enter fully into the Tax Rental Agreements of either 1947 or 1952.

Despite being in a period of somewhat chaotic financial arrangements, by the middle of the 1950s Ontario politicians had come close to perfecting a new strategy in federal-provincial negotiations. For more than a decade, Ontario had been avoiding the confrontational approach that had characterized the intergovernmental relationship in the years before the Second World War. Instead, Canada's largest and wealthiest province was positioning itself as the protector of the national interest, the articulator of an alternative pan-Canadian vision to that offered by the federal government. Whenever Ottawa officials introduced a proposal dealing with fiscal arrangements, or constitutional amendments, or social policy, Ontario politicians invariably countered with an alternative proposal of their own – one that generally addressed its unique position as provincial behemoth, but was also attuned to the particular needs of other provinces. Occasionally, Ottawa seemed reluctant to take action in a particular policy field, and in these cases, Ontario's proposal often filled the perceived vacuum and thus established the foundation for intergovernmental debate. This strategy of making alternative suggestions, wooing as much provincial support as possible, and attempting, essentially, to take Ottawa's place as the protector and articulator of the national interest, was not always successful. It always served, however, to keep Ontario's position front and centre, and must in no way be regarded as a forfeiture of its tradition role as guardian of provincial autonomy. The discussions surrounding the federal–provincial fiscal relationship, begun in 1955, thus followed a pattern that had been being drawn since the aborted Dominion-Provincial Conference on Reconstruction: Ottawa made a proposal, Ontario countered with one of its own, and all other participants were essentially forced to decide which was the more attractive. In this case, however, Ontario demonstrated a political willingness to entertain equalization payments that ultimately forced the provincial government to back away from its own tax-sharing proposal.

The Tax Rental Agreements, which were really a peacetime extension of the Wartime Tax Rental Agreements, did not establish a permanent procedure for sharing the direct tax fields between the federal and provincial governments. The arrangements lasted five years, and were then renegotiated. The complexities of the issues involved ensured that the two levels of government were in a near-constant state of fiscal negotiation. The 1952 agreements, therefore, would expire in 1957; the intergovernmental discussions on this renewal began in 1955. At this meeting, Prime Minister Louis St Laurent recommended some form of equalization, albeit in a somewhat obtuse manner: 'The type of plan which we are inclined to favor is one in which the payments to be made to each province would be determined by the amounts which need to be added to the yield of a set of standard taxes in that province to bring the revenue per capita up to some specified level defined in terms of what all provinces or certain provinces might obtain from those sources.'[19] Ontario's Premier Leslie Frost was more concerned with negotiating a fair provincial share of the direct tax yields than with equalization, but he nevertheless also addressed the issue. 'We do not question,' he stated, 'the desirability of the Federal government paying subsidies to provinces which need them. We are heartily in accord with the payment of such subsidies, but the amount of these subsidies should be determined in light of sound principles.'[20] Discussion over just what those sound principles would be continued for the next two years.

Three months after the formal federal-provincial conference and following consultation with provincial officials, the Liberal government in Ottawa was prepared to make a 'definite proposal.' It offered equalization payments that would top up the combined yield of income, corporate, and death taxes 'to the level of the average per capita yield of these taxes in the two provinces which have the highest per capital combined yields in these three fields.'[21] This system had been the brainchild of John Deutsch in the federal Department of Finance, who was convinced that providing equalization payments, regardless of whether or not a particular province rented its tax fields to the national government, would be a way of ending the isolation of Quebec. Under this new scheme, 'Quebec could therefore continue to impose its own taxes and be eligible for the equalization grant without having to sign any agreement with Ottawa.'[22] Moreover, as the prime minister pointed out, 'these proposals provide revenues to the provinces somewhat greater than those available under the present tax-rental system ... and they guarantee a measure of stability in this sector of provincial revenues more effectively than do the present arrangements.'[23] Interestingly, the very provinces for whom the equalization payments were so necessary – the chronically poor Atlantic provinces – were not singled out as benefactors of the program or as the reason that equalization was contemplated in the first place.

It is therefore not surprising that the proposal was found wanting. The premiers of have-not provinces Nova Scotia, New Brunswick, and Saskatchewan all 'expressed regret that the federal government was not able to accept suggestions ... for a wider application of the fiscal need principle.' In the face of this criticism, St Laurent maintained that 'there is a very substantial recognition of fiscal need involved in the equalization payments we have proposed.'[24] In contrast, Frost argued that the equalization payments proposed were too generous:

> It appears to us that the basic formula which uses the weighted average of the per capita tax yields of only Ontario and British Columbia – to all intents and purposes this means Ontario – does not recognize the heavy financial burdens that are imposed on this Province and its municipalities in servicing a rapidly growing population and industry which produce such a large proportion of the Federal Government's revenue. In view of the enormous obligations and commitments that we face, we feel strongly that a formula that provides a special payment to all the provinces except Ontario fails to meet the special needs of this Province. As a first step in this approach, we believe that the equalization payments should be calculated on the basis of the four provinces having the highest per capita tax yields.[25]

Another meeting would clearly be necessary to sort out the conflicting views on how, or indeed whether, equalization grants would be calculated.

Early in March, the first ministers got together for a face-to-face meeting. The night before discussions began, New Brunswick's delegation was 'somewhat hopeful that something special might be arrived at on the morrow.' The hope was that there would be some form of adjustment grant made available to those provinces in which 'per capita income was below 85% of the national average' – like New Brunswick, with a per capita income of only 55 per cent of that of Ontario.[26] Ontario's delegation also had high expectations for the 9 March meeting, during which Leslie Frost presented the Ontario government's alternative vision of tax-sharing and equalization. The premier reiterated his belief that the poorer provinces should receive equalization payments that would yield the average of the taxation income in the four richest provinces. He also advocated an increase in the rental fees that the federal government would pay for the opportunity to occupy the direct tax fields and, because of their particularly precarious financial situations, a $10 million annual subsidy to both New Brunswick and Nova Scotia.[27]

Supporters of the St Laurent government and those generally in favour of a greater degree of centralization in the Canadian federation were appalled by Frost's comments. Explaining that the Ontario scheme would see tax revenue, which Ontario would receive, increase, and equalization payments, which Ontario would not receive, decrease, *Winnipeg Free Press* journalist Grant Dexter accused Frost of becoming 'about as cooperative as an irritated porcupine.' He described the Ontario proposal as the most 'selfish and grasping policy ... [that has] ever been advanced since 1941.'[28] The exaggerated rhetoric of those offended by Frost's suggestion, however, may have had more to do with attempts to shift attention from the increasingly arrogant and complacent behaviour of the Liberals in Ottawa than on the relative merits of the Ontario scheme.[29]

This was not a view that was uniformly held, however. In fact, Ontario's vocal opposition to what even Dexter acknowledged was the 'detail, rather than the principle'[30] of the federal offer earned it an unlikely ally in the province of New Brunswick, where any earlier hopes of an advantageous offer from the federal government had been 'badly shattered' at the 9 March meeting.[31] According to the provincial secretary-treasurer in Fredericton, 'The formula as it stands is going to make "the rich get richer and the poor get poorer"... The provinces to get the largest percentage increase are Quebec, Ontario and Alberta.' However, Ontario could not be criticized too vigorously, as Frost had demonstrated himself to be 'particularly concerned about the future of New Brunswick and Nova Scotia.'[32] The $10 million Ontario proposed sounded both enticing and reasonable, as it was 'really very little by comparison with what the Federal Government takes out of the provinces.'[33] Therefore, not wanting to criticize the only government that made a proposal that was at all agreeable, the New Brunswick minister made it clear that he supported the argument that Ontario should receive even *more* money, as 'the cost of growth is a serious matter.'[34]

Ontario's rather vocal defence of the idea of an adjustment grant of some kind for the most destitute of provinces was an interesting strategy and led to much speculation about motive. In Ottawa, Frost's unexpected criticism of the federal government gave rise to suggestions that he had decided not to pursue a career in federal politics, and had opted instead to become federal Conservative leader George 'Drew's Ontario lieutenant ... and take the platform in the next Federal election, proclaiming the "grievances" of Ontario.' This tactic would ensure the support of Premier Duplessis and resurrect the old Ontario-Quebec axis; it was also 'the worst possible interpretation of what is happening' from the federal perspective.[35] Frost's popularity in Ontario was something of a threat to the Liberals in Ottawa, but as long as he continued to distance himself from the national Conservative party and its leader, George Drew, there was little need for real concern. The pronouncements against the new tax proposals, however, combined with various sightings of Drew and Frost together, elicited more anxiety than usual in the Liberal backrooms.[36]

But rather than getting suspicious, the federal Liberals would have been better off noticing the pattern in Ontario's actions. The Ontario government had been, for more than a decade, positioning itself as the articulator of an alternative national interest in areas of intergovernmental relations. Frost's behaviour at the 9 March meeting was in keeping with a much more long-standing approach than commentators like Grant Dexter seemed to acknowledge. The key for Frost was to extract from the federal government a more generous sharing of tax fields than had been the case with either the 1947 or the 1952 Tax Rental Agreements. Ontario had greater taxing capacity than any other province, given the area's general stability and number of industries, and access to a higher percentage of the income, corporate, and succession tax fields would necessarily mean more money for the provincial government. After securing an arrangement that was clearly in Ontario's best interest, the Frost government was prepared to propose incentives to other provinces to achieve their agreement to the scheme. Ten million dollars a year to both Nova Scotia and New Brunswick, each of which coincidentally was operating under a Conservative government, was a small price to pay for their acceptance of the Ontario proposal for the division of tax fields.

The Ontario tax-sharing proposal, with its related equalization component, achieved two goals. First, Frost was able to identify Ontario as the principal proponent of an alternative national vision to that offered by Ottawa. Other provinces, most significantly Saskatchewan, one of the other have-not provinces, fell into line behind Ontario in pressing the federal government for 'some recognition ... of the fiscal need of the Maritimes.'[37] It seemed to be a position that it would be ill-advised to dispute. Second, Frost seemed to win provincial allies in New Brunswick, at least: as Conservative party organizer Dalton Camp remarked, 'That the Maritime Provinces should now find their cause being championed and upheld by the Premier of Ontario rather than the Federal Government [is] ... more than somewhat ironic.'[38] The plight of the Maritimes might find another spokesperson in the national Conservative leader George Drew, who thought 'that the Maritimes Provinces have been badly let down.' Recognizing the power of the Ontario electorate, however, he also felt compelled to add 'that Ontario is in an impossible position, as Les Frost has been pointing out with increasing vigour.'[39] Drew's concern over Maritime prospects was not, in the long run, as important as the Ontario premier's concern.

By the summer of 1956, Ontario's determination to change the basis of calculating tax-sharing arrangements had become even firmer. In a series of confidential memos produced around the time that the federal legislation was introduced in Parliament on 16 July, Ontario officials outlined their opposition to the framework of the existing scheme. 'As an earning province,' they wrote, 'Ontario is required to provide a great array of services for industry. The tax revenue from this industry makes it possible for the Federal government to pay equalization fiscal need assistance to the other provinces. There are two ways of providing equity. One is to allow Ontario an amount in compensation for the costs of servicing industry which other provinces, receiving a tax dollar by way of subsidy, are not obliged to provide to the same extent. The second method would be to adopt, as the basis for determining the equalization payments, the average per capita yield of four provinces instead of two, and with increased rates. These rates should be at least 15, 15 and 50.'[40] Still, the federal government refused to budge from its initial logic that the provinces could have access, without imposing double taxation, to 10 per cent of the personal income tax yield within their boundaries, 9 per cent of the corporate tax yield, and 50 per cent of the succession taxes.[41]

Debate raged in the House of Commons over the tax bill, known as Bill 442 and informally called 'Plan C,' during the summer of 1956. Equalization was, at least according to some, its 'chief purpose.'[42] Its passage marked the official beginning of a legislative system by which tax yields for the poorer provinces were brought up to a national standard – in this case, much to the dismay of the Ontario government, the average yield in British Columbia and Ontario. The figures for 1957–8, the first year for which equalization payments would be available, showed a per capita tax yield average in the two wealthiest provinces of $38.20; all other provincial tax yield averages would thus be brought up to this level.[43] Still, the Frost government continued its critique, arguing that the financial burdens of managing such a prosperous economy necessitated levying 'special corporate taxes and, as in the past, have them treated under Federal tax law as an expense without any offset by the Federal Government.'[44] St Laurent's government was not convinced by the argument, forcing Frost to continue to impose provincial death taxes and, in his provincial budget of early 1957, to introduce a new corporate tax of 11 per cent.[45] The Ontario premier, however, had other tricks up his sleeve.

George Drew's ill-health or, perhaps more accurately, his election failures, led him to resign from the Conservative leadership; the convention held in mid-December 1956 to replace him had an important effect on Ontario's position on fiscal relations. Frost had thrown his support behind leadership candidate John Diefenbaker, widely expected to win the position. Diefenbaker's victory at the convention marked the beginning of an uncommon period of alliance between the federal and provincial wings of the Conservative party and suggested that Ontario's position on the fiscal arrangements might find a stronger proponent in Ottawa than had been the case for quite some time.[46] Certainly, Diefenbaker's first few months in the office of leader of the Progressive Conservative party suggested that he was eager to redress Ontario's tax grievances. Late in February 1957 he asked his advisor, Roland Michener, 'to recommend a course of action for our Party, national in outlook but incorporating the general consideration which brought about the new [corporate] taxation measures in Ontario.'[47] A rethinking of the fiscal arrangements was especially important 'now that the Government of Ontario has come out so strongly for Provincial taxation rights.'[48] Leslie Frost's support of Diefenbaker's leadership aspirations would not soon be forgotten.

Meanwhile, the federal government's tax agreements for 1957–1962 were being put into place, despite the failure to achieve agreement in full from either Ontario or Quebec. Of course, the most interesting component of the accord was that 'the Federal Government will pay annually to nine Canadian provinces an unconditional tax equalization payment.'[49] Ontario's continued pressure for an alternative arrangement, despite being motivated by a demand for increased provincial tax room and therefore a higher degree of provincial autonomy, could not ignore the plight of the have-not provinces. Thus, as had been the case since the province first began promoting its alternative vision, the Ontario position contained promises of an adjustment grant to the chronically poor Atlantic provinces. This became an increasingly important component of the Ontario scheme, not only because it softened the overt tax-grab component of the first part of the Ontario plan, but also because it fit so comfortably with Diefenbaker's own new 'National Policy' rhetoric. Taken too much further, arguments about '"prior rights" in the field of direct taxation' might lead to a 'national policy for provincial autonomy,' but most in Ontario seemed to understand the incompatibility of this position with the needs of the poorer prov-inces.[50] The provincial position was therefore a fine balance between Ontario's needs and those of the rest of the country.

So effective was Frost at driving home his twin messages – more tax room for the wealthier provinces, equalization grants for the poorer provinces – that fiscal concerns became identified as a key battlefield in the federal election called for June 1957. Introducing Diefenbaker at a rally in Toronto, Frost reiterated that 'it is not a matter of the Fed-eral Government giving Ontario or the Provinces anything. That is the patronizing attitude in Ottawa. All that we ask is a reasonable part of our own.'[51] This speech caught the attention of premiers in the Mari-times, who asked Frost 'to appear at public meetings in Fredericton and Halifax with the respective premiers to discuss the subject of a fair division of the national tax dollar.'[52] The result was a strange fed-eral election campaign, according to Grant Dexter at least, who argued that in making 'the tax agreements the vital issue in the campaign' the real conservative leader on the campaign trail was Frost. All appear-ances suggested that 'Mr Frost is in control of Federal Conservative policy.'[53]

He certainly played an extraordinary role in the national election campaign and elevated tax policy to a staggering level of public in-terest. Louis St Laurent, campaigning only half-heartedly and clearly showing his age, was forced to 'express regret' that the fiscal arrange-ments had become an election issue. Frost's was an animated reply:

> Where under all the circumstances does he think it should be brought up? Goodness only knows it has been discussed often enough in Federal-Provincial Conferences and elsewhere. Surely in view of the plight of our tax payers, it should be considered now. Why are none of the Provinces satisfied? Why are some of them desperate? Why do the Maritimes, New-foundland, Prince Edward Island, New Brunswick and Nova Scotia meet in conference and express dissatisfaction? It all begins with the fact that the whole arrangement and all of the adjustment payments to the other provinces are premised on a sharing arrangement with Ontario. If this sharing arrangement does not meet the requirements of Ontario, how pos-sibly could it meet the requirements of the other provinces?[54]

Although it came as a surprise to the Liberal establishment, compla-cent after twenty-two years in office in Ottawa, Diefenbaker won the election of 1957, largely as a result of the impressive support he received not only from Leslie Frost, but also from his provincial machine. Once in office, though, Diefenbaker would have to move quickly to address the tax concerns if he expected Frost's goodwill to last.

Early in his mandate, Diefenbaker did elect to reopen the 1957–1962 Tax Rental Agreements, calling a conference of first ministers for November 'to review the present pattern of tax sharing arrangements.'[55] Ontario's leadership in calling for a renegotiation of these agreements was instrumental in the decision to call the meeting in the first place, and the particular features of Ontario's position also had an important impact on the outcome of the conference, although perhaps not exactly the outcome that Frost had imagined. Much of the time that the premier was allotted for his opening statement was spent outlining the terrible expenses that Ontario incurred managing and servicing the buoyant post-war economy that was the envy of all the other provinces. Towards the end of his remarks, he noted that 'Ontario is concerned with the problems of the other Provinces. We recognize that all the difficulties do not lie in the Provinces having the greatest concentration of industry and population. We support adjustment payments to the other Provinces and have gone even further. We believe that such adjustments are necessary.'[56] In general, the conference opened with 'an atmosphere more hopeful than that which has prevailed at any previous Dominion-Provincial conference.'[57]

The hopefulness was perhaps a charade for the press. The federal position, after some last-minute shifts in policy, was not to present a clear proposal but rather to solicit input from the provincial premiers on the structure of the tax arrangements. It was destined to be another fact-finding conference, and Frost was getting increasingly weary of the absence of any decisions on issues of federal-provincial concern.[58] There was only one tangible result of the conference – an agreement to supplement the tax yields of the Atlantic provinces by providing an adjustment grant. While other provinces complained, in the aftermath of the conference, that Diefenbaker had forced them to accept 'better terms' for the Atlantic provinces without 'time to prepare a full and studied' response, Ontario remained silent.[59] In fact, at a conference characterized by a relative absence of support for the national interest, the fact that Ontario's premier had publicly supported adjustment grants earned him the position of the only 'giver' present at the conference.[60] Had Ontario not made further grants to the poorest provinces such a key component of its own proposed tax sharing plan, there is no question that Diefenbaker could not have made the offer he did in the fall of 1957. It was not exactly the result that Premier Frost had anticipated, but it pointed in the direction that fiscal arrangements would take for the next half century.

Thanks to the work of the government and bureaucracy of Ontario, equalization was on the table and would remain so. Clearly, however, this was not because of any great generosity of the part of Leslie Frost or his team. Instead, they had taken a calculated gamble: in an effort to negotiate a higher provincial share of direct taxes, the have-not provinces would be wooed with further money. But this was a strategy that could successfully be employed only by the national government, and despite any illusions in Ontario, it remained simply one of ten provinces. Thus only part of Ontario's two-pronged strategy was adopted, and equalization became part of the political landscape while a 50:50 sharing of all the direct tax fields did not.

During the next round of fiscal negotiations, both the federal and Ontario governments tried to wiggle out of some of the commitments that had been made in the 1957–62 tax rental series. By 1960, Frost was warning his fellow first ministers 'that equalization needed a good look because it could become too burdensome to the federal government. It could actually make it impossible,' he warned, 'for the federal government to carry out the 15/15/50 formula because of the added costs involved.'[61] As it turned out, the federal government was finding the expense of equalization onerous. The director of the federal–provincial relations division of the federal Department of Finance noted that there were 'several weaknesses' with the 1957–62 calculation of equalization, commenting particularly on the 'impossible burden on the regions from which the transfers are made.'[62] Ontario representatives would agree wholeheartedly with this assessment, but it unfortunately did not translate into tangible benefits. The new tax-sharing arrangements were based on the federal vacation, rather than rental, of the direct tax fields, but Ottawa would withdraw only from the personal, corporate, and succession taxes to the 14/9/50 per cent rates that had been the formula before. Ontario was no closer to achieving the equal division of taxes that had been its goal since entering into a fiscal sharing arrangement with the federal government during wartime, yet had been instrumental in securing further equalization payments to all other provinces. The original gamble may not have paid off for Ontario, but the benefits were high for other regions and the nation as a whole.

Ontario's support of the principle of equalization was an absolute prerequisite of any form of institutionalized program being put into place.

It was the wealthiest province by far, and the federal funds necessary to support poorer provinces could not help but come from the tax base in central Canada. Almost two decades of wartime and post-war tax sharing arrangements had introduced the concept of a federal role in the direct tax fields, and had gone some way towards undermining provincial autonomy. Since the hearings of the Rowell-Sirois Commission in the late 1930s, Ontario had been a vocal critic of the federal incursion into what provincial politicians regarded as their rightful tax fields – the areas of personal, corporate, and succession taxes. This viewpoint did not change, but Ontario's strategies for dealing with the federal position became more artful. Calls for a more equitable sharing of the tax fields themselves would be combined with a carrot to induce other provinces to support the Ontario position. This inducement took the shape of support for the principle of equalization, so long as it was calculated on something other than the average tax yield of the two wealthiest provinces. When that failed, or at least seemed to be going nowhere, Ontario shifted to calling for a more equitable division of the direct tax fields combined with support for top-up grants to the most depressed areas. This latter strategy meshed nicely with the views of the Conservative governments in power in the Maritimes, and with the policies of the new leader of the national Progressive Conservative Party. When the inducement was accepted, but not the general principle of greater access to tax fields for the provincial government, Frost was stymied. He felt betrayed by Diefenbaker to a certain degree, but unable to withdraw his loudspoken, and much-appreciated, support of the Atlantic Adjustment grant. It was a major step towards agreeing to equalization, and one that has, thus far, tied Ontario to the principle.

NOTES

1 Robert Vipond, 'From Provincial Autonomy to Provincial Equality (Or, Clyde Wells and the Distinct Society),' in *Is Quebec Nationalism Just? Perspectives from Anglophone Canada*, ed. Joseph Carens (Montreal and Kingston: McGill-Queen's University Press, 1995), 105.
2 Nova Scotia Premier John Hamm to Nova Scotia Chamber of Commerce, 24 October 2000, http://www.gov.ns.ca/fairness/speecha.htm; Stephane Dion, minister of intergovernmental affairs, in *Globe and Mail*, 13 July 2001.
3 Alexander Brady called the report at the time 'one of the most comprehen-

sive public inquiries undertaken in the modern British Empire.' 'Report of the Royal Commission on Dominion-Provincial Relations,' *Canadian Historical Review* 21, no. 3 (1940): 245–53.

4 Doug Owram, *The Government Generation: Canadian Intellectuals and the State, 1900–1945* (Toronto: University of Toronto Press, 1986), 242–3.

5 John T. Saywell, *'Just Call Me Mitch': The Life of Mitchell F. Hepburn* (Toronto: University of Toronto Press, 1991), 379–84.

6 Thomas J. Courchene, *Equalization Payments: Past, Present and Future* (Toronto: Ontario Economic Council, 1984), 27.

7 Ontario Bureau of Statistics and Research, 'Facts Pertinent to Dominion-Provincial Relations,' 16 July 1945, 39–48, file: Dominion–Provincial Relations, Department of Finances: Policy Division Subject Files, box UF 22, RG 6-44, Archives of Ontario (AO).

8 'An Examination of the Financial Proposals of the Government of Canada with Ontario's alternative plans,' n.d., file: Dom-Prov Re: Taxation and D-P Coordinating Cttee, 1942–1945, box 4, Office of the Premier: Frost Premier's Correspondence, AO.

9 Dexter to George Ferguson and Bruce Hutchinson, 26 September 1945, file: 100, box 15, Grant Dexter Papers, Queen's University Archives (QUA). According Marc Gotlieb, the Ontario Treasury Department was 'shocked' by the federal government's use of population to determine subsidies. 'George Drew and the Dominion-Provincial Conference on Reconstruction, 1945–1946' *Canadian Historical Review* 66, no. 1 (1985): 35.

10 Ontario Bureau of Statistics and Research, 'Facts Pertinent to Dominion–Provincial Relations,' 16 July 1945, 44, 46, file: Dominion-Provincial Relations, box UF 22, Department of Finances: Policy Division Subject Files, RG 6-44, AO.

11 Ibid., 48.

12 Telephone conversation between Colonel George Drew and Premier Hart, 1:30 p.m., 16 November 1945, file: Dominion-Provincial Conference, British Columbia, 1945, box 5, Department of Finance Papers: Dominion-Provincial Conferences, 1935–1955, AO; 'An Examination of the Financial Proposals of the Government of Canada with Ontario's Alternative Plans,' n.d., file: Dom-Prov Re: Taxation and D-P Co-ordinating Cttee, 1942–1945, box 4, Office of the Premier: Frost Premier's Correspondence, AO.

13 'Speech by Premier George A. Drew before the Canadian Club, Toronto, October 1, 1945,' file: Prime Minister no. 18, Canadian Club, vol. 27, RG 6-15, Department of Finance Papers, AO.

14 Ibid.

15 Wilfrid Eggleston, 'The Ottawa Letter,' *Saturday Night*, 26 January 1946.

16 H.M. Robbins to Drew, 26 January 1946, file: Dom-Prov General, 1945, 1946, box 3, Office of the Premier: Frost Premier's Correspondence.

17 FitsRandolph to McNair, 14 January 1946, file: Background Material for NB Delegation to Dom-Prov Conf., 1944–1946, box C5, RS 414, John McNair Papers, Public Archives of New Brunswick (PANB); and WB Trites to JJ Doone, 21 January 1946, file: Correspondence relating to Dominion-Provincial Conference, 1946, John McNair Papers, PANB.

18 Canada, *House of Commons Debates* (27 June 1946), p. 15; Courchene, *Equalization Payments*, 29.

19 Canada, *Proceedings of the Federal-Provincial Conference, 1955* (Ottawa: Queen's Printer, 1955), 16–17.

20 Ibid., 21.

21 St Laurent to Frost, 6 January 1956, file: Dominion-Provincial Conference, January 6, 1956, 1955, 1956, box 8, Office of the Premier: Frost Premier's Correspondence, RG 3-24, AO.

22 J.W. Pickersgill, *My Years with Louis St Laurent: A Political Memoir* (Toronto: University of Toronto Press, 1975), 309.

23 St Laurent to Frost, 6 January 1956, file: Dominion-Provincial Conference, January 6, 1956, 1955, 1956, box 8, Office of the Premier: Frost Premier's Correspondence, RG 3-24, AO.

24 St Laurent to Frost, 18 February 1956, file: 121, box 16, Grant Dexter Papers, Queen's University Archives (QUA).

25 Frost to St Laurent, 22 February 1956, file: Dominion-Provincial Conference, January 6, 1956, 1955, 1956, box 8, RG 3-24, AO.

26 Don Patterson to George Drew, 30 April 1956, file: Federal-Provincial Fiscal Arrangements, vol. 239, Drew Papers, Library and Archives Canada (LAC).

27 'Statement of the Hon. Leslie M. Frost … on March 9th, 1956,' file: Dominion-Provincial Conference (Statement LMF), vol. 38, Office of the Premier: Frost Premier's General Correspondence, RG 2-23, AO.

28 Draft, 'Plan C2,' March 1956, file: 121, box 16, Dexter Papers, QUA.

29 See Patrick H. Brennan, *Reporting the Nation's Business: Press–Government Relations during the Liberal Years, 1935–1957* (Toronto: University of Toronto Press, 1994), 157–64.

30 Draft, no title, March 1956, file: 121, box 16, Dexter Papers, QUA.

31 Don Patterson to George Drew, 30 April 1956, file: Federal-Provincial Fiscal Arrangements, vol. 239, Drew Papers, LAC.

32 William Kinmond, 'Frost's New Tax Formula Would Bring In an Extra $250,000,000,' *Globe and Mail*, 10 March 1956.

33 Ibid.

34 Don Patterson to Thomas Bell, 13 March 1956, file: Federal-Provincial Arrangements, vol. 239, MG 32 C3, George Drew Papers, LAC.
35 Draft, 'Plan C2,' March 1956, file: 121, box 16, Dexter Papers. On the postwar history of alliances between Ontario and Quebec, see P.E. Bryden, 'The Ontario-Quebec Axis: Postwar Strategies in Intergovernmental Negotiations,' *Ontario since Confederation: A Reader*, ed. Edgar-André Montigny and Lori Chambers, 381–408 (Toronto: University of Toronto Press, 2000).
36 Roger Graham, *Old Man Ontario: Leslie M. Frost* (Toronto: University of Toronto Press, 1990) 26.
37 'Frost Indicates Province Would Re-Enter Tax Fields,' *Globe and Mail*, 13 March 1956.
38 File: Federal–Provincial Relations, 1953–1956, vol. 411, MG 28 IV 2, Progressive Conservative Party Papers, LAC.
39 Drew to Don Patterson, 24 April 1956, file: Federal-Provincial Fiscal Arrangements, vol. 239, MG 32 C3, George Drew Papers, LAC.
40 'Criticism of Federal Proposal on Fiscal Arrangements,' 10 July 1956, file: Dominion-Provincial Conference, July 11, 1956, box 8, RG 3-24, AO.
41 'Dominion-Provincial #4,' August 1956, file: 121, box 16, Dexter Papers, QUA.
42 Ibid., no title, August 1956.
43 Ibid.
44 Memorandum on Federal-Provincial Relations Submitted by the Government of Ontario, August 13, 1956, file: Dominion-Provincial Conference, July 11, 1956, box 8, RG 3-24, AO.
45 See J. Harvey Perry, *A Fiscal History of Canada: The Postwar Years* (Toronto: Canadian Tax Foundation, 1989), 537; and, by the same author, *Background of Current Fiscal Problems* (Toronto: Canadian Tax Foundation, 1982), 59.
46 See Rand Dyck, 'Links between Federal and Provincial Parties and the Party System,' in *Representation, Integration and Political Parties*, ed. Herman Bakvis, vol. 14 of the research studies, Royal Commission on Electoral Reform and Party Financing (Toronto: Dundurn, 1991), 148; Denis Smith, *Rogue Tory: The Life and Legend of John G. Diefenbaker* (Toronto: Macfarlane Walter & Ross, 1995), 203–4.
47 Diefenbaker to Michener, 28 February 1957, file: Diefenbaker, John – correspondence, n.d., 1957, vol. 88, MG 32 A4, Roland Michener Papers, LAC.
48 Diefenbaker to Michener, 28 February 1957 [#2].
49 File: IV 6b – Tax Rental Agreements, 1946–1960, R.37, CM Fines Papers, Saskatchewan Archives (SA).
50 Merril Menzies to Diefenbaker, 10 April 1957, file: 391.8, vol. 22, reel M-5777, MG 26 M, John Diefenbaker Papers, LAC.

51 'Notes on Remarks by the Hon. Leslie M. Frost, QC, at Massey Hall,' 25 April 1957, file: 364, vol. 18, reel M-5555, John Diefenbaker Papers; 'Diefenbaker Offers Tax Cut, New Deal for Municipalities,' *Globe and Mail*, 26 April 1957.
52 Allister Grossart to Frost, 6 May 1957, file: Frost, 1954–57, vol. 341, PC Party Papers, MG 28 IV 2, LAC.
53 Tax Agreements #1, 11 May 1957, file: 122, box 16, Dexter Papers.
54 Frost press release, 5 June 1957, file: Elections, Press Clippings, 1957, box 14, RG 3-24, AO.
55 Diefenbaker to Frost, 16 September 1957, and Diefenbaker to Frost, 31 October 1957, file: Dominion-Provincial Conference, Nov. 1957, vol. 38, RG 3-23, AO.
56 *Dominion-Provincial Conference, 1957* (Ottawa: Queen's Printer, 1957), Frost, p. 18.
57 William Kinmond, 'Frost Key Figure at Talks with Bid for $100,000,000,' *Globe and Mail*, 25 November 1957.
58 Graham, *Frost*, 335–6.
59 Douglas Campbell, premier of Manitoba, to Diefenbaker, 18 December 1957, file: Federal-Provincial Correspondence, 1958, box 11, UC container 11-12, RG 6-115, AO.
60 R.M. Burns, *The Acceptable Mean: The Tax Rental Agreements, 1941–1962* (Toronto: Canadian Tax Foundation, 1980) 169; interview, Dalton Camp, 19 February 1997.
61 Notes on In Camera Proceedings of Federal-Provincial Conference of July 25–27, 1960, file: FP – 11th Continuing Committee, Sept. 1960, box 16, UC container 15-16, RG 6-115, AO.
62 A.S. Abell on Federal-Provincial Tax Arrangements, panel discussion, *Report of the Proceedings of the Fifteenth Annual Tax Conference*, Montreal, 21–2 November 1961, 305.

4 'As the Indians were wards of the Dominion Government': The Anishinabe of McIntyre Bay in the Hepburn-King Constitutional Battles

MARK KUHLBERG

Jack Saywell devoted the last half-century to dissecting the litany of constitutional battles that have shaped our federation since 1867. He focuses special attention on the caustic conflicts that marked relations between the Liberals in Toronto and Ottawa during the 'Hepburn-King era.' In doing so, Saywell highlights the subjects – such as hydro and taxation powers – over which the most important campaigns were fought. In these disputes, he underscores how each side took a 'no holds barred' approach to outdoing the other.

The battles between 'Mitch' and King were not limited to these jurisdictions, however, as they also included dealings with First Nations in Ontario. This reality is poignantly illustrated by the experience of the McIntyre Bay Reserve in Northwestern Ontario during the 1930s and 1940s. By the early part of the Depression, the local Indian agent had created a self-sufficient community on this reserve by establishing a timber harvesting and processing operation there. Although the endeavour proved to be a smashing success, its continuation required the province's cooperation, specifically in terms of providing a tract of Crown timber. While initially Ontario was willing to accommodate the Natives, it changed its mind after recognizing the golden opportunity that serendipity had placed in its lap. It could use the Aboriginals as pawns in dealing with the Dominion government, with the complementary goal being to tweak Ottawa's nose on jurisdictional issues and take a swipe at the federal government at a time when relations between Hepburn and King had reached a low ebb. The result is a tale that sheds light on but one aspect of the structural fetters that hamper efforts to resolve the challenges that face Canada's Aboriginals.

Battles between Ontario and Ottawa regarding First Nations are nothing new. Prior to 1867, the British government had entered into treaties with Aboriginals in what is now Ontario. In exchange for gaining 'legal' title to the First Nations' land, the agreements that dealt with central and northern Ontario essentially confined the Aboriginals to reserves within the large tracts of land they surrendered. The government also promised to protect certain Aboriginal off-reserve rights and privileges, particularly hunting and fishing. Under the British North America Act, Canada remained responsible for 'Indians and lands reserved for Indians.' The problem arose because the BNA Act also created the provinces and gave them jurisdiction over Crown lands. In other words, Ottawa was now responsible for the Aboriginals on the reserves *and* upholding its promise to protect their off-reserve rights, but Ontario had jurisdiction over the land surrounding the reserves. Moreover, the province was keen to see non-Natives exploit the resources that were found in its hinterland. Not surprisingly, conflict resulted.[1]

It was within this context that the McIntyre Bay Reserve came into being. By the mid-nineteenth century, the United Province of Canada had been anxious to acquire the land north of the upper Great Lakes in order to facilitate development by non-Natives. To achieve this end, it had entered into the Robinson-Superior Treaty in 1850 with the 'Ojibewa Indians'[2] who inhabited 'the Northern Shore of Lake Superior.' The treaty set out a number of reserves for the Ojibwa. Although McIntyre Bay was not among them, a group of Anishinabe (part of the Red Rock Band to the south) who had traditionally taken up summer residence in Grand or McIntyre Bay on the south shore of Lake Nipigon continued to live there. After the Anglican Church established a mission on the site in the 1880s, Ontario tacitly approved the reserve's existence by surveying its boundaries. On the eve of the First World War, Ontario determined that the land it had set aside for 'the Indians' under the Robinson-Superior Treaty exceeded that allotted for the purpose. It thus cancelled two reserves, one of which was McIntyre Bay. Ontario promised, however, 'that the Indians residing on the said two reserves are not to be disturbed in the occupation of the same as improved and occupied by them at the present time.' In 1919, W.R. Brown, the local Indian agent, proposed turning the McIntyre Bay Reserve into a quarantine and palliative care centre, specifically 'a supervised camp for the care of the sick, aged and destitute Indians in that District especially because of the Spanish Influenza Epidemic with its concomitant exactions.' Ontario was sympathetic to the request. It granted the Department of Indian Affairs (DIA) full title to the roughly six hundred–acre plot, with the caveat that the land would revert to Ontario if the DIA did not carry out the project or ceased to use the land 'for the purposes for which the grant is made.'[3]

During the 1920s, the Aboriginals around Lake Nipigon saw their living conditions deteriorate, and Ontario was at least partly to blame for this growing crisis. Jerry G. Burk was the Indian agent for Port Arthur, which encompassed this part of northern Ontario, and he continually reminded the DIA about the numerous challenges the local Anishinabe faced. His reports stressed that they had traditionally survived by hunting and fishing and that they could no longer do so because the 'natural heritage of the Indians has been to[o] exploited in recent years by the advance of civilization and industry; commercial fishing in inland waters; and in a more pronounced way by invasion of white hunters; resulting in scarcity of fur bearing animals ... [I]n my opinion,' he predicted, 'if this situation is allowed to become progressively worse, it is only a matter of a comparatively short time until the Indian will be driven to extinction.' Burk added that the culprit and remedy were, in his mind, clearly identifiable. As he put it, 'I would suggest that the Robinson Treaty which states; "Indians may trap and hunt as long as the river flows, grass grows, and the sun shines"; be upheld, or that the Ontario Government make some concessions by which the Indian may derive a living.'[4]

Faced with this emergency, Burk proposed a plan to Ottawa to concentrate the Anishinabe around Lake Nipigon at the McIntyre Bay Reserve where they could take up farming. Burk had already determined that this location held the greatest agricultural potential. He thus implored the DIA to provide the requisite practical support in the form of horses, farming implements, and instruction, and ask the Ontario government to expand the size of the reserve to accommodate the anticipated population influx. Burk also asked Indian Affairs to fund the construction of new housing for the Anishinabe who would take up residence at McIntyre Bay. In presenting his case to headquarters, Burk argued that, if his superiors implemented his plan, 'both Father Couture [the Agency's missionary] and myself feel confident that the Indians ... could in time become self-supporting.'[5]

To Burk's delight, the decision-makers in this instance gave the project the green light. By mid-June 1931, Indian Affairs had approved the effort and written the Ontario government to gain its support. A.F. MacKenzie, the DIA's secretary, asked the province to assent to the

DIA's plan to use the McIntyre Bay Reserve 'for the purpose of improving their [i.e. the local Natives'] living conditions.' Within short order, Walter C. Cain, Ontario's deputy minister of lands and forests, had conveyed the good news; the province agreed with Burk's concept in principle, and would permit the reserve to be used for this effort. Cain would not entertain the notion of expanding the reserve's size, however.[6]

Burk ignored this minor setback and drove aggressively ahead, but it soon became apparent that an activity other than farming was becoming the community's economic lifeline. Because it was prohibitively expensive to ship building materials for the new homes from the Lakehead to McIntyre Bay, Burk had recommended – and the DIA had approved – purchasing a small sawmill and associated wood-finishing machinery to process the trees found on the reserve and turn them into the numerous products needed for constructing houses. And when he reported to headquarters in the fall of 1931 – only a few months after the project had begun – that more land was being cleared for farming, this story was dwarfed by tales that described the community's production of lumber and the advantages accruing from it. The sawmill had arrived in November, and within one month it was operational along with an edger, shingle mill, and four-sided planer. In short order, the facility had produced enough timber to construct roughly one dozen houses, and the value of the building material alone was worth more than twice the DIA's $2,500 investment in the equipment. In addition, the Natives had begun turning the smaller pieces of lumber they produced into boxes; these were used to ship (on ice) to Toronto the surplus fish they were catching. The sawmill's success soon attracted the attention of the local media, and it also drew more Aboriginals from around Lake Nipigon to McIntyre Bay, necessitating the construction of additional houses beginning in the spring of 1932. In no uncertain terms, if the changing local circumstances had closed the door on survival based upon the Anishinabe's traditional existence, their lumbering operations offered a highly promising means of adapting to a new way of life.[7]

It proved to be far more than promising. While the Canadian economy was suffering through the nadir of the Depression over the course of the early and mid-1930s, the Aboriginals at McIntyre Bay were riding a wave of prosperity because of their forest industry. It attracted an ever-increasing number of local Aboriginals to what the DIA had proudly christened the 'McIntyre Bay Experiment.' Not only were the Natives running practically the entire operation themselves, but they were also erecting houses and ancillary buildings for their community. In addition, they soon captured a major contract (12,000 units the first year and 22,000 the second) to produce boxes for the local non-Native commercial fishermen, and began selling some of their surplus lumber to nearby reserves. And when fires destroyed the sawmill in 1935 and again the next year, the DIA was uncharacteristically prompt in funding its reconstruction. As Indian Agent Burk boasted to his superiors in summarizing his initiative, he had overseen the migration of the local Aboriginals – many of whom had previously been 'tubercular,' on relief, and 'living in most unsanitary conditions' – to McIntyre Bay. Now, he described how they were 'living in properly constructed homes, receiving sufficient food, and ... working for a living.'[8]

By early 1936, however, the project's continued success depended upon receiving the Ontario government's cooperation. The sawmill on the McIntyre Bay Reserve had been processing logs for four seasons. During this time, it had been supplied by timber – largely white, red, and jack pine – that the community had been harvesting from its own reserve. But the supply of merchantable trees on the reserve had been practically exhausted; the reserve's small size – 585 acres – meant there was a relatively small volume of wood to cut. In fact, Burk had been aware of this looming bugbear from the outset, and had augmented the Natives' wood supply by salvaging logs lost by a local contractor on the south shore of Lake Nipigon. This stop-gap measure could not hide the fact that the Anishinabe needed more wood, and the only source from which it could come was provincial Crown land adjacent to the McIntyre Bay Reserve.[9]

This prompted Burk to take up the matter with the Ontario Department of Lands and Forests (ODLF). In February 1936, Burk spoke with Thorsten Ehn, the ODLF's supervisor of timber operations. Ehn invited Burk to Toronto to discuss the matter with Peter Heenan, the province's minister of lands and forests. Ehn believed that Heenan would be inclined to assist the Natives in acquiring a small piece of timberland that abutted the McIntyre Bay Reserve.[10]

Burk soon learned that Ontario's cooperation would come at a price, but it was one that Burk was willing to pay, and with good reason. After his trip to Toronto, Burk reported to Ottawa that the province was 'prepared to lease or sell to the McIntyre Bay Reserve 2,000 acres of timber.' But, he stressed, 'because of the fire hazard caused by our steam boiler,' Ontario hesitated 'granting this limit unless a sawmill powered with a Diesel motor which would automatically eliminate [the] fire hazard' was installed on the reserve. Considering the previous two years had seen major blazes destroy much of the Anishinabe's wood-processing operation, the province's request seemed both reasonable and a desirable one to meet. As a result, over the summer of 1936 the DIA approved both the purchase and installation of a used diesel engine at McIntyre Bay and the upgrading of the community's sawmill. By the end of July, the new machinery was ready and awaiting a supply of sawlogs to be cut that winter. Moreover, the pressure to acquire a new source of wood mounted after Burk lined up an additional contract for railway ties and boxcar lumber with the Canadian National Railway for the McIntyre Bay operation.[11]

After the DIA had fulfilled its end of the bargain, Ontario seemed willing to do likewise. In mid-September 1936, Burk officially applied to the Ontario government for roughly five square miles of timberland in Innes Township that bordered the McIntyre Bay Reserve on its eastern end. In doing so, Burk stressed that the Natives' cutting privileges ought to extend over a minimum of three years, if not much longer; his goal was to provide long-term employment by harvesting only as much timber each season as was absolutely needed. F.J. Dawson, the province's local district forester, assessed Burk's application and pointed out that 'the timber from the reservation is cut out. Therefore in order to keep the mill operating, he [Burk] asks that the Department give his application due consideration.' Dawson added, 'I would recommend that the Department look favourably on this application.'[12]

Ontario then attached another caveat to granting the DIA's request for this timber limit, and again Burk went the extra mile to meet it. The area for which Burk had applied was within a pulpwood concession that the provincial government had leased to Nipigon Corporation, a subsidiary of the pulp and paper giant, Canadian International Paper Company (CIP). Ontario thus insisted that Indian Affairs 'deal with the concessionaires' to obtain permission to harvest the tract in question, a directive the DIA followed to the letter. By the last week of October, Indian Affairs had received the company's formal permission to cut the red, white, and jack pine (i.e., sawlogs) in this small area. It finally seemed that Ottawa had met all the province's conditions for acquiring this tract. In fact, Burk was downright convinced that gaining official permission to cut it was a fait accompli. A telegram to his superiors in early November explained that he had not taken any more action with the ODLF regarding the matter because provincial officials had 'informed me Nipigon Corporation had full authorization to lease the timber limit stop timber on reserve exhausted have started operations on new limit.'[13]

By this time, however, a new factor had already entered into the equation, one that would prove ruinous to the Anishinabe at McIntyre Bay and was tarred with more than a hint of political skulduggery. O.R. Greer was a small-scale timber contractor who had recently begun operating in the Sioux Lookout area, a 250-mile train ride from the south shore of Lake Nipigon. In early October 1936, he had applied to the ODLF for permission to cut the white and red pine from the identical, five-square-mile timber limit for which Indian Affairs had applied. Greer explained that he was motivated by his desire to fill a contract for railway ties that he had secured from the Canadian National Railway.[14]

Greer's application was stupefying for numerous reasons. In November 1935, he had won a tender for the jack pine timber on a roughly eight-square-mile tract near Sioux Lookout. It would have provided him with more than enough wood to manufacture tens of thousands of railway ties – the product he wished to make – for at least a few seasons. Moreover, there were numerous other timber limits available throughout the Lakehead area. Why would Greer now be interested in obtaining another limit – precisely the one that Indian Affairs sought – on the shore of Lake Nipigon that was both so far from the one he already controlled and so isolated and difficult to access? Finally, jack pine was the species from which railway ties were made in Ontario. Why, then, was Greer interested in the same tract as the Anishinabe, particularly after a cursory cruise carried out by the Ontario government's forest rangers at this time revealed that red and white pine made up roughly 75 per cent of the merchantable timber on the limit adjacent to the McIntyre Bay Reserve?[15]

Indian Affairs had little time to worry about answering these questions, especially after it learned that Ontario favoured Greer's application over the DIA's. On 9 November, Vernon E. Johnson, the woodlands manager for CIP, the pulp and paper company within whose pulpwood concession the timber limit in question was located, conveyed startling news to A.F. MacKenzie, the DIA's secretary. Johnson informed MacKenzie that not only had another party applied for the timber tract in Innes Township, but Johnson also explained that the Ontario government was pressuring CIP to grant the wood to Greer instead of the Anishinabe of McIntyre Bay. MacKenzie countered by arguing that Indian Affairs had begun pursuing this matter several months earlier, and that, at that time, the Ontario government had indicated that 'it would be necessary to apply to your company for the necessary cutting rights. You were good enough to give your consent and our agent was instructed to advise the Department [of Lands and Forests] at Toronto. The Indians at McIntyre Bay,' MacKenzie's plea continued, 'are greatly in need of this timber for their small saw-mill, so as to supply themselves with building material etc., and I think you will agree that our application should be given the preference both by reason of priority and urgency.' MacKenzie closed by urging Johnson to emphasize these points when the former responded to the Ontario government.[16]

As word of what had happened spread, the DIA faced increasing external and internal pressure to take steps to rectify the situation. Dan McIvor, the member of Parliament for Fort William, wrote T.A. Crerar, the minister of Indian affairs, to point out that CIP had already given its permission to the DIA to harvest in this area, but now the Ontario government was indicating that it was going to tender the limit and 'Big Contractor O.G. [sic] Greer expects to get it.' McIvor's telegram closed by stressing that 'immediate action is required to protect Indians' interest if lease [i.e., to the timber limit] is cancelled entire Band will be on relief.'[17] Fearful of being sideswiped by this unfolding story, Crerar's office asked the DIA for a full report. H.J. Bury, the DIA's supervisor of Indian timber lands, composed a precis on the subject for the minister. The nub of the matter, Bury asserted, was that four days ago CIP had advised Indian Affairs that 'Hon. Peter Heenan had suggested to them [i.e., CIP] that they should give their consent to Mr Greer, and retract that which they had already given to the Department on behalf of the Indians.' Bury thus implored the 'Hon. Superintendent General [i.e., the minister] to write to Hon. Peter Heenan, and urge that the consent given by the [CIP] be recognized.'[18]

By this time, Ontario had already slyly taken steps to render superfluous any protest from Indian Affairs. On 6 November, the province advertised a tender for the right to cut the pine timber from the six-square-mile tract 'on the Innes Section of Lake Nipigon.' The DIA was undoubtedly dismayed by this news, but it was downright irate upon learning that Ontario had ensured that the tender's terms precluded the Aboriginals at McIntyre Bay from *ever* harvesting this timber. The tender declared, for example, that the winning bidder had to construct 'by the 30th June, 1937, a saw mill having a minimum capacity of Thirty thousand feet per diem, such mill to be erected on the East shores of Lake Nipigon in Orient Bay, or in the vicinity thereof.' This provision prohibited the Anishinabe at McIntyre Bay from processing the timber in their existing sawmill. Moreover, the tender called for the timber to be cut and removed by 31 March 1938, and for a minimum of 75 men to be employed in harvesting it. In contrast, the DIA had asked for at least three seasons to cut the wood (and probably much longer), and the Aboriginals at McIntyre Bay would also have been hard-pressed to assemble a gang of more than three dozen bush workers, let alone seventy-five. Finally, the tender set a moderate minimum or 'upset' price for the wood ($7.50/Mfbm was where the bidding started) and included the extraordinary provision that 'the upset price or price bid on this timber, shall not, in any way, be subject to reduction.'[19]

Word of the tender and its terms incensed J.G. Burk, the Indian agent at the Lakehead who had been the driving force behind the McIntyre Bay project. He thus exhorted his superiors in Ottawa to push the Ontario government into aborting the public sale and awarding the wood to the Aboriginals. In a letter to the DIA's secretary on 11 November, Burk stressed that the 'McIntyre Bay reserve is surrounded by a large area of muskeg land, with the exception of that portion where we have applied for a timber limit. This portion is the only available timber adjacent to the reservation.' He also stressed that the DIA would not realize its goal of making this group of Indians 'self-supporting' if the Anishinabe did not 'secure this limit.' To buttress his case, he enclosed a map of the Thunder Bay District that illustrated the 'numerous other timber limits, which could be obtained from the Ontario Government,' and argued that it was thus 'only fair that the limit adjacent to the McIntyre Bay reservation, be reserved for the Indians.' He closed by expressing his hope that Indian Affairs would 'be able to have this order [i.e., to tender the wood] cancelled and that the limit will eventually revert back to the Indians of the McIntyre Bay Reserve.'[20]

Burk's efforts precipitated a meeting in Toronto to discuss the matter, but it was there that he learned that Ontario was playing a game in which Ottawa was about to draw the 'provincial rights card.' Burk led an entourage of prominent Lakehead officials (including future Senator Norman M. Paterson and Dan McIvor, the aforementioned MP from Fort William) who met with Peter Heenan, Ontario's minister of lands and forests. During their get-together, Burk explained the desperate plight of many of the Aboriginals in the 'Robinson-Superior' area and the dire necessity of acquiring the timber limit in question. Burk reported that Heenan had then taken centre stage and 'intimated that, as the Indians were wards of the Dominion Government, it was up to that Government to support them and that if they so desired they could put in a tender for this timber limit.' As a result, Burk relayed the news that 'Heenan refused to show any leniency and would not consider post-poning the sale of this timber.'[21]

As a last resort, T.A. Crerar, the superintendent general (i.e., minis-ter) of Indian affairs, took the matter up with Heenan on 21 November, only six days before the tender was set to close. Crerar recounted that the DIA had the consent of the local pulp and paper firm to allow the Anishinabe to harvest the pine timber from the tract in question. 'I un-derstand,' Crerar continued, 'that the pine timber on this area is now being offered for sale by tender under such terms of operation as will be impossible for the Indians to comply with ... These Indians experience, at the best of times, difficulty in supporting themselves, and if they are deprived of the opportunity of securing this small limit, their mill will have to close down and they will have no means of support.' For these reasons, Crerar pleaded with Heenan to postpone selling the timber un-til the DIA had another opportunity to present its case to the province.[22]

Predictably, Crerar's plea fell on deaf ears, and Ontario went ahead with the tender. There were only two bids, and while Greer submitted one of them – he offered a 'bonus' of 52¢/Mfbm for the wood – Indian Affairs did not. The other bidder, and the party who walked away with the tender, was Charles W. Cox, whose bid of $2.50/Mfbm had bested Greer's by a long shot.[23]

Cox's involvement in this incident would have come as no surprise to anyone familiar with his modus operandi. A veteran timber contrac-tor at the Lakehead, he had a long history of harvesting wood from Indian reserves in Northwestern Ontario dating back to the early 1920s. In this regard, his record was strewn with misdemeanours. On numer-ous occasions during the 1920s and early to mid-1930s, the DIA had investigated his activities in order to defend the Aboriginals' interests, but it had never taken effective action to shut Cox down.[24]

The evidence suggests that Cox's remarkable impunity was largely a function of his political influence. By the time of the tender in No-vember 1936, he was a crucial member of Hepburn's government, hav-ing sat as the MPP for Port Arthur since 1934. What made Cox such a prized political asset was his contention – credible enough to send chills down the spines of several high-profile Tories – that he had se-cured incriminating information that, if revealed, would condemn the 'Ferguson Conservatives' to the dustbin of history, and maybe even jail. Hepburn demonstrated his high regard for Cox's support by amend-ing legislation to override a challenge to Cox's electoral victory in 1934 and giving Cox remarkable latitude to exploit Ontario's Crown timber resources in order to profit personally.[25]

Hepburn was anxious to line up his allies in the mid-1930s as relations between Ottawa and Toronto soured. 'Mitch' had thrown himself into the 1935 federal election on behalf of the King Liberals in the hopes that a Grit victory in Ottawa would translate into 'a better deal' for Ontario in particular and the provinces in general. Although pundits judged the sweeping Liberal victory of mid-1935 to have been more Hepburn's than King's, King made it clear that Ottawa did not share Hepburn's vision for a reconstituted federalism. In practice, this meant that King refused to assume responsibility for implementing an effective relief plan to deal with the Depression. Predictably, thereafter the premier's affection for the prime minister dissipated. The deteriorating situation culminated with Hepburn's declaration on the eve of the Ontario election in the fall of 1937 that he was not 'a Mackenzie King Liberal.'

In this battle with Ottawa, Hepburn cherished Cox as an ally, one whom he did not wish to lose to King. Hepburn knew that Cox had forged a strong tie to C.D. Howe, Cox's federal counterpart in the Port Arthur riding and a politico whose star was rising. To protect his claim on Cox's allegiance to the provincial team, Hepburn named Cox minister without portfolio in late 1936, even though it broke the premier's pledge never to appoint officials to this sinecure.[26]

If there was any doubt about Cox's potential value in battling Ottawa, he put them to rest beginning in the fall of 1936. He was the central figure in a cunning plan, one that almost certainly went forth with the premier's approval, to remind Ottawa that two could play the game of refusing to help out in the realm of providing social assistance. While the federal government was free to choose – and had chosen – to be obstinate on this issue, in doing so it had seemingly forgotten that it needed the provinces' help, especially Ontario's, in caring for 'Indians.' Hepburn's government clearly recognized its opportunity to hit at Ottawa's Achilles heel, and Cox was the person who knew just how to deliver a stinging blow.

This was clear from the manner in which Ontario handled its sale of the timber in Innes Township in November 1936. It will be recalled that the tender obliged the winning bidder both to build a sawmill at or near Orient Bay on the eastern shore of Lake Nipigon and process the wood there. Coincidentally, from the early to late 1920s, Cox had harvested timber from the Gull Bay Reserve on the west side of Lake Nipigon. In order to get his timber to market, in 1925 he had leased from the Ontario government a parcel of land in Orient Bay that was *the* ideal location for both landing and processing logs that were cut around Lake Nipigon and loading them onto the railway. By the eve of the Depression the site was known as 'Cox's spur.' In other words, anyone wishing to win the tender in 1936 would have to deal with Cox to gain access to his site. Moreover, events would soon reveal that Cox had also probably prodded Greer to apply for the pine in Innes Township in an effort to stymie Indian Affairs' plan.[27]

While there was no love lost between Cox and Peter Heenan, Ontario's minister of lands and forests, the guiding principle on this occasion was the desire to give Ottawa some of its own medicine. In early December 1936, Heenan took great delight in rubbing salt into Ottawa's wound when he wrote the DIA to inform it officially of the outcome of the tender in Innes Township. Heenan admitted that the 'situation with respect to the desire of the Indians to acquire timber was presented on different occasions to this Department by your Indian Agent.' At the same time, he was adamant that 'it was quite clearly and distinctly pointed out to him that if the Dominion Government – responsible for the welfare of the Indians – was desirous on behalf of the Indians of bidding on timber that might be offered for sale in accordance with the Regulations, and did so and became the successful tenderers, there was no reason why the operations should not be undertaken by or on behalf of the Indians.' Moreover, Heenan stressed that Ontario did not deem it desirable 'to grant to Indians privileges that are denied the regular timber operators, who are in the business and who are regularly subject to market competition.'[28]

Witnessing first-hand the devastating toll the Ontario government's actions were taking on the Anishinabe at McIntyre Bay, Indian Agent Burk again took up the cudgels against the province. He reported fully on the situation to H.W. McGill, the director of Indian affairs, in late February 1937, reminding McGill that some time ago the Natives had 'secured a timber limit adjacent to the reserve … Unfortunately,' Burk lamented, 'the timber berth was cancelled, and, unless action can be taken to recover this timber limit, it will become necessary to place the entire band on relief through shortage of timber for the sawmill by means of which these Indians had become self-supporting.' The problem was compounded, Burk pointed out, by the fact that 'this timber was the only available timber adjacent to McIntyre Bay reserve,' and the terms of the tender 'were such that it was compulsory to cut the entire timber berth in two years. The same amount of timber would keep this entire band for the next 50 or 100 years.' As a result, he pleaded for the DIA to 'recover this timber berth, and thus eliminate further relief.'[29]

What made the situation especially grating for Burk and the McIntyre Bay Aboriginals was news that Cox had not even operated in Innes Township over the winter of 1936–7. Instead, he had arranged to have the Ontario government literally give him a large timber limit near Sioux Lookout (i.e., it was not tendered, as the law required). He also saw to it that Greer, who had lost the tender in Innes, received equally favourable treatment; this suggests that Cox and Greer had acted in concert in the Innes tender. Over the course of the winter of 1936–7, both of them had conducted large operations on these tracts in the far northwest.[30] As a result, even though the tender for the timber in Innes Township had required the licensee to complete his harvesting operations by the end of March 1938, by the time spring had arrived, Ontario's local forest officials had reported that they had 'found no signs of any operations being carried out in this area or any camp buildings, nor does it appear that any operations are contemplated this season.'[31]

The evidence suggests that Cox had only acquired the Innes Township licence to gain leverage in dealing with the DIA. Cox's timber operations on the Long Lac and Lac Seul reserves at this time were eliciting ever louder howls of dissatisfaction from both the disaffected Aboriginals and officials within Indian Affairs.[32] With pressure growing on Ottawa to provide answers to some troubling questions about Cox, the DIA began squeezing him for answers. Over the first half of 1937, for example, the department refused to release the railway ties Cox had cut from the Lac Seul Reserve the previous season until he cleared his outstanding debts and submitted the requisite paperwork for his operations. The DIA even threatened to have 'the whole account placed in the hands of the Department of Justice' if Cox refused to co-operate. By acquiring the licence to the timber that the DIA desperately sought in order to sustain the Anishinabe at McIntyre Bay, then, Cox had won himself an invaluable bargaining chip that he could barter in exchange for leniency.[33]

And Cox was prepared to barter. In mid-April 1937, the DIA met with representatives from the ODLF to review the matter. During the discussion, the ODLF suggested to Indian Affairs that the latter 'make some arrangements with C.W. Cox to obtain relinquishment of [his] rights on such portions of the timber limit as are required to keep our [i.e., the DIA's] mill in operation.' By early May, Indian Agent Burk had opened negotiations with Cox. The latter quickly agreed to sell the licence to the DIA while the DIA would pay Cox $3,500 to cover the cost of the deposit he had made when he had won the tender.[34]

When the DIA then approached Ontario about the tender's 'objectionable terms,' Ontario agreed to acquiesce but only partially and only in a manner that snidely implied that helping the Natives had always been the province's intent. On 7 May 1937, Walter Cain, the ODLF's deputy minister, informed Burk that Ontario was prepared to amend some of the terms under which the wood could be cut. The province agreed specifically to 'waive the condition regarding the new saw mill' and to extend the time frame for cutting the wood to one that 'may be deemed fair and reasonable.' In extending this olive branch, Cain disingenuously declared that he hoped this 'arrangement can be consummated [i.e., with Cox] and thus place the Indians in an independent position for some years to come. When this timber was offered for sale it was expected that the Indian Department would have tendered.'[35]

Buttressing the view that Ontario was not sincere in its inclination to help the Anishinabe in this instance was its decision to stop short of meeting all their needs. Indian Agent Burk wrote headquarters in mid-May 1937 and described how Cain had been willing to cooperate 'to some extent.' The problem, Burk underscored, was that Cain had refused to reduce 'the timber dues offered by Cox,' that is, his bid of $2.50/Mfbm in addition to the 'upset' price of $7.50/Mfbm that Ontario had set meant the wood would cost $10/Mfbm. Burk was adamant that this 'would be an impossible amount for the Indians to pay,' and he thus urged the DIA to take this final matter up with provincial officials.[36]

So once again, Indian Affairs renewed its battle against Ontario, this time to persuade the province to lower the stumpage dues the Aboriginals from McIntyre Bay would pay to cut the wood from the Innes Township limit. With the DIA's secretary pointing out to Burk that the 'whole transaction hinges on this vital point,' officials from Indian Affairs took the matter up with W.C. Cain, the ODLF's deputy minister.[37]

While they appeared to win their case, Cain ensured that Ontario still retained the upper hand in its dealings with Ottawa. J.C. Caldwell, the director of the DIA's Lands and Timber Branch, summarized the situation in general and the province's perspective in particular in a letter he sent H.W. McGill, the head of Indian affairs, in mid-May 1937. Caldwell indicated that everything had been arranged with regard to the timber licence 'with the exception of the matter of price to be paid for the timber.' He added that Cox's tender had been for $10/Mfbm, and Cain had made it clear in recent conversations with officials from

Indian Affairs that 'this price would have to prevail.' At the same time, Cain had dangled a carrot stick in front of the DIA. Caldwell explained that Cain had also 'intimated that within a reasonable time, subsequent to the transfer, this Department [i.e., Indian Affairs] might, if considered advisable, submit representations to his Department requesting a revision of the purchase price and if such action should be taken, Mr Cain indicated that undoubtedly a reasonable and satisfactory re-arrangement would be made.'[38]

It was now Cox's turn to tease Indian Affairs. On 15 May, he had formally indicated to the Ontario government his willingness to transfer his licence to the DIA. Five days later, the DIA had written him expressing its willingness to pay him $3,500 to cover his deposit, but it made handing over the cheque contingent upon both Cox completing the legal documentation regarding the transfer and the province approving the deal. While Cox had the paperwork before him at this time, he refused to sign it. Repeatedly over the course of late May and early June, the DIA pressed Cox on the matter, but to no avail.[39]

While both Ontario and Cox continued to toy with Indian Affairs, the Anishinabe at McIntyre Bay were suffering from being left in this lurch. Thomas McGookin, the inspector of Indian agencies, put the case forcefully before the DIA in mid-June after he had investigated conditions at McIntyre Bay. 'Splendid progress has been made both from an economic and health view point,' McGookin explained with reference to McIntyre Bay, and the 'community has become entirely self-supporting through the operation of a saw mill, snow shoe, boat and canoe factory and a co-operative scheme.' The problem, he emphasized, was that the 'sawmill is idle at the moment owing to lack of timber.'[40]

Cox finally caved in late June. His motive in transferring the licence to Indian Affairs at this time is difficult to determine with certainty, but there are a few possible explanations. In February 1937, Cox suffered severe burns to his face when an alleged 'affair gone wrong' caused the aggrieved party to throw acid at him. Although he was back to work within a few months, he could hardly be faulted for wishing to get his 'business affairs' in order.[41] In addition, Cox was in arrears to the Ontario government for timber dues, and it was pressing him to clear the debt. Finally, shortly after Cox transferred the licence near McIntyre Bay to Indian Affairs, the DIA reversed its hard-line stance in dealing with Cox's licence to the timber on the Lac Seul Reserve. Cox's acquiescence at McIntyre Bay may have been one end of a simple quid pro quo with the DIA.[42]

Nevertheless, even though Indian Affairs now controlled the licence it had long sought – Burk proclaimed in September 1937 that securing the new timber limit would mean that 'work can be provided permanently for all the Indians on the reservation' – Ottawa soon learned that its victory was a Pyrrhic one. In May 1938, the DIA contacted Indian Agent Burk with a burning question. Why, after all the fuss to obtain the tract from the Ontario government, did the Aboriginals not cut any timber from it over the 1937–8 season? Burk responded by reminding his superiors that Cain, Ontario's deputy minister of lands and forests, had promised to 'give consideration to a reduction on timber dues for 1938. Mr Caine [sic] suggested that when our timber operations were completed this spring [i.e., 1938] that I call at his office and discuss the question of dues.' Burk then pointed out, however, that Ontario's refusal to reduce the stumpage dues on the timber meant that the Anishinabe from McIntyre Bay could not afford to cut the wood.[43]

While this was Burk's official line, apparently he had already devised and implemented a novel – albeit illegal – solution to this problem. Over the winter of 1937–8, the Anishinabe at McIntyre Bay cut their reserve's remaining scattered merchantable timber.[44] More importantly, at some point during that same winter, they also began harvesting white and red pine on their Innes Township tract. They also cut a very large volume of jack pine, which they desperately needed in order to fill a large railway tie contract for the CNR (worth nearly $20,000). The problem, however, was that the DIA's timber licence to Innes Township was limited to white and red pine. Because Ottawa was not licensed to harvest jack pine, the Aboriginals had broken the law and Ontario was in a position to levy costly penalties.[45]

While Ontario took an uncharacteristically sympathetic view of Ottawa's transgression on this occasion, the province refused to budge on the issue of the dues it had set for the white and red pine, the two dominant merchantable species on the Innes Township licence. Determined to address the latter matter, Burk wrote the Ontario government in October 1938 and provided a litany of reasons why it ought to lower the dues on the white and red pine. 'It is impossible to operate' for these two species, Burk explained, 'as it is a well known fact that the price was bid up in order not to allow any other firm to secure the Limit.' In response, Ontario obstinately declared that 'no reduction can be made.' Moreover, provincial officials noted that the Natives' operation in 1937–8 had consisted 'almost entirely of jack pine, which class is not included in the license. This, however, will not be regarded as a trespass, and a rate of $6.60 per M. inclusive of dues, has been set and the account will go out shortly.'[46]

Burk's solution was but an interim measure, and it left Indian Affairs little choice but to go down a road that Burk had tried to avoid for the better part of a decade. Ontario was clearly uninterested in budging with regard to lowering the dues on the white and red pine, and the Anishinabe from McIntyre Bay had now cut most of the jack pine from their licence in Innes Township. The challenge was thus to find gainful employment for these Natives, and Burk devised a two-pronged plan to achieve this end. He negotiated deals with two major pulp and paper firms at the Lakehead that agreed to employ a limited number of the Aboriginals around Lake Nipigon to cut small volumes of pulpwood on the concessions the mills leased from the Ontario government. This solution would not address the problem of the Innes Township licence, however. In this regard, Indian Affairs believed it would be necessary to team up with a non-Native contractor whose profit margin could absorb the high dues Ontario was demanding be paid for the white and red pine. As a DIA memorandum on the subject read, Ottawa could either team up with an outside operator to cut this wood, 'or throw up the timber berth [i.e., licence] and absorb the loss that that will entail.' While various parties expressed interest in the cooperative enterprise, the DIA eventually decided to align itself with C.E. McDevitt.[47]

These latest initiatives were undeniably creative means of solving the problem, but they represented a monumental blow for the Anishinabe of McIntyre Bay. Previously, these Natives had essentially been 'in business for themselves.' Granted, a non-Native had worked as a millwright on the project. Apart from that very limited outside help, however, the Aboriginals had handled practically all aspects of their endeavour. More importantly, the Natives had earned good wages while cutting and processing their own wood. In addition, they had been able to sell their wares off-reserve for a profit. Their tie project in 1937–8, for example, had taken in over $4,000 more than it had cost, and this was just one phase of a single season's operation. But as a result of the new direction in which the Anishinabe were now compelled to move, they were reduced to being mere subcontractors confined to the harvesting end of the business. They sold only their labour and the logs they cut to outside interests. While this work was better than none at all, this new means of operating undermined their independence and pinned their future economic well-being on the backs of non-Natives.

The lobby for lowering the dues on the Innes Township licence continued for a few years, and this sustained effort was noteworthy because it mentioned with increasing frequency the force that had derailed Burk's master plan for gaining autonomy for the Anishinabe. In late January 1940, C.E. McDevitt, the contractor with whom the Aboriginals were now working, provided Peter Heenan, Ontario's minister of lands and forests, with some insight into Cox's original interest in this tender. 'It is apparent,' McDevitt informed Heenan, 'that Mr Cox when he bid this Norway [i.e., red pine] in at $10.00 per thousand had no intention of living up to the terms of the sale and was quite ready to have the Indian Department releive [sic] him of the limit. Evidently Mr Cox makes a practice of doing this as I am informed that he bid in an area around Jellico, recently, that was put up for the Geraldton lumber, at the exorbitant price of $12.00 per thousand.'[48]

Ontario would ultimately grant the reduction in the fall of 1940, but by then the damage had been done. Heenan conveyed the good news to Ottawa in early October that Ontario would lower the dues from $10 to $8/Mfbm. He added that a committee had been struck to study timber prices in the area to determine if additional reductions were warranted.[49] Over the next half dozen or so seasons, the Anishinabe of McIntyre Bay would be involved in cutting nearly 6 million fbm of white and red pine from the Innes Township licence. While this accomplishment was certainly a testament to a successful make-work project for the Natives, the fact that they had been reduced to mere hewers of wood indicated that their role in the local timber trade was a far cry from the independent operation for which Burk had laid the groundwork many years earlier.[50]

The spectre of Ontario's reluctance to facilitate Anishinabe participation in the region's timber economy would reappear soon enough. In February 1952, Reverend A. Rolland of the Lake Nipigon Indian Missions contacted the DIA in an effort to secure a relatively miniscule tract of Crown timber for two small-time Aboriginal lumbermen. Rolland strategically asked for a parcel that was relatively worthless to the large, non-Native timber firms, pointing out that 'it's a cut area, but there is enough left to keep the boys going 3 or 4 years.' At the same time, the minister was sensitive to the obstacles Ottawa faced in dealing with Toronto about this matter. 'It's for a small portion of small people and involves highest politics and powers,' he declared exasperatingly.[51]

Rolland had accurately identified one of the fundamental problems that the Anishinabe faced in northern Ontario after Confederation. The division of powers outlined in the BNA Act emasculated Ottawa in terms of providing the means by which the Aboriginals had traditionally sustained themselves. This anomalous situation was highly conducive to Ontario toying with Ottawa when it came to dealing with Indian Affairs. As the events at McIntyre Bay during the 1930s and 1940s demonstrate, the province's predilection in this regard was acute during the Depression when the Hepburn Liberals pounced upon a golden opportunity to do unto the King government as it had done unto them.

While elected officials at Queen's Park may have seen this simply as an amusing distraction and a chance to snicker at their colleagues on Parliament Hill, there was – and continues to be – a tragic aspect to this state of affairs. The Aboriginals who are caught in the crossfire suffer immeasurably as politicians in Toronto and Ottawa place expediency ahead of addressing pressing concerns about the Natives' welfare. In some ways this problem is even greater today than it was at the time of the McIntyre Bay affair, as there is now a significant overlap whereby both federal and provincial governments provide social services to Native communities. This has only heightened the mud-slinging between the two levels of government each time news of the Aboriginals' generally deplorable living conditions make the headlines. 'A battle between the federal and Ontario governments over who is to blame for a tainted-water crisis at a remove [sic] native reserve intensified yesterday,' the *Globe and Mail* reported in the fall of 2005 with regard to the Kashechewan Reserve in northern Ontario, 'as the first twin propeller planes landed on the community's gravel runway and began airlifting ill residents to safety.' As politicians in Toronto and Ottawa trade sound bites in an effort to one-up their rivals, sadly the Anishinabe are the losers in this perpetual dual that is Canadian federalism.[52]

NOTES

1 The most celebrated legal case was *St Catharine's Milling v. The Queen* in the mid- to late 1880s. See Bradford W. Morse, ed., *Aboriginal Peoples and the Law: Indian, Metis and Inuit Rights in Canada* (Ottawa: Carleton University Press, 1985), 57–9; Anthony J. Hall, 'The St Catharine's Milling and Lumber Company vs. The Queen: A Study in the Relationship of Indian Land Rights to Federal–Provincial Relations in Nineteenth Century Canada,' in *Aboriginal Resource Use in Canada: Historical and Legal Aspects*, ed. Kerry Abel and Jean Frisen, 267–86 (Winnipeg: University of Manitoba Press, 1991).

2 The 'Ojibwa' spelling of this word will be used in the text of this article, and 'Anishinabe' will be used to refer to the Aboriginals around Lake Nipigon.

3 Documents germane to the establishment of the McIntyre Bay Reserve, with the citations taken from C. Stewart to W.R. Brown, 21 October 1914; and A. Grigg to J.D. McLean, 7 June 1919, 9/30-1, 10429, RG10, Library and Archives Canada (LAC); Copy of OC [24 October 1919 re: creation of McIntyre Bay Reserve] 492/3-6, 10429, RG10, LAC.

4 J.G. Burk to DIA, 2 September 1931, 10009-9, 7594, RG10, LAC.

5 J.G. Burk to D.C. Scott, 30 May 1931, 10009-9, 7594, RG10, LAC.

6 F.H. Paget to D. Robertson, 22 June 1931; A.F. MacKenzie to W.C. Cain, 23 June 1931; and Cain to MacKenzie, 24 July 1931, 10009-9, 7594, RG10, LAC.

7 Documents from October 1931 to May 1933, especially J.G. Burk to DIA secretary, 6 May 1932, 10009-9, 7594, RG10, LAC.

8 Documents from spring 1933 to early 1936, with the citation taken from J.G. Burk to DIA secretary, 17 March 1934, 17009-9 pt. 1, 7624, RG10, LAC; Burk to DIA secretary, 2 April 1932, 10009-9, 7594, RG10, LAC; *Annual Report of the Department of Indian Affairs for the Year Ending March 31 1934*, 8–9.

9 J.G. Burk to DIA secretary, 10 May 1933, 10009-9, 7594, RG10, LAC.

10 J.G. Burk to H.W. McGill, 24 February 1936; and T. Ehn to A.F. MacKenzie, 26 February 1936, 17009-9 pt. 2, 7624, RG10, LAC.

11 J.G. Burk to DIA secretary, 7 April 1936; and correspondence from June and July 1936 regarding the acquisition and installation of the new equipment at McIntyre Bay, 17009-9 pt. 2, 7624, RG10, LAC; A.F. MacKenzie to Burk, 30 April 1936, 492/3-6, 10429, RG10, LAC.

12 J.G. Burk to J.F. Dawson, 18 September 1936; and Dawson to W.C. Cain, 18 September 1936, 110381, RG1-246-3, Archives of Ontario (AO).

13 H.C. Draper to F.J. Dawson, 24 September 1936, 110381, RG1-246-3, AO, from which the first citation is taken. Dawson to J.G. Burk, 2 October 1936; A.F. MacKenzie to W.B. Daley, 9 October 1936; MacKenzie to Burk, 10 and 23 October and 5 November 1936; Burk to MacKenzie, 10 October 1936; MacKenzie to V.E. Johnson, 20 October 1936; and Johnson to DIA secretary, 22 October 1936, 30,009-9X, 7547, RG10, LAC. Finally, Burk to MacKenzie, 6 November 1936, 30,009-9X, 7547, RG10, LAC, from which the second citation is taken.

14 J.F. Sharpe to H.C. Draper, 5 October 1936; and O.R. Greer to P. Heenan, 1 November 1936, 110381, RG1-246-3, AO.

15 W-9-264, vol. 10, RG1-E-4-B, AO; and F.J. Dawson to deputy minister, 22 October 1936, 110381, RG1-246-3, AO; D.A. Wood to Dawson, 30 October

1936, 110381, RG1-246-3, AO; and Dawson to W.C. Cain, 3 and 4 November 1936, 110381, RG1-246-3, AO.

16 H.J. Bury to J.C. Caldwell, 9 November 1936; as well as A.F. MacKenzie to V.E. Johnson, 5 November 1936, 30,009-9X pt. 1, 7547, RG10, LAC, from which the citations are taken.

17 D. McIvor to T. Crerar, 9 November 1936, 30,009-9X pt. 1, 7547, RG10, LAC.

18 W.J.F. Pratt to H.W. McGill, 9 November 1936; H.J. Bury to J.C. Caldwell, 9 November 1936 (from which the citations are taken); and McGill to superintendent general, 12 November 1936, 30,009-9X pt. 1, 7547, RG10, LAC.

19 'Sale of Red and White Pine Timber,' 6 November 1936, vol. 3, 61303, RG1-246-3, AO.

20 J.G. Burk to DIA secretary, 11 November 1936, 30,009-X pt. 1, 7547, RG10, LAC.

21 J.G. Burk to DIA secretary, 19 November 1936, 30,009-X pt. 1, 7547, RG10, LAC.

22 T.A. Crerar to P. Heenan, 21 November 1936, 30,009-X pt. 1, 7547, RG10, LAC.

23 O.R. Greer to P. Heenan, 27 November 1936; C.W. Cox to Heenan, 27 November 1936; deputy minister to Heenan, 28 November 1936; and W.C. Cain to F.J. Dawson, 28 November 1936, 110381, RG1-246-3, AO.

24 Mark Kuhlberg, '"Nothing it seems can be done about it': Charlie Cox, Indian Affairs Timber Policy, and the Long Lac Reserve, 1924–1940,' *Canadian Historical Review* 84, no. 1 (2003): 33–64; Kuhlberg, 'Disturbing Synergy between Inspector and Inspected: The Gull Bay Case, 1916–1932, in *Papers of the Thirty-Fifth Algonquian Conference*, ed. H. C. Wolfart, 207–38 (Winnipeg: University of Manitoba Press, 2004).

25 Jack T. Saywell, *'Just Call Me Mitch': The Life of Mitchell F. Hepburn* (Toronto: University of Toronto Press, 1991), 209, 300–1.

26 Saywell, *'Mitch,'* 222–359.

27 C.W. Cox to T.A. Cummins, 29 May 1925; and T.A. Cummins to W.C. Cain, 2 June 1925, 58868, RG1-246-3, AO.

28 P. Heenan to T.A. Crerar, 10 December 1936, 30,009X, 7547, RG10, LAC.

29 J.G. Burk to DIA secretary, 30 November 1936; and Burk to H.W. McGill, 24 February 1937, 30,009X, 7547, RG10, LAC.

30 OC220/433, OC220/432A, and OC223/457, RG75-57, AO.

31 W.C. Cain to C.W. Cox, 11 January 1937; Cain to F.J. Dawson, 12 February 1937; Dawson to Cain, 16 February 1937; and finally F.E. Rowe to Dawson,11 March 1937, from which the citation is taken and it is enclosed in M.R. McDonell to Cain, 11 March 1937, 110381, RG1 246 3, AO.

32 J. Chapais and councillors to DIA, 12 March 1936; H.J. Bury to J.C. Cald-

well, 24 April 1936; W.J.F. Pratt to H.W. McGill, 22 August 1936; G. Gonthier to deputy minister, 23 February 1937; J.G. Anderson to DIA secretary, 10 June 1937; T.R.L. MacInnes to Anderson, 14 June 1937; and T. McGookin, memorandum, 23 July 1937, 30009-5 pt. 2, 7805, RG10, LAC.

33 *Port Arthur News-Chronicle*, 20 and 21 March 1936; T.R.L. MacInnes to C.W. Cox, 9 February 1937, enclosing 9 February 1937 Account with C.W. Cox for Lac Seul Contract Only; MacInnes to F. Edwards, 15 April 1937; MacInnes to Cox, 16 April 1937; and MacInnes to G.P. MacLaren, 3 May 1937, 30144-7 pt. 3, 7850, RG10, LAC.

34 T.R.L. MacInnes to H.W. McGill, 26 April 1937; W.C. Cain to McGill, 3 May 1937; McGill to Cain, 3 May 1937; and Cain to J.G. Burk, 7 May 1937, 30,009-X pt. 1, 7547, RG10, LAC.

35 Cain to J.G. Burk, 7 May 1937, 30,009X pt. 1, 7547, RG10, LAC.

36 J.G. Burk to DIA secretary, 13 May 1937, 30,009X pt. 1, 7547, RG10, LAC.

37 T.R.L. MacInnes to J.G. Burk, 17 May 1937; and Burk to DIA secretary, 19 May 1937, 30,009X pt. 1, 7547, RG10, LAC.

38 J.C. Caldwell to H.W. McGill, 20 May 1937, 30,009X pt. 1, 7547, RG10, LAC.

39 C.W. Cox to W.C. Cain, 15 May 1937; Cain to Cox and T.R.L. McGinnis [sic], 20 May 1937; MacInnes to Cox and Cain, 20 May 1937; Cain to McInnes and Cox, 7 June 1937; and MacInnes to Cain, 8 June 1937, 110381, RG1-246-3, AO; J.G. Burk, Requisition for $3,500, 27 May 1937; T.R.L. MacInnes to Burk, 29 May and 10 June 1937; J.C. Caldwell to Burk, 1 June 1937; Cox to MacInnes, 2 and 24 June 1937; MacInnes to Cox, 2, 14, and 16 June 1937; Cain to MacInnes, 7 June 1937; MacInnes to Cain, 8 June 1937; Burk to DIA secretary, 12 June 1937 (from which the citation is taken); and Cox to Caldwell, 21 June 1937, 30,009X pt. 1, 7547, RG10, LAC.

40 J.G. Burk to DIA secretary, 12 June 1937, 30,009X pt. 1, 7547, RG10, LAC; T. McGookin to Headquarters, Report re: McIntyre Bay #54 and Grand Bay, 23 July 1937, 17009-9 pt. 2, 7624, RG10, LAC.

41 The story can be followed in the local papers and is described in A.W. Rasporich, '"Call Me Charlie," Charles W. Cox: Port Arthur's Populist Politician,' Thunder Bay Museum Historical Society, *Papers and Records* 19 (1991): 2–20.

42 T.R.L. MacInnes to C.W. Cox, 3 August and 17 September 1937; Accounting from Charles W. Cox, Limited, 19 July 19[3]7; and MacInnes to G.P. MacLaren, 16 September 1937, 30144-7 pt. 3, 7850, RG10, LAC; MacInnes to W.C. Cain, 26 June 1937, 30,009X pt. 1, 7546, RG10, LAC; Assignment of Timber Licence from C.W. Cox Limited to the Dominion Government, 22 June 1937, 110381, RG1-246-3, AO.

43 J.G. Burk to DIA secretary, 14 September 1937, 32009-9, 7874, RG10, LAC

(from which the first citation is taken); Burk to DIA secretary, 8 May 1938, 30,009-9X, 7546, RG10, LAC.

44 [Forest Projects for Anishinabe in Port Arthur District], ca. October 1937, 30,009-1-2, 7546, RG10, LAC.

45 Entry for Licence 48 to Innes Township, vol. 55, RG1-E-9, AO; correspondence between September 1937 and October 1938, 30009-9, 7805, RG10, LAC; H.W. McGill to J.P. Mertz, 21 September 1938, 30,009-9X, 7546, RG10, LAC; McGill to deputy minister, 8 November 1938, 30009-9 pt. 2, 7546, RG10, LAC; Report on Sawmill and Equipment, June 1938, 17009-9 pt. 2, 7624, RG10, LAC.

46 J.G. Burk to F.J. Dawson, 13 October 1938; and J.F. Sharpe to Dawson, 20 October 1938, 110381, RG1-246-3, AO.

47 Memorandum to Dr McGill re: The McIntyre Bay Tie Operation, 29 September 1938, 30,009-9X, 7547, RG10, LAC; H.J. Bury to DIA director, 22 June 1938, 30009-9 pt. 1, 7805, RG10, LAC (from which the citation is taken); correspondence from fall 1938 to fall 1939, 30,009-1-2, 7546, RG10, LAC; Memorandum to McGill, 29 September 1938; and R.J. Prettie to G. Burk, 3 October 1938, 30,009-9X pt. 1, 7547, RG10, LAC.

48 C.E. McDevitt to P. Heenan, 27 January 1940; and J.G. Burk to Heenan, 27 January 1940, 110381, RG1-246-3, AO; H.W. McGill to Heenan, 5 February 1940, 30,009-9X pt. 1, 7547, RG10, LAC.

49 T.A. Crerar to P. Heenan, 27 September 1940; and Heenan to Crerar, 3 October 1940, 110381, RG1-246-3, AO; Licence Reference Sheet, W-9-373, RG1-E-3-B, AO.

50 Cutting Record, W-9-373, RG1-E-3-B, AO; Memorandum of Meeting among C.E. McDevitt, J.G. Burk, F.A. Macdougall, and J.F. Sharpe, 18 March 1943; and acting minister to N.O. Hipel, 25 May 1943, 110381, RG1-246-3, AO.

51 A. Rolland to Major MacKay, 24 February 1952, 492/20-7-0-54 pt. 1, 7054, RG10, LAC.

52 Karen Howlett and Bill Curry, 'Tempers Flare with Ottawa As Airlift of Natives Begins,' *Globe and Mail*, 27 October 2005.

5 From 'On-to-Ottawa' to 'Bloody Sunday': Unemployment Relief and British Columbia Forests, 1935–1939

RICHARD A. RAJALA

Canadian political history, Jeremy Mouat notes, 'is often little more than the history of federal–provincial relations writ large.'[1] Mouat's observation caught my eye in considering British Columbia's Depression-era forest relief projects, a subject that supports his contention. While Ottawa's interest in the revenue generated by BC forest exploitation has remained constant, direct federal involvement has waxed and waned over the years in response to a host of influences. During the latter years of the Great Depression, massive unemployment called for a measure of federal spending in support of the province's effort to cope with the western tide of jobless transients. That said, it is less the constitutional aspects of the story that drew me than the social and environmental dimensions.

In placing public lands and forests under provincial jurisdiction, the 1867 British North America Act dictated a limited role for Ottawa in BC woodlands. With the exception of the Railway Belt, under federal control until 1930, policies set by provincial governments set the terms of forest exploitation. Other instances of federal involvement prior to 1930 included the Commission of Conservation's pioneering survey of BC forests published in 1918, the establishment of a forest products laboratory at the University of British Columbia in 1917, and research on early-twentieth-century bark beetle outbreaks by Dominion entomologists. During the Second World War federal funding supported the assignment of conscientious objectors to forest improvement and fire protection work supervised by the BC Forest Branch. Passage of the 1949 Canada Forestry Act brought millions of federal dollars to provincial forestry programs for two decades during the post-war economic boom, before Ottawa's 'proclivity to hide behind its constitutional skirts'[2] prompted a retreat to the less costly research field. The Forest Resource Development Agreements of the 1980s signalled a brief renewal of federal interest in response to timber supply concerns, but as the above suggests, Canadian federalism has defeated efforts to create a consistent national forest policy.[3]

Forestry may not have topped the list of grievances that the 'spoilt child of Confederation' has presented in the quest for better terms, but the flow of tax dollars generated by BC's dominant industry to Ottawa fit nicely alongside demands for greater understanding in controversies surrounding federal immigration, tariff, and transportation policy. And the province's disproportionate share of the national unemployment crisis during the second half of the Dirty Thirties enabled Premier T. Dufferin Pattullo to convince Mackenzie King that conditions on the West Coast were, indeed, exceptional. Pattullo would fail to convince both R.B. Bennett and King that the solution to joblessness lay in a national unemployment insurance scheme. Nor, when given the chance in 1941, was Pattullo himself willing to grant Ottawa the additional financial powers needed to transfer constitutional responsibility for welfare from provincial to federal jurisdiction. Nevertheless, between 1935 and the onset of the war Pattullo's faith in state activism and King's caution combined to find space within the rigidities of federalism for relief programs that saw the unemployed undertake a wide range of work in BC forests. The results were mixed in both human and ecological terms, but analysis of this largely unknown chapter of BC's Depression era should provide insights of value to labour, environmental, and political historians.[4]

Despite fine scholarship on unemployment policy and social protest in BC during the 1930s, the period separating the On-to-Ottawa Trek of 1935 and Vancouver's 'Bloody Sunday' of 19 June 1938 is not well understood. Clarification demands that the focus widen from Vancouver to take in the province's forestlands, the site of two sorts of relief efforts administered by the BC Forest Branch. The first, known as the Young Men's Forestry Training Plan (YMFTP), began in 1935 without Ottawa's direct financial assistance. Inspired by Franklin D. Roosevelt's Civilian Conservation Corps, the YMFTP provided young male residents of the province with training in woodscraft during the summer months. The absence of organized protest suggests that the carefully selected YMFTP enrolees exchanged their labour for relief in a generally congenial atmosphere, reflecting well on T.D. Pattullo's government. Ottawa would draw on BC's example in national youth training efforts, culminating in the 1939 National Forestry Program.

The second, much leaner, and more contentious program arose out of Mackenzie King's decision to close the Department of National Defence (DND) camps in 1936 without long-term provision for transient relief on the West Coast. These wintertime Forest Development Projects (FDP) took in the country's single unemployed, many of them hardened veterans of the DND camps and the Ottawa trek. Together, the two programs provided a poorly funded Forest Branch with a welcome source of labour – forced labour in the case of the FDP workers. YMFTP and FDP camps constructed forest experiment stations and nurseries, carried out forest protection improvements, built roads, developed the provincial park system on Vancouver Island, and even planted a few trees as the province began to confront a massive backlog of cutover land. Aside from their significant environmental legacy, the forest relief projects command attention for what they reveal about relations between the governments of Duff Pattullo and Mackenzie King, the capacity of the single unemployed and their allies to wring concessions out of these administrations, and the limits of Depression-era reform in our federal system.

Canada's export-driven economy was highly vulnerable to the collapse of international commodity markets, which triggered the Great Depression. Western provinces experienced the most acute suffering, per capita incomes falling more steeply than in other regions between 1929 and 1933. BC's forestry sector, devastated by slack demand and American tariffs, sputtered along at less than half its capacity during the early 1930s. Seasonal and cyclical transience had been a feature of the national economy since the late nineteenth century, but the idling of the West's farms, mines, logging camps, and sawmills saw the traditional resource proletariat joined by thousands of jobless engaged in a restless search for jobs or relief.[5]

BC attracted large numbers of these men, as it had in previous slumps, most ending up in Vancouver where the most unfortunate took shelter in a series of makeshift 'jungles.' But the almost 11,500 interprovincial transients who had registered for relief at the province's Pender Street relief centre by February 1932 occupied an unenviable position in Canada's rickety welfare system. Under the British North America Act, responsibility for welfare rested with the provinces, which shifted the relief burden downward to their municipalities. Vancouver officials responded by adopting a one-year residency requirement in 1930, arguing that the Dominion and the province should accept responsibility for the single unemployed and the interprovincial transients. In leaving home, then, the migrants had cut themselves off from aid beyond perhaps a meal and bed for a night's rest.[6]

Newly elected Prime Minister R.B. Bennett turned down provincial and municipal demands to take responsibility for the homeless, instead offering grants to the provinces while waiting in vain for his tariff policies to stimulate recovery. Such funds were used to initiate shared-cost public works projects, and in the fall of 1931 BC Premier Simon Fraser Tolmie established over two hundred relief camps for single unemployed provincial residents and transients. The federal Parks Department also received funding for national park development in the West, but by the summer of 1932 the Bennett government faced widespread condemnation from the new Cooperative Commonwealth Federation, the Communist Party's National Unemployed Workers' Association, and local unemployed councils around the country. Bennett only deepened the crisis in 1932 when his Relief Act rejected public works in favour of the less costly alternative of direct relief. The country's estimated seventy thousand single unemployed drifted back to the cities, where protests for more humane treatment grew in scale and intensity.[7]

Fearing that the single jobless would fall easy prey to radical organizers, the Bennett government made an ill-fated effort to take temporary responsibility for their upkeep. Anxious to remove the transients from communist influences in the cities, in October 1932 Cabinet approved Department of National Defence administration of a national series of relief projects designed to, as Laurel Sefton MacDowell puts it, 'salvage youth and reduce the danger of disorder.'[8] By 1933 DND camps had opened in every province except Prince Edward Island. BC's road camps were transferred to DND jurisdiction, and the establishment of others brought the province's total to fifty-three. By 1934 they held 7,000 men, over one-third of the national total.[9]

The story of the unrest, protests, and strikes that plagued the DND camps, which federal Minister of Labour Norman Rogers later termed 'a ready-made forum for the propagation of subversive doctrines where teachers and pupils were given shelter, food and clothing at the expense of the government,' is well known. The Communist Party's Workers' Unity League quickly chartered the Relief Project Workers' Union (RPWU) to organize collective protest. Some 1,200 supporters participated in a late-1934 general strike in the BC camps, setting the stage for a much larger April 1935 protest for better conditions, higher wages, and an end to military control. The ensuing 'On-to-Ottawa Trek' and Regina riot ultimately discredited both the DND scheme and Bennett's government. Mackenzie King would close the camps in 1936, but in BC a more innovative approach to work relief, although similar in inspiration, had already entered its second year of operation.[10]

BC's YMFTP swung into action in the spring of 1935, providing a few months of woods work at nominal wages for youths. Explicitly ignoring the transients, the program sought to address the unemployment problem among a select group of male residents of the province, provide the Forest Branch with a means to initiate much-needed protection and development projects, and prepare enrolees for work in the forest industry. A masterstroke of public policy modelled on Franklin D. Roosevelt's Civilian Conservation Corps, the relief experiment would generate approval of T.D. Pattullo's Liberal government by rebutting growing criticism of Crown forest management and fostering the impression of government activism on the unemployment front.

The keys to the YMFTP's success lay in careful selection of participants, a general perception among both those involved and taxpayers that their work had value, and its emphasis on training and education. The last feature dictated some sacrifice of efficiency, but lent the program a purpose and legitimacy lacking in the DND camps. With no activists to contend with, project supervisors experienced only isolated disciplinary problems, and none of the collective resistance to authority that discredited Bennett's 'slave camps.'

Elected in November 1933 on a platform of 'Work and Wages,' but unable to persuade either Bennett or Mackenzie King to initiate a massive public works program, Pattullo used his faith in state activism to introduce his own 'little New Deal.' Roosevelt's CCC, which employed over five hundred thousand by late 1935, provided a nearby model for its forestry component. Over two hundred camps operated in the Pacific Northwest, engaged in planting trees, building forest protection roads and trails, and laying telephone line between ranger stations in the national forests. BC foresters could only look on in envy as their own agency withered away under staff reductions and salary cuts, unable to conduct anything more than the most rudimentary revenue collection and protection tasks.[11]

Cowichan Leader editor and independent MLA Hugh Savage created the initial impetus for BC to borrow from Roosevelt's CCC in February 1935, proposing a series of 'Hope Stations' to provide work for young unemployed males in provincial forests. *Comox Argus* publisher Ben Hughes agreed that 'young men eating their hearts out in idleness would be a thousand times better off helping the foresters.' Seizing an opportunity to improve his agency's fortunes, Chief Forester P.Z. Caverhill endorsed the idea of using 'unemployed older boys' to clear forest protection trails and undertake work at the Cowichan Lake, Green Timbers, and Aleza Lake experimental stations.[12]

By early April Forest Branch and provincial Department of Labour officials had agreed to go forward with a Youths Employment and Forestry Corps, offering woods training that would leave participants 'more self-reliant and with a saner outlook towards the future.' In addition to the stated objective of opening opportunities for youths in logging, administrators hoped that the program would diminish reliance on immigrant labour, suspected of radical tendencies. The Forest Branch received an initial allotment of $80,000 from the province's Unemployment Relief Fund to administer the YMFTP, with an original goal of employing 350 young men from mid-June to mid-September. Eligibility requirements, strictly enforced at the outset and then gradually relaxed, restricted openings to physically fit unmarried men in 'necessitous circumstances' aged twenty-one to twenty-five, resident in the province for at least ten years, with a high school education.[13]

In the end, roughly five hundred young men took part that summer, earning a wage of $1.75 per day, less 75 cents a day for board, transportation, and blankets. Kenneth McCannel immediately obtained information on CCC procedures after being named YMFTP supervisor. He organized three fifty-man crews at the experiment stations, which also served as clearing centres where enlistees were evaluated prior to assignment to sixteen smaller crews consisting of ten to twelve men each. These mobile crews cleared forest protection trails, built bridges, laid telephone line, and constructed patrol cabins in the five forest districts. Another hundred men assisted Rangers at stations around the province. The Forest Branch insisted on the authority to 'dispense with the services of anyone whose work and conduct are not satisfactory,' but the YMFTP's status as a training program dictated that the agency exercise this right with considerable restraint. The emphasis on 'character building' also resulted in the provision of recreational and educational opportunities. One-half day each week was devoted to fishing, swimming, or organized sports, and the branch offered some rudimentary instruction in forestry.[14]

Pattullo's 9 May 1935 announcement of the YMFTP and a smaller companion program in placer mining sparked widespread interest. He pledged to continue pressing for a solution to the transient problem, emphasizing the need for a Dominion-financed works program along the lines of Roosevelt's $500 million Federal Emergency Relief Administration, the Civil Works Administration, and the CCC. Provincial Minister of Labour George Pearson insisted that only those 'with a sincere desire to benefit from the training ... be considered for the YMFTP.' Since one of the scheme's main objectives was to 'make these young men desirable material for timber operators to draw from,' Forest Branch supervisors would keep records of individual performance, detailing 'physical ability to stand up under work, his working capacity [and] general character.'[15]

Early reports from the projects were generally encouraging. Cowichan Lake Superintendent Charles Schultz described his Cowichan Lake crew as 'very keen,' and his Aleza Lake counterpart C.L. Anderson found his men to be of 'a very high standard.' Nelson District foresters praised their assistant rangers as 'boys of an excellent type ... willing, keen, and gluttons for work.' Inevitably, of course, problems arose as young men of various backgrounds confronted the reality of physical, outdoor labour. A couple of 'poor specimens' left a Nelson trail crew after a short time. 'These gentry were most highly indignant at the very idea that ultra-refined examples of humanity like themselves should be expected to perform such lowly tasks as manual labour,' reported a *Forest Branch Newsletter* correspondent.[16]

Throughout the 1935 season administrators monitored signs of discontent closely to head off conflict that might produce criticism and diminish chances of funding in subsequent years. When the foreman of a Vancouver Forest District trail crew fired a man for unspecified reasons, the case reached the desk of Acting Chief Forester E.C. Manning. Conceding that under normal circumstances the foreman was justified, Manning pointed out that in the YMFTP camps 'sympathetic handling of the youths is desirable and we are expected to take more of a personal interest in them.' After determining that offenders in CCC camps often received a second chance, Manning offered the man reinstatement at Green Timbers.[17]

Despite efforts to promote a paternalistic employment relationship, isolated incidents of acrimony became more frequent as the summer waned. Deteriorating weather, inadequate blankets, and leaky tents led to grumbling among some trail crews. But, while Manning maintained a policy of 'getting rid of agitators as fast as possible,' only seven men were discharged during the season. As the summer neared its end, Forest Branch officials made systematic efforts to meet their mandate of securing employment for men in the timber industry. By the end of August, twenty-six 'distinctly suitable men' had been placed with Vancouver Island logging firms, leading the B.C. *Workers News* to describe the YMFTP as little more than a government effort in training youths to serve as scab labour or 'stool pigeons' in the event of strikes. Loggers should educate the newcomers and transform them from 'a weapon of the lumber barons' into supporters of the Lumber Workers' Industrial Union.[18]

The program wrapped up in mid-October to widespread editorial praise. Manning had even arranged for UBC professor Malcolm Knapp to present a series of forestry lectures at Cowichan Lake and Green Timbers. Hugh Savage praised the government's implementation of his idea. The operators' Pacific Logging Congress and the Canadian Society of Forest Engineers commended Pattullo's enlightened policy. All agreed the YMFTP should be reintroduced in 1936. Manning, now chief forester after Caverhill's late-1935 death, described the program as 'a complete success in every respect.' At the experiment stations, crews had made progress on the installation of water systems, telephone lines, firebreaks, and roads. Trail crews had improved or established 382 miles of packhorse trail, put in miles of telephone line, and built several cabins for protection purposes. But however impressive the YMFTP's accomplishments, its focus on provincial residents did not address the larger menace posed by the homeless men now congregated again in the DND camps after the Regina Riot. They represented a national problem, one demanding federal action.[19]

When William Lyon Mackenzie King's Liberal party returned to national power late in 1935, the new prime minister moved ahead with a campaign promise to close the DND camps. Anticipating the eventual closure of the federal camps, BC's Department of Labour asked the Forest Branch in early December to formulate a scheme for the winter employment of three to four thousand single homeless men. Forester F.D. Mulholland prepared a plan for the utilization of transient labour in developing nurseries at the existing Green Timbers site, Campbell River, and Prince Rupert, along with the preparation of 50,000 acres of cutover land for planting by the spring of 1938. Manning, however, was ambivalent about the prospect of operating relief camps for the transients. Not only was the labour 'largely undesirable,' carrying out forestry work during a typical coastal winter would be problematic. Nevertheless, a reforestation crisis loomed on the lower coast, and a less ambitious plan involving reforestation, protection, and campground construction was feasible so long as government did not demand 'real returns on the expenditures.'[20]

Events in Ottawa dictated that Manning would not confront the mixed blessing of the DND men until the following winter. King's Labour Minister Norman Rogers worked out an arrangement with the Canadian National Railway and Canadian Pacific Railway to employ up to ten thousand former DND inmates on track work that summer, and a farm placement scheme absorbed a smaller number. With these measures in place, Rogers announced that the federal camps would close by 1 July 1936. But the government placed only 8,700 of the 20,467 camp workers with the railways, and a paltry 641 accepted seasonal farm work. The remaining 10,000 began drifting back to the cities in July, to be joined by the others when the railway jobs ended. Thus, by the time the relief camps closed, 'the makings of a new relief crisis were readily apparent,' James Struthers observes.[21]

Pattullo, worried about the inevitable influx of men to Vancouver, cited the YMFTP's success in pressing King to create 'a generous program of public works.' The prime minister, determined to balance the federal budget, declined. Nor would he commit funds for a second YMFTP in 1936. By April Manning was hopeful, but not yet certain, that monies would be made available for another season's work. Later that month provincial Relief Administrator E.W. Griffith told Manning to set up the administrative apparatus, but go no further until Ottawa agreed to loans necessary for BC to meet its share of relief costs. Finally in late May Pearson announced that the YMFTP and mining program would resume with an initial allotment of $100,000. The 1936 YMFTP took shape under a broader base of eligibility; officials lowered the minimum age to eighteen, and the residency requirement from ten to five years. About a thousand applied for one of the 500 positions that promised four months' work.[22]

Manning's desire to make some progress in the multiple use of provincial forests and appeals from local business interests for development of areas with the potential to attract tourists and recreationists enabled the Forest Branch to make its first foray into park development that summer. McCannel authorized a fourteen-man crew for Elk Falls Park near Campbell River, assigned to construct a trail to the falls from a nearby road. Manning received a number of requests for such undertakings, but remained wary of large projects that might plunge his agency into the sort of conflict that plagued the DND camps. A main YMFTP objective, he told the Parksville and District Board of Trade in response to a plea for a Little Qualicum Falls project, was to 'take men out of the "camps" and give them a chance under suitable supervision on isolated jobs as far removed from any suggestion of relief and paternalism as possible.'[23]

On the national scene, King's National Employment Commission spent the summer of 1936 contemplating the problems posed by the single homeless, initiating a Canada-wide registration of relief recipients in September. Hoping that finances could be arranged to begin a 12,000-man national youth training program along CCC lines in 1937, federal Director of Forestry D. Roy Cameron asked Manning to submit estimates for a 2,000-man enrolment. Now completing the second season of YMFTP operation, Manning attributed its 'unqualified success' to several principles that any federally financed scheme should follow. First, the government 'must profit by honest labour value for every dollar spent.' Second, the scale of the enterprise should not exceed Forest Branch capabilities. Manning went on to emphasize the importance of athletics, occupational training, morale-building, and job placement in preventing 'the suggestion of relief' from tainting BC's YMFTP program. Concerned that federal funding might be accompanied by 'divided authority,' he emphasized his agency's sole responsibility in implementing the plan.[24]

Turning to the province's participation in a national program, Manning suggested that his understaffed agency could manage a 1,000-man initiative embodying the above principles. 'Is it not possible,' he cautioned Cameron, 'that the 12,000 man plan is too ambitious, will become just another relief scheme, with its attendant waste and adverse criticism?' Manning, then, was anxious to avoid entangling his agency in any measure that would damage its reputation or generate negative public opinion. 'I foresee very great benefits to forestry in Canada through the present proposal if we have the strength of mind to refuse too much,' he concluded. 'We can overstep our resources in efficient administration and work rapidly toward criticism, dissatisfaction, investigations, and the same end as the relief camps. Or we can confine ourselves to a moderate scheme with outstanding success.'[25]

If press reports are any indication, the Forest Branch had distinguished its YMFTP from the DND scheme. These were not relief camps, wrote the *Daily Colonist*'s John B. Tompkins, 'but outdoor units of a large college of ambitious youths being tutored in the elements of forestry by experienced forest men and university professors.' The *Victoria Daily Times* enthused that graduates left with 'fresh self-respect, new-found hope, a fresh outlook on life.' The Elk Falls project, with a public appeal that transcended the more mundane field of forest protection, came in for special praise. By season's end the crew there had disposed of a good deal of slash and fallen snags, and constructed an observation platform, drawing an expression of 'hearty appreciation' from the Campbell River and District Board of Trade.[26]

Manning's report to the Legislative Assembly in November 1936 drew attention to the YMFTP's social value in rehabilitating unemployed youths and the province's '100 percent' return on the $100,000 invested. Thanks in large part to industry's endorsement, the legislature's forestry committee recommended the program's continuation the following summer. In the interim, however, Manning and his agency would be drawn into a larger and much more contentious relief effort. The nation's slow recovery, coupled with large-scale protest by the unemployed in BC, forced the federal and provincial governments to cooperate in a plan for the wintertime relief of the single homeless men who had inhabited the DND camps. Manning's agency would thus confront the activists who had organized those camps, and who were dedicated to continuing their struggle in the new Forest Development Projects.[27]

Mackenzie King's decision to close the DND camps in July 1936 without provisions for long-term transient relief triggered another crisis in Vancouver that autumn. Pattullo once again called on Ottawa to care for the single unemployed as some took to the streets selling artificial flowers, precipitating obstruction arrests and demonstrations. Facing a winter of disorder in western cities and continued provincial insistence that the transients were federal responsibility, Dominion officials turned to relief proposals submitted by King's National Employment Commission. Since BC's agricultural sector would not absorb great numbers, the commission suggested that the Dominion and province share the cost of employment in basic industries such as forestry and mining. After Cabinet approval, King's Labour Minister Norman Rogers asked his BC counterpart George Pearson to submit plans that would enable Ottawa to 'obtain public support' when it cut men who refused work off relief.[28]

BC joined most of the other provinces in signing up for the farm placement plan, but could place no more than a few hundred men. Considering Rogers's request for other winter employment proposals, Pearson placed the blame for the province's unemployment problem on the interprovincial transients. Some six thousand might arrive in Vancouver by mid-winter, he warned, their exposure to the 'radical element' making a dismal scenario potentially explosive. The Dominion should remove the non-residents and place them on farms in their provinces of origin, Pearson declared; BC anticipated having to provide relief for up to nine thousand of its own single homeless men that winter. To provide for this class, Pearson proposed the provision of six thousand jobs in forest and mine development and public works for the November–April period, the $1.5 million cost to be shared equally.[29]

As the Forest Branch simultaneously wrapped up the YMFTP and drafted plans for a winter works program, Pattullo and Pearson continued to insist that the primary responsibility for unemployment rested with Ottawa, and that BC should not be burdened with the jobless from other provinces. Thus, when Relief Administrator E.W. Griffiths travelled to Ottawa for discussions, he carried a plan dealing only with BC's single homeless. Federal officials rejected the province's position, and the threat of disorder in Vancouver pushed the negotiations to a conclusion on 16 November, when the governments agreed to share the cost of a $1.5 million forest development relief scheme running to April 1937. Twenty-one camps would be established along the coast, employing 3,800 men at thirty cents an hour on a forty-four-hour week. Each man would have a portion of his wages held back, to be paid at four dollars per week after leaving the projects. All those who could prove arrival in BC prior to 15 November were eligible, a compromise designed to address Dominion concerns while discouraging further westward migration by interprovincial transients.[30]

The BC Forest Branch faced daunting challenges in administering a winter work relief program for the single unemployed. The new Forest Development Projects (FDP) differed in at least two fundamental respects from the YMFTP. A strict enterprise in social containment, these were labour camps pure and simple. No training, education, or organized recreation component would be afforded the enrolees. Second, the FDP took in former inhabitants of the DND camps, including the militants who had organized the Ottawa trek. These camps – eleven on Vancouver Island and the remainder on the lower coast – would be contested terrain from the start.

Experiment station improvement, park development, road building, and watershed protection received priority under Ken McCannel's administrative authority. Green Timbers and the UBC Demonstration Forest hosted seventy-five-man camps to undertake clearing, road and trail work, and nursery development. A crew of equal size carried forward YMFTP efforts at the Cowichan Lake Experiment Station. A hundred men were assigned to Elk Falls Park, and smaller gangs began developing the potential of Qualicum River Falls, Englishman River Falls, Skutz Falls, John Dean, and Thetis Lake parks on Vancouver Island. The Capilano, Seymour Creek, Nanaimo, and Victoria watersheds accepted forty-man road and trail building projects, and a number of similar forest protection initiatives occupied other camps.[31]

Reaction to the FDP plan ranged from the delight expressed by Vancouver officials to the ambivalence of Communist organs critical of low pay and the wage holdback policy. The Single Unemployed Protective Association (SUPA) denounced the 'dastardly' wage holdback, voting to accept the FDP program and organize on the job for better conditions. The CCF called the scheme a step in the right direction, but suggested a training component.[32]

While McCannel and his staff rounded up foremen and arranged for the supplies, provincial Department of Labour officials registered the single unemployed. Reluctant applicants learned that participation was a condition of relief eligibility. Moreover, the employment form the men signed included a declaration that dismissal from the projects 'for cause' meant forfeiture of the right to further aid. 'If they do not want to go to these camps, well, it is just "root, hog, or die,"' Pattullo said. 'There will be no more single relief for them.'[33]

Contingents of men began arriving at the projects at regular intervals through December, reaching a total of seven hundred by the end of the year. The typical fifty-man camp included fourteen sleeping tents, cookhouse, dining hall, wash house, supply tent, meat house, and recreation tent where the men could play checkers and cards, listen to a radio, and read magazines and newspapers. McCannel instructed his foremen to 'assure comfort and sanitation of the men,' but to demand a full day's work. Anyone found 'undesirable on any score' should be evicted immediately.[34]

Initial reports from foremen pleased McCannel, although the absence of carpentry skills forced some to hire local workers to put the finishing touches on camps. The arrival of many men in poor health also caused problems in the early days, despite medical examinations prior to assignment to the projects. McCannel, worried that the presence of idle men would weaken camp discipline, required those claiming illness to undergo a second examination. Enrolees ruled fit would do their share of the work or face dismissal.[35]

The government made clear its intention to tolerate no 'subversive' influences in the projects. Having provided fair living and working conditions, officials were determined not to 'permit discordant elements ...

to agitate for unreasonable demands.' From the outset, however, FDP enrolees demonstrated a capacity for solidarity when those in authority treated one of their number unfairly, failed to maintain adequate conditions, or challenged their dignity as workers. Hoping to prevent the RPWU from gaining a foothold, but recognizing the wisdom of allowing a forum for the expression of grievances, the Labour Department authorized foremen to meet with elected grievance committees if no 'outside influences' were involved and their membership changed weekly. Another approach to RPWU containment that drew discussion but no immediate action involved rounding up all known agitators for assignment to a single, isolated project.[36]

That idea began to gain more support after early January brought a number of firings for malingering and protests over food quality and camp conditions. Mainland Project Supervisor J. Pedley showed a willingness to compromise when presented with 'legitimate kicks' rather than trigger mass walkouts and adverse press coverage. For example, when the UBC Demonstration Forest project foreman fired a man for loafing, a sympathy strike erupted. Pedley considered the malingering charge valid, but after meeting with the crew agreed that the man should have received a warning before his discharge. Pedley ordered his reinstatement, achieving what he considered an honourable settlement by emphasizing the foreman's full authority to discharge the lazy. 'I told them we were trying to give them a fair deal,' Pedley explained to McCannel, 'but would insist that they in turn do the same for us.'[37]

The wage holdback policy provided the RPWU with a rallying point that transcended individual camp management issues. Protesting this affront to the principle of full payment for work performed, several camp locals urged Pattullo to drop the plan to withhold a portion of earnings for distribution in four-dollar instalments to sustain men for a few weeks after leaving the projects. The union also called on the premier to observe his own minimum wage law, to abandon the plan to rotate crews out of the camps to make room for a second wave, and to extend the projects until economic conditions permitted regular employment. Pattullo and Pearson refused all such demands, and by mid-January the RPWU announced a vote on what action should be taken to achieve payment of wages in full and recognition of grievance committees.[38]

Over the next week the struggle over authority in the camps became more heated. Over half of the Green Timbers crew struck in sympathy with a discharged worker on 20 January and were evicted by provincial

police. That same day at Cowichan Lake four RPWU members presented Foreman A. Gordon with a list of grievances, including overcrowd-
ed bunkhouses, poor breakfast fare, and the wage holdback. Gordon
called in three provincial police constables from Duncan and fired the
protesters, two of whom were reportedly veterans of the On-to-Ottawa
Trek. Pearson declared that all strikers would be paid off, barred from
the projects, and denied further relief. Moreover, if a rumoured general
strike occurred on 1 February, he would shut the camps down entirely
and cut the single unemployed off relief.[39]

Pearson's threat to close the camps in the event of a rumoured general strike elicited shrugs from RPWU officials. 'It's news to me,' Secretary Eric Cumbler replied when asked about a possible strike. Pearson,
he charged, hoped to provoke a walkout through a campaign of intimi-
dation against union men seeking to better their working conditions.
Indeed, ample evidence suggests that the government sought to purge
the camps of agitators in early 1937, and Cumbler cautioned Pattullo
that 'pursuance of this idiotic policy' would produce only further protests. Pearson expressed the government's willingness to address 'tri-
fling' grievances such as meal quality or overcrowding, but gave no
ground on the issues of union recognition, the wage holdback, or the
crew rotation plan.[40]

Pearson's stand drew approval from major newspapers, the *Province*
praising his 'refusal to be coerced or bamboozled by agitators,' but the
RPWU continued to mobilize resistance when grievances arose. Eighteen men refused to work in heavy snow at the Campbell River Ranger
Station in early February and were escorted off the premises by police.
A week later the firing of 7 men at Englishman River Falls triggered a
sympathy strike, leading to the eviction of 23 workers. Pearson blamed
the incidents on 'professional agitators,' and prepared to evacuate the
projects in late February to make way for the second rotation of 1,800
men who had been collecting direct relief. According to the government, the original contingent would have accumulated sufficient wages and holdback payments to sustain them until early May.[41]

As the released men returned to Vancouver, government press releases emphasized their financial well-being and success in securing
employment. The SUPA and RPWU, conversely, stressed the lack of
jobs and impossibility of getting by on only a few four-dollar holdback
cheques. The RPWU urged Pattullo to initiate a summer public works
program for the single unemployed, scoring something of a victory
when Ottawa authorized a one-month extension of the projects until
the end of May.[42]

The announcement, unfortunately, came only after a soliciting campaign had begun on the streets of Vancouver by men who had exhausted their holdback payments. Over fifty received one-month jail terms for obstruction, although the prosecutor later admitted that no charges would have been laid had he known of the government's intention to readmit these first-rotation men to the extended projects. Canadian Labour Defence League attorney Garfield King later secured pardons for the offenders, but only those with clean FDP employment records received the opportunity to re-enlist.[43]

The approaching provincial election, set for 1 June, 1937, heightened concern as rumours continued to circulate about a general strike set for 17 May. McCannel instructed his foremen to immediately discharge any who challenged their authority, expressing confidence that Pearson would execute his policy of closing the camps in the event of a walkout. No doubt wishing to prevent demonstrations by the unemployed during the last days of the campaign, Pattullo authorized the projects to remain open for an unspecified period. Sensing correctly that the FDP's new lease on life would be brief, the RPWU called for a post-election extension, but on 26 May McCannel instructed his staff to begin laying off the men on 2 June, the day after the election, to make way for YMFTP crews. The Liberals won the election, taking thirty-one of the legislature's forty-eight seats, announcing the closure of the FDP camps a couple of days later. The RPWU, CCF, and trade unions appealed the decision to cut the single unemployed from the relief rolls for the summer, but to no avail.[44]

A total of 2,809 men had taken part in the FDP program from late November until early June, about 1,200 of them transients from other provinces. BC contributed $249,284 of the total $460,539 expenditure, and enrolees accumulated $305,946 in wages. Gross earnings averaged $109, less $41 in board deductions. McCannel described the majority as 'willing workers' who 'returned to their homes ... better fit to secure employment.' Although 75 were discharged and another 50 quit in sympathy, the diverse nature of the work helped avoid the demoralization that plagued the DND camps, he reported, as did the enrolees' 'realization of the constructive value of their own labour.' Roderick Haig-Brown agreed with this assessment after inspecting Elk Falls, where crews had cleared underbrush and fallen snags, installed restrooms, fireplaces, and picnic tables, and cleared a playing field. 'The park is already a brighter, more cheerful place' the author and conservationist remarked, describing discipline as 'firm, but unobtrusive and reasonable.'[45]

While wrapping up the FDP project and expressing hope for a renewal in 1938, McCannel prepared for a less stressful season of YMFTP work. Although Pattullo's pleas for an aggressive federal public works program continued to go unheeded, the King administration did provide $1 million to allow the provinces to follow BC's example in youth training during the summer of 1937. Federal Minister of Labour Norman Rogers informed Pattullo in mid-May that Ottawa would contribute up to $100,000, on a 'dollar-for-dollar basis' toward the cost of provincial schemes for the training of unemployed young people in forestry, placer mining, and a few other fields. The transients would be left to fend for themselves. The province ultimately spent $75,000 on the YMFTP that summer, providing work for 585 of the 1,009 applicants. Manitoba, Ontario, Saskatchewan, and Nova Scotia also took part, and several other provinces provided work relief opportunities that winter.[46]

BC's 1937 YMFTP program followed the established pattern, with the addition of a few extra crews for recreational development at Tweedsmuir Park, Kokanee Park, Silvertip Falls, and Hollyburn Ridge. At the conclusion of the summer Manning called for the YMFTP to be made 'a permanent factor in the development and protection' of the province's forest resources. McCannel and his foremen, no doubt welcoming the respite from workplace strife, discharged only nine men between June and the end of September. The early departure of students bothered Labour Department officials, but Manning cited survey results indicating that 90 per cent of enrolees were anxious to take up some aspect of forest work as a livelihood.[47]

The suggestion that logging jobs were available for the taking misjudged or misrepresented a bleak employment picture. Although trade agreements had provided new access to commonwealth and American markets during the mid-1930s, the 'Roosevelt Recession' of 1937–8 caused exports to slump badly again. Thus, the province succeeded only in inviting a summer of protest when it closed the FDP camps and lopped the single homeless from the relief rolls at the beginning of June. By late August 1937 over a hundred had been arrested on obstruction charges for soliciting funds on Vancouver streets, according to one estimate. Honest prosecutors would have 'charged the boys simply with being poor,' the RPWU's Cumber declared in pressing Pattullo for a genuine program of work and wages.[48]

As summer turned to autumn, rumours of another winter works program drew more transients to Vancouver, where over three hundred 'tin-canners' eventually faced sentencing. An FDP resumption depended entirely upon the conclusion of negotiations with Ottawa, Pearson asserted, but arrests following a mid-October sit-in at the Woodwards Department Store taxed Vancouver's jail capacity. With Vancouver citizens warning of the serious situation developing in the city, and reports circulating that the jail overflow would be held in prison camps, federal officials still preferred to delay an FDP announcement until November to avoid triggering a flood of unemployed west from the prairies.[49]

BC officials, concerned by late October that the pressure from relief applicants in Vancouver had become 'so great as to be embarrassing and possibly dangerous,' pressed for an immediate opening of the camps. Rogers consented on 26 October, announcing an $800,000 shared-cost FDP program for twenty-four camps and an estimated 1,800 enrolees extending to April. The late addition of a Mount Douglas Park project in Victoria brought the number to twenty-five. Ottawa and Victoria also agreed to pardon the jailed 'tin-canners' so that they could be sent to the camps. The RPWU welcomed the announcements but pledged to campaign to have the camps remain open until economic recovery provided jobs for all and to abolish the wage hold-back.[50]

Within a few days nearly seventeen hundred 'single, homeless, destitute' men had registered, lining up in the rain outside provincial employment offices in Vancouver and Victoria. Those unable to prove residence in BC prior to 1 November were invited to return to their province of origin. McCannel and his staff once again hurried to prepare camps for occupation – a task complicated by limited carpentry skills. 'Who in hell picked that bunch for a camp construction crew?' asked the foreman at Williams Lake. 'Not a damned one of them can drive a nail, let alone cut a rafter.' His colleague at the established Cowichan Lake Experiment Station had an easier time of it, reporting that 'the comrades seem to be well pleased with the camp.'[51]

Relations with the men and their union also had to be worked out again. Manning instructed foremen to first warn and then discharge any 'physically able' enrolee found unwilling to 'give a reasonable return on the money paid him.' Lack of skills could not be held against the men, but those judged lazy should be sent packing after a warning. Labour Minister Pearson left the decision on the RPWU's right to hold meetings in recreation tents up to the foremen, but left no doubt about the government's refusal to recognize the union. 'The ordinary employer–employee relationship did not exist in the relief camps,' he asserted. Since no basis for a union existed, the question of recognition was settled.[52]

Pearson's intellectual gymnastics in explaining away the RPWU notwithstanding, the union constituted a daily reality for foremen and supervisors who had to tread carefully to avoid provoking organized protest. Initial reports conveyed an impression of general harmony. Some minor troubles had arisen due to agitation by RPWU members, a Labour Department investigator noted, but most men seemed satisfied and put in a fair day's work. The dismissal of four alleged malingerers at Green Timbers in early December produced some unrest, and the cookhouse fare at Shawnigan Lake prompted about half of the eighty-man crew to demand the cook's immediate dismissal. Nearby at Saht-lam the foreman allowed use of the recreation tent for Sunday morning union meetings, but fired an RPWU organizer for a secret gathering in his tent.[53]

The second winter of FDP operation saw the previously discussed policy of isolating suspected agitators in a single camp implemented. RPWU members pardoned from their 'tin-canning' sentences appear to have qualified automatically for shipment to FDP No. 10, near Powell River on the mainland coast. McCannel routinely arranged transfers there for others labelled troublemakers. Alternatively, foremen might request the retention of strong FDP loyalists to counter the union influence at their camps. While the strategy of concentrating RPWU organizers may have been sound in principle, it triggered the season's first major confrontation at Thetis Lake in mid-December. The attempted transfer of two activists to Powell River prompted a walkout, bringing the provincial police to the scene. Ultimately, fourteen men were discharged, sacrificing their relief eligibility rather than return to work.[54]

With the assistance of the provincial police, which regularly monitored lower-Island projects, government officials sought to stifle any expression of collective discontent. No recognition would be extended to grievance committees, although those organized for recreational purposes were tolerated. Individuals should be free to register 'reasonable' complaints without fear of discrimination, Relief Administrator E.W. Griffith instructed McCannel, but organized demonstrations of resistance called for a decisive response. Unfortunately, it would be impossible to confine benign committees to acceptable functions. The 'social committee' at the Harrison Hot Springs camp complained frequently about meal quality, for example, and the performance of the cook at Englishman River Falls prompted the entire 104-man crew to demand his immediate departure. McCannel, arriving accompanied by a squad of provincial police, blamed the whole episode on RPWU troublemakers and discharged seven alleged ringleaders. Twelve others quit in sympathy, thereby terminating their relief eligibility as well.[55]

Isolated conflicts continued to erupt in the new year, as the Forest Branch prepared to rotate the first contingent out to make room for fresh crews in early February. Pearson blamed these outbreaks on a small number of 'trained agitators' from other provinces who valued the camps as a 'breeding ground of Communistic teachings.' The RPWU countered by calling a 12 February conference in Victoria to discuss wages and conditions, organization issues, and strategies to ensure an FDP extension. Twenty camps sent delegates despite the threat of dismissal, but Pearson offered few concessions when confronted with a long list of resolutions; the government would investigate legitimate grievances but close the camps rather than relinquish control to the men and their union.[56]

A post-conference meeting involving Pearson and a delegation of trade union and RPWU representatives produced two reforms, although the more significant fell short of initial expectations. First, Pearson agreed to readmit the Victoria conference delegates to the camps. Then, discussions between the Labour Department and Forest Branch produced what seemed a more significant policy reversal. Readmittance would be granted to some of the FDP workers who had left of their own accord or quit out of sympathy with discharged activists. The RPWU hailed this apparent easing of the blacklist, but in the end officials ruled against those discharged for malingering and agitation, along with their sympathizers. Of the eighty-one applications for reinstatement, only thirty-one received approval.[57]

Estimates of the RPWU's strength varied after the Victoria conference. The provincial police reported that the union had fifteen camps fully organized, with the remainder rapidly being 'whipped into shape' by the RPWU's John Matts, Eric Cumber, and several new organizers. Three-quarters of the camp enrolees had joined the union, the police asserted. McCannel doubted that membership amounted to 50 per cent in mid-February, but solidarity among camp workers forced the government to back down twice in the coming weeks as the program neared its end. When the entire Harrison Lake crew struck in support of a man discharged for malingering, Labour Department officials had him assigned to light duty rather than risk the departure of a hundred angry project workers to Vancouver. Four Nanaimo Lakes project workers, fired for refusing to work in heavy rain, were reinstated after strikers forced negotiations.[58]

With little to lose as the date for closure of the projects approached, then, workers grew more militant as administrators scrambled to preserve control. But what would happen when the projects came to an end? According to government assertions the four dollars a week in deferred pay would hold the men until mid-May, coinciding with an expected seasonal economic upswing. Fearing a long summer of protest, Vancouver officials no doubt hoped that the senior levels of government would grant the RPWU's demand for an extension. Pearson declined on 7 April, however, explaining that the province had exhausted all funds and prolonging the projects would only bar men from securing private-sector jobs. A total of 4,700 men had been admitted to the camps over the winter, Pearson said, in a 25 June radio broadcast. Some 1,600 had come to BC the previous autumn, and 1,000 had left the camps on their own or been discharged. Thus, only 2,100 participants had over a year's residence in the province, and they could reasonably be expected to provide for themselves over the summer. The CCF blasted both the King and Pattullo administrations for their indifference and buck-passing, but it seemed certain that the end would come quickly.[59]

As foremen prepared to clear the camps of the single unemployed, their end-of-project reports reveal that a good deal of useful work had been accomplished. Progress was apparent in expanded nursery capacity at Green Timbers and improved access to the Cowichan Lake research station. At Elk Falls crews had felled snags, had constructed trails, fireplaces, and picnic tables, and had planted trees. A new bridge above the falls opened up the Sayward Forest Reserve for future planting. Residents of Victoria could now reach the summit of Mount Douglas, where a new seawall enhanced the park. Capilano, Stamp Falls, Little Qualicum Falls, Englishman River Falls, John Dean, and Medicine Bowls near Courtenay all benefited from similar park improvements. New roads created better access to the Greater Vancouver and Nanaimo watersheds.[60]

Commentators and local interests placed special value on accomplishments that promised increased tourist traffic. Journalist Leslie Fox praised the FDP men for making Vancouver Island a better place for residents and future tourists who would 'leave their golden harvest.' The *Comox Argus*'s Ben Hughes expressed similar enthusiasm for the work that had brought 'nature's wizardry' at Medicine Bowls into public view. The new stairway linking Elk Falls to a viewpoint, built by

Saskatchewan farm boy Peter Skaret, was 'a thing of beauty,' the editor declared, and the 60,000 seedlings planted there would provide a model for much-needed provincial reforestation. The efforts of the single unemployed restored faith in the future, Hughes concluded. Writer and conservationist Roderick Haig-Brown travelled the short distance from his Campbell River home to inspect Elk Falls. Placing the changes seen there in a broader provincial history of 'tearing down, despoiling and exploiting nature,' Haig-Brown presented the FDP workers in hopeful terms, as representative of a new commitment to 'putting the land back to production and bringing it to a new and planned beauty.'[61]

With little time for such reflection, the single unemployed and their supporters launched a campaign for an immediate FDP extension. Up to five thousand men gathered in Vancouver, their deferred pay vouchers providing subsistence funds to mid-May, if one believed government press releases. Again the CCF called on King to take responsibility for unemployment, as some three thousand jobless paraded through Vancouver in late April, trying to win public support for a works program. When the RPWU issued an early-May warning that the men would take 'definite action' when their deferred pay ran out, Pearson gave the standard answer: funds were unavailable and jobs awaited in private industry.[62]

Pressure continued to build, however, with a Vancouver Mothers' Council picnic in Stanley Park and a mid-May tag day. The proceeds from that event would sustain 'the boys' for only a couple of days, John Matts told Pattullo, but instead of initiating a new works program Ottawa and Victoria agreed to share the cost of sending the transients who had participated in the 1937–8 FDP back to their province of origin. The RPWU rejected that offer when it failed to include a provision for prairie employment, setting the stage for the 20 May occupation of the Hotel Georgia, Art Gallery, and Post Office. Only seventy-five transients had accepted transportation home. The refusal of the majority to search for work outside Vancouver or accept return to their province of residence had culminated in a 'revolt against constituted authority,' one orchestrated by a small group of radicals, Pearson charged. In the aftermath of the violent 'Bloody Sunday' eviction of 19 June, Pattullo told a CCF delegation that the single unemployed would have to 'do the best they can' until winter offered the possibility of another FDP venture. His reform energies waning, the premier could only urge the jobless to scour the province for work while expressing regret at the way people's expectations of the state had risen since his childhood.[63]

In fact, as Robin Fisher notes, King's steadfast refusal to accept responsibility for unemployment left Pattullo with few options. His mounting frustration showed in an acrimonious meeting with representatives of the single unemployed. Blaming his problems on the interprovincial transients, he ended the discussion with a terse 'no change in policy.' But behind the tough front he maintained toward those who had caused his government such public embarrassment was a conviction that the real fault lay elsewhere. He had, Pattullo confessed to MP Ian Mackenzie, 'felt for some time on the defensive' for Ottawa's treatment of the homeless. Recent layoffs and shutdowns had aggravated unemployment, public sympathy for the men ran high, and the need for a national public works initiative had not passed.[64]

With little hope that King would adopt a 'broad and expansive' program of federal-provincial cooperation for transient relief, Pattullo emphasized the threat to law and order in communicating his immediate needs to the prime minister. His government would take steps to preserve the peace, but only quick federal action would 'prevent the smouldering fire from bursting into conflagration of flames.' Ottawa should stem the tide of incoming transients and offer those already in the province subsistence relief. 'It is not our responsibility to provide for every penniless person who may come here from the rest of Canada,' Pattullo asserted. Public support for government declarations that the jobless 'should get out and rustle' had vanished. King responded in typical piecemeal fashion, agreeing to provide emergency relief to prairie transients until 15 August, pending their acceptance of transportation home to take up harvest employment. Pattullo accepted, making the routine request for a long-term national public works initiative.[65]

BC's forestry programs continued to the outbreak of the Second World War. YMFTP camps operated under joint funding in the amount of $135,000 during the summer of 1938, giving way to another FDP scheme that winter. Rather than invite a repeat of the previous year's protests during the visit of King George V and Queen Elizabeth to Vancouver, additional funding kept the projects open through the summer of 1939. They coincided with the Dominion's most ambitious Depression-era effort to link forest conservation, relief, and youth training: the $1 million National Forestry Program (NFP). Drawing directly upon the example set by BC's YMFTP and the CCC, the NFP briefly combined 'training and employment of young unemployed men with protection of Canadian forest and wildlife conservation.'[66]

All nine provinces participated in the shared-cost program, providing three months of summer employment for almost five thousand youths, BC offering 860 jobs in conducting both NFP and its own Youth Forestry Training camps. The province's effort was 'not surpassed anywhere in Canada,' Dominion Forester D. Roy Cameron remarked after an inspection tour, but the outbreak of war dashed his hopes for a permanent NFP. Enlistments and economic revival eroded support for Canada's first truly national forest policy, the usual constitutional barriers to federal-provincial cooperation legitimating Dominion withdrawal.[67]

War would provide another sort of national emergency, bringing conscientious objectors west to take the place of the relief workers in forest conservation and park development. But the Depression-era programs merit a good deal more attention than they have received. The camp workers made a significant contribution in fire protection, the development of research and nursery facilities, and the foundation for BC's park system. While modern sensibilities might consider our historic devotion to forest fire suppression, artificial regeneration, and landscape modification in pursuit of tourism revenues misguided, enlightened contemporaries such as Roderick Haig-Brown considered it progressive in the context of traditional approaches to resource exploitation.

These projects are also noteworthy for what they reveal about the capacity of the downtrodden and apparently powerless to produce positive social policies. The camps, for all their shortcomings, were better than the alternative of life in Vancouver's jungles. They would not have existed, even seasonally, had not Communist and CCF activists and the unemployed themselves pressed for some measure of relief in the face of federal government intransigence. That every concession, each extra measure of dignity and fair treatment came only through struggle and resistance, merely highlights how high were the obstacles to the making of humane social policy. Sadly, neither Bennett nor King acknowledged the need for national answers to national problems.

In the end, Pattullo and his foresters took what they could squeeze from Ottawa, turned it to advantage in managing provincial forests, and avoided the malaise of the DND experience. The YMFTP even provided, during the summer of 1939, the model for national forest conservation. And while the winter projects for the single homeless were never free of conflict, these were not 'slave camps.' The Vancouver sit-ins of late spring 1938 erupted in response to their closure, after all. That the protest yielded violent repression rather than enlightened policy is

142   Richard A. Rajala

clear evidence that the transients had hit the wall of federal jurisdiction, an obstacle neither they nor Pattullo could move.

NOTES

Abbreviations

BCLW   B.C. Lumber Worker
BCWN   B.C. Workers News
DC   Daily Colonist
DP   Daily Province
PA   People's Advocate
VDT   Victoria Daily Times
VS   Vancouver Sun

1 Jeremy Mouat, *The Business of Power: Hydro-Electricity in Southeastern British Columbia, 1897–1997* (Victoria: Sono Nis, 1997), 142.
2 D.I. Crossley, 'Canadian Forestry and the Canadian Forester,' *Forestry Chronicle* 42 (1906): 335.
3 Monique M. Ross, *Forest Management in Canada* (Calgary: Canadian Institute of Resources Law, 1995), 60–3; Thomas L. Burton, *Natural Resource Policy in Canada: Issues and Perspectives* (Toronto: McClelland and Stewart, 1974), 97–100; Kenneth Johnstone, *Timber and Trauma: 75 Years with the Federal Forestry Service, 1899–1974* (Ottawa: Minister of Supply and Services, 1991), 48–9, 106–11; Richard A. Rajala, 'The Vernon Laboratory and Federal Entomology in British Columbia,' *Journal of the Entomological Society of British Columbia* 98 (December 2001): 177–88; Richard A. Rajala, *Feds, Forests and Fire: A Century of Canadian Forestry Innovation* (Ottawa: Canada Science and Technology Museum, 2005), 101–2; D.I. Crossley, 'Canadian Forestry and the Canadian Forester,' *Forestry Chronicle* 42 (December 1966): 335. For an overview of the federal role in BC forests, see Richard A. Rajala, 'A Political Football: The History of Federal-Provincial Cooperation in British Columbia Forests,' *Forest History Today* (Spring/Fall 2003): 29–40.
4 Donald E. Blake, 'Managing the Periphery: British Columbia and the National Political Community,' in *A History of British Columbia: Selected Readings*, ed. Patricia E. Roy (Toronto: Copp Clark Pittman, 1989), 174–90; Robin Fisher, 'The Decline of Reform: British Columbia Politics in the 1930s,' *Journal of Canadian Studies* 25 (Fall 1990): 81; George M. Abbott, 'Pattullo, the Press, and the Dominion-Provincial Conference of 1991,' *BC Studies* 111 (Autumn 1996): 37–59.

5   Kenneth Norrie and Douglas Owram, *A History of the Canadian Economy* (Toronto: Harcourt, Brace, Jovanovich, 1991), 411–506; J.F. Conway, *The West: The History of a Region in Confederation* (Toronto: Lorimer, 1994), 98–104; C.J. Taylor, *The Heritage of the British Columbia Forest Industry: A Guide for Planning, Selection and Interpretation of Sites* (Ottawa: Environment Canada, 1987), 181–3; David Avery, *Dangerous Foreigners: European Immigrant Workers and Labour Radicalism in Canada, 1896–1932* (Toronto: McClelland and Stewart, 1979), 16–38.

6   Patricia E. Roy, *Vancouver: An Illustrated History* (Toronto: Lorimer, 1980), 95–9; John D. Belshaw, 'The Administration of Relief to the Unemployed in Vancouver during the Great Depression' (MA thesis, Simon Fraser University, 1992), 40, 91–2; Marion Elizabeth Lane, 'Unemployment during the Depression: The Problem of the Single Unemployed Transient in British Columbia, 1930–1938' (undergraduate essay, University of British Columbia, 1968), 11; James Struthers, 'Canadian Unemployment Policy in the 1930s,' in *Readings in Canadian History: Post-Confederation*, ed. R. Douglas Francis and Donald B. Smith (Toronto: Harcourt Brace, 1994), 380; John Herd Thompson and Allen Seager, *Canada, 1922–1939: Decades of Discord* (Toronto: McClelland and Stewart, 1986), 193–7; Lorne Brown, 'Unemployed Struggles in Saskatchewan and Canada, 1930–1935,' *Prairie Forum* 31 (Fall 2006): 193–216.

7   Margaret Ormsby, *British Columbia: A History* (Toronto: MacMillan, 1958), 445–6; Bill Waiser, *Park Prisoners: The Untold Story of Western Canada's National Parks* (Saskatoon: Fifth House, 1995), 52–84; James Struthers, *No Fault of Their Own: Unemployment and the Canadian Welfare State, 1914–1941* (Toronto: University of Toronto Press, 1983), 79–82; Norman Penner, *Canadian Communism: The Stalin Years and Beyond* (Toronto: Methuen, 1988), 109; Ivan Avakumovic, *The Communist Party in Canada: A History* (Toronto: McClelland and Stewart, 1975); John Manley, '"Starve, Be Damned!": Communists and Canada's Urban Unemployed, 1929–39,' *Canadian Historical Review* 79 (September 1998): 466–91; Thompson and Seager, *Decades of Discord*, 226–35; Ian D. Parker, 'Simon Fraser Tolmie: The Last Conservative Premier of British Columbia,' *BC Studies* 11 (Fall 1971): 21–36.

8   Laurel Sefton MacDowell, 'Relief Camp Workers in Ontario during the Great Depression of the 1930s,' *Canadian Historical Review* 76, no. 2 (1995): 209.

9   See Lorne A. Brown, 'Unemployment Relief Camps in Saskatchewan, 1933–1936,' in *Canadian Working Class History: Selected Readings*, eds. Laurel Sefton MacDowell and Ian Radforth (Toronto: Canadian Scholars Press, 1992): 523–46; Laurel Sefton MacDowell, 'Relief Camp Workers in Ontario

during the Great Depression of the 1930s,' *Canadian Historical Review* 76 (June 1995): 205–28; Laurel Sefton MacDowell, 'Survey of Federal Relief Activities since 1930,' *Labour Gazette* 35 (May 1935): 487–88.

10 'The National Attack on Unemployment,' *Labour Gazette* 37 (January 1937): 26; Avakumovic, *The Communist Party*, 73; Penner, *Canadian Communism*, 110; Lane, 'Unemployment during the Depression,' 85–92; Irene Howard, *The Struggle for Social Justice in British Columbia: Helena Gutteridge, the Unknown Reformer* (Vancouver: UBC Press, 1992), 170–1; Ronald Liversedge, *Recollections of the On-to-Ottawa Trek*, ed. Victor Hoar (Toronto: McClelland and Stewart, 1973); Ronald Liversedge, *The 60th Anniversary of the On-to-Ottawa Trek* (Regina: Saskatchewan Federation of Labour, 1995); Ronald Liversedge, 'Camp Boys on to Ottawa,' *B.C. Workers News* (hereafter *BCWN*), 31 May 1935, 1; Ronald Liversedge, 'Fight against Slave Camps Continues,' *BCWN*, 12 July 1935, 1.

11 Margaret A. Ormsby, 'T. Dufferin Pattullo and the Little New Deal,' *Canadian Historical Review* 43 (December 1962): 277–97; Gerald W. Williams, 'The Civilian Conservation Corps (CCC) Contribution to Forests in the Pacific Northwest,' in *History of Sustained-Yield Forestry: A Symposium*, ed. Harold K. Steen, 48–57 (Durham: Forest History Society, 1984). For discussion of Depression-era forestry concerns in the province, see Richard A. Rajala, *Clearcutting the Pacific Rain Forest: Production, Science and Regulation* (Vancouver: UBC Press, 1998).

12 'Selective Logging and Work Given to Youths Suggested,' *Daily Colonist* (hereafter *DC*), 19 February 1935, 2; 'Forest Cadets,' *Comox Argus*, 21 February 1935, 2; 'Another Slave Camp Scheme Is Proposed,' *BCWN*, 1 March 1935, 3; P.Z. Caverhill, 'Memorandum to the Minister of Labour Re: Employment of Unemployed Older Boys on Forest Projects,' 3 April 1935, GR1441, file 0120053, reel B3976, BC Department of Lands Records, BC Archives (hereafter BCA).

13 'Forest Plan Stirs Hopes,' *Victoria Daily Times* (hereafter *VDT*), 18 May 1935, 1; 'The Young Men's Employment Branch of the B.C. Forest Branch,' *British Columbia Lumberman* 19 (November 1935): 50; P.Z. Caverhill, Memorandum to the Relief Administrator, 7 May 1935; E.W. Griffith, Memorandum for the Chief Accountant, Public Works, 20 May 1935, GR1441, file 0120053, reel B3976, BCA.

14 Harry Forse, 'The Young Men's Forestry Training Plan,' *B.C. Forest History Newsletter* 23 (April 1990): 1–2; *Forest Branch Newsletter* 1 (27 May 1935): 2; P.Z. Caverhill, Memorandum to the Relief Administrator, 7 May 1935, GR1441, file 0120053, reel B3976, BCA.

15 'Forest and Mine Jobs for Youths; Work for Married,' *VDT*, 10 May 1935;

E.W. Griffith to Government Agents, Employment Superintendents, etc., 15 May 1935; Applications for Employment, Young Men's Forestry Training Plan; E.W. Griffith to K.C. McCannel, 21 May 1935, GR1441, file 0120053, reel B3976, BCA.

16 C.D. Schultz to K.C. McCannel, 19 June 1935; C.L. Anderson to McCannel, 3 July 1935, GR1441, file 0120053, reel B3976, BCA; *Forest Branch Newsletter* 2 (12 July 1935): 2; *Forest Branch Newsletter* 3 (10 Aug. 1935): 2.

17 K.C. McCannel to the Minister of Labour, 20 August 1935; E.C. Manning to District Forester, Vancouver, 17 August 1935, GR1441, file 0120053, reel B3976, BCA.

18 E.C. Manning to E.W. Griffith, 16 September 1935; K.C. McCannel to A. Gordon, 21 August 1935; McCannel to the Minister of Lands, 20 August 1935, GR1441, file 0120053, reel B3976, BCA; 'Work in Forests,' *BCWN*, 30 August 1935, 2.

19 'Forest Training for Youth,' *VDT*, 13 September 1935, 4; 'B.C. Forest Work Lauded,' *Vancouver Sun* (hereafter *VS*), 26 October 1935, 28; 'Praises Plan,' *DC*, 18 October 1935, 6; E.C. Manning, Memorandum to the Minister of Lands, 31 October 1935, box 10, GR1222, BCA; BC, *Report of the Forest Branch for the Year Ending Dec. 31, 1935* (Victoria: King's Printer, 1936), 29–30.

20 F.D. Mulholland, 'Proposed Employment of Relief Labour in the Provincial Forests,' 2 December 1935; E.C. Manning Memorandum to E.W. Griffith, 3 December 1935, GR1441, file 0120053, reel B3976, BCA.

21 Struthers, *No Fault of Their Own*, 145–7; Stephen Ryback, 'A Hasty Patching Up: An Examination of Unemployment and Relief Programs as They Affected Canada's Transient and Single Homeless' (MA thesis, Concordia University, 1976), 47–50; 'Closure of Relief Camps and Measures for Re-employment,' *Labour Gazette* 36 (March 1936): 219.

22 T.D. Pattullo to W.L.M. King, 4 February 1936, box 75, MSS 3, T.D. Pattullo Papers, BCA; Robin Fisher, *Duff Pattullo of British Columbia* (Toronto: University of Toronto Press, 1991), 286–7; King to Pattullo, 24 February 1936, box 75, MSS 3, BCA; E.W. Griffith, Memorandum for E.C. Manning, 24 April 1936; K.C. McCannel to District Foresters, 19 May 1936, GR1441, file 0120053, reel B.3976, BCA; 'Forestry Training Plan for Young Men To Continue This Year,' *Province*, 8 April 1936, 4; 'Government Issues Call To Volunteer Forestry Training,' *DC*, 22 May 1936, 5; 'Many Eager for Training,' *DC*, 11 June 1936, 11.

23 'Bad Roads near Campbell River,' *Comox Argus*, 18 June 1936, 1; K.C. McCannel to District Forester, Vancouver, 29 June 1936; R.W. Yates to A. Wells Gray, March 1936; E.C. Manning to Yates, 17 March 1936, GR1441, file 0120053, reel B3976, BCA. For discussion of tourism in BC during the

period, see Michael Dawson, 'Taking the "D" Out of Depression": The Promise of Tourism in British Columbia, 1935–1939,' *BC Studies* 132 (Winter 2001/2002): 31–56.

24 D. Roy Cameron to E.C. Manning, 8 September 1936, GR1441, file 0120053, reel B3976, BCA.

25 E.C. Manning to D. Roy Cameron, 12 September 1936, GR1441, file 0120053, reel B3976, BCA.

26 John B. Tompkins, 'B.C. Forest School Attracts Thousands of Youth,' *DC*, 23 August 1936, 7, magazine section; 'Forestry Training Opens New Life for Youths,' *VDT*, 7 November 1936, 1, magazine section; 'Forestry Workers at Elk Falls,' *Comox Argus*, 24 September 1936, 6; H.J. Watters to District Forester, Vancouver, 3 October 1936, GR1441, file 0120053, reel B3976, BCA.

27 'The Proceedings of the 1936 Forestry Committee,' *British Columbia Lumberman* 20 (December 1936): 16; 'Wider Forest Work Urged,' *VDT*, 19 November 1936, 10.

28 'Starving Youth Get Callous Treatment,' *BCWN*, 25 September 1936, 1; 'Twenty-Six Single Unemployed Arrested for Selling Flowers,' *BCWN*, 7 October 1936, 5; Struthers, *No Fault of Their Own*, 159–60; N. Rogers to G.S. Pearson, 10 September 1936, box 136, GR1222, BCA.

29 G.S. Pearson to Chairman, National Employment Commission, 8 October 1936, box 136, GR1222, BCA.

30 G.S. Pearson to T.D. Pattullo, 29 October 1936, box 97; J.G. Gardiner to Pearson, 29 October 1936; Pearson to Gardiner, 30 October 1936, 'Memorandum of Agreement,' 16 November 1936; G.S. Pearson, 'File Note,' 17 November 1936, box 136, GR1222, BCA; 'Work for 6,000 Men,' *VS*, 19 November 1936, 1.

31 'Plan Many Duties for Workless Men,' *Daily Province* (hereafter *DP*), 1 December 1936, 1.

32 'Relief for Single Men,' *VS*, 19 November 1936, 6; 'Forestry Camps, Should We Commend or Condemn?' *Federationist*, 23 December 1976, 10; 'Jobless Accept Forestry Work,' *BCWN*, 4 December 1936, 1.

33 'Few Apply Here for Forest Jobs,' *VDT*, 9 December 1936, 15; E.W. Griffith to A.S. Thompson, 25 November 1936, GR1441, file 0126835, reel B4017, BCA; 'Join Army Pattullo Advises Single Jobless,' *Federationist*, 23 December 1936, 2.

34 'Relief and Forest Camps Tied in New Provincial Policy,' *DC*, 2 December 1936, 3; 'Tents and Buildings Required for a Fifty-Man Camp,' K.C. McCannel, 'Forest Development Projects, 1936–7, Instructions for Project Foremen,' GR1441, file 0126835, reel B4017, BCA.

35 'Finds Progress in B.C. Camps,' *VDT*, 29 December 1936, 13; K.C. McCannel to J. Pedley, 17 December 1936, GR1441, file 0126835, reel B4017, BCA.

36 J.T. Gawthrop to E.W. Griffith, 5 January 1937, GR1441, file 0126835, reel B4017, BCA.
37 J. Pedley to K.C. McCannel, 5 January 1937, GR1441, file 0120835, reel B4017, BCA.
38 A.A. Staub to T.D. Pattullo, 9 January 1937; R.J. Porter to Pattullo, 10 January 1937, box 145, GR1222, BCA; 'All Forest Camps Open,' *VDT*, 11 January 1937, 5.
39 'Jobless Leave Surrey Forest Camp,' *British Columbian*, 22 January 1937, 1; 'Blame Agitators for Camp Strike,' *News-Herald*, 22 January 1937, 1; 'Four Island Camp Men Dismissed,' *VS*, 23 January 1937, 1.
40 'Pearson Threatens To Close Camps,' *BCWN*, 22 January 1937, 1; 'Men out of B.C. Camps,' *VDT*, 22 January 1937, 1; E. Cumber to T.D. Pattullo, 22 January 1937, box 145, GR1222, BCA; 'Camp Policy Is Unaltered,' *VDT*, 22 January 1937, 11.
41 'The Forestry Camps,' *DP*, 22 January 1937, 4; 'Objected To Work,' *DC*, 4 February 1937, 6; 'Camp Walkout at Errington,' *VDT*, 16 February 1937, 5.
42 'Camp Men Secure Jobs,' *VDT*, 26 February 1937, 15; 'Week's Work: Seven Cents,' *BCWN*, 5 March 1937, 1; Relief Project Workers Union to T.D. Pattullo, 21 April 1937, box 146, GR1222, BCA; E.W. Griffith, Memorandum to the Chief Forester, 23 April 1937, GR1441, file 012835, reel B4017, BCA.
43 'Month for Panhandlers,' *VS*, 4 May 1937, 1; 'B.C. Officials Hushed Facts as 50 Boys Jailed – G. King,' *Federationist*, 6 May 1937, 8; 'Destitute Men Are Freed from Oakalla on Order from Ottawa,' *B.C. Lumber Worker* (hereafter *BCLW*), 12 May 1937, 1.
44 K.C. McCannel, Circular No. 15 to Superintendents and Foremen, 26 May 1937, GR1441, file 0126835, reel B4017, BCA; Fisher, *Duff Pattullo*, 297; Relief Project Workers' Union to T.D. Pattullo, 7 June 1937; Local 204, Pile Drivers, Dock and Wharf Builders Union to Pattullo, 21 June 1937, box 145, GR1222, BCA; 'Jobless Face Starvation,' *People's Advocate* (hereafter *PA*), 11 June 1937, 1; 'B.C. Project Men Stranded Here,' *Federationist*, 17 June 1937, 1.
45 K.C. McCannel, 'Forest Development Project, Annual Report, 1937'; 'Forest Development Projects, 1 Nov. 1936 to June 1937, Average Earnings of Men Regularly Enrolled,' GR1441, file 0126835, reel B4017, BCA; R.L. Haig-Brown, 'B.C. Youth Develop Beauty around Elk Falls,' *DP*, 24 April 1937, 5, magazine section.
46 Fisher, *Duff Pattullo*, 302; 'Establishment of Unemployed Youth,' *Labour Gazette* 37 (April 1937): 414–15; N. Rogers to T.D. Pattullo, 15 May 1937; G.S. Pearson to Pattullo, 9 Aug. 1937, box 145, GR1222, BCA; 'Youth Plans Negotiated,' *VDT*, 8 June 1937, 11; 'YMFTP Projects – 1937,' GR 1441, file 0120053, reel B3977, BCA; Struthers, 'Canadian Unemployment Policy,' 386–7.

47 BC, *Report of the Forest Branch of the Department of Lands for the Year Ended Dec. 31, 1937* (Victoria: King's Printer, 1938), 8–9; BC, *Annual Report of the Department of Labour for the Year Ended Dec. 31, 1937* (Victoria: King's Printer, 1938), 92.

48 Norrie and Owram, *A History of the Canadian Economy*, 506; 'Jobless Rap Government Policy,' *People's Advocate*, 27 August 1937, 2; 'Relief Head Raps Government's Unemployment Policy,' *Federationist*, 23 September 1937, 1.

49 'Single Unemployed Denied by Pearson,' *Federationist*, 7 October 1937, 1; 'Hungry Youths Taxing Capacity of City Jail,' *BCLW*, 20 October 1937, 1; J. Hart to G.S. Pearson, 21 October 1937; Pearson to Hart, box 145, GR1222, BCA.

50 E.W. Griffith to T.D. Pattullo, 25 October 1937; N. Rogers to Pattullo, 26 October 1937, box 145, GR1222, BCA; 'Men Joining Forest Camps,' *VDT*, 27 October 1937, 1; 'Ottawa Frees Jailed Youths,' *BCLW*, 3 November 1937, 7; 'Single Jobless Win Aid from Government,' *Federationist*, 28 October 1937, 1.

51 'Forestry Camps' Men Total 1,658,' *VDT*, 6 November 1937, 3; E.W. Griffith to W.G. Stone, 13 November 1937, GR1441, file 0126835, reel B4017, BCA; Foreman, FDP #22, Williams Lake, to K.C. McCannel, 23 November 1937, GR1441, file 0126839, reel B4020, BCA; D. Calder to F.S. McKinnon, 1 November 1937, GR1441, file 083211, reel B3728, BCA.

52 E.C. Manning, 'Forest Development Projects, 1937–1938'; G.S. Pearson to R. Smeal, 29 November 1937, GR1441, file 0126835, reel B4017, BCA.

53 F.G. Hassard, Memorandum for G.S. Pearson, 20 December 1937, GR1441, file 0126839, reel B4029, BCA; F.G. Hassard, 'Report: Camp 5, Shawnigan Lake,' 10 December 1937; F.G. Hassard, 'Report: Camp 17, Sahtlam Road,' 15 December 1937, GR1441, file 0126835, reel B4017, BCA.

54 K.C. McCannel to F.V. Webber, 21 December 1937; A. Gordon to Webber, 21 December 1937; J.T. Gawthrop to McCannel, 18 January 1938; H. Ferguson to McCannel, 7 February 1938, GR1441, file 0126840, reel B4021, BCA; W.C. Murray, 'Labour Conditions – Thetis Lake, B.C.,' 16 December 1937, GR1441, file 0126839, reel B4020, BCA.

55 E.W. Griffith to K.C. McCannel, 20 December 1937; McCannel to Griffith, 24 December 1937, GR1441, file 0126835, reel B4017, BCA; F.G. Hassard, Memorandum for G.S. Pearson, 20 December 1937; K.C. McCannel, Memorandum to the Minister of Labour, 7 December 1937, GR1441, file 0126839, reel B4020, BCA.

56 'To Close Camps if Men Not Satisfied,' *VDT*, 2 February 1937, 1; 'Relief Project Workers Union: Conference Call,' GR1441, file 0126839, reel B4020, BCA; 'Camp Men to Meet Here,' *VDT*, 11 February 1938, 15; 'Not Continu-

ing Forest Camps,' *VDT*, 14 February 1938, 1; 'Pearson Promises Grievance Redress,' *PA*, 18 February 1938, 5.

57 'Project Union Secures New Concessions,' *Federationist*, 17 February 1938, 1; J.T. Gawthrop to W.R. Bone, 24 February 1938, GR1441, file 0126835, reel B4017, BCA; R. Fogle to J.T. Gawthrop, 12 March 1938, GR1441, file 0126840, reel B4012, BCA.

58 J. Mullin to K.C. McCannel, 16 February 1938; Mullin to McCannel, 17 February 1938; McCannel to E.W. Griffith, 18 February 1938; J. Russell, 'Report re. Forest Camp Project #25,' 18 March 1938, GR1441, file 0126839, reel B4020, BCA; Griffith to McCannel, 3 March 1938, GR1441, file 0126835, reel B4017, BCA.

59 'Winter Camps Closing Down,' *VDT*, 29 March 1938, 1; 'Closing Camps To Bring Relief Crisis Here,' *Federationist*, 31 March 1938, 1; 'Reopening of Camps Asked,' *PA*, 8 April 1938, 1; G.S. Pearson, 'Radio Speech, CFCT: Transient Single Unemployed Situation,' 25 June 1938, box 146, GR1222, BCA; 'Camps Will Not Be Permanent,' *VDT*, 8 April 1938, 1.

60 'Brief Resume of Work Undertaken by Forest Development Projects, Nov. 1, 1937 to Mar. 31, 1938,' GR1441, file 0126839, reel B4020, BCA.

61 Leslie Fox, 'Opening Up Island Playgrounds,' *VDT*, 30 Apr. 1938, 1, magazine section; 'Medicine Bowls Camp Closed,' *Comox Argus*, 31 March 1938, 1; 'Something To Be Proud Of,' *Comox Argus*, 31 March 1938, 2; R.L. Haig-Brown, 'A Forestry Project,' *DC*, 19 June 1938, 5, magazine section.

62 'The Single Unemployed,' *Federationist*, 28 April 1938, 1; 'Jobless Demonstrate for Works Scheme,' *PA*, 29 April 1938, 1; 'Declare Men Seek Action,' *VDT*, 5 May 1938, 1.

63 N. Rogers to G.S. Pearson, 14 May 1938, box 145, GR1222, BCA; 'Jobless Refuse To Be Shipped East,' *Federationist*, 19 May 1938, 1; 'Words Can't Satisfy Hunger,' *PA*, 20 May 1938; Pearson, 'Radio Speech'; 'Proceedings at Conference between the Honourable T.D. Pattullo, Premier of British Columbia, and a Delegation from the Cooperative Commonwealth Federation,' 20 June 1938, box 146, GR1222, BCA. For accounts of 'Bloody Sunday,' see Pierre Berton, *The Great Depression, 1929–39* (Toronto: Anchor Canada, 2001), 447–57; Sean Griffin, ed., *Fighting Heritage: Highlights of the 1930s Struggle for Jobs and Militant Unionism in British Columbia* (Vancouver: Tribune, n.d.), 85–110.

64 Fisher, *Duff Pattullo*, 306–8; 'Proceedings at Conference between the Honourable T.D. Pattullo, Premier of British Columbia, and a Delegation from the Single Unemployed,' 20 June 1938, box 147, GR1222, BCA; T.D. Pattullo to I. Mackenzie, 22 June 1938, box 75, ADD MSS 3, BCA.

65 T.D. Pattullo to W.L. Mackenzie King, 23 June 1938, box 73; Pattullo to

King, 24 June 1938, box 70; Pattullo to King, 25 June 1938, box 70; Pattullo to King, 6 July 1938, box 70; King to Pattullo, 6 July 1938, box 70; Pattullo to King, 11 July 1938, box 70; Pattullo to King, 12 July 1938, box 73, ADD MSS 3, BCA.

66 E.C. Manning, Memorandum to District Foresters, 16 May 1939, GR1441, file 0126841, reel B7971, BCA; D. Roy Cameron, 'National Forestry Program,' *Forestry Chronicle* 16 (January 1940): 54; 'Youth Training and National Forestry Programs,' *Labour Gazette* 39 (May 1939): 456–7; Rajala, *Feds, Forests, and Fire*, 60–2.

67 Harry B. Forse, 'British Columbia,' *Forest and Outdoors* 36 (January 1940): 12–13; D. Roy Cameron, 'Inspection Report, British Columbia,' GR1441, file 0120053, reel B3977, BCA; Rajala, 'A Political Football,' 32–3.

6 Canada and the Implementation of International Instruments of Human Rights: A Federalist Conundrum, 1919–1982

MICHAEL BEHIELS

'As in the case of labour conventions, so in the case of human rights, any broad Canadian participation in and adherence to international instruments depends on federal acquisition, by constitutional amendment or constitutional decision, of an independent treaty-implementing power.'[1]

Introduction

Canadian governments and Parliament have confronted a fundamental federalist conundrum since 1919 when Prime Minister Borden signed the Treaty of Versailles along with the treaties creating the two institutions that flowed from it, the League of Nations and the International Labour Organization (ILO). As Canada achieved control over its foreign policy, Cabinet's treaty-making powers were questioned and eventually challenged. Provincial rights advocates contended that Parliament's treaty-implementing powers were constrained by the distribution of powers delineated in sections 91 and 92 of the British North America Act, 1867.

Following the First World War, an ongoing series of political crises proved increasingly embarrassing for Canada in the eyes of the international community. These involved the implementation of ILO covenants, and Canada's ambivalent approach to the negotiations over the creation of the United Nations Charter in 1945, the Universal Declarations of Human Rights in 1948, and the International Covenants on Civil and Political Rights and Economic, Social and Cultural Rights, 1948–1966. These crises accumulated because the federal Cabinet had plenipotentiary treaty-making powers while both Parliament and the provincial legislatures held treaty-implementing powers. Constitutional convention dictated that Cabinet and Parliament – working together to ratify and implement treaties and multilateral international agreements – could not bind provincial governments and legislatures in areas of provincial jurisdiction. Throughout this debacle, several constitutional scholars and political scientists proposed solutions to resolve the conundrum. Provincial governments, backed by constitutional convention, rejected all the overtures.

The crisis was accentuated in 1960 with the advent of Quebec's 'Quiet Revolution' of state-building. Ottawa was confronted with successive Quebec governments' incessant demands for treaty-making powers in their areas of jurisdiction. Ottawa politicians and mandarins were determined to prevent provincial cabinets from obtaining, de facto or de jure, treaty-making powers in areas of provincial jurisdiction, especially in crucial matters pertaining to individual rights and freedoms as well as the rights of Canada's official language minority communities.

Prime Minister Pierre Elliott Trudeau's government took the initiative of thwarting the international constitutional ambitions of the provincial governments led by Quebec, Alberta, and Ontario. Trudeau pushed for a Canadian Charter of Rights and Freedoms, based in large measure on international human rights instruments that Canada helped formulate after 1945. A constitutionally entrenched Canadian Charter of Rights and Freedoms, protecting citizens from discrimination by the state, would be binding on the executives, Parliament and the provincial legislatures, and the courts. Trudeau believed that an entrenched Charter of Rights and Freedoms would engender, in the words of an eminent human rights advocate and colleague, Maxwell Cohen, a greater sense of community among all Canadians.[2] Such a development, Trudeau hoped, would assist Canada in resolving the longstanding conflict between Ottawa's executive treaty-making powers, and Parliament's and the provincial legislatures' treaty-implementing powers in the crucial field of fundamental rights and freedoms for individuals and minority groups. The Charter, by recognizing and strengthening Canada's human rights movement, would make it more difficult for premiers to veto the implementation of international instruments of human rights. Conversely, the Charter would enhance Canada's role in the international arena of human rights.

Canada's human rights scholars and lawyers making use of an entrenched Charter would have recourse to legal scholarship, international human rights instruments, and the full array of international and nation-state juridical decisions to influence the interpretation as well as the implementation of the Canadian Charter of Rights and Freedoms by the executives and their bureaucracies, the legislators, and the Canadian judiciary. Indeed, this is what transpired following the proclamation of the Constitution Act, 1982, with its Canadian Charter of Rights and Freedoms.[3] Finally, the federalist conundrum became more amenable to resolution, thereby fostering a mutually reinforcing interplay between the Canadian Charter and Canada's international human rights commitments.[4]

The International Origins of Human Rights and Canada's Federalist Conundrum

A decade before an embryonic Canadian human rights movement emerged during the Great Depression,[5] Canada became a permanent member the League of Nations and the International Labour Organization. The League was created, in part, to advance universal human rights and world peace, while the ILO's mandate focused on developing international standards on working conditions for industrial working men and women.[6] Like other federal states, Canada became embroiled in a heated controversy over the issue of ratification and implementation of ILO conventions. Given their experience with what can be termed 'imperial' federalism, the British proposed a formula whereby ratification of conventions, if they contained provisions within the legislative jurisdictions of the sub-states, required separate ratification and implementation by each of the sub-states. Once these were achieved, the convention would be deemed ratified by the central government of that federal state. This formula was rejected because it undermined the sovereignty of the nation-state in international affairs. Instead, following the United States' proposal, article 19 of the League's constitution called for federal state ratification of conventions with a subsequent obligation to obtain legislative implementation by the sub-states if the matters involved in the convention pertained to their jurisdiction.

Prime Minister Robert Borden's initial response was to resort to Cabinet's authority. Bolstered by the BNA Act's section 132 dealing with Canada's ratification and implementation of British imperial treaties, and section 91(1), the 'Peace, Order and Good Government' clause, he argued that the executive made treaties while Parliament implemented treaties, even if these involved areas of provincial jurisdiction. When it came time to implement the ILO covenants and recommendations, the Borden and Arthur Meighen governments adopted a more 'federal' approach by referring them to the provincial governments when they contained provisions falling within provincial jurisdiction. In December 1925, the cautious Mackenzie King Liberal government referred the thorny question of Ottawa's treaty-implementing powers to the Supreme Court of Canada for a ruling. In its 1925 *Legislative Jurisdiction over Hours of Labour* case, the Supreme Court ruled that if ILO conventions involved matters of provincial jurisdiction, they had to be referred to provincial legislative assemblies for deliberation and appropriate enabling legislation. Consequently, the Canadian government ratified only four of forty-four ILO conventions prior to 1935 – the four dealing with federal jurisdiction in the maritime field.

For a brief period in the mid-1930s, it appeared that this jurisdictional conundrum might be overcome. Early in 1935 a beleaguered Prime Minister Bennett – encouraged by favourable rulings by the Judicial Committee of the Privy Council (JCPC) in the 1932 *Aeronautics*[7] and *Radio*[8] cases and pressured by the growing economic, social, and political crises – attempted to enforce three ILO conventions by passing federal legislation pertaining to weekly rest for workers, minimum wages, and limitation of hours of work.[9] A watertight-compartments classical federalist, Liberal Prime Minister Mackenzie King, who replaced Bennett after the 1935 election, considered the laws unconstitutional and referred them to the Supreme Court. Stacked with strong provincialist justices, the extensive hearings culminated in a three-three tie that set off a firestorm of criticism from progressive-minded academics, politicians, and journalists.[10] The outcry was a prelude to an even greater denunciation of Canada's outmoded 'imperialistic' judicial system.[11] Upon appeal, the JCPC, under the leadership of an outspoken imperialist and provincialist, Lord Atkin, ruled in the highly contentious 1937 *Labour Conventions* case that the Parliament of Canada could not use its treaty-making powers to expand its treaty-implementing powers in areas of provincial jurisdiction. How was the dilemma to be resolved? The JCPC opined that Parliament and the provincial legislative assemblies, working in concert, must use the 'totality of legislative powers' to achieve comprehensive implementation of treaties negotiated and signed by Ottawa when such treaties concerned matters of provincial jurisdiction.[12]

The *Labour Conventions* case set in motion a powerful Canadian nationalist movement of politicians, citizens groups, and academic legal realists that campaigned to abolish all appeals to the JCPC. It took over a decade for the movement to achieve its goal in 1949.[13] The abolition of appeals to the JCPC did not resolve the conflict over Ottawa's right to make and implement international human rights instruments. But abolition ensured that the conundrum would be resolved in Canada and not the United Kingdom.

One of the most outspoken academics, Frank Scott, a McGill constitutional law professor and social democrat, denounced the JCPC's emasculation of the Canadian state. He was convinced that the abolition of appeals would enable Parliament, with the backing of Canada's Supreme Court, to ratify and implement all ILO conventions dealing with areas of federal jurisdiction. Beginning with the supposition that Parliament had the power to amend the Constitution and using the concept of 'public rights of Canadian citizens,' Scott argued that Ottawa's constitutional powers over the implementation of civil liberties extended well beyond section 91. Scott argued that Ottawa, proceeding judiciously, could use the concept of 'public rights of Canadian citizens' to expand its treaty-implementing powers into areas that were heretofore considered exclusively a provincial jurisdiction under the property and civil rights clause.[14]

Other academics, H.F. Angus and James Eayrs, were concerned that Scott's overly robust and centralist interpretation of Ottawa's treaty-making and Parliament's treaty-implementing powers would transform the Canadian federation into a unitary state or embroil Canada in a prolonged constitutional crisis that would cripple its ability to negotiate, ratify, and implement crucial international conventions and agreements. Angus, very cognizant of a rapidly changing world, insisted that Canada must be able to play an effective role in advancing the cause of global security, social and economic development, and human rights. These crucial areas, he maintained, should be designated 'a special class of treaty,' one that required rapid implementation by all member states of the United Nations, including problematic federal states. Angus argued that Ottawa and the provinces, to avoid further embarrassment and delay, had to amend the obsolete section 132 of the BNA Act, 1867, in a way that empowered the Canadian government to 'enact legislation designed to implement Canadian treaties' while requiring it 'to secure ratification of these treaties by some process designed to protect the provinces.'[15]

Eayrs decried the Canadian government's naive and hypocritical approach to the negotiations surrounding the creation of the United Nations. Prime Minister Mackenzie King trumpeted the creation of the

United Nations as long as its high-minded Charter did not impose any obligations, international or domestic, that Canada, because of its federal constitution, would not be able to fulfil. Canada wanted the mandate of the Economic and Social Council to be limited to studies, reports, and recommendations. Canada's representatives, backed by their U.S. colleagues, objected unsuccessfully to the use of the term 'full employment' in article 55 dealing with equality rights and self-determination of peoples, but they did managed to ensure that implementation of Article 56 did not impose any binding obligations, especially in areas of provincial jurisdiction.[16] Given its inability to act in matters of security due to the Cold War, the work of the United Nations' Economic and Social Council and its numerous commissions was paramount. Canada, because of its dysfunctional federal constitution, Eayrs argued, could not in good faith sign on to any more multilateral international conventions because it lacked the authority to implement them. Ottawa's approach – a 'messenger-boy' between the United Nations and the provinces – was interpreted by those in the know as 'a deliberate attempt to shirk international responsibilities by taking refuge in a constitutional *impasse*.'[17] Eayrs hoped that Ottawa's hypocritical approach – advocating human rights principles while objecting to their specifics and implementation – would fuel international pressures on Canada to amend its anachronistic Constitution, despite the 'haughty priests of the provincial rights cult.'[18]

Allan Gotlieb characterized the 1940s and 1950s as an era of hesitancy and retrenchment. Rebuffed and humiliated by the JCPC, parliamentarians made no further efforts to implement international instruments of human rights when these involved the provinces. Canada signed four ILO covenants, three involving federal jurisdiction. Given the premiers' categorical rejection of the Rowell-Sirois Report's recommendation urging a constitutional amendment enabling provinces to delegate legislative powers to Ottawa to implement treaties, and given the climate of rising Canadian nationalism propelling Ottawa to act unilaterally, the King and St Laurent Canadian governments eschewed the 'totality of powers' approach to achieve implementation of its international human rights commitments. Canada continued to participate in international discussions on the lack of implementation of ILO conventions by federations but firmly rejected the suggestion that sub-states of be allowed to ratify these conventions. Instead, Canada proposed, along with the United States, a fractional or partial ratification by sub-states. Pressure on Canada increased when, during the 1946 International Labour Conference in Montreal, delegates removed the right of federations to consider these conventions mere recommendations rather than obligations. Delegates also strengthened reporting procedures as well as implementation actions required of all federal states that had signed on to conventions and recommendations.[19]

Canada's Ambivalent Strategy

While Canadian governments refused to act domestically, they played a self-serving role – for reasons of enhanced status and a greater role on the world scene based on the functional principle – in the international debate over the formulation of the United Nations Charter and the Universal Declaration of Human Rights (UDHR). The Charter's clarion call for the 'realization of human rights and fundamental freedoms for all without distinction as to race, sex, language, or religion' was reiterated ad nauseam. The King government continued to support the Charter's international idealism in the hope that another world war could be averted. Canadians could pursue their economic interests on the world stage while remaining united at home.

The long shadow of the *Labour Conventions Case* and the continued hesitancy to act on signed agreements influenced Canada's role during the extensive drafting stages of the non-binding Universal Declaration of Human Rights – a process overseen by a Canadian, John P. Humphries. According to a recent revisionist account,[20] the St Laurent Liberal government's attitude was fraught with skepticism and overt hostility. With the backing of a joint committee of Parliament and the Canadian Bar Association, Ottawa's representatives used the pretext of provincial jurisdiction to express Canada's very strong opposition to the entrenchment in the UDHR of substantive norms of human rights, including the freedom of religion and of association and social and economic rights. To the shock of many, in the vote in committee on the UDHR Canada abstained at the third session of the General Assembly in 1948. When the UDHR was put to a vote in the Plenary Assembly, Canada was shamed into voting in favour, while reiterating its abstention on educational and cultural rights. William Schabas argues, with convincing evidence, that a combination of very strong opposition to substantive rights, glaring indifference, and the absence of a 'human rights culture' among Canada's governing elites explain Canada's very reluctant embrace of the UDHR in 1948.[21] In the end, Canada accepted the UDHR because it was a non-binding symbolic educational instrument, one that would not create unwanted conflict between Ottawa and the provincial governments, especially with the troublesome Quebec government of Maurice Duplessis, which trampled on human rights with impunity.

Canada continued its practice of walking a fine line between its strong advocacy of human rights while refusing to sign on to specific human rights obligations that it objected to and/or would prove impossible to implement. This bifurcated approach explains but does not justify its role of reluctant activist in the discussions and negotiations of the international covenants for the protection of civil and political rights and of economic, social, and cultural rights as well as other human rights instruments. These lengthy and difficult negotiations got underway in 1948 in the Commission on Human Rights and proceeded until they were finalized in the Third Committee of the General Assembly in 1966. In order to forestall any international embarrassment over Canada's future ratification of the two binding covenants when it was patently obvious that implementation would be difficult if not impossible to achieve, Canada's representatives steadfastly insisted on a 'federal states' clause. Without such a clause, Canada put everyone on notice that it would not ratify the binding covenants.[22]

In the wake of Canada's vote for the Universal Declaration of Human Rights, the drafting of several new human rights instruments, and the 1947–8 Joint Committee of the Senate and the House of Commons' rejection of an entrenched bill of rights, the impatient civil liberties advocate Frank Scott revisited the controversial matter of Ottawa's jurisdiction over individual rights and freedoms. Scott, a strong believer in the myth of parliamentary supremacy, was critical of the Joint Committee's recommendation that the proposal for an entrenched bill of rights be referred to the Supreme Court to determine Parliament's jurisdiction. Such weighty constitutional matters should be decided by governments, not the courts. While not opposed to an entrenched comprehensive bill of rights, Scott believed this option was not realistic, given the absence of an amending formula, the lack of the bill's comprehensiveness, the prospect of judicial review, and the need for enforcement mechanisms. On the other hand, a federal statutory bill of rights would be largely symbolic and limited to federal jurisdiction, and could be repealed at will.[23] Another Canadian conundrum in the making.

Proceeding on the assumption that many fundamental rights already existed in the BNA Act, Scott demonstrated that a committed federal government had the undeniable jurisdictional authority to undertake positive action on virtually every article in the UDHR and, perhaps, move beyond the limitations of the declaration's rights. Scott challenged the conventional wisdom that 'civil liberties' and 'fundamental freedoms' fell within the purview of section 92, 'Property and Civil Rights in the Provinces.' Section 92, he argued, dealt with *private* law rather than *public* law, which resided under Ottawa's jurisdiction.[24] In analysing the Constitution, Scott revealed a vast array of federal powers over human rights and fundamental freedoms, including the right to make treaties and implement treaties within federal powers. Canadá could, Scott suggested, use Ottawa's authority over public law to expand its treaty-implementing powers over unnamed jurisdictions as well as over aspects of those areas considered exclusively in the provincial sphere. Scott also concurred with the suggestion that Ottawa, applying the necessary distinction between private and public law, could resort to a revitalized 'Peace, Order and Good Government' clause as authority for a federal bill of rights that protected and promoted the 'public rights of Canadian citizens everywhere.'[25]

A bill of rights, functioning as a defensive shield, was necessary but not sufficient. Scott urged Parliament to endorse the UDHR, to establish a standing committee to review existing and new statutes to ensure they did not violate fundamental rights and freedoms, and to establish a civil rights section in the Department of Justice responsible for overseeing the application of all criminal law. Scott had a truly visionary conception of the state in which the executive, legislative, and judicial branches all cooperated as guardians of fundamental freedoms and human rights.[26] It was an audacious approach that, alas, fell on deaf years.

Abolition of appeals to the JCPC in 1949 and the passage of the British North America Act (No. 2) 1949. which granted Parliament a general power to amend the constitution except in areas of provincial jurisdiction, raised expectations that a constitutional solution was perhaps not out of reach. The perceptive Frank Scott was very disappointed that the 1949 amendment could not be construed to confer authority on Parliament to amend section 132 of the BNA Act, 1867 – it had been rendered obsolete by the JCPC – so as to confer on Parliament the authority to implement all treaties and international multinational agreements negotiated and signed under Cabinet's authority.[27] Scott contended that if Canada was going to be able to contribute to the new world order, it had to chose between 'two values, one of local sovereignty, the other of world peace.'[28]

Other constitutional law specialists interested in human rights matters struggled to solve Canada's federalist conundrum. G.J. Szablowski, a McGill law graduate influenced by Scott, in a 1956 seminal article analysed the seemingly irresolvable problem pertaining to the creation and implementation of treaties in the Canada federation. With the Statute of Westminster, the 1939 Seals Act, and the Letters Patent of 1947, the United Kingdom had transferred 'all powers' to the Governor General-in-Council of Canada. This meant that Cabinet had unlimited authority to ratify treaties and intergovernmental agreements that could be put to Parliament for its assent before ratification.[29] But once Canada gained complete independence, most legal scholars and the courts concurred that the Canadian government and Parliament lost their exclusive ability to implement treaties when these trenched on areas of provincial jurisdiction, because section 132[30] applied only to 'Empire Treaties' and had been rendered obsolete.

Szablowski, contending that this was a misleading and strained interpretation of section 132, argued that its broad intent was to create 'a central authority competent in law and in fact to deal effectively with all matters of general or national interest.'[31] It was a power distinct from sections 91 and 92 and intended to override them. These international 'Obligations of Canada,' as a separate class of subjects, were not part of the distribution of powers scheme but rather under the heading 'Miscellaneous Provisions, General.' He maintained that section 132 created a permanent 'aspect' for all matters coming under international agreements because it raised these matters from a purely local 'aspect' to a national 'aspect.' Sections 91 and 92 were not frozen jurisdictions but rather fluid and overlapping areas that were determined by the 'aspect' of a matter. The use of an international agreement to add a national dimension to what was heretofore a local matter under exclusive provincial jurisdiction was not an amendment. 'Parliament does not gain additional jurisdiction other than that which it possessed *ab origine* to make laws for "Peace, Order and Good Government."'[32]

His analysis of the operation of section 132 revealed that it overrode the distribution of powers scheme and was used to invalidate provincial laws. As well, in the 1932 *Aeronautics* case, Lord Sankey used section 132 to rule in favour of Ottawa on the grounds that the 'aspect' of the matter was national in scope. And yet Canadian governments ignored section 132, opting for political reasons to proceed with flawed treaty ratification and implementing procedures that made any subsequent recourse to section 132 politically impossible. The constitutional door was slammed shut by the JCPC in its 1932 *Radio* and 1937 *Labour Conventions* cases. Intent on weakening the Canadian government, the JCPC deliberately misinterpreted section 132. In an ironical twist, the Privy Council justices refused to accept that an independent Canadian government could continue to exercise the same powers of treaty performance that it had exercised as a member of the British Empire.[33]

How then could this debilitating federalist conundrum be resolved? Szablowski wondered if the 'Peace, Order and Good Government' clause could be used to reinstate Ottawa's treaty-implementation powers. Of course this meant that the legitimacy and scope of POGG had to be restored, following its highly strained and overly narrow interpretation by the JCPC. It was highly improbable that residual clause would be used to authorize Parliament's implementation of treaties. Nor, in his estimation, should it be used because it involved trenching between sections 91 and 92. Yet there was hope. The Supreme Court was showing signs of moving beyond the straitjacket of sections 91 and 92 toward a proper application of the aspect rule, one that would enable Parliament to implement treaties, conventions, and other international agreements if their substance was truly national in scope. This evolution should be consolidated by a constitutional amendment vesting in Parliament – as was the case with section 132 – 'exclusive power to legislate in relation to matters coming within a ratified treaty,' if the matters involved were of national concern. As one of the guardians of the Constitution, the courts would have the power to review all treaty-implementing legislation to ensure that the matters involved were inherently national in character and scope. The grounds for invalidation would not be found in sections 91 and 92 but rather on whether the matters within dealt strictly with a national aspect involving individual rights and freedoms. The prospect of judicial review would ensure that Parliament would fulfil its role of guardianship of the Constitution so as not to be discredited by the courts.[34]

By the late 1950s Canada's ability to implement international human rights instruments had hit a major roadblock. This was readily acknowledged by F.H. Soward in his judicious overview of the severe limitations that federalism placed on Canada's ability to fulfil its international obligations. While Soward's outline of the crisis over implementation of international human rights instruments mirrored that of Szablowski and Professor James McLeod Henry of Dalhousie University,[35] he nonetheless maintained that Canada's dismal record in this regard was amply offset by its active participation in the work of various United Nations committees and agencies as well as its significant contribution to NATO and several peacekeeping missions. Federalism, for Soward, played a complicating but not a disabling role in the implementation of Canada's international obligations.[36]

Nevertheless, the record by the late 1950s was a far cry from the myth trumpeting Canada's highly positive role in creating the UN Charter and formulating the UDHR, a myth that would become central to the populist movement in favour of an entrenched Canadian Charter of Rights and Freedoms in the 1970s. Ottawa's fear of alienating the provincial governments, especially the Duplessis government of Quebec, was very real, considering that it required their support to implement the comprehensive range of non-binding political, civil, legal, social, and economic rights outlined in the UDHR document. In the immediate post-war years, the plea for a constitutional amendment fell on deaf ears as several of the premiers vigorously contested Ottawa's determination to use its taxing and spending powers to control the Canadian economy by putting in place a wide range of economic and social programs in areas of provincial jurisdiction.

Ottawa Encounters Mounting Pressures to Act

The 1960s and 1970s witnessed the development of a Canadian human rights movement. Canadian civil liberties and equality rights organizations, propelled by increasing incidents of home-grown discrimination and a radicalized American civil rights movement, became much better organized and more outspoken, thereby expanding their appeal among urban, middle-class Canadians. Initially, Prime Minister Pearson's Liberal government showed little interest in Canada's ongoing participation in the comprehensive discussions and negotiations leading up to the final drafts of the Covenants on Civil and Political Rights and Economic, Social and Cultural Rights in 1966. When asked in the House on 19 January 1967 if Canada intended to sign and ratify the covenants that its UN representatives had voted for, a bemused prime minister said he was not even aware of the covenants but would look into the matter of their ratification. Pressured by parliamentarians to take action, Pearson announced a few days later that his government would begin negotiations with the provinces concerning implementation. Once provincial agreement was forthcoming, Ottawa would sign and Parliament would ratify the covenants.[37]

Ottawa's decision to move forward met stiff opposition from increas-

ingly powerful provincial executives, some federal and provincial political parties, and a considerable number of legal organizations. The
emergence of the Québécois neo-nationalist and secessionist movements fuelled the Quebec government's drive for treaty-making powers
to complement its treaty-implementation powers. These developments
threatened Canada's jurisdiction over foreign policy as well as national
unity. They compelled Ottawa's political leaders and senior mandarins
to seek a common solution to the domestic crisis in federal–provincial
relations as well as its inability to implement international instruments
of human rights in areas of provincial jurisdiction. Prime Ministers
Pearson and Trudeau shared the view that an entrenched Charter of
Rights and Freedoms, based in large measure on international human
rights instruments and fully binding on Parliament and provincial executives and legislatures, would assist in shoring up national unity and
resolving the longstanding and increasingly humiliating federalist conundrum of non-implementation of international human rights instruments. An entrenched Charter would respond to the emerging 'rights
revolution' throughout Canada while resolving the dilemma.

Ottawa's insistence on a 'federal-state' clause prevailed throughout
the Diefenbaker and Pearson administrations. In 1964, legal scholar and
future Supreme Court justice Bora Laskin noted that 'Canada's limited
constitutional competence to implement international agreements is reflected in its practice in international negotiations.'[38] Personnel in the
Department of External Affairs accentuated Canada's participation in
United Nations commissions and agencies, believing that it was important to expand and strengthen international standards for the protection of human rights. In 1957 Canada accepted the Convention on
the Political Rights of Women (1953) but with a reservation concerning
provincial rights. It had representatives on the Commission on the Status of Women, 1958–61, and the Commission on Human Rights, 1963–5.
While they voted in favour of several non-binding declarations dealing
with the rights of children (1959), the elimination of racial discrimination (1963), and discrimination against women (1967), these declarations were not always reported to Parliament. When feasible, Ottawa
legislated these new standards and numerous conventions when they
involved areas of exclusive federal jurisdiction. It continued to pressure
provincial governments, with little success, to do likewise for all those
matters within their jurisdictions.[39]

On the matter of ILO conventions dealing with a wide range of human rights issues, Ottawa's behaviour continued to be framed by the

1937 *Labour Conventions* case decision requiring provincial implementation. Consequently, by 1961 Canada had ratified only 19 of 116 conventions. Laskin, like Scott, doubted that Ottawa's powers were as narrow as the Canadian government asserted. While he concurred with Scott that current judicial decisions remained ambivalent, he suggested that greater federal-provincial cooperation might be one way of achieving implementation.[40] The Pearson government, in the spirit of cooperative federalism, negotiated with provincial governments to accelerate the process. With provincial consent, Ottawa ratified the ILO Convention 111 against Discrimination in Employment in 1964, Convention 45 concerning Employment of Women in Mines in 1966, and Convention 122 on Employment Policy in 1966.[41] When, by the mid-1960s, the spirit and practice of cooperative federalism broke down, the possibility of provincial agreements vanished.

Bora Laskin examined the possibility that a coterie of judicial decisions – the 1932 *Aeronautics* and *Radio* cases, the 1951 *Johannesson* case, and, the far-reaching 1956 *Pronto Uranium Mines Ltd v. Ontario Labour Relations Board* – could be interpreted as expanding 'the dimensions of federal power by reason of the international aspects of a particular matter.' If the political will existed in Ottawa, the aspects doctrine – founded on the central government's residual power to make laws for the peace, order, and good government – could eventually be used to reverse the *Labour Conventions* case, providing Ottawa with 'an over-riding treaty implementing power.'[42] Laskin concurred with Scott's 1949 rejection of the traditional interpretation of the provincial 'property and civil rights' head of power to limit Ottawa's treaty-implementing powers. Laskin characterized the view that the provincial power in relation to 'property and civil rights in the Province' embraces the civil and political freedoms as one based 'on a misreading of constitutional history, on a wishful transference to Canadian constitutional significance of a phrase (civil rights) which is United States currency, and, above all, on an unjustified attenuation of the federal general power, especially in its contact with the public-order aspects of criminal law.'[43]

Clearly Ottawa's long-standing reliance on a questionable interpretation of 'property and civil rights' to avoid federal-provincial conflicts over the implementation of international human rights instruments and ILO conventions was being systematically undermined by a maturing Canadian legal scholarship. Yet it was going to take far more than legal scholarship to change the paradigm. In 1966, Canada, dropping its insistence on a 'federal-state' clause, voted for the Covenant on Civil and Political Rights along with its Optional Protocol and the Covenant on Economic, Social and Cultural Rights. Yet Canada continued to play its usual game. Well aware that both covenants contained strong implementation procedures, Ottawa delayed ratification of both covenants until it had obtained the approval of the provincial governments, a process that took the Trudeau government a full decade.[44]

Quebec's Quiet Revolution of state-building put severe pressures on Ottawa to resolve the conundrum over its lack of ability to implement international instruments of human rights. Successive Quebec governments' quest to obtain treaty-making powers in areas of provincial jurisdiction altered the substance of the debate and threatened the very core of Ottawa's international persona as a nation-state speaking with one united voice. A reluctant Premier Jean Lesage was pressured by several militant Cabinet members, led by his minister of education, Paul Gérin-Lajoie, to carve out a role for Quebec on the international stage.[45] The crisis began soon after General Charles de Gaulle became president of France's Fifth Republic in January 1959. Fully briefed about Quebec's 'Quiet' and 'not-so-quiet' revolutions, De Gaulle, backed by the 'Quebec Mafia' in Paris, developed a keen interest in the possibilities that an independent Quebec could offer to advance France's international interests. Following several years of transatlantic visits by French and Quebec intellectuals, journalists, academics, officials, and political leaders, the crisis became public. On 27 February 1965 in Paris, the Lesage Quebec government – represented by its minister of education, Paul Gérin-Lajoie – and Charles de Gaulle's French government, in the absence of Ottawa's delegate, signed an 'Entente entre le Québec et la France sur un programme d'échanges et cooperation dans le domaine de l'éducation.'[46] It was trumpeted by Lesage, Gérin-Lajoie, and the francophone media as a major advance in Quebec's quest for an international role.

Reacting immediately, Canada's minister of external affairs, Paul Martin, warned France's ambassador that only Canada had the legal authority to speak for Canadians on the international stage and that the Cabinet had the exclusive power to make treaties with other states. Yet, hoping to avoid a full-blown conflict with Quebec and France, Martin indicated that on the practical level the exchange agreement met with Ottawa's approval. He was naive and short-sighted. Gérin-Lajoie, in a 12 April 1965 speech to Montreal's Consular Corps reported in Le Devoir, elaborated what became the Gérin-Lajoie doctrine of Quebec's External Affairs. He indicated that the Quebec state was determined to take its rightful place on the world stage to fulfil the aspirations of a rising generation of middle-class Québécois. In its areas of jurisdiction, all central to modern state-building, it was imperative that the Quebec Cabinet acquire the power to make treaties to complement the National Assembly's power to implement treaties. He concluded, 'It was no longer acceptable, either, for the federal State to exercise a sort of surveillance and monitoring of Quebec's international relations.'[47] In his 22 April speech to French, Belgian, and Swiss academics at the National Assembly, Gérin-Lajoie declared that the Quebec state, because of its heavy responsibility for the future of the Québécois collectivity, required constitutional special status empowering it to negotiate and implement treaties with other countries.[48]

The minister of external affairs felt compelled to respond on 23 April via a press release and a statement to the House. Martin reiterated the Canadian government's position that only independent states had the authority to ratify treaties. His ministry was willing to facilitate every provincial government wanting to enter into an agreement with another state in areas of its jurisdiction, as long at it was clearly understood that only Ottawa had the treaty-making power to formalize any and all such agreements. Gérin-Lajoie restated Quebec's position a few days later.[49] Prime Minister Pearson and Premier Lesage met to exchange views on the conflict but failed to agree on a solution. Their senior bureaucrats and ministers were mandated to develop a framework or 'umbrella' agreement, one that respected Ottawa's prerogatives while giving Quebec a circumscribed and monitored role in its developing ties with France in matters of language, education, and culture. The Canada-France framework agreement was finalized in late September 1965. Quebec, opting to ignore the document, insisted on negotiating and signing a France-Quebec Cultural Entente, which, while approved by Ottawa, was quickly trumpeted as another major victory. Ottawa had been outmanoeuvred yet again. Lesage's successor after the election of 1966, Premier Daniel Johnson, proved to be even more insistent on an unfettered role for Quebec in international affairs.[50]

In 1962, a Québécois legal scholar in the Faculty of Law at l'Université de Montréal, Jacques-Yvan Morin, addressed the role of Canadian provinces in the negotiation of international agreements in the light of comparative law. He reviewed Canada's dilemma over treaty-making and treaty-implementing powers but categorically rejected the solutions proposed by various English-language scholars.[51] Following an analysis of different federal models, he concluded that Canada could find a solution to its impasse over the implementation of international instruments of human rights by adopting the approach of the Federal Republic of Germany, which allowed its sub-states, the Länder, to negotiate, ratify, and implement treaties in their areas of jurisdiction.[52] Quebec's new and pressing needs required innovative solutions. He favoured a constitutional 'special status' for Quebec in international relations, but, contrary to Gérin-Lajoie, he proposed that the Supreme Court had the authority to ensure, via judicial review, that all Quebec's international agreements were constitutional, that is, they respected the division of powers.[53] Morin, along with several other legal scholars,[54] was called upon to provide advice to Quebec governments on how they should and could proceed in their struggle for 'special status' in international relations.

Following the election of Premier Daniel Johnson in 1966, having proclaimed 'égalité ou independence' for Quebec, Prime Minister Pearson's minority Liberal government was strongly encouraged by three newly elected Quebec MPs – Jean Marchand, Gérard Pelletier, and Pierre Elliott Trudeau – and several Cabinet members and legal scholars to adopt a much firmer approach with the Johnson Quebec government on the issue of treaty-making and Quebec's role on the international stage. In spring 1965, law professor Bora Laskin, a member of the Ontario Advisory Committee on Confederation, addressed the central legal question. He asked 'whether the central government could exercise the executive power of dealing internationally with matters which were domestically within the exclusive provincial competence, and whether the central Parliament could legislate on those matters so far as necessary to carry out international obligations.'[55] Only Parliament, under section 3 of the Statute of Westminster, 1931, has the authority to enact extraterritorial legislation. Does this prohibition of a provincial legislative power extend to provincial extraterritorial executive power? Constitutional convention and practice since 1931 'led to acceptance of the national government of Canada as the spokesman for Canada in international affairs.'[56] There is no provision in the Canadian Constitution granting provinces treaty-making powers with or without the consent of the national government. Acknowledging that the *Labour Conventions* case rendered section 132 obsolete, Laskin agreed that neither Ottawa's residual power nor the principle of the exhaustiveness of legislative power, alone or in tandem, was adequate to empower

Parliament with unlimited treaty-implementing powers. This did not mean, in Laskin's opinion, that a province could make an enforceable treaty – it had no means of validating the treaty by implementing legislation – with a foreign state, since it would have no international validity. If a foreign state recognized the treaty, such action would constitute a declaration of independence and thereby a denial of Ottawa's exclusive treaty-making power. Ottawa had the option of delegating, for a specific purpose, a treaty-making power to a province, but it would retain the international responsibility. Like Lord Wright, who in 1955 expressed publicly his original dissent with the 1937 *Labour Conventions* case, and Chief Justice Kerwin in *Francis v. The Queen* [1956], who mused about the need to reconsider the landmark case, Laskin clearly relished the opportunity to partake in such a case.[57] His appointment to the Ontario Court of Appeal and eventually to Canada's Supreme Court opened that door.

When in early 1968 the Pearson government began mega-constitutional negotiations with the premiers, Ottawa's position on federalism and international relations was clearly outlined by Secretary of State for External Affairs Paul Martin in a document submitted to the conference. Canadian sovereignty on the international level was and would remain indivisible to ensure the unity of Canada: 'In Canada the constitutional authority to conclude international agreements is a part of the royal prerogative and, with respect to treaties, is exercised in the name of Canada by the Governor-General, usually on the advice of the Secretary of State for External Affairs.'[58] Ottawa acknowledged the longstanding dilemma about its comprehensive treaty-making powers and the provincial legislatures' treaty-implementing powers involving their jurisdictions. It also recognized that Canadian foreign policy had to reflect the federal nature of Canada, its two linguistic communities, its expanding cultural diversity, and provincial interests. The document proposed a wide-ranging set of procedures and structures that would allow provincial representatives to participate in international organizations, and to be consulted on treaty-making and treaty-implementation while not undermining Canada's domestic or international sovereignty and thereby the unity of the country.[59] Ottawa raised the possibility of resolving the dilemma via a constitutional amendment. There were two options: granting the federal government comprehensive treaty-implementing powers in areas of provincial competence, or granting the provinces treaty-making powers. Ottawa rejected the second option as extremist because it would entail the disintegration of Canada. On the other hand, the first option could be effectively achieved only as part of a far more comprehensive process of constitutional renewal.[60] A follow-up document on international conferences on education by Mitchell Sharp, the new secretary of state for external affairs, reaffirmed Ottawa's position.[61]

The battle lines hardened. Quebec's Ministry of Intergovernmental Relations led the counter-attack. Its Delegation of Officials to the Constitutional Conference, led by Deputy Minister Claude Morin, provided a sharp rebuttal rejecting Ottawa's reaffirmation of its exclusive jurisdiction over treaty-making. Drawing upon the work and advice of legal scholars, including Professor Edward McWhinney, the Quebec government based its claim to treaty-making powers in its own jurisdictions on the silence of the BNA Act on international powers, on Quebec's urgent need to exercise all of its powers to the fullest, on the 1937 *Labour Conventions* case, which it claimed Ottawa deliberately misinterpreted by relying on the Supreme Court decision leading to the reference to the JCPC, on its categorical rejection of the constitutionality of the Letters Patent 1947, and on the general principles governing the exercise of the royal prerogative. The provincial governments' constitutional right to make treaties with other countries in their areas of jurisdiction, Quebec concluded, should be spelt out clearly in the new Canadian constitution. Federations were created and functioned on the principle of the division of internal sovereignty and this principle had to be extended to the division of sovereignty over treaty-making powers.[62]

Professor McWhinney, very supportive of Quebec's position along with other scholars,[63] penned a scathing indictment of Ottawa's outmoded concepts and attitude about intergovernmental relations that led to destabilizing symbolic wars with Quebec over its demand to exercise treaty-making powers. A strong proponent of a pragmatic and experiential British approach to 'living law,' he called upon Ottawa to accept the 'de facto changes, which are already ripening through sustained practice and observance, into Conventional constitutional law.'[64] Following a lengthy debunking of Ottawa's legal arguments, a favourable analysis of transnational provincial activities, a harsh critique of the France-Canada Framework Agreement as legal surplusage, and a lament over Ottawa's rejection of 'Associate State' or 'special constitutional' status for Quebec, McWhinney recommended that Canada adopt a variant of the model and practice of the German Federal Republic pertaining to the Länder's treaty-making powers, an approach based on the principle of federal comity. The operative term for Canada was pragmatic cooperative federalism pursued on the domestic and international levels.[65]

Ottawa Seizes the Initiative

Pierre Elliott Trudeau – minister of justice in the Pearson government and then leader of the Liberal Party and prime minister in 1968 – took charge of the process of mega-constitutional reform that, while culminating initially in the failed Victoria Charter of 1971, would add a new paradigm to Canada's constitutional framework by 1982.[66] Under his influence, the Canadian government initiated the arduous task of transforming the way Canadian citizens perceived their constitution, the British North America Act, 1867. For a century, Canadians viewed the British statute as belonging exclusively to the executive and judicial branches of government. In sum, it was an instrument whose primary role was to delineate the respective powers of the federal and provincial governments, and, if disputes arose, to call upon the JCPC and then Canada's Supreme Court after 1949 to resolve them.

The addition of a second, competitive paradigm to Canadian constitutionalism was hinted at by Prime Minister Pearson at the 1968 Conference.[67] This Canadian constitutional 'revolution,' featuring a wholesale democratization of the constitution, was expanded upon in Trudeau's *The Constitution and the People of Canada* at the second conference in mid-February 1969. Ottawa's proposals for constitutional renewal focused primarily on the interrelationships between Canadians and their governments because 'the rights of people must precede the rights of governments.' The proposals outlined 'how the aspirations of Canadians may best be expressed in the objectives and principles of the Constitution, their rights as individuals safeguarded, their right to participate in democratic processes assured, and their interests as residents of both a vast country and of a particular region adequately represented in our federal structures.'[68] The primary objective of Confederation was no longer just the delineation of powers between Ottawa and the provinces[69] but rather 'the maintenance through the Constitution of a democratic society, a society in which the ultimate sovereignty of Canada is to be found in the people which comprise it. It means that the whole of the Constitution and the institutions of government it creates ought to reflect and to protect those concepts of freedom, equality, and the dignity of the individual which surely characterize Canada.'[70]

At the centre of Trudeau's constitutional 'revolution' was an entrenched, comprehensive, hybrid charter of rights and freedoms, one comprising fundamental human values, linguistic rights, and minority rights.[71] This constitutional charter, by virtue of its overriding nature and stability, would guarantee fundamental principles and rights by placing a check on the exercise of power by the state.[72] A thoroughly democratized citizens' Constitution, reformed governmental institutions, and a comprehensive, hybrid charter of rights and freedoms would contribute to strengthening the bonds of nationhood. A stronger, united Canada would empower Canadians and Ottawa to play an enhanced role on the international stage in an increasingly interdependent world.[73] Once Canadians embraced a democratized and Canadianized constitution, one with a citizens' charter of rights and freedoms at its very core, it would be much easier for the Canadian government to obtain their support for the implementation of international instruments of human rights. Once a mature Canadian human rights movement was in place, Trudeau believed that it would be easier for Ottawa to convince provincial governments to implement international instruments of human rights. The new dynamic would assist Ottawa in overcoming one of the longstanding conundrums of Canadian federalism.

The Trudeau government's approach to constitutional renewal altered the dynamic of the debate on Canada's implementation of international instruments of human rights. Walter Tarnopolsky, a human rights law professor at the University of Ottawa, declared that it was high time Canada had a charter of human rights.[74] Louis Sabourin, a political scientist and director of the Institute of International Cooperation at the University of Ottawa, understood the potential 'revolutionary' nature of Trudeau's entrenched charter of rights and freedoms. Furthermore, since most states, including recent federal states, rejected the use of a 'federal state' clause, Canada was refusing to sign multilateral treaties without inserting reservations allowing it to derogate from certain aspects of the treaties.[75] How could Canada's federal dilemma be resolved? Until a constitutional solution was forthcoming, it was unlikely that Canada would sign on to the groundbreaking 1966 International Covenant on Civil and Political Rights with its Optional Protocol and the International Covenant on Economic, Social, and Cultural Rights. Canada's representatives had helped formulate both. Could the political, social, psychological, cultural, religious, ideological, administrative, and legal impediments to these covenants be overcome via constitutional reform?[76] While the entrenchment of a charter would not guarantee a greater respect for fundamental freedoms, Sabourin argued that it would create a more receptive climate, one that would encourage the recognition and respect for the principle of the equality of citizens throughout Canada.[77]

While it was clear that important fundamental rights and freedoms were under federal jurisdiction, many others fell under provincial jurisdiction. Was it possible for Trudeau to obtain provincial agreement for an entrenched charter, including linguistic rights, binding both levels of government? Several premiers categorically rejected Trudeau's entrenched charter on the grounds that it undermined federalism, parliamentary sovereignty, and the constitutional monarchy.[78] A sanguine Sabourin recommended three approaches. He suggested that Trudeau and the premiers negotiate a federal-provincial charter of rights and freedoms, one that would accelerate Canada's signing, ratification, and implementation of both UN covenants. If this approach failed, a constitutional conference could establish a set of phasing-in procedures with all the provinces for the various rights and freedoms set out in the covenants, depending on whether these fell under federal, provincial, or shared jurisdiction. Finally, Ottawa and the provincial governments could agree to joint ratification and implementation of the covenants. Once this process was complete, it would by relatively easy for all governments to agree upon a Canadian charter of rights and freedoms, one that was neither federal or provincial, but supra-institutional because it would be based on international instruments of human rights.[79]

The Trudeau government pursued the first two approaches simultaneously, setting aside the third option because it would create a patchwork quilt of rights and freedoms. Seizing the initiative from the premiers, between 1968 and 1970 the Trudeau government launched a fundamental constitutional renewal based on its comprehensive proposals and agenda.[80] Phase one of Canada's mega-constitutional politics, contends Peter Russell, generated intense conflict between federal and provincial governments and between citizens and their political leaders. Why? Because the process went beyond the merits of specific proposals and addressed 'the very nature of the political community on which the constitution is based.'[81] Determined to retake control of the agenda, the premiers, led by Quebec and Alberta, insisted that discussions and agreement on a new distribution of powers, beginning with Ottawa's use of taxing and spending powers in provincial jurisdictions, must take precedence over patriation, an amending formula, and a charter of rights. The longstanding paradigm of executive federalism, one entailing a closed-door, elite-driven federal-provincial diplomacy, failed to arrive at a consensus on either substance or procedure.[82]

By late 1969 Trudeau was eager to bring a quick end to an intense and prolonged emotional debate over matters of 'identity and the fundamental principles of the body politic,'[83] which was undermining national unity by fuelling the growing secessionist movement in Quebec led by René Lévesque, a very popular former member of Jean Lesage's 'Quiet Revolution' government, 1960–6. Seeking a way around the premiers in order to bring closure to the government's first stage of constitutional renewal, Trudeau adopted a dual strategy. Early in 1970, he called upon a special joint committee of the Senate and the House of Commons on the Constitution of Canada to gather evidence and testimony, via extensive public hearings in all provinces and territories, from experts and ordinary citizens, and then report back to Parliament on their and its responses to the government's comprehensive proposals. This process of participatory democracy, Trudeau hoped, would garner much broader public support for his vision of Canada based on shared values and a common citizenship. It would then be easier to convince Canadians that his constitutional renewal package was the only way to achieve this vision.[84] In sum, substance would drive the process to a successful conclusion.

In the interim, Trudeau and his justice minister, John Turner, lobbied the premiers, including the newly elected Liberal premier of Quebec, Robert Bourassa, to accept for the sake of national unity a limited reform package reflecting Ottawa's vision of a liberal democratic, pluralistic, bilingual Canada in which sovereignty resided in the people, and citizens' rights could not be trumped by the power of the state. The Victoria Charter, hammered out by the prime minister and the premiers during their 14–17 June 1971 Federal-Provincial Conference in Victoria, included patriation, a region-based amending formula without provincial vetoes, entrenchment of the Supreme Court of Canada with a provincial role in the selection of justices, and a mini charter of rights and freedoms guaranteeing only fundamental 'Political Rights,' not equality rights, as well as linguistic rights for Canada's two official language minorities.[85] The Victoria Charter, agreed to by all the premiers, crashed on the shoals of Québécois neo-nationalism when several organizations, including the militant union centrals, held public rallies to denounce the agreement, which, ironically, granted Quebec and Ontario vetoes over constitutional change. Premier Bourassa was threatened with the resignation of several senior Cabinet ministers, led by his irascible minister of social affairs, Claude Castonquay. They denounced the premier's failure to obtain exclusive provincial control over social programs with the taxing powers to pay for them. To quell the Cabinet revolt, Bourassa informed an irate and frustrated prime minister that his government would not put the Victoria Charter to the National Assembly for ratification.[86]

Human rights organizations and their supporters were not pleased with the very narrow 'political rights' guaranteed in the Victoria Charter. They used its demise to push for a far more comprehensive charter of rights and freedoms. The Special Joint Committee of the Senate and the House of Commons on the Constitution of Canada in its extensive 1972 report wholeheartedly endorsed the democratic vision outlined in the Trudeau government's comprehensive constitutional reform package. Feedback from a wide spectrum of Canadians and myriad organizations convinced the Molgat-MacGuigan Committee that Trudeau's democratic vision had considerable support. It concluded that this vision, as reflected in an expanded charter of rights and freedoms, would garner even broader support. It was imperative that it include, alongside all fundamental civil rights, a full range of equality rights prohibiting all and any forms of discrimination based on sex, race, ethnic origin, colour, or religion in the public and private sectors. A new constitution had to recognize the special place of Native and Metis peoples and respect their right of self-determination by not amending the terms of section 91(24), concerning 'Indians, and Lands Reserved for the Indians,' without their consent.[87] On the sensitive matter of international relations and implementation of human rights instruments, the report reaffirmed the existing theory and practice. It recommended that a new 'Constitution should make it clear that the Federal Government has exclusive jurisdiction over foreign policy, the making of treaties, and the exchange of diplomatic and consular representatives.' The committee recommended that the provinces, in cooperation with Ottawa and subject to its veto power, should have the right to enter into a wide range of administrative agreements with foreign states and/or their sub-states in areas of their jurisdiction.[88]

When Prime Minister Trudeau took office in 1968, his primary goal was to undermine the Québécois secessionist movement by entrenching a charter of rights and freedoms in a renewed Constitution. When the Victoria Charter failed in 1971, growing pressure from MPs, senators, increasing numbers of civil and equality rights organizations, and citizens forced the government to turn its attention to the ratification of the UN covenants. In late December 1971, Trudeau 'issued a comprehensive and unequivocal statement of support for ratification, and called on recalcitrant provinces to agree.' Negotiations began among federal and provincial officials and ministers leading up to the 1975 federal-provincial conference on ratification and implementation of the covenants. A federal Cabinet committee was advised that any possible conflicts between the Covenant on Civil and Political Rights and domestic law were manageable and 'the Covenant would provide a catalyst for review of conflicting laws in future.'[89] While parliamentary and public interest in and support for human rights continued to grow, there was still not enough pressure to convince reluctant premiers to agree to implement aspects of the covenants under their jurisdiction.[90] Stymied, but determined to force the hand of the premiers by generating an expansive public debate on international human rights, the Trudeau government decided to ratify and implement the Covenant on Civil and Political Rights and the Optional Protocol in May 1976 just months after they had come into force.[91]

Within a very short time, both the Canadian and provincial governments and their officials were drawn into the international human rights process when the UN committee agreed to evaluate individual complaints. The minister of justice and the secretary of state for external affairs and their senior officials cooperated fully with the committee in its investigation of complaints from Canadians who availed themselves of the procedures set out in the Optional Protocol. Both levels of government cooperated extensively in the mandatory Optional Protocol reporting process to the UN Human Rights Committee responsible for the Covenant on Civil and Political Rights.[92] Indeed, Canada produced the best quality and most comprehensive reports. Canada managed to get Walter Tarnopolsky elected to the committee. He contributed to the expansion of the committee's powers and duties as well as to its professionalism. In doing so, he raised Canada's international profile in the expanding debate over human rights matters.[93]

The covenants had an important influence on the growing debate over a Canadian charter of rights and freedoms. In 1977, following a long period of gestation, Canada finally passed the Canadian Human Rights Act and set up a human rights commission to oversee its administration.[94] By the end of the 1970s, the UN covenants, Canada's extensive first report, and the committee's evaluation of individual Canadian cases energized an expanding human rights culture and movement throughout Canada. In 1978 Don Jamieson, secretary of state external relations, acknowledged the impact of the covenants. 'Consultations related to Canada signing and ratifying the important human rights covenant,' he claimed, 'has a catalytic effect on the evolution of human rights legislation in Canada. It encouraged, as well, the establishment of statutory human rights agencies at the federal and provincial levels. The international obligations we have assumed by ratifying the covenants ensure a continuing review of domestic performance judged against the covenants' standards.'[95]

Yet it was patently clear to close observers that until full implementation was achieved at the federal and provincial levels, Canadians would not benefit from all the rights spelt out in the covenants.[96] Canada required a domestic solution, preferably a constitutional charter that bound both governments. During the 1979 federal election, Prime Minister Trudeau gave top priority to renewing Canada's constitution, beginning with what he termed was the people's package – patriation, the Victoria amending formula, and an entrenched, comprehensive, hybrid Canadian charter of rights and freedoms. His Liberal government was defeated but was returned to office in the federal election of 1980 soon after Prime Minister Joe Clark's Conservative government was defeated on its budget. The Trudeau government played the central role in the defeat by a margin of 60 to 40 per cent of the Parti Québécois government's referendum on secession in May 1980.[97]

Having promised to renew Canada's Constitution along the lines he had been discussing since 1968, Prime Minister Trudeau and his minister of justice, Jean Chrétien, immediately initiated negotiations with all ten premiers to assess their willingness to accept the people's package. When it became apparent before and during the federal-provincial conference of September 1980 that the premiers were not willing to cooperate, the Trudeau government decided to take unilateral action. A 'Proposed Resolution for a Joint Address to Her Majesty the Queen respecting the Constitution of Canada,' comprising a charter of rights and freedoms, was put before a joint committee of the Senate and the House for Commons for debate. Following very extensive televised testimony from a wide range of witnesses in late fall 1989 and early winter 1981, the government responded by greatly improving the charter. Nonetheless, passage of the amended resolution was stalled when three provincial governments challenged the process in their courts of appeal. The Manitoba and Quebec courts ruled the resolution constitutional, while the Newfoundland Court of Appeal ruled the resolution unconstitutional. All three provincial governments filed appeals to the Supreme Court of Canada for a final ruling in what became known as the 1981 Patriation Reference. On 16 April 1981, hoping to undermine the political legitimacy of Ottawa's resolution, which was supported by the premiers of

Ontario and New Brunswick, the remaining premiers, soon dubbed the Gang of Eight, proposed their own constitutional accord, which included patriation and Alberta's amending formula, but no charter.[98]

Several months later the Supreme Court justices ruled that the resolution was legal but unconstitutional in a conventional, that is, political, sense. To ensure the political legitimacy of Parliament's and then Westminster's passage of the resolution, the Supreme Court opined that while unanimity was not required, the resolution must have the consent of a substantial number of provincial governments.[99] Trudeau reconvened the premiers in November 1981 for one last desperate attempt to achieve a compromise. Following several days of very difficult negotiations, a breakthrough deal was struck. Trudeau agreed to Alberta's general amending formula, one based on provincial equality and requiring seven provinces with 50 per cent of the Canadian population. The traditional paradigm of Canadian constitutionalism, federalism, was reaffirmed. In return, the premiers accepted Trudeau's new paradigm, a comprehensive hybrid charter of rights and freedoms, including education rights for the official language minorities, but with a notwithstanding clause – renewable every five years – that could be used by legislatures and Parliament to override fundamental rights but not the rights of the official language minorities. All the premiers, except Quebec's René Lévesque, accepted the amended resolution. The deal was almost derailed when section 28 on gender rights and section 35 on Aboriginal rights were dropped from the amended resolution. These sections were reinserted when the national and provincial organizations representing women and Aboriginal communities successfully pressured the premiers to drop their opposition.[100] The Canada Act, 1982 – which incorporated Schedule B, the Constitution Act, 1982, with the Canadian Charter of Rights and Freedoms – was approved by the Canadian and UK Parliaments and given royal assent by Queen Elizabeth II on 17 April 1982.[101]

Conclusion

Following nearly two decades of fractious debate, Canadians acquired their own Constitution with the Canadian Charter of Rights and Freedoms, one binding on both levels of government. In becoming a sovereign people, Canadians had resolved one important dimension of the longstanding conundrum facing Canadian federalism. In the context of a mature and expansive human rights community backed by an entrenched charter, the Canadian government had acquired the political capacity, if it wishes to exercise it, to implement international instruments of human rights. This is especially so concerning rights that converge with Canada's domestic Charter of Rights and Freedoms. It is now far more difficult for provincial government to hide behind the Constitution and veto implementation of international instruments of human rights already recognized in Canada. Henceforth the Canadian and provincial governments can, if they so desire, proceed simultaneously with the further development of human rights on both the international and domestic levels. Indeed, the Supreme Court is leading the way in linking international and domestic instruments of human rights in their role judicial review of the Charter.[102]

Since 1919, Canada's treaty-implementing powers in the emerging field of human rights were severely constrained by a constitutional convention, reinforced by the JCPC's 1937 *Labour Conventions* case, pertaining to provincial treaty-implementation powers in areas of their own jurisdiction. It took legal scholars decades to challenge successfully the conventional wisdom that the provincial head of power over 'Property and Civil Rights' incorporated the lion's share of both the public and private conceptions of fundamental individual civil rights and equality rights. It became increasingly evident that Ottawa, because of its vast constitutional powers over criminal law especially, could legislate effectively in the realm of human rights. The quick fixes recommended by various scholars failed to gain traction among Ottawa's political leaders and senior mandarins.

A combination of international and domestic factors finally compelled Ottawa to seize the initiative in the mid-1960s. During the postwar years, Canadian representatives helped formulate the 1948 UDHR, a statement of general principles, and the UN Covenants on Civil and Political Rights and Economic, Social and Cultural Rights, which spelt out the specifics of the UDHR principles. Unfortunately, fearful of challenging the premiers, Ottawa would not sign, ratify, or attempt to implement these instruments – that is, until the mid 1970s when international pressures became too embarrassing. This enabled Trudeau to place more pressure on the provinces. Once Quebec's Quiet Revolution got underway, increasingly powerful neo-nationalist and secessionist movements and political parties pressured successive Quebec governments to demand treaty-making powers in areas of provincial jurisdiction. This development proved most troubling for Ottawa, which was determined to protect Canada's sovereignty in international affairs.

The Trudeau government launched two unsuccessful rounds of mega-constitutional negotiations, 1968–71 and 1978–9, in order to obtain an entrenched charter of rights and freedoms, one that bound both states. An entrenched charter binding on both levels of government, Trudeau hoped, would assist Ottawa in signing, ratifying, and implementing UN covenants and conventions dealing with human rights. Following his return to office in 1980 and the defeat of the Quebec government in the May 1980 referendum, Trudeau's controversial third attempt at mega-constitutional politics succeeded, thanks to his astute political manoeuvring based on a keen understanding of Canadian society at large. The development during the 1960s and 1970s of a broadly based, well-organized, better-funded, urban middle-class human rights movement – one comprising civil and equality rights as well as minority rights – played a determining role in assisting the Trudeau government in cajoling recalcitrant premiers into supporting a national instrument of human rights and freedoms, one that reflected while expanding upon the international instruments of human rights.

NOTES

Special thanks to my research assistant, Irma Sirvinskaite, for her contribution in the collection and analysis of the voluminous sources involved in this most complex of topics. I am grateful to Barry Strayer for his very helpful insights and comments.

1 Bora Laskin, 'Some International Legal Aspects of Federalism: The Experience of Canada,' in *Federalism and the New Nations of Africa*, ed. David P. Currie (Chicago: University of Chicago Press, 1964), 413.

2 Maxwell Cohen, 'Human Rights: Programme or Catchall? A Canadian rationale,' *Canadian Bar Review* 46 (1968): 558–61. Pessimistic about a Charter, Cohen called for an integrated human rights program.

3 James B. Kelly, *Governing with the Charter: Legislative and Judicial Activism and Framers' Intent* (Montreal and Kingston: McGill-Queen's University Press, 2005).

4 Maxwell Cohen and Anne Bayefsky, 'The Canadian Charter of Rights and Freedoms and Public International Law,' *Canadian Bar Review* 61 (1983): 265–313.

5 Ross Lamberston, *Repression and Resistance: Canadian Human Rights Activists, 1930–1960* (Toronto: University of Toronto Press, 2005).

6 Margaret MacMillan, *Paris 1919: Six Months That Changed the World* (New York: Random House, 2001), 94–5.
7 *In re Regulation and Control of Aeronautics in Canada* (1931) [1932] A.C. 54.
8 *In re Regulation and Control of Radio Communication in Canada* [1932] A.C. 304.
9 Allan Gotlieb, 'The Changing Canadian Attitude to the United Nations Role in Protecting and Developing Human Rights,' in *Human Rights, Federalism, and Minorities*, ed. Allan Gotlieb, 19–22 (Toronto: Canadian Institute of International Affairs, 1970).
10 *References re The Weekly Rest in Industrial Undertakings Act, The Minimum Wages Act and The Limitation of Hours Act*, [1936] S.C.R. 461.
11 For a full analysis of the crisis created by the treaty-implementation legislation and subsequent legal cases, consult John T. Saywell, *The Lawmakers: Judicial Power and the Shaping of Canadian Federalism* (Toronto: University of Toronto Press, 2002), 203–5.
12 *A.G. Canada v. A.G. Ontario*, [1937] A.C. 326, known as *Labour Conventions* case.
13 Saywell, *The Lawmakers*, 226–37.
14 F.R. Scott, 'The Privy Council and Mr Bennett's "New Deal" Legislation,' *Canadian Journal of Economics and Political Science* 3 (1937): 238-41; F.R. Scott, 'Constitutional Adaptations to Changing Functions of Government,' *Canadian Journal of Economics and Political Science* 11, no. 3 (August 1945): 329–41.
15 H.F. Angus, 'The Canadian Constitution and the United Nations Charter,' *Canadian Journal of Economics and Political Science* 12, no. 2 (May 1946): 133.
16 James Eayrs, 'Canadian Federalism and the United Nations,' *Canadian Journal of Economics and Political Science* 16 (1950): 173–7.
17 Ibid., 179–80.
18 Ibid., 182–3.
19 Gotlieb, 'The Changing Canadian Attitude,' 26–31. On the rationale for a 'federal-states' clause, consult Max Sörensen, 'Federal States and International Protection of Human Rights,' *American Journal of International Law* 46 (1952): 195–218.
20 Adam Chapnick, *The Middle Power Project: Canada and the Founding of the United Nations* (Vancouver: UBC Press, 2005).
21 William A. Schabas, 'Canada and the Adoption of the Universal Declaration of Rights,' *McGill Law Journal* 43, no. 2 (1998): 403–41.
22 Gotlieb, 'The Changing Canadian Attitude,' 38–40.
23 F.R. Scott, 'Dominion Jurisdiction over Human Rights and Fundamental Freedoms,' *Canadian Bar Review* 27, no. 5 (May 1949): 497–505, 531–3.
24 Ibid., 508–11.

25 Ibid., 511–33.

26 Ibid., 533–6.

27 F.R. Scott, 'The British North American Act (No. 2), 1949,' *University of Toronto Law Journal* 8 (1949–50): 206.

28 F.R. Scott, 'Centralization and Decentralization,' *Canadian Bar Review* 29 (1951): 1113.

29 G.J. Szablowski, 'Creation and Implementation of Treaties in Canada,' *Canadian Bar Review* 34 (1956): 28–36.

30 Section 132 states, 'The Parliament and Government of Canada shall have all Powers necessary or proper for performing the Obligations of Canada or of any Province thereof, as Part of the British Empire, towards Foreign Countries arising between the Empire and such Foreign Countries.'

31 Szablowski, 'Creation and Implementation of Treaties in Canada,' 37.

32 Ibid., 38–40.

33 Ibid., 42–8.

34 Ibid., 49–58.

35 James McLeod Hendry, *Treaties and Federal Constitutions* (Washington: Public Affairs, 1955). He recommended that s. 132 be amended to grant Parliament 'all the necessary implementing powers, subject again to judicial control, and that should it be deemed that the legislation in fact amends the Constitution, the legislation is invalid' (180).

36 F.H. Soward, 'External Affairs and Canadian Federalism,' In *Evolving Canadian Federalism*, ed. A.R.M. Lower and F.R. Scott, 126–60 (London: Cambridge University Press, 1958).

37 Cathal J. Nolan, 'The Influence of Parliament on Human Rights in Canadian Foreign Policy,' *Human Rights Quarterly* 7 (1985): 378.

38 Laskin, 'Some International Legal Aspects of Federalism,' 402.

39 Ibid., 403; Gotlieb, 'The Changing Canadian Attitude,' 41–3.

40 Laskin, 'Some International Legal Aspects of Federalism,' 404–6; F.R. Scott, 'Federal Jurisdiction over Labour Relations – A New Look, *McGill Law Journal* 6 (1960): 153.

41 Gotlieb, 'The Changing Canadian Attitude,' 43–4.

42 Laskin, 'Some International Legal Aspects of Federalism,' 408–11, quotations 408, 410.

43 Ibid., 412.

44 Gotlieb, 'The Changing Canadian Attitude,' 45–6.

45 For an overview, consult Dale C. Thomson, *Jean Lesage & the Quiet Revolution* (Toronto: Macmillan, 1984), chap. 20, 'International Ventures.'

46 J.F. Bosher, *The Gaullist Attack on Canada, 1967–1997* (Montreal and Kingston: McGill-Queen's University Press, 1999), 22–37.

47 Thomson, *Jean Lesage*, 436–7.

48 Jacques-Yvan Morin, 'La conclusion d'accords internationaux par les provinces canadienne à la lumière du droit comparé,' *Annuaire canadien de Droit international* 3 (1965): 173–5, 181.

49 Thomson, *Jean Lesage*, 437–8.

50 Ibid., 440–52.

51 Morin, 'La conclusion d'accords internationaux, 127–44.

52 Ibid., 144–73.

53 Ibid., 179–86.

54 J. Brossard, A. Patry, and E. Weiser, *Les pouvoirs extérieurs du Québéc* (Montreal: Presses de l'Université de Montréal, 1967).

55 Bora Laskin, 'The Provinces and International Agreements,' in *Background Papers and Reports*, Ontario Advisory Committee on Confederation (Toronto: Queen's Printer, 1967), 1:105.

56 Ibid., 108. The federal position was supported by Gérald La Forest, 'May the Provinces Legislate in Violation of International Law?' *Canadian Bar Review* 39 (1961): 78–91.

57 Ibid., 107–13.

58 Paul Martin, *Federalism and International Relations* (Ottawa: Queen's Printer 1968), 15.

59 Ibid., 30–42, 44–5.

60 Ibid., 29–30, 45–6.

61 Mitchell Sharp, *Federalism and International Conferences on Education* (Ottawa: Queen's Printer, 1968).

62 Quebec, Ministère des affaires intergouvernemental, 'Working Paper on Foreign Relations,' submitted to the Constitutional Conference Continuing Committee of Officials, 5 February 1969.

63 Ronald G. Atkey, 'Provincial Transnational Activity: An Approach to a Current Issue in Canadian Federalism,' in *Background Papers and Reports*, 2:153–88; R.J. Delisle, 'Treaty-Making Power in Canada,' in *Background Papers and Reports*, 2:115–47.

64 Edward McWhinney, 'Canadian Federalism: Foreign Affairs and Treaty Power,' in *Background Papers and Reports*, 2:118–19.

65 Ibid., 119–42.

66 Pierre Elliott Trudeau, 'Toward a Constitutional Bill of Rights,' *Canadian Forum* (October 1967): 158–9; and Trudeau, *A Canadian Charter of Human Rights* (Ottawa: Queen's Printer, 1968).

67 Lester B. Pearson, *Federalism for the Future: A Statement of Policy by the Government of Canada; The Constitutional Conference, 1968, Ottawa, February 5, 6 and 7* (Ottawa: Queen's Printer, 1968).

68 Pierre Elliott Trudeau, *The Constitution and the People of Canada: An Ap-*

proach to the Objectives of Confederation, the Rights of People and the Institutions of Government (Ottawa: Queen's Printer, 1969), 4.

69 Any new division of powers, sections 91 and 92, should strengthen the economic union and 'enable the Parliament of Canada to contribute to the social and cultural development of the country' (ibid., 10). In his initial discussion of a Charter, Trudeau showed greater concern with provincial jurisdiction over equality rights and suggested that a staged implementation process might be needed. *A Canadian Charter of Human Rights*, 116–17.

70 Trudeau, *The Constitution and the People of Canada*, 6.

71 Michael D. Behiels, 'Pierre Elliott Trudeau's Legacy: The Canadian Charter of Rights and Freedoms,' in *The Canadian Charter of Rights and Freedoms: Reflections on the Charter after Twenty Years*, ed. Joseph Magnet, Gerald A. Beaudoin, Gerald Gall, and Christopher Manfredi, 139–73 (Toronto: Butterworths, 2003).

72 Trudeau, *The Constitution and the People of Canada*, 14, 16, 18, 20, 22.

73 Ibid., 10, 12.

74 Walter Tarnopolsky, *The Canadian Bill of Rights* (Toronto: Carswell, 1966); 'Why Canada Must Have a Charter of Human Rights,' *Globe and Mail*, 4 March 1968.

75 Louis Sabourin, 'Le Fédéralisme et les conventions internationales des droits de l'homme,' in *Human Rights, Federalism and Minorities*, ed. Allan Gotlieb (Toronto: CIAA, 1970), 67–70.

76 Ibid., 86–91.

77 Ibid., 79.

78 Ibid., 99–100.

79 Ibid., 105–7.

80 Trudeau, *The Constitution and the People of Canada*, Appendix, 46–86.

81 Peter Russell, *Constitutional Odyssey: Can Canadians Become a Sovereign People?* 2nd ed. (Toronto: University of Toronto Press, 1993), 75.

82 Richard Simeon, *Federal-Provincial Diplomacy: The Making of Recent Policy in Canada* (Toronto: University of Toronto Press, 1972).

83 Russell, *Constitutional Odyssey*, 75.

84 Canada, Special Joint Committee of the Senate and the House of Commons on the Constitution of Canada, *Final Report* (Ottawa: Queen's Printer, 1972), 1–101. Co-Chairs: Gildas L. Molgat and Mark MacGuigan.

85 Paul Fox, ed., *Politics: Canada*, 4th ed. (Toronto: McGraw-Hill Ryerson, 1977), 22–32.

86 Russell, *Constitutional Odyssey*, 85–91; Edward McWhinney, *Quebec and the Constitution 1960–1978* (Toronto: University of Toronto Press, 1979), 49–51;

Michel Vastel, *The Outsider: The Life of Pierre Elliott Trudeau* (Toronto: Macmillan of Canada, 1990), 174–8.

87 Canada, *Final Report*, 1–26.

88 Ibid., 68–9.

89 Barry Strayer, memo to author, 20 June 2007. Mr Strayer was the senior justice person involved in the preparation of Canada's First Report.

90 Nolan, 'The Influence of Parliament,' 379.

91 Hugo Fischer, 'The Human Rights Covenants and Canadian Law,' *Canadian Yearbook of International Law* (1977): 46–5; Egon Schwelb, 'Entry into Force of the International Covenants on Human Rights and the Optional Protocol to the International Covenant on Civil and Political Rights,' *American Journal of International Law* 70 (1976): 511–19.

92 Barry Strayer, memo to author, 20 June 2007.

93 Cathal J. Nolan, 'The Human Rights Committee,' in *Human Rights in Canada's Foreign Policy*, ed. Robert O. Matthews and R. Cranford Pratt (Montreal and Kingston: McGill-Queen's University Press, 1988), 107–9.

94 Barry Strayer, memo to author, 20 June 2007. Mr Strayer, as an ADM in the Justice Department, was responsible for the development of the Act beginning in 1973.

95 Cited in ibid., 110; Canada, Secretary of State for External Affairs, *International Covenant on Civil and Political Rights: Report of Canada on Implementation of the Provisions of the Covenant* (Ottawa: Secretary of State, 1979).

96 Fischer, 'Human Rights Covenants and Canadian Law,' 72–83.

97 Behiels, 'Pierre Elliott Trudeau's Legacy,' 153–5.

98 Michael D. Behiels, 'Premier Peter Lougheed, Alberta and the Transformation of Constitutionalism in Canada, 1971–1985,' in *Forging Alberta's Constitutional Framework*, ed. Richard Connors and John Law (Edmonton: University of Alberta Press, 2005), 433–4.

99 *Re Resolution to Amend the Constitution* [1981 1 S. C. R. 753].

100 Behiels, 'Pierre Elliott Trudeau's Legacy,' 155–8.

101 Canada, Department of Justice, *A Consolidation of the Constitution Acts 1867–1982* (Ottawa: Ministry of Supply and Services Canada, 1989), 57–80.

102 The Supreme Court, in *Baker v. Canada* [1999] 2 S.C.R. 817, ruled that Canada's *Immigration Act* should be interpreted consistently with the UN *Convention on the Rights of the Child*, which the Canadian government had signed but was never legislated by the federal or provincial governments.

7 Cars, Conflict, and Cooperation: The Federalism of the Canadian Auto Industry

DIMITRY ANASTAKIS

The automobile is a central fact of modern Canadian life. Few Canadians can imagine their world without the ubiquitous and pervasive influence of the car, and all it represents. The automobile industry that builds these cars, too, is a central fact of the Canadian economy. The early twenty-first century auto sector is Canada's leading employer, its largest exporter (and importer), and unquestionably the country's most important economic sector.[1] At the same time, while Canadians might be hard-pressed to imagine a world without cars, imagining a world without the auto industry itself is all too easy – and all too dismal, given the thousands of jobs at stake and importance of the sector upon Canada's economy.

Federalism is also a central fact of modern Canadian life. For the vast majority of Canadians, federalism is far less tangible than the automobile or its industry, yet just as pervasive in its reach and impact. Indeed, the interaction of federal and provincial governments (and increasingly, municipal governments) shapes our society and the way we understand it in fundamental ways. Federalism, of course, influences the economy through the jurisdictional consequences of road building, or trade issues, or labour issues, and a host of other matters. It is much more than some abstract recitation of sections 91 and 92 of the British North America Act.

The interaction of the Canadian automotive industry and Canadian federalism brings together these two central facts. This essay examines, in broad terms, the role that the automotive industry has played within Canadian federalism from the beginnings of the sector to the present. In doing so, the article makes two main arguments. The first is that the changing nature of the federalism of the automotive industry can be explained in three very broadly defined periods. Each period is characterized by intra-state conflict, consensus, and interstate cooperation, respectively. Certainly there are exceptions to these different themes, but this overarching survey makes the case that the auto industry's relationship to federalism can best by seen by specific episodes within these periods. This episodic approach also allows us to understand the transformations between each of these broader periods.

The first period, before the Second World War, was marked by intra-state conflict, largely over the question of the tariff and the automobile. This was essentially a conflict of regionalism, which mirrored the tariff debate more generally, and was reflected in the political fight between Liberals, Progressives, and Conservatives, which reached a crescendo in the 1920s. In an era when automotive consumption and production were utterly intertwined through the tariff, the battle over auto tariffs during the Roaring Twenties became a political fight between a consuming West and the producing East. As an intra-state battle, this fight took place almost exclusively within the federal sphere of national politics between federal parties and politicians, and was eventually eased by a shift in automotive tariffs, which again mirrored the broader intra-state responses to regional unhappiness about protectionism.

The period after the Second World War was one of consensus on the auto sector. In an era marked by prosperity for consumers and producers alike, with little concern over tariffs, and a general golden age in the North American auto sector, there were few instances of conflict either within the federal arena or between governments over the industry. The consensus from both levels from government was to leave well enough alone, and the period was one of inactivity when it came to auto policy-making (in sharp contrast with federal-provincial conflict in other areas, such as social policy or fiscal federalism). Governments did not wish to rock the auto sector boat. However, by the end of the 1950s, with new difficulties emerging in the sector stemming from economic dislocation, technological challenges, and trade difficulties, this consensus was slowly breaking down.

The solutions to these difficulties ushered in a third era, one of interstate cooperation in the automotive field, beginning in the 1960s. Most importantly, the 1965 Canada-US Automotive Products Trade agreement – known as the Auto Pact – was pivotal in reshaping the federalism of the Canadian auto industry. The Auto Pact fundamentally altered the federal-provincial dynamic within the auto field. It also marked the emergence of sub-national governments as key players in industrial policy directed at the auto sector. Before 1965, the Ontario government was largely absent from questions surrounding the automotive industry, which it considered a tariff issue outside its jurisdiction. From 1965 onwards, interstate relations became paramount in the federalism of the auto sector: provincial governments – chiefly Ontario's – were players in the automotive field in a manner that they had never been before, and along with the federal government were central in automotive decision-making. This was especially true on the paramount issue of automotive investment. As a result of this altered dynamic, Ottawa and Ontario began to work together to ensure the health of the Canadian auto sector. The Auto Pact created a new strain of asymmetric interstate cooperation, largely focused on intergovernmental relations between the federal state and the Ontario government.[2]

This broader argument about the periodic evolution of the auto industry points to one other development that emerges in the examination of the federalism of the Canadian auto industry. The second argument this article makes concerns the growth of the state apparatus dealing with the auto industry, both provincially and federally. The emergence of this new strain of asymmetric interstate cooperation after 1965 created an extensive federal-provincial bureaucracy centred on the auto industry. The Auto Pact sparked its own quiet revolution in the growth, sophistication, and necessity for both federal and provincial apparatuses for dealing with the auto industry. The 1960s witnessed the emergence of a federal Department of Industry (1963), accompanied by growth in the Ontario Ministry of Economic Development and Trade in the 1970s. By and large, these growing Ottawa and Ontario state automotive apparatuses worked in cooperation to address questions within the automotive field, from nurturing the Auto Pact, to cross-border competitions for auto investment, to periodic crises within the industry, such as the Chrysler bailout.[3] The historic development of this automotive bureaucracy at both the federal and Ontario level remains central to understanding the recent successes in attracting investment to Canada's automotive heartland.[4]

Given the importance and centrality of the automotive sector in Canadian development over the course of the twentieth century, social and economic historians have examined many issues related to cars and their industry.[5] Much of this work, however, has looked at the period before the Second World War, when the automobile's influence was first being felt. Most notable is the work of Tom Traves, who has explored the political economy of the tariff, with particular attention to the auto industry.[6] While this paper considers the pre-war period, it adds to our understanding of the federalism of the auto industry by closely examining the transformations that have occurred since the 1940s. In doing so, the paper attempts to take a broad survey of the issue, as opposed to the micro-histories of the political economy of the more recent Canadian auto industry.[7]

Finally, owing to the vastness of the auto sector and its connections with so many central questions of Canadian history, the article considers only a few episodes that are central to the industry's role and interaction within Canadian federalism. As such, it does not, for instance, examine in any detail, the period around the two World Wars, during which auto companies boosted war-related production or were drafted for wartime purposes. Nor does the paper examine many important business, labour, technological, political, or social aspects of the automotive industry in Canadian life. There are many elements to the larger story, but it is not the purpose of this paper to detail all the aspects of the industry during these tumultuous times. The focus is thus on utilizing particular episodes to understand the broad sweep of the industry's role as a factor in Canadian federalism.

A 'Creature of the Tariff': Intra-State Conflict in the Canadian Auto Sector, 1904–30

The auto industry in Canada emerged, in the words of historian Tom Traves, as 'a creature of the tariff.'[8] Conservative Prime Minister John A. Macdonald's 1879 National Policy of tariff protection predated the auto industry, but was the key element in the creation of an auto sector. An 1897 tariff rate of 35 per cent on carriages, the auto industry's closest precursor, set the mould for the auto trade. As in so many other industries, the policy was designed to ensure that a high tariff wall would protect the Canadian industry from imports, and perhaps nurture some local, infant, auto makers. As a result, in the first few pioneering years of the auto industry, a number of indigenous attempts to create a viable Canadian motor car company emerged, but most failed. Canadian firms often lacked technological capabilities, were short on capital, or were simply unable to sell enough of their product in such a small, scattered, and poorly linked market.[9] Even with the high protection of 35 per cent, Canadian companies were hard-pressed to remain solvent. A few Canadian firms attempted to survive by importing cheaper American parts, since the 30 per cent duty was less than that for completed autos. But by 1921 the last of these, Gray-Dort, was out of business after its American parts-maker had closed its doors. By the late 1920s, there were no strictly Canadian-owned concerns left in the industry.[10]

The inability of the tariff to suckle a precarious Canadian-owned auto sector to life did not represent the end of a Canadian auto industry, however. While Canadian automotive ventures met with near-universal failure, this was not the case for the branch plant operations of US companies, set up in Canada to circumvent the tariff.[11] Canada, or more specifically, southern Ontario, had the good fortune to be located adjacent to the emerging 'motoropolis' of Detroit. The archetypal story of Henry Ford and Michigan's pivotal place in the creation of the mass automotive industry and market is well known.[12] Canada's place in that story is becoming better known, especially the role of Gordon McGregor and the Ford Motor Company of Canada, among others.[13]

Canada's automakers were staunch protectionists.[14] When the tariff was threatened, as it was during the 1911 federal election, automakers led their own insurrection against free trade, in conjunction with Toronto industrialists.[15] Wilfrid Laurier's agreement with the Americans generated responses such as the front page *Globe* letter to the editor by R.S. McLaughlin, whose company, McLaughlin Motors, would eventually become General Motors (GM) of Canada. McLaughlin 'did not support reciprocity.' 'I believe', wrote the automaker, 'from a national as well as a local viewpoint that when this pact is worked out to its ultimate completion, that it is anti-Canadian, and entirely opposed to the best interests of Canada's national life and welfare.'[16] In 1911, free trade was defeated, to the relief of automakers, if not their customers.

After the war there were quite a few more customers, however, especially in the West. With the impact of Laurier's boom finally being felt, the West grew by leaps and bounds, and this growth was in many ways tied up in the automobile, as much as the railway. Farmers in the West were among the earliest adapters and most committed auto users. In sprawling Saskatchewan, for instance, Model T Fords were ideal for work on the farm or getting products to town or market. By the early 1920s, Saskatchewan boasted the highest per capita ownership of automobiles in Canada, and one of the highest rates of automobile ownership anywhere in the world.[17] Ontario might have been the heart of the automobile industry, but the booming Prairie West was the heartland of the Canadian car-buying public.[18]

This new generation of Westerners, proud of their accomplishments and growing numbers within the federation, were determined to challenge the regional unfairness of protectionism.[19] Automobiles were protected under the tariff while Western wheat was not, and became a daily reminder of the injustices of the federal system. Westerners drove their costly Canadian-built cars to political meetings where they agitated against the banks, the interests, and the manufacturing East – whose greatest industrial facility was Ford's Windsor plant, the British Empire's largest by 1921. Automobiles exacerbated the existing regional conflicts over protectionism, and the battle over the tariff – particularly the auto tariff – became a dominant theme of 1920s federal politics.[20]

The auto tariff battle was largely fought out within the federal House of Commons, and reflected an attempt to mitigate the regional differences over the tariff within the federal sphere. The chief actors in this episode of automotive federalism were the Progressives and Mackenzie King, with the Conservatives playing the role of automotive-building Ontario's defender, as the party of protection. The Progressives represented mostly Westerners (and consumers in general, they argued) who were tired of the tariff, and targeted automobiles as a particularly odious example of protectionism.[21] Mackenzie King, on the other hand, walked the fine line in bringing the Progressives along (famously calling them 'Liberals in a hurry'), attempting to remain true to traditional free trade Liberalism while slowly whittling down the tariff.

The main phase in this intra-state regional battle occurred after the election of 1925. Although Mackenzie King's Liberals had been returned with a bare majority in 1921, for the first time in Confederation a 'third party' graced the halls of Parliament. The Progressives, born in the fires of Western protest, emerged as a significant force, and were keen to exact changes to the tariff, and to the auto tariff in particular. With fifty MPs in 1921, the Progressives could do little but rail at Mackenzie King to lower tariff rates.[22]

But the election of 1925 changed the dynamic dramatically. Although the Progressives had been reduced to twenty-four members, the party actually held the balance of power, as King's, and Canada's, first minority government teetered on the brink. The Progressives' leading speaker on the issue was G.G. Coote of Alberta, whose anti–auto tariff admonitions had been ignored in the last Parliament. He had railed against the obscene profits being made by automakers, most of which were finding their way into their American stockholders' pockets, and the fact that the auto was no longer a luxury, but a necessity. But most importantly, Coote emphasized the plight of farmers, who needed autos to survive: 'It is impossible,' argued Coote, 'for a railway company to build railways within ten miles of our settlers, and any man who had to haul his wheat, his cream and all his produce to market is certainly in need of a motor truck.'[23] Ignored in the last session of Parliament, Coote was now being listened to by Liberals, fearful of their shaky position.

This essentially regional debate was pushed not only by Western Progressives, but also fermented by the largely Ontario-based Conservatives. Tory Raymond Morand, representing East Essex, where the Ford company's sprawling facilities were located, was clear in his position: he could not be expected 'to be very enthusiastic' to the idea of lowering the duty on autos. Ontario jobs would be wiped out if the auto tariff were lowered, allowing the massive American industry to export to Canada undisturbed. Moreover, Morand had 'listened during this session to a discussion of Maritime rights and to the Western lament, and after listening to them both for a long time began to wonder whether we in central Canada had any rights at all.' When it came to the auto tariff, Ontarians, Morand argued, 'have some small right at least, and they should be protected.'[24]

Out of this sectional fight, Mackenzie King and the Liberals attempted to forge a compromise. In an effort to keep the Progressive rump onside, the 1926 James Robb budget created a new auto tariff schedule. Instead of a general 35 per cent rate, the auto tariff was made dependent on the price of cars. Autos priced at $1,200 and under would have a general rate of 20 per cent, while those valued at $1,200 and over would have a tariff of 27.5 per cent. Thus, the effective general rate became 26 per cent when added excise taxes were factored in.[25] King also agreed to create a non-partisan tariff board, which was intended to de-politicize the issue of tariffs. These measures were designed to placate anti-tariff Progressives and to also still provide some measure of protection for the automakers.

In this sense, the Western insurrection of G.G. Coote and his Progressive colleagues was successful. As Robb told the House of Commons, the new tariff structure recognized that there was 'a pronounced sentiment throughout Canada that the automobile industry enjoys more protection than is needed to maintain it on a reasonably profitable basis.'[26] At the same time, the Robb measures had made only a small dent in the industry's protection. In typical King fashion, the Liberals had attempted to placate both Western consumers and Eastern producers.

Instead, King's compromise provoked a tremendous backlash from Ontario automakers and their political patrons. In the House, Conservative leader R.J. Manion decried the new tariff structure as an attack on democracy. Since more Canadians, 'with the exception probably of those in the Prairie provinces,' had voted for the Conservatives and protection in the 1925 election, 'this government is not in agreement with the people of Canada generally, and you may take it for granted as a political axiom that when a government differs from the people of a country, the people are right and the government is wrong.'[27] Ontario Conservative Hugh Guthrie was even more sharp in his sectional attack on the plan: 'Speaking for the province of Ontario,' he declared, 'I say that we are a great industrial province; we have a tremendous force of organized labour in this province, and we know where the labouring men stand in regard to the question of reduction of duty.'[28]

Guthrie's words were soon transformed into actions. A day after the new tariff measures were announced, GM closed its massive plant in Oshawa, and sent out all the workers. A few days later, representatives of over two hundred auto and parts manufacturers met in Toronto, from where they sent a deputation to Ottawa, over three thousand strong and led by Oshawa's mayor, to protest the changes.[29] King was not swayed by the automakers' protests. The precarious prime minister thought the GM plant closing 'all a bluff,' and felt that the pro-tariff Ottawa march would have been surpassed if deputations had been sent out asking those in favour of the changes to come to the capital.[30]

The tariff changes and the Robb budget of 1926 both passed, and a tariff board was eventually created.[31] These measures did not stop King's government from falling on the infamous Beauharnois scandal, but they did reflect efforts to alleviate regional strains by the federal government. For now, Canadians had worked within the bounds of a strained federal system to work out an uneasy compromise over the issue of automotive tariffs. For most of the next two decades, the auto issue would recede into the background, as Canadians battled the Great Depression and fought a world war.

Consensus: Canada in the Golden Age of the North American Automobile, 1945–60

The late 1940s and 1950s were something of a golden age for the North American auto sector. During the Second World War, consumer products were restricted in order to meet the necessities of wartime output. But after the war, pent-up demand led to an automotive surge, as veterans returned, suburbs were built, and Canada's car and car-buying population exploded. By the late 1940s the Canadian auto industry was booming as it had been in the 1920s. Between 1946 and 1954 production of vehicles increased from 92,000 to 375,000. Employment in the industry increased as well, from 22,000 to 29,000.[32]

The post-war automotive production boom was fuelled by more than Canadian consumer demand. In the ten years between 1946 and 1955, the Canadian Big Three of GM, Ford, and Chrysler exported nearly 175,000 autos to Europe and parts of the commonwealth, as much of the globe recovered from the war. In Canada the number of plants increased and the value of the auto industry in terms of parts and vehicle production was the most significant industrial aspect of the Canadian economy. Labour problems, which had wracked the industry since the 1930s, had become much less prominent as auto workers gained the benefits of the well-functioning industry. The 'Treaty of Detroit,' which signalled this labour peace and automotive progress, reflected a period of consensus and prosperity in the sector, and the growth of Canada's middle class.[33] In the glow of the post-war boom the auto industry had become the cornerstone of the Canadian economy.

With widespread prosperity, the passionate automotive tariff battles of the pre-war period faded into the past, and there remained little regional or intra-state conflict over the operation of the industry. On the one hand, Canadian consumers continued to purchase cars in astronomical numbers. In 1950, there were fewer than two million cars registered in Canada; by 1960, that figure had more than doubled to over four million cars. By the late 1950s, Canadians were the second most enthusiastic users of cars on the planet, after Americans.[34]

On the other hand, the Canadian industry continued to operate relatively smoothly. The pre-war tariff schedule, which remained in place, had the effect of facilitating much Canadian production, though the cars made in Canada were usually significantly more expensive than their US equivalents. At the same time, the duty-free status granted to any parts of a 'class or kind' not made in Canada allowed the major manufacturers to import substantial quantities of expensive parts from their US parent firms. These major parts included main body stampings and complex transmissions, which were not built in Canada because the smaller Canadian economies of scale made such production prohibitively expensive. This tariff structure did not slow down the Canadian producers, who by the mid-1950s were still producing nearly half a million vehicles per year – double the pre-war high in the 1920s. Sales, production, employment, and exports all reached historic highs in the early and mid-1950s. The industry saw the expansion or building of dozens of new assembly and parts facilities, including the 1954 construction of Ford Canada's sparkling new headquarters just west of Toronto in Oakville, Ontario.[35]

Yet the Canadian auto industry faced serious structural challenges that began to emerge towards the end of the decade. These difficulties stemmed not from regional conflicts over the tariff as had characterized the pre-war period, but from the operation of the industry itself. Most prominent was the decline of export markets for Canadian producers. By the end of the decade, the export market had almost entirely dried up, as Europe's automakers (particularly those in Great Britain) re-emerged from the rubble of war. In 1952 Canadian firms had exported nearly eighty thousand vehicles; by 1959 this figure had declined dramatically to fewer than nineteen thousand.

At the same time, the number of foreign cars coming into Canada skyrocketed. This change was true not only of US auto imports (Canadian branch plants could import some makes that were not built in Canada duty-free), but also of imports from Great Britain, which had since 1936 entered Canada duty-free. In 1952, Canadians bought 38,000 foreign-built cars; in 1959 they bought 165,000.

There were also problems on the production side: Canadian plants could not produce the latest complex technologies, such as automatic transmissions, nor did they have the economies of scale to produce these new technologies effectively, even if they mastered the production methods.[36] When the inevitable cyclical downturn in the post-war economy occurred, as it did after 1958, the Canadian auto sector was particularly hard hit. The tariff structure and production model the industry operated upon was no match for the complexity of the modern automotive industry and the new challenges it faced.

Nor were the politicians or their state apparatuses capable of dealing with the modern realities of the auto sector. When the auto industry ran smoothly, as it had for more than a decade, governments paid little attention to it. But when things turned sour, governments, particularly the Ontario government of premier Leslie Frost, did not respond well. This became apparent in March 1958, in one of the few battles that the provincial government had with the industry. When a sudden spike in job losses in Windsor reflected the industry's downturn, Frost lashed out at the industry's apparent short-sighted management, focusing on Chrysler's employment practices. Frost felt that Chrysler had simply hired too many people, and too many people from outside the province (who would now need relief of some sort), and that the company should have seen the downturn coming. Frost's objection was 'not the fact that the auto manufacturers are not now able to employ all the people who had been engaged in motor vehicle production, but the fact that these people were hired a few years ago in what the auto industry should have recognized were excessive numbers.' In response, Chrysler President Ron Todgham challenged the notion that the company's moves were short-sighted and the assertion by Frost that the company 'collected people from all over the country in Windsor.'[37]

The premier betrayed his profound misunderstanding of the realities of the new industry. Canadian consumers demanded the full range of auto styles and models offered in the United States, which Canadian manufacturers attempted to meet. Yet Frost attacked the industry, in which, 'in a wild race to expand sales, many methods of sales enticement were used – scores of types and colours of cars, bigger and wider bodies and more horse power.' Unlike the car-buying public, Frost felt that 'these frills are not needed by the average car driver.' As a result, Frost continued, 'It should have been obvious to the auto industry that the pace of 1955 and 1956 could not be maintained forever and that when sales slackened, large numbers of workers in the motor vehicle and supplier industries would have been out of work. And this is exactly what has been happening.'[38] Frost's position reflected an unwillingness to engage the auto sector in thinking about ways to alleviate the structural problems of the industry, which were quickly becoming apparent. Canada's small-scale branch plants simply could not keep up with the demand of consumers, or the full model lines offered by their parent companies.

This disconnection between the Ontario government and the new automotive industry realities became plain in 1960, Frost's last year as premier. With employment falling and the sector's problems mounting, stakeholders within the industry pleaded for provincial government assistance. D.S. Wood, leader of the Automotive Parts Manufacturers Association of Canada (APMA), began a campaign to bring the auto issue more forcefully to the attention of the Ontario premier. Wood felt that the premier and 'members of the Ontario legislature would wish to be informed of this problem which is facing many of their constituents.'[39] Wood's admonitions were soon followed by those of auto advertising executive William Gent. Gent, a Conservative supporter, was forthright in his plea for help for the industry: 'It is obvious to me as I am sure it will be to you, that ... the in-roads made in the Canadian market of foreign made automobiles, trucks, and the necessary parts for their continued operation, have seriously affected not only employment in Canada, but basically employment in the Province of Ontario.'

Frost was not moved. The APMA's Wood and Gent attached a brief that outlined measures that the premier might take to alleviate the problems of the industry. They pleaded 'with the hope that our own Ontario government might not only agree with the brief ... but that you might lend the weight of the Provincial government to some means of a fair and more equitable tariff arrangement for Canadian industry and the Canadian worker.' The premier's response was coldly jurisdictional: Frost responded that 'most of the recommendations relate to the tariff structure, which, as you are aware, comes under the jurisdiction of the Federal Government.' With that, he dismissed the matter.[40]

Building a New Automotive State: The Auto Pact, 1961–78

Unlike Premier Frost and the government of Ontario, the federal government was far more responsive to the challenges faced by the changing automotive industry. Although he was unsuccessful in convincing Frost to aid the sector, auto parts lobbyist D.S. Wood also pursued Progressive Conservative Prime Minster John Diefenbaker. Diefenbaker was sensitive to the fact that the auto industry, because of the tariff, had always been seen as a 'federal issue.' Diefenbaker was also made sensitive to the issue by vocal representations of Canadian auto workers, the Canadian United Auto Workers Union (UAW), and the constant attacks he faced on the issue in the House of Commons from Liberal MP Paul Martin, who represented auto-dependant Windsor.[41]

Diefenbaker realized that something had to be done about the troubles in the sector. In 1960 he appointed Vincent Bladen of the University of Toronto to head a one-man royal commission. The Bladen Report, as it came to be known, resulted in a number of small steps to alleviate the structural problems in the industry. The most important of these was the creation of a duty-remission program to spur growth in the Canadian sector by providing tariff drawbacks on transmissions imported into Canada by GM, Ford, or Chrysler, if these companies boosted their exports of other parts.[42]

The Liberals, too, were keen to improve the auto industry, and took an even more interventionist approach than Diefenbaker after their electoral victory in 1963. Their initiatives began a process that resulted in nothing less than an entirely new regime for the Canadian auto industry, and the creation of a vibrant new automotive bureaucracy to oversee that regime. Under the aegis of activist ministers such as Walter Gordon and Charles Drury, these measures included the creation of the Department of Industry and an expansion of the Diefenbaker duty-remission plan to include all parts.[43]

Eventually these measures resulted in an entirely new policy: the 1965 Canada-US Automotive Products Trade Agreement, or Auto Pact. Negotiated under the threat of a trade war because of the adverse American reaction to the duty-remission programs (which shifted some Big Three purchasing to Canada from the United States), the Auto Pact created a new model of trade. It contained an element of protection for the Canadian industry sought by the Pearson government (local content requirements and production targets), and at the same time eliminated duties on the cross-border auto trade, which was sought by US negotiators, and the US Big Three. The Auto Pact heralded a new, borderless North American auto industry, one that proved to be immensely beneficial for the Canadian industry, which grew significantly in the years after 1965.[44]

The new approach by the Liberals towards auto policy was accompanied by a new bureaucratic apparatus to implement and oversee the operation of the Auto Pact. This emerging 'automotive bureaucracy' centred upon the new Department of Industry. To some degree, the department had been spun off from the interdepartmental 'Industry Committee,' which itself had emerged from an effort to examine the Bladen Commission in 1962. By 1963 many of the people who would direct government policy on the auto industry were working in other departments (mostly Finance and Trade and Commerce) and would take up temporary or permanent positions in Industry. Simon Riesman, for instance, was assistant deputy minister in finance until 1964, when he took over the auto negotiations and the position of deputy minister of industry. Initially led by Riesman, this dynamic cadre of civil servants worked to ensure a robust automotive sector from the 1960s onwards.[45]

Notwithstanding their vibrant approach to auto issues, the federal government's automotive strategy in the early 1960s also reflected the utter lack of communication between the two levels of government on the industry. All the automotive measures enacted by both the Diefenbaker and Pearson governments, including the Auto Pact itself, were initiated with virtually no communication between Ottawa and Queen's Park. Worse yet, even with the new regime created by the Auto Pact, both governments remained tied to a 'watertight compartments' view of the industry – that neither government could, or should, address auto sector issues outside of its jurisdiction.

This became abundantly clear when the Studebaker car company was in its final death throes in 1966. Studebaker, founded in 1897 and based in South Bend, Indiana, was one of the last surviving independent car companies. But by the 1960s the post-war auto industry required large capital expenditures, massive economies of scale, and costly product development. Without a large percentage of the market, independents such as Studebaker had trouble remaining profitable. Merging with Packard in 1954 had not helped, as poor quality, work stoppages, and cut-throat competition from the Big Three ravaged the company. By 1962 the company accounted for only 1.33 per cent of the American market and had not made a profit in years.[46]

In 1963 Studebaker ceased production in the United States and moved manufacturing operations to its plant in Hamilton, Ontario.[47] The plan was to give Studebaker some benefit in taking advantage of the Canadian remission plans, and the company's chief executive proudly proclaimed the emergence of a truly Canadian auto company. In reality the company's move north was a ploy to ensure that Studebaker avoided lawsuits from its over-extended network of dealers in the event of the end of production. It could do so because its Canadian subsidiary would continue even though production had ceased at the US parent plant.[48]

Even with the remission plans and the Auto Pact, Studebaker could not survive. By 1966, the company was on its last legs. In a final plea for help, Studebaker President Robert Growcock wrote to John Robarts, begging the Ontario premier to help the company by investing directly in the plant in order to save hundreds of jobs. Robarts was unmoved by the dying company's spokesman. In response, Robarts treated Growcock to the traditional federal-provincial jurisdictional brush-off: 'If anything in this connection is done, I should think the government at Ottawa should be the jurisdiction which is concerned.'[49]

Within ten years, however, Ontario's approach would utterly change from Robarts's jurisdictional indifference towards Studebaker. As one of the key auto-producing jurisdictions in North America, Ontario was now vulnerable to the vagaries of a continentalized auto industry under the Auto Pact regime. Initially, the Ontario government's response to the new automotive reality in North America was slower in coming than Ottawa's. But by the mid-1970s the province took a much more vocal and active role in the sector.

This was reflected by the activist approach of new Ontario premier Bill Davis after his election in 1971. As Davis represented Brampton in the provincial legislature, home to the American Motor Corporation's Canadian plant, he was keenly sensitive to automotive issues. As a result, the new premier ensured that Ontario's voice was heard during sensitive Canada-US discussion on the future of the Auto Pact: in 1971, when reports began to circulate that the federal government was considering changes to the agreement at the behest of the administration of Richard Nixon, Davis asked Prime Minister Pierre Trudeau 'not to yield to any pressures in this direction.' He also suggested that 'in view of the singular importance of these matters to the people of Ontario, representatives of my government would welcome an opportunity to participate in discussions.'[50] This was the first time that an Ontario premier had asked to have a direct say in auto industry matters.

Davis's newfound interest was accompanied by the growth of an Ontario automotive apparatus similar to the one that had emerged in Ottawa in the 1960s. By the early 1970s, it was clear to senior Ontario civil servants such as James Fleck that the province needed to build a capacity to deal with auto industry issues. Fleck, a former Harvard Business School and York University instructor, was appointed executive director of the Ontario government's new Committee on Government Productivity in 1969, with a mandate to streamline some of the industrial policy apparatus that emanated from Queen's Park. As a result, Fleck, with the support of Davis's Secretary to Cabinet Edward Stewart (who himself was from Windsor – his father had worked in the auto industry), worked to secure new personnel and authority to expand the provincial state's auto capacity.

Eventually centred in the Department of Industry and Tourism, the emerging automotive node at Queen's Park drew personnel and expertise from other departments, notably Treasury. Treasury had up to this point provided most of the economic policy formulation impetus within the Ontario government. By the early 1970s, some of this impetus shifted to the Industry and Tourism node. In this way, Ontario mimicked the earlier development in Ottawa, where automotive personnel in the new Department of Industry were drawn from the Finance Department. In both governments, Finance and Treasury had each hitherto retained the main analytical and policy capacities for economic measures.[51] Now, each government's industry ministry was given more responsibility over automotive policy. Thus, the 1978 appointment of Lynton Wilson as deputy minister of industry was, in a sense, history repeating itself along federal-provincial lines. In much the same way that Reisman was appointed deputy minister of industry in Ottawa at the start of the Auto Pact negotiations and era, Wilson took the helm of Ontario's own nascent automotive mandarinate as it was about enter a dynamic new phase, one that changed the federalism of Canada's automotive industry profoundly.

Cooperation: Inter-State Collaboration, 1978–2005

A new cooperative approach exhibited by the federal and Ontario governments towards the auto sector after 1978 reflected the growing importance of the Canadian auto industry under the Auto Pact regime. By the mid-1970s, automotive production in Canada had grown spectacularly. In 1965, Canada had produced 853,000 vehicles. By 1976, production had doubled to 1.6 million vehicles, nearly 80 per cent of which were exported south of the border.[52] Exports, imports, and employment had all increased significantly from the pre–Auto Pact era. The auto sector had come to represent the single most important industry in the Canadian economy. As such, governments in both Ottawa and Toronto were extremely sensitive to the operation of the industry. While there was no formal arrangement between the two governments on working together on auto issues, an emerging 'automotive cooperative federalism' can be seen by examining two important episodes.

The first episode marked one of the very first cases of locational competition over automotive investment in North America. With the Auto Pact regime, manufacturers could establish plants in any jurisdiction in North America and produce for the whole continent. This differed from the pre–Auto Pact period in that tariff barriers constrained production locales. Now, states and provinces competed for a plant that could build for all of North America. This dynamic meant that capital in the auto industry flowed 'beyond borders,' as one leading scholar of the new dynamic has termed it.[53] While Ontario was somewhat protected by the production guarantees contained in the Auto Pact, there was no guarantee that the province was assured new automotive investment.

In early 1978, the Ford Motor Company announced that it planned to build a new engine plant somewhere in North America. The company publicly stated that the plant could go to either Windsor, Ontario, or Lima, Ohio. As the Canadian auto sector had faced a downturn in the mid-1970s,[54] both the federal and Ontario governments were keen to advocate for the plant, as was Ford of Canada. During a meeting at the

Calgary Stampede that year, Davis, Trudeau, and Ford Canada President Roy Bennett agreed that the two governments should make a proposal to the company, with Ford Canada's support.[55] But, Ford argued, this pitch needed to be backed by significant incentives if Windsor was to beat out Ohio. Working together, the two governments' automotive bureaucracies hammered out a proposal to provide Ford with $68 million in incentives for the plant – $40 million from Ottawa, and $28 million from Queen's Park. Thus, out of the company's total investment of approximately $533 million for the Essex Engine Plant, the two governments had provided about 13 per cent of the money, or $26,000 for each of the 2,600 jobs generated.[56]

Ford's decision to build the Essex Engine Plant in Windsor represented a number of important outcomes. First, this was the first incident in which Canadian and US jurisdictions directly competed for auto investment by providing such significant subsidies. Ford had auctioned the plant to the highest bidder, and in doing so had created a precedent – auto investment was no longer constrained by national or sub-national boundaries, but drawn by government subsidies. As a result, the Essex plant precedent sparked severe US displeasure towards the bidding war, and the Ohio loss. In the wake of Ford's decision, in 1978–9 US officials unsuccessfully attempted to negotiate an agreement between Canada and the United States prohibiting investment incentives.[57]

Second, the decision marked a growing realization that investing in Canada was good under the Auto Pact regime: by 1978, the low Canadian dollar, lower health care costs, and higher productivity made Canadian locations attractive to companies such as Ford, even if it meant that their products were no longer 'made in the USA.' According to L.R. Wilson, the Ontario deputy minister of industry key to making the deal, the Ford investment put Ontario 'on the map.' Finally, the decision also reflected Ford's concerns in meeting its Auto Pact requirements in the future. Beyond the benefits associated with the incentive package and the Canadian cost advantages, Ford of Canada argued that not building the plant in Canada might mean that the company would miss its Auto Pact requirements, thus requiring payment in millions in duties.[58]

For this paper's purposes, the Ford decision represented a significant step in the creation of a cooperative automotive federalism between Ottawa and Toronto. Although the final amount each government was to provide was arrived at only after contentious negotiations, the Ford deal was pivotal in engaging the provincial and federal governments to work together to achieve auto investments. For the first time, auto experts from each government worked together to consummate an incentive package offer that was designed to build the Canadian sector.

The second important episode that reflects the new cooperation between the two levels of government is the somewhat more famous bailout of the Chrysler Corporation in 1979–80. Like other car makers, by the late 1970s Chrysler was buffeted by government regulations, high gas prices and interest rates, the penetration of cheaper and more fuel-efficient Japanese imports, and a cyclical downturn in the auto sector. As the smallest of the Big Three, Chrysler was less able to weather these problems than GM or Ford. The company also hurt itself by having poor-quality products, a dependence on large gas-guzzling vehicles, and unprofitable overseas operations. By 1979, the company lost $1 billion, owed $4 billion, and was bleeding market share and customers. In desperation, Chrysler hired Lee Iacocca, who pleaded for government loan guarantees to survive long enough to bring new products on the market.[59]

The Chrysler bailout differed in that the two levels of government worked together to provide an aid program, as opposed to the Ford incentive package of a year before. Nonetheless, this required the cooperation of both governments' automotive apparatuses, working together to develop a small but essential part of Chrysler's overall recovery plan. In the fall of 1979 and the spring of 1980, the two governments met on a number of occasions to determine their respective positions on Chrysler. In this case, for political reasons (federal ministers Herb Gray and Eugene Whelan both represented Windsor-area ridings, and pushed for the aid), Ottawa pledged aid first. The Ontario government, hoping to build the province's research and development capacity, held out to the last possible moment, necessitating a dramatic late-night meeting between government officials and Lee Iacocca in a Toronto hotel room in late 1979. Eventually, the federal government provided $200 million in loan guarantees, while Ontario agreed to co-fund a research facility with Chrysler.[60]

Conclusion

Clearly, the shift from intra-state conflict to interstate cooperation was marked by a number of key developments. First, continentalism in the auto industry has had the effect of strengthening interstate cooperation. The single most important factor in restructuring the federalism of the auto industry has been the advent of a continentally integrated North

American auto industry. The end of the tariff on autos, first through the 1965 Auto Pact and further enforced through the 1989 Canada-US Free Trade Agreement and 1993 North American Free Trade Agreement, fundamentally altered the relationship between the industry and the federal and provincial states. Before the Auto Pact, the discourse focused on intra-state regional battles between consumers and producers of automobiles. After the end of tariffs, auto issues engaged provincial governments (chiefly Ontario's) to work with the federal government in ensuring a healthy auto industry within a continentally competitive dynamic.[61]

A second factor is the growth and nature of state activism. Although these episodes illustrate the two governments' willingness to work together on auto files, there was not always a happy cooperation between the two. For instance, during the Chrysler bailout negotiations, the Ontario government held out in their talks with Ottawa, and refused to acquiesce to loan guarantees, which the federal government expected.[62] Yet this should not obscure the fact that there was cooperation nonetheless, and there continues to be so. The two automotive bureaucracies regularly meet and consult on a wide range of subjects and projects, from launching industry-government initiatives such as the Canadian Automotive Partnership Council (CAPC, in 2002), or simply to exchange information.[63] Just as importantly, the two governments have continued to work together to attract billions of dollars of automotive investment to Ontario.

Third, the context of the period under examination is significant. In the first period, federal intra-state conflict over autos fit within the broader framework of East-West regional conflict.[64] Similarly, in the second period, the automotive consensus reflected the general lack of conflict within Canadian federalism in the period. In the 1970s, auto cooperation fit within the context of broader Ontario-federal cooperation on a number of fronts, including energy, the constitution, and generally warm personal relations between Premier Davis and Prime Minister Trudeau. Although the early continentalization of the auto industry remains unique, as does the sector's pre-eminent place within North America's economy, the evolution of the federalism of the auto industry does not deviate dramatically from that of the broader story of Canadian federalism.

In charting the evolution of the federalism of the automotive industry, the article has examined the regionally based intra-state conflict that emerged over automotive tariff rates in the 1920s. The article then addressed the period from the Second World War into the 1950s, an era of consensus in the auto industry. Further, the paper explored the key shift in state policy towards the automotive industry, the creation of the 1965 Auto Pact and the new era of cooperation between the emerging federal and provincial bureaucratic apparatuses surrounding the operation of the auto industry. The creation of this 'automotive cooperative federalism,' and its emergence over the last three decades is essential to understanding both the mechanics of the auto industry itself, and the evolution of Canadian federalism in this central element of Canadian life.

NOTES

1 According to Industry Canada, the auto sector employs over half a million Canadians. http://strategis.ic.gc.ca/epic/internet/inauto-auto.nsf/en/Home

2 This dynamic was also present in Quebec, where a much smaller auto sector than Ontario's existed. This essay focuses upon Ontario, because the province's automotive sector is clearly preeminent within Canada.

3 A third argument, beyond the scope of this paper, also comes into view as a consequence of the emerging 'automotive bureaucracy.' The creation and expansion of federal and provincial state capacities to address the post-1965 dynamic was, at the same time, accompanied by a corresponding growth in the auto industry's own apparatus within the new Auto Pact framework. In the eras of intra-state conflict and consensus, industry leaders dealt directly with the federal government, and could expect little cooperation from Ontario. In the post-war period, especially after 1965, lobby groups such as the Motor Vehicle Manufacturers' Association (MVMA) or the Automotive Parts Manufacturers' Association (APMA), became more sophisticated and expanded their efforts to lobby both the federal and Ontario governments. The emergence of this growing 'automotive lobby' is another consequence of the evolution of the federalism of the auto industry.

4 In 2006 *Foreign Direct Investment* magazine awarded Ontario Premier Dalton McGuinty the title of 'Personality of the Year' for bringing $7 billion in new automotive investment to Ontario in 2003–6.

5 See, for instance, Robert E. Ankli and Fred Frederiksen, 'The Influence of American Manufacturers on the Canadian Automobile Industry,' *Business and Economic History* 9 (1981): 101–13; Gerald T. Bloomfield, 'No Parking Here to Corner: London Reshaped by the Automobile, 1911–61,' *Urban*

History Review 18, no. 2 (1989): 139–58; Stephen Davies, '"Reckless Walking Must Be Discouraged": The Automobile Revolution and the Shaping of Modern Urban Canada to 1930,' *Urban History Review* 18, no. 2 (1989): 123–38.

6 Tom Traves, *The State and Enterprise: Canadian Manufacturers and the Federal Government, 1917–1931* (Toronto: University of Toronto Press, 1979).

7 John Kirton, 'The Politics of Bilateral Management: The Case of the Automotive Trade,' *International Journal* 36 (1980–1): 36–69; James F. Keeley, 'Cast in Concrete for All Time? The Negotiation of the Auto Pact,' *Canadian Journal of Political Science* 16, no. 2 (June 1983): 281–98.

8 Traves, *State and Enterprise*, 101.

9 For views of the early Canadian auto industry, see Donald F. Davis, 'Dependent Motorization: Canada and the Automobile to the 1930s,' in *The Development of Canadian Capitalism*, ed. Douglas McCalla, 191–218 (Toronto: Copp Clark Pitman, 1990); O.J. McDiarmid, 'Some Aspects of the Canadian Automobile Industry,' *Canadian Journal of Economics and Political Science* 6 (February–November, 1940): 258–74; Tom Traves, 'The Development of the Ontario Automobile Industry to 1939,' in *Progress without Planning: The Economic History of Ontario from Confederation to the Second World War*, ed. Ian Drummond, 208–23 (Toronto: University of Toronto Press, 1987); Traves, *The State and Enterprise*, chap. 6, 'The Political Economy of the Automobile Tariff'; James G. Dykes, *Background on the Canada–United States Automotive Products Trade Agreement* (Toronto: Motor Vehicle Manufacturers Association, 1979). A non-academic view can be found in James G. Dykes, *Canada's Automotive Industry* (Toronto: McGraw Hill, 1970).

10 See Ankli and Frederiksen, 'The Influence of American Manufacturers.'

11 And to take advantage of Canada's imperial preferences. In the 1904–30 period of the Canadian auto industry, a major portion of production by American branch plant firms went to other imperial/commonwealth destinations. This was particularly true of Ford Canada, a company that exported and created its own branch plants around the world.

12 See, for example, Douglas Brinkley, *Wheels for the World* (New York: Viking, 2003).

13 On Canada's early branch plant auto industry, see Dimitry Anastakis, 'From Independence to Integration: The Corporate Evolution of the Ford Motor Company of Canada, 1904–2004,' *Business History Review* 78, no. 2 (Summer 2004): 213–53; David Roberts, *In the Shadow of Detroit: Gordon M. McGregor, Ford Canada and Motoropolis* (Detroit: Wayne State University Press, 2006); Heather Roberts, *Driving Force: The McLaughlin Family and the Age of the Car* (Toronto: McClelland and Stuart, 1995).

14 Although Roberts makes the case that Ford Canada founder Gordon Mc-

Gregor was unconcerned about the tariff issue (80), Ford Canada sought to retain tariffs. In the 1930s, when Henry Ford argued for free trade, and tariff reform threatened the company's protection, Ford Canada released a pamphlet, *Some General Aspects of the Canadian Customs Tariff, the National Economy, and the Automobile Industry in Canada* (Windsor: Ford Motor Company of Canada, 1938) defending the tariff.

15 For a view of the Toronto 18, see Robert Cuff's seminal article, 'The Toronto 18,' in *Ontario History* 57, no. 4 (1965): 169–80, originally written for John Saywell's senior seminar at the University of Toronto.

16 'Mr Robert McLaughlin's Letter,' Toronto *Globe*, 13 September 1911.

17 Davies, '"Reckless Walking Must Be Discouraged,"' 136.

18 Ford Canada recognized this reality by establishing a satellite plant in Winnipeg to assemble partially knocked down (PKD) Model Ts shipped from Windsor in 1922.

19 By the 1920s, the regional inequalities of the National Policy had produced political movements on both flanks of the country. Maritimers, incensed at central Canadians' neglect and mistreatment of their concerns, and fearful of a rapidly populating West, agitated for lower rail rates and the reinvigoration of Atlantic ports. This Maritime Rights movement was barely mollified by the King government, which created a royal commission in an attempt to address their concerns.

20 Kenneth Norrie and Douglas Owram criticize the National Policy and emphasize the regional inequalities that grew from the policy. See their *History of the Canadian Economy*, 2nd ed. (Toronto: Harcourt Brace Canada, 1996). Another famous critique of the National Policy came from economic historian J.H. Dales, who referred to John A. Macdonald as 'the first great Canadian non-economist' for attempting to build a wealthy country by lowering the standard of living of its population.' Dales, 'Canada's National Policies,' in *The Protective Tariff in Canada's Development* (Toronto: University of Toronto Press, 1956), 144, 146.

21 On the Progressives, see W.L. Morton, *The Progressive Party in Canada* (Toronto: University of Toronto Press, 1950).

22 At the end of the 1925 parliamentary session, on 16 March 1925, G.G. Coote, a Progressive member from the Alberta riding of Macleod, moved a motion in the Commons that read, 'That, in the opinion of this House, a substantial reduction should be made in the customs tariffs on automobiles and motor trucks.' The motion was defeated. Canada, *House of Commons Debates* (hereafter *Debates*), p. 1178.

23 *Debates*, 29 March 1926, p. 2001.

24 *Debates*, 29 March 1926, pp. 2006–7.

25 Reductions were also made to the intermediate and British preferential

tariff. *Debates,* 15 April 1926, p. 2450; McDiarmid, 'Some Aspects of the Canadian Automobile Industry, 261; Traves, *State and Enterprise*, 104. See figure 1.

26 *Debates,* 15 April 1926, p. 2450.

27 *Debates,* 20 April 1926, pp. 2626–7.

28 *Debates,* 15 April 1926, p. 2450.

29 *The Canadian Annual Review* 1925–6 (Toronto: Annual Review, 1927), 77.

30 Of the protest, in his diary Mackenzie King wrote, 'This has been a gala day. The Tories have been staging a huge demonstration from Oshawa against reduction of duties on automobiles, all kinds of dire prophecies made as to it storming the city etc. About 3,000 or more came in special trains …' After meeting 'as many of the deputation as possible, I think I succeeded in turning the whole business to our advantage.' *Mackenzie King Diary*, 23 April 1926, and *The Canadian Annual Review*, 1925–6, 77, J13, MG 26, LAC.

31 The rather impotent version of the Tariff Board created by King in 1926 was dismantled by R.B. Bennett in 1930. In 1936 the *Tariff Act* was significantly altered following an examination by a reconstituted Tariff Board. The new most-favoured-nation (MFN) tariff rate was 17.5 per cent for all autos and most parts. The most important change was the creation of a sliding scale for duty-free entry based on the amount of commonwealth (essentially Canadian) content a company was including in its production of cars. It also reduced the duties on imported British cars to zero.

32 Dominion Bureau of Statistics figures cited from Sun Life Assurance Company of Canada, *The Canadian Automotive Industry* (Ottawa: Sun Life, 1956), 3.

33 For the post-war labour issues surrounding the auto industry, see Sam Gindin, *The Canadian Auto Workers: The Birth and Transformation of a Union* (Toronto: Lorimer, 1995); Don Wells, 'The Impact of the Postwar Compromise on Canadian Unionism: The Formation of an Auto Worker Local in the 1950s,' *Labour/Le Travail* 36 (Fall 1995): 147–73; Charlotte Yates, *From Plant to Politics: The Autoworkers Union in Postwar Canada* (Philadelphia: Temple University Press, 1993).

34 Motor Vehicle Manufacturers' Association, *Annual 1971.*

35 On the operation of the post-war auto industry, and post-war automotive statistics, see V. Bladen's *Report on the Royal Commission on the Automobile Industry* (Ottawa: Queen's Printer, 1961), 101–4.

36 On the problems of the late 1950s Canadian auto sector, see the Bladen Commission *Report.*

37 R. Todgham, president of Chrysler Canada, to Frost, 6 March 1958, file 12-G, box 7, Leslie Frost Papers, RG 3-25, Archives of Ontario (hereafter AO). In responding to Frost, Todgham wrote, 'Premier, during these recent

years which form the basis of your criticism, our company has paid out in wages, salaries, and benefits an average of 16 million dollars *more* each year to sustain local employment and to maintain a high level of prosperity in this area, than was paid during the period prior to our expansion.'

38 Frost to Todgham, 10 March 1958, file 12-G, box 7, Leslie Frost Papers, RG 3-25, AO.

39 Wood to Frost, 12 May 1960; acknowledged by R.A. Farrell, executive officer to the premier, 17 May 1960, file 12-G, box 7, Leslie Frost Papers, RG 3-25, AO.

40 William Gent, president, Gent Advertising Limited, to Frost, 12 July 1960; Frost to Gent, 14 July 1960, file 12-G, box 7, Leslie Frost Papers, RG 3-25, AO.

41 On the Canadian UAW's approach towards the auto industry in this period, see Dimitry Anastakis, 'Between Nationalism and Continentalism: State Auto Industry Policy and the Canadian UAW,' *Labour/Le Travail* 53 (Spring 2004): 89–126.

42 On the Bladen Commission and the duty remission schemes, see Dimitry Anastakis, *Auto Pact: Creating a Borderless North American Auto Industry, 1960–71* (Toronto: University of Toronto Press, 2005), chap. 1.

43 *Debates*, May 16 1963, p. 7.

44 On the creation of the Auto Pact, see Anastakis, *Auto Pact*.

45 From 1963 onwards, there would be close interdepartmental cooperation among government officials on the auto issue, though the core of this group worked out of the industry department. Drury, the minister of defence production, became the first minister of industry. He was Finance Minister Walter Gordon's brother-in-law. N.B. Macdonald, director of the Mechanical Transport Branch, was listed in the organizational charts of both Industry and Defence Production, as were a number of other industrial sector branches. *McGraw-Hill Directory and Almanac of Canada* (Toronto: McGraw-Hill, 1967), 210–19; C.M. Drury, 'The Canadian Department of Industry,' *Addresses of the Empire Club of Canada: 1963–1964* (Toronto: Empire Club of Canada, 1964).

46 Donald T. Critchlow, *Studebaker: The Life and Death of an American Corporation* (Bloomington, IN: Indiana University Press, 1996), 131–40; Studebaker Corporation, *Annual Report for 1962*, 16 October 1962, Historical Collections, Baker Library, Harvard Business School.

47 'Studebaker Auto Making Ended Except in Canada,' 'Studebaker Corporation Traces Its Origin Back to 1852 and an Oak-Sided Wagon,' 10 December 1963, 'Canada Applauds Studebaker Move,' 16 December 1963, *New York Times*.

48 Gordon Grundy, president, Automotive Division, 'A Special Report on Canadian Automobile Manufacturing: Studebaker,' 13 December 1963, October 1963–May 1964, vol. 1, Department of Foreign Affairs and International Trade (hereafter DFAIT); Critchlow, *Studebaker*, 182.

49 Robert Growcock, president of Studebaker Canada, to Robarts, 17 March 1966, file: January 1966 to December 1966, box 350, John P. Robarts Papers, RG 3-26, AO.

50 William Davis to Pierre Trudeau, 14 October 1971. Trudeau wrote back, 'My colleague, the Minister of Industry, Trade and Commerce [Jean Luc-Pépin] welcomes this offer and I would suggest that you let him know the names of your reps who might meet with federal officials to discuss matters relating to the auto, so that specific arrangements can be made for appropriate consultations,' Trudeau to Davis, 5 November 1971. Both letters from Representations, 1964–1971, part 1, file 8705-04, vol. 5624, RG19, Library and Archives Canada (LAC).

51 Fleck eventually became secretary to the Cabinet in 1974, and was deputy minister of industry from 1976 to 1978. Treasury's Dennis DesRosiers was Ontario's first automotive analyst when he joined the government in 1974. He would go on to become Canada's leading private sector automotive analyst. Author's interview with Dennis DesRosiers, 1 August 2006; author's interview with L.R. Wilson, 27 June 2006.

52 *DesRosiers Automotive Yearbook 2000* (Richmond Hill, ON: DesRosiers, 2001), 114.

53 Kenneth P. Thomas, *Capital beyond Borders: States and Firms in the Auto Industry, 1960–94* (New York: Macmillan, 1997). For another view of the changes to the automotive investment regime, see David Lleyton-Brown, 'A Mug's Game? Automotive Incentives in Canada and the United States,' *International Journal* 35 (Winter 1979–80): 170–84.

54 The difficulties in the sector prompted the creation of another one-man royal commission to look at the industry, this time headed by Auto Pact negotiator Simon Riesman, in 1978.

55 Author's interview with L.R. Wilson, 27 June 2006.

56 Thomas, *Capital beyond Borders*, 115.

57 Minutes of Automotive Incentive Meeting, 3–4 May 1979, Washington, D.C., F3881-02, pt 4, vol. 5348, RG 19, LAC; 'Automotive Investment Incentives: Meeting with USA,' Washington Embassy to Ottawa, 7 May 1979, file 37-7-1-USA-2, vol. 39, Department of Foreign Affairs and International Trade.

58 For an insightful view of this episode, see Paul Weaver, *The Suicidal Corporation* (New York: Publisher, 1989), 34–8.

59 On Chrysler's difficulties in this period, see Charles Hyde, *Riding the Roller Coaster: A History of the Chrysler Corporation* (Detroit: Wayne State University, 2003).

60 On the Canadian story of the Chrysler bailout, see Dimitry Anastakis, 'Industrial Sunrise? The Chrysler Bailout, the State, and the Reindustrialization of the Canadian Automotive Sector, 1975–86,' *Urban History Review* 35, no. 2 (Spring 2007): 37–50.

61 This development also shows that while continentalism has pushed Ontario to become more of an economic 'region state' within North America, and loosened the bonds of federalism, there are instances where federal-Ontario cooperation has increased under continentalism. See, for instance, Thomas Courchene with Colin R. Telmer, *From Heartland to North American Region State: The Social, Fiscal and Federal Evolution of Ontario* (Toronto: Centre for Management, University of Toronto, 1998).

62 'Chrysler,' A.S. Rubinoff to Ian A. Stewart, 10 April 1980, part 7, file 8705-04-2, V5959, RG 19, LAC. 'Chrysler Canada,' J.D. Girvin to L.R. Wilson, 10 April 1980, file: Chrysler–1979, box DM, Acc. 22206, RG 9-2, AO.

63 The author can attest to this practice, as he was a member of the Automotive Office, Ministry of Economic Development and Trade, in the Ontario government from 2001 to 2002.

64 It should be noted, however, that the regionalism of automotive federalism is not entirely dead. Some Western observers complained that Ontario's auto plants were granted unfair exemptions under the federal government's plans to cut greenhouse gas emissions.

8 Ottawa, the Provinces, and the Evolution of Canadian Trade Policy since 1963

BRUCE MUIRHEAD

Let me begin with a proposition articulated by James Rosenau with which I agree, that politics is no longer happening in discrete spheres of governance – international and domestic. Rather, Rosenau suggests, there are intense political contests happening in the space *between* these spheres of governance. In short, 'politics is happening along the domestic-foreign frontier.'[1] This development presents a challenge to Canada's federal system, as it has been based upon the compartmentalization of responsibility and jurisdiction into what were conceived of as 'watertight' compartments. This certainly applies to the evolution of the country's trade policy since 1867, but more particularly, from the early 1960s.

The development and implementation of Canadian foreign economic policy is an area of responsibility stuck by the Fathers of Confederation, at least according to constitutional practice as well as in the popular mind, in the federal area of responsibility. Section 91(2) clearly delineated the trade and commerce power, while the British North America Act's residual clause, citing the federal responsibility for peace, order, and good government (POGG), was another weapon in Ottawa's arsenal to assert its will in this area, if such were ever needed. And there it remained for almost a century, as the provinces were more or less content to let Ottawa map out the main avenues of the country's foreign trade. Relatively speaking, when it came to trade issues, the provinces did not count for much.[2] That said, as Kim Richard Nossal has pointed out, the BNA Act did not, contrary to accepted wisdom, explicitly assign absolute responsibility over foreign affairs and foreign economic policy-making to Ottawa.[3] Nor did the 1982 patriation of the constitution change that fact. In an odd way that this chapter will discuss, this turned out to be a very grey and problematic area as Canada's international obligations became more encompassing. This play started off in slow motion in its first act in 1963, picking up speed as the decades passed and the plot developed.

A number of protagonists helped to write the general storyline. For example, the courts, but in particular the London-based Judicial Committee of the Privy Council (JCPC), the final court of appeal for Canada until 1949, contributed to what might be called confusion in this area.[4] It erred on the side of what became known as dual federalism, which allowed distinct communities to live independently, in watertight compartments, sealed off from one another and preserve their cultural traditions while enjoying the benefits of a larger political union. This is not what the Fathers of Confederation had had in mind when creating Canada out of four small colonies in 1867, but it was the spirit in which the JCPC interpreted the British North America Act.[5]

While dual federalism observed a sharp division and distinction between the domestic and the foreign, assigning the latter to the federal level, it is also true that at times the two collided in a confusing way. The 1937 *Labour Conventions* reference to the Privy Council established that the central authority could conclude treaties in Canada's name but that such treaties could not modify internal, provincial law. The implementation of a treaty must respect the distribution of legislative powers as defined by the BNA Act. Parliament could implement treaties relating to federal matters; if the substance of a treaty negotiated with a foreign country fell under provincial jurisdiction, provincial legislatures were responsible for implementing legislation.[6] And if they refused, the international treaty was, presumably, not applicable to that province! Ottawa could not enact legislation where provincial interest collided with foreign obligation.

That ruling, however, did not deter the federal government from becoming more activist in the pursuit of *Canadian* objectives. The Second World War changed the dynamic of Canadian federalism, and the government in Ottawa emerged in 1945 much the stronger. Provinces, it seemed, did not count for much, and for the next two decades it did not consult with them on trade matters or with respect to foreign affairs more generally, nor evince much concern about what they might have considered to be their interests in various General Agreement on Tariffs and Trade (GATT) negotiations, designed to reduce the incidence of tariff protection among contracting parties that began in 1947.[7] It was also true, however, that the provinces themselves did not intrude into trade policy. The fact that provincial interest largely coincided with federal in this area was fortuitous and made for constitutional peace, at least here.

Ottawa also had some support from the Supreme Court of Canada (SCC) after 1949. As the JCPC had tended to favour provincial rights, the SCC more often sided with the national government. For example, in maintaining the distinction between the two levels of government, in *Attorney-General Ontario v. Scott* (1956), the court ruled that international agreements between *provinces* and foreign governments were allowed only if they did not involve treaty obligations but 'merely reciprocal or concurrent legislative action.'[8] The future chief justice of the SCC, Bora Laskin, wrote in almost the mirror image of the *Labour Conventions* reference, 'If a province ... purported on its own initiative to make an enforceable agreement with a foreign state on a matter otherwise within provincial competence, it would either have no international validity, or, if the foreign state chose to recognize it, would amount to a declaration of independence ... [and] to a denial of the exclusive juridical competence of Canada as such in the field of foreign affairs.'[9] That position was untenable and had, of course, tremendous implications for trade and the possibility of independent negotiation with others on the part of provinces. Nor, despite the gentle drift of some judicial interventions in the pre-1970s world, has any provincial claim to independent treaty negotiation been recognized by Ottawa; the right remains specifically allocated to the latter.[10]

The relatively comfortable federal-provincial world that prevailed during the twenty-five years following the late 1940s, however, came to an end. As Canadians of a certain age will know, federalism and its practice became a contact sport as Toronto, Victoria, Edmonton, and Quebec City, among others, began to assert a position in certain jurisdictions that had formerly been the preserve of Ottawa, and vice versa. Over this period, provinces discovered that the practice of Canadian federalism, if they pushed the limits, allowed them greater flexibility to act against the desires of Ottawa if they so wished, even in areas that might be considered federal jurisdiction. By the 1970s, the evolution of Canada's federal structure made it mandatory for the federal government to at least consult with the provinces in reaching any trade agreement that might possibly interfere with the prosperity and happiness of voters who, while at one level were citizens of Canada, but at another were British Columbians, Nova Scotians, Ontarians, or Quebeckers. Moreover, the provinces began to demand it.

Further, as a new political and economic paradigm, neo-conservatism and globalization became the gospel, governments at both levels were forced to respond, and this has generally favoured Canadian provinces. As national governments have surrendered authority to supranational institutions, sub-national jurisdictions have gained in importance and relevance for international treaty making.[11] Hamish Telford has also correctly pointed out that, given this situation, 'the vertical model of dual federalism, in which the federal government assumes responsibility for international affairs and the provinces look after local affairs, ... no longer seems tenable.'[12] Leakage occurred, and in Canada, some provinces were not slow to take cognizance of that new reality, as will be seen below.

For their part, as Francois Rocher and Richard Nimijean have pointed out, given new international economic arrangements often of their own making, 'national governments must ... come to grips with the new conditions of governance: they must recognize that they no longer dispose of the same degree of political sovereignty. Their power to act is constrained by the nature of the new international political economy,' and into that partial vacuum the provinces could expand.[13] It is also true, however, that the national government is the one with which foreigners make their first contact. Ottawa is also the level that remains the focus of many citizens, tasked to solve many of the old problems continuing to plague Canada; paradoxically, then, and for the present, '[it] alone [has] the legitimacy.'[14] In Canadian federalism, it is all very confusing.

This chapter will address the practice of federalism, the development of Canadian trade policy, and how they have clashed and evolved to the point where now one could almost speak of co-responsibility. This area remains contentious, however, and change has come slowly, forced upon a reluctant federal government by ambitious and aggressive provinces. This paper will examine two examples of provincial intrusion into what had been solely federal jurisdiction to make that point: Canada's domestic strategy with respect to the 1970s GATT Tokyo round of negotiations, and the provincial role in the free trade discussions with the United States during the mid-to-late 1980s. These are critical to understanding the growing provincial interest where before there had been very little. What followed with the North American Free Trade Agreement in 1994, the Uruguay round of the General Agreement that resulted in the establishment of the World Trade Organization, and various softwood lumber disputes, merely add substance to the point made above.

The federal-provincial conference held in November 1963 marked the beginning of what might be called the modern era in Canadian constitutional meetings. By those attending, it was also called 'a landmark – the most important in [Canada's] history ... The conference was to decide the future of Canada.'[15] This was the first such meeting convened following the election victory of Lester Pearson and his Liberals in April 1963, when they had won a minority government. It also witnessed the first official use of the phrase 'cooperative federalism,' which was used to describe Canadian practice.[16] The communiqué suggested that 'the diversity of Canada creates unusual and differing problems which can be solved only by concerted federal-provincial action involving close and continuing consultation and cooperation between the two levels of government on all matters of common interest.' The new prime minister believed that the gathered premiers and his government could begin to write a new chapter in the book of Canadian federalism. As an indication of what he meant, he told the gathering that 'in one case – trade – the jurisdiction is specifically federal,' but it was also a national problem that intimately concerned the provinces.[17] He would involve them more in trade negotiations, canvassing their opinions on Canadian policy in the GATT's Kennedy round. In the afterglow of the federal election campaign that saw off the Diefenbaker Conservatives, it seemed that experimentation was possible.

Of course, in 1963 that did not happen, nor did most of the provinces seem overly concerned; theirs was not a world of trade discussion. Not even a new and critical departure in Canadian–American economic relations like the Auto Pact could provoke Ontario's interest in the intricacies and process of negotiation; Toronto seemed completely oblivious that this new instrument taking shape would fundamentally change the provincial economy. While at President Lyndon Johnson's Texas ranch for the signing, Pearson correctly called the agreement 'one of the most important accords ever signed between our two countries in the trade field.'[18] Everything about the Auto Pact, from its conception to its completion, was a federal operation and amazingly, no matter how essential the final result might turn out to be for Ontario's prosperity, the latter stayed clear.[19]

Still, one province was becoming increasingly concerned about the evolution of Canadian federalism and forced the federal government to take note of a changing climate as the 1960s ground on. The Quiet Revolution in Quebec had really set the provincialist cat among federalist pigeons and, in some ways, anticipated issues that would arise between Ottawa and the other provinces during the 1970s. Quebec was the first to establish a full ministry to coordinate federal–provincial relations a year after the election of the Jean Lesage government in 1960.[20] It also began transforming the province's international policy into a role where Quebec would be treated as an international actor. This reflected the so-called Gérin-Lajoie doctrine, first expressed in a speech by the then minister of education, Paul Gérin-Lajoie, on 12 April 1965 to foreign consular officials in Montreal.

Over the next decade, and partly pushed by Quebec, the period of so-called cooperative federalism was coming to an end. This was superseded by 'executive federalism,' characterized by the exercise of more and more authority at the executive level. This was followed by a significant increase in the work of interprovincial and intergovernmental committees of ministers, including first ministers, to resolve jurisdictional disputes. It also implied more equality between the two levels of government. Later, this coincided with a new phase, intra-state federalism, connoting 'the principle that interdependence between the orders of government in a federation required adequate formal representation of the governments, or at least the concerns and interests, of the federated units within the institutions of the federal government.'[21] This new idea was given shape by those provinces keen to immerse themselves in the minutia of trade policy formation on a global level.

By the 1970s, the bigger provinces were more and more espousing the concept of intra-state federalism, even though they might not as then have had any intellectual hook on which to hang it. They were in feisty moods about presenting a certain point of view on trade matters, especially as the Canadian economy began to suffer. Federal investment rules, symbolized by the Foreign Investment Review Agency, the process and the results of the Tokyo round (1973–9) of negotiations under the GATT, the general decline of economic vitality as oil crises and stagflation came to characterize the later 1970s, and the election of the Parti Québecois government of René Lévesque in November 1976 were instrumental in transforming federalism. All of these stimulated the provinces to become more assertive in their relations with Ottawa. With foreign trade generally, as Douglas Brown has written, it was increasingly important to provinces, given the deleterious economic situation, and 'finding a voice on trade policy matters meant that the provinces became more sensitized than they had been to the importance of trade policy and trade relations to provincial interests.'[22] *Canadian* policy became more than just federal policy, as also reflecting provincial interest became important.

As the Tokyo round of the GATT got underway in 1973, the provinces were put on notice. While all previous General Agreement negotiating sessions had been focused on reducing the direct incidence of tariff protection, the new objective was to begin the attack on non-tariff barriers (NTBs) to trade. And that made the provinces particularly vulnerable, as some had erected instruments to assist their citizens. The milk marketing board in Ontario, hog and egg marketing boards in western Canada, or turkey marketing boards in eight provinces were concrete expressions of agricultural supply management that had yielded benefits to certain sectors but which Canada's trading partners found to be contrary to their interests. As well, control of the sale and distribution of liquor was a provincial responsibility, and Canada was to take a number of body blows from putative trading partners during the negotiations over protectionist provincial interests. Similarly, Ontario's interest in the Auto Pact also became more focused in the years after 1973, resulting in Toronto ensuring that nothing was done that could in any way detract from its provisions.

In the Tokyo round, relations between the provinces and the federal authority became more regularized as formerly watertight compartments of constitutional jurisdiction began to leak. The Canadian Trade and Tariffs Committee, chaired by a federal deputy minister, was the mechanism in place in 1973 where the provinces could make their views known.[23] This was later replaced by a federal-provincial committee of deputy ministers that was 'more political and more continuous,' and was also perceived by the provinces as not having any determining influence over the Canadian bargaining position. By August 1977, this had proved to be inadequate, leading Ottawa to appoint a Canadian coordinator for trade negotiations to harmonize input from federal departments, industry, and the provinces. Further, four provinces – Alberta, British Columbia, Ontario, and Quebec – sent representatives to Geneva to take in the negotiations, although the federal delegation did not accept them as equals. Still, by the time the GATT negotiations wound up, Canadian provinces were at least in the process of becoming more involved in developing strategy and vigorously pushing their own agendas.

That involvement at home was partly reflected by the establishment of provincial offices abroad; by 1985 seven provinces had established over thirty-five offices on three continents.[24] Six years later, in a class by itself, Quebec had twenty-six, most in the usual places in Europe and the United States, but some also in Africa, the Middle East, and South America. Almost all of these bureaus were to represent and promote provincial trade interests. As has been pointed out, however much Ottawa might work to suggest another interpretation, 'these … Canadian provinces [were] international actors which challenge[d] the conventional concept of sovereignty and the federal view of a national monopoly in foreign policy.'[25]

This foray into what had been an exclusive federal preserve was significant; more and more, the provinces were finding that in an increasingly globalized world, their interests needed to be promoted and protected by their own representatives abroad, if not in Ottawa. As well, the economic climate of the later 1970s and earlier 1980s was hardly conducive to economic growth – interest rates set by the Bank of Canada in 1982 reached 20 per cent, an absolutely crippling figure that contributed to the worst recession in a half century. The political context underlying this disastrous economic situation was also revealing; with the election of Joe Clark's Conservative minority government in the May 1979 vote, there was not a Liberal government left sitting anywhere in the country.[26]

With Clark's defeat in December of that year and the re-election of the Trudeau Liberals in May 1980, there was one. This condition contributed to federal-provincial suspicion and disharmony, especially as the new government undertook to enact some policies, among them the hated National Energy Program, designed to accomplish a number of objectives but, in the perception of Western Canadians, to 'rip off' oil resources to benefit central Canada. Even bumper stickers expressed Western outrage – 'Let Eastern bastards freeze in the dark.' The dispute that eventually escalated between Alberta's Premier Peter Lougheed and the federal government was very destabilizing for, and destructive of, national unity.[27]

A similar situation prevailed in Quebec. The election of René Lévesque's Parti Québecois government in 1976 had set the province on the track toward its first referendum on sovereignty. While the 'No' side won in 1980 with about 60 per cent of the vote, it was, again, a very destabilizing and demoralizing exercise. These two events, combined with the recession, aggressive provincial governments, a distant Liberal federal one, and a general sense of malaise that permeated the country contributed to Canadians questioning their future. Citizens could not be faulted for believing that provincial capitals, as opposed to the national one, represented their interests better. By 1983, the percentage of those polled who said they favoured the opposition Conservatives stood at 62 per cent. The government as a source of inspiration and a focus of Canadian loyalty, it seemed, had disappeared, with consequent implications for the sense of national unity.

In 1984, the Conservatives of Brian Mulroney won power, undertaking to change the relationship of the federal government with ordinary Canadians. It had also campaigned on a no-free-trade plank, which soon changed. By 1985 and with the release of the *Final Report* of the Royal Commission on the Economic Union and Development Prospects for Canada, free trade became a viable proposition, seized upon by Ottawa as perhaps a panacea for some of its ills.

The negotiations with the United States began in 1986. In February, the federal government discussed the issue at the Regina First Ministers' Conference. In his opening remarks, the new prime minister, Brian Mulroney, told the assembled premiers that his 'objective ... was to encourage the key actors in the Canadian economy to recast their dialogue in terms that made issues into shared concerns, not jurisdictional disputes.'[28] Clearly, he had in mind that the eleven governments in attendance would work together in securing a satisfactory conclusion to this momentous project.[29] The conference communiqué, later known as the Regina Accord, committed those governments to meet together at least once per year to, among other things, review the state of the Canadian federation, consult on the state of the economy, and consider broad objectives for governments in Canada. One government, at least, established a new department, the Ministry of International Trade and Investment, to reflect this new-found cooperation. As British Columbia's finance minister noted on that occasion, his province 'want[ed] to be an active partner with Ottawa and with the other provinces in ensuring that the trade policy environment in Canada reflects aims, aspirations and interests of all regions,' but perhaps of most importance, those of his own province.[30]

Later, given the reassurance of Regina, all provinces demanded full participation in the negotiations, whatever that meant. And meaning became critical. For Ottawa, the obligation was met by informing and negotiating with the provinces only on matters that involved provincial jurisdiction, which, admittedly, were many, from government procurement through agricultural marketing boards to matters pertaining to liquor sales. This reflected the decision in the *Labour Conventions* case of 1937. As has been pointed out by several involved in the negotiations, the federal negotiator, Simon Reisman, 'took the view that he would consult to the fullest extent possible with the provinces and would seek to negotiate an arrangement in which they would see it in their own interests to accept obligations in areas of provincial jurisdiction. In no circumstances, however, would he accept a provincial presence in the negotiations or on his team.'[31]

Conversely, most provinces believed that the chief negotiator 'would derive his instructions from the federal and provincial governments and that provincial representatives would be present at the negotiating table.' Perhaps the provincial position reflected the situation with the GATT meetings that were occurring in Montevideo, Uruguay, in September 1986 – on the federal delegation were provincial officials to advise and negotiate with their federal counterparts. Nine provinces viewed the prime minister's commitment at Regina as 'ironclad,' and would not budge from the notion of total and complete provincial input into Canada's negotiating strategy. Even prior to the Saskatchewan meeting, the provinces had laid out their position that reflected the notion of national reconciliation that had followed the Mulroney election victory in the summer of 1984 – 'the establishment by all first ministers of a joint mandate and joint control over Canada's chief negotiator; full provincial representation on the Canadian negotiating team, including the option of being "in the room" with the Americans; full participation in the negotiating strategy; and full information sharing in confidence with the federal negotiators.'[32]

To ensure that their intentions were realized, most of them, and all of the big ones – Alberta, British Columbia, Ontario, and Quebec – engaged senior people from either the public or private sectors to attend the Continuing Committee on Trade Negotiations to represent their interests. As well, the provinces 'revamped old bureaucracies [and] developed new ones,' sending ministers and officials to Washington to speak with Congress and the Administration.[33] Some did this more assiduously than others, among them Alberta and Quebec, which remained wholeheartedly favourable to an agreement, and that was welcomed in federal circles. As Ian MacDonald has pointed out, 'The alliance between Quebec and Alberta was the heart of the Mulroney political coalition, and would be critical to his prospects of winning the next election.'[34] Those two, at least, would be jollied along.

On the other hand, Ontarians and their premier, David Peterson, were not thrilled with the direction of negotiations throughout their entire sweep. His province, of course, had, potentially, the most to lose from any free trade agreement. As Peterson told other first ministers, 'Ontario [is] not against secure and enhanced access to the US market. We are only against a hasty and uninformed approach to the issue. We do not expect benefits without costs. But we do expect benefits to exceed costs.'[35] Ontario comprised the bulk of Canada's manufacturing capability as well as the Auto Pact, the crown jewel in the provincial diadem. With rumours of its sacrifice to the gods of continentalism, he told CBC's Wendy Mesley that the pact 'must never be tampered with ... there was no *Canadian* response on the issue, at least there better not be.'[36] So great was his concern over its future that he had flown to Washington in January 1987 in an attempt to convince American officials to keep it off the table. Indeed, it remained a major point of contention between Toronto and Reisman.

As for the others, Mulroney was able to co-opt them, if such was needed, in part through the holding of quarterly meetings to update premiers on progress and process. As well, federal officials continuously briefed provincial representatives.[37] Reisman, one participant remembered, spent more time with the provincial premiers during the first year of negotiation than he did with the Americans. While the agenda was Ottawa's (or Washington's), provincial leaders were involved, to the point where Michael Hart, then a participant in this process, noted that 'it was not unusual for the premier of Ontario to be informed of the details of a negotiating session before any ministries or deputies in Ottawa had been debriefed, often in detail.'[38] And while Ontario and Manitoba might remain opposed, given this stroking and the identification of provincial interests with free trade, the others were generally supportive. Had more provinces been opposed, the discourse during, and perhaps the result of, the 1988 federal election campaign might have been very different. The Free Trade Agreement (FTA) came into force as of 1 January 1989. Obviously, the FTA process witnessed what has been called a 'quantum leap' in the extent to which the provinces participated in trade negotiations.[39] Admittedly, that leap began from a relatively low place, and Ottawa continued to insist upon federal primacy in the practice of foreign trade relations, even despite the obvious reality with which it was confronted.

The FTA was followed in due course by the North American Free Trade Agreement (NAFTA), which came into effect as of 1 January 1994 and which included Mexico. As well, the old General Agreement on Tariffs and Trade was transformed into the World Trade Organization, partly at the urging of Canada, which began life on 1 January 1995, one of the accomplishments of the Uruguay round. For both of these agreements, the 'new' Canadian way of operation, seen tentatively during the Tokyo round, and given more substance during the FTA discussions, of continuing federal consultation with the provinces over trade policy formation, was further entrenched.

The FTA and the NAFTA also fundamentally changed the country's trade relationship with implications for Canadian federalism and national unity. Rather than a national state, by the earlier 1990s the outlines of provincial/regional groupings was clear. In the ancient history of the 1980s, more than half of every province's trade went to another part of Canada. By 1995, for every province except Manitoba, more than half of provincial trade went to the United States. Clearly the forces of continentalism had sped up, and this has left sub-national governments much less dependent on the centre.

This stark integration of the North American economy is represented in Canada's top six export sectors to the United States: cars and parts, oil, machinery and equipment, agriculture, and fish products.[40] These reinforce the integration of the two economies on a regional, or provincial, basis. Ontario is a good example: its merchandise exports to the world in 2005 were about CAN$200 billion, of which CAN$180 billion went to the United States! In the case of Quebec, the numbers were equally astounding. In 1989, just as the FTA was being implemented, exports to other Canadian provinces accounted for about 21 per cent of gross domestic product, and to the United States approximately 16 per cent. By 2001, this had changed dramatically – Quebec's north/south exports had increased to 34 per cent of its GDP, while those to other provinces had fallen to 19 per cent.[41]

As Thomas Courchene points out, 'Because Canada's provinces/regions tend to differ industrially more from each other than their cross-border counterparts, the provinces' attempt to enhance their prospects in North America will tend to result naturally in an enhanced degree of policy decentralization and operational asymmetry.'[42] This has led to the emergence of North American region states with shrinking ties and allegiance to Canada and a much greater interest in Washington and its policies. In the medium term, this can only change the nature of Canadian federalism, trade policy included, as provinces seek to establish mini-embassies in the US capital, undeterred by Ottawa's demand that it alone represent Canada and its parts in that city.

This is also demonstrated by the Canadian, or perhaps more accurately, the *provincial*, response to an ongoing softwood lumber dispute. This has been an area of conflict between Canada and the United States since the nineteenth century, but it picked up steam in the late twentieth century as American producers saw their northern neighbours taking too large a proportion of their market. Part of the Canadian competitive advantage lies in how their forests are organized; most are owned by either federal or provincial governments. In the case of British Columbia, Canada's largest producer, 95 per cent are provincially owned, 1 per cent are controlled by Ottawa, and 4 per cent by the private sector. The provinces administer the tenure systems and provide harvesting rights on provincial and federal land to the provincial lumber industry. US industry has challenged the Canadian stumpage program under both the WTO and NAFTA, claiming that the stumpage fees set by the provincial governments are too low, resulting in unfair subsidies to Canadian producers and injury to those in the United States.

Following negotiations among Ottawa, Victoria, Edmonton, Toronto, and Quebec City, the federal government signed the US-Canada Softwood Lumber Agreement in April 1996. It obliged the Canadian government to impose an export tax on Canadian businesses exporting softwood lumber to the United States from the provinces of British Columbia, Alberta, Ontario, and Quebec, should exports exceed a set threshold of 14.7 billon board feet. This agreement was in effect until April 2001. Following its expiration, the United States again filed suit against Canadian producers and on 22 March 2002 the US Department of Commerce found that unfair subsidies had been provided, and a few months later, the US International Trade Commission levied a countervailing duty of 18.79 per cent – a decision that, incidentally, was successfully appealed by Canada.

Through many twists and turns and appeals to NAFTA tribunals and WTO panels that need not concern us here, a 'deal' of sorts was reached in April 2006. On 1 July 2006, the agreement was signed by Canada's international trade minister, David Emerson, and the US trade representative, Susan Schwab. Emerson told the press that he hoped to have Parliament's agreement by 1 October, making the accord law.[43] Clearly, he could certainly gain federal legislative approval for the softwood lumber agreement, but would the provinces agree? In the rather confused state of the constitutionality of trade policy, the answer remained unclear throughout the summer, especially as provincial lumber organizations in BC, Alberta, and Quebec, as well as the BC government, expressed significant concerns over it. Indeed, Victoria, in concert with the provincial association, wrote to Ottawa on 30 June 2006, noting that 'the current draft agreement has not met some of our key requirements. We will, therefore, not be able to offer our support.' When appearing before a parliamentary committee investigating the softwood lumber issue, Emerson told members that, so far, he had 'not had a good summer' because of ongoing concerns.[44] Although, in the end, affected provincial governments did sign on following vigorous federal lobbying, it is interesting that their disagreement threatened to compromise the accord. The Canada-US softwood lumber agreement came into effect on 12 October 2006, with federal legislation following in December.

Clearly, this sort of issue will become more challenging. Indeed, following the Uruguay round of trade negotiations, the Japanese penned an interesting and sophisticated analysis of Canadian practice. In a case that raised red flags for them, British Columbia had imposed restrictions on the export of high value Douglas fir, spruce, and red cedar logs. Because these quantitative restrictions were designed to protect the domestic industry, it was highly likely, or so thought the Japanese, that they violated article 11 of the GATT. But herein lay the rub, which complicated what otherwise might have been a relatively straightforward situation: 'these measures are implemented by a *provincial government not directly committed to obligations under the WTO Agreements.*' It lay with the government of Canada, according to World Trade Organization rules, to 'take such reasonable measures as may be available to it to ensure observance of the provisions.'[45] If reasonable measures were not enough, however, where did that leave Canada's obligations and Japanese concessions? Trade policy development and conflicting spheres of jurisdiction continue to muddy the waters, and it may be that, in the future, a federal government will have to take cognizance of provincial objectives before it enters into any negotiations.

The search for continuing improvements (or not) to the practice of Canadian federalism and the division of jurisdiction and power between the two levels goes on. In July 2003, provincial premiers gathered in Charlottetown, PEI, to adopt a plan 'to revitalize the Canadian federation and build a new era of constructive and cooperative federalism,' the centrepiece of which was the creation of the Council of the Federation.[46] This council would comprise the 13 sub-national government leaders in Canada, and would have regular meetings. It would not, however, include the prime minister, but would meet with the federal government once per year. The sub-national legislatures would also increasingly occupy space that was once the preserve of the federal government. Rather than function within the old divisions of federal and provincial, Canada would become 'multi-centric,' with the inclusion as well of Aboriginal and local governments.[47] As well, a trade agreement signed between Alberta and BC on 28 April 2006 could represent, or so Margaret Kopala suggested in the *Ottawa Citizen*, 'a tectonic shift' in Canadian federalism.[48] 'Could it,' she asks, 'lead to the creation of a BC-Alberta superprovince-cum-region state with the challenge that that connotes to Canadian federalism and trade practice? Sure it could,' she concludes. In short, things have become much more complex with, presumably, implications for trade policy development.

Federal–provincial relations have evolved dramatically from their beginnings as 'cooperative federalism' following Pearson's election in 1963, when, with the exception of Quebec, most provinces took little interest in Canadian trade policy. By the 1970s, however, provinces, motivated by Canada's deleterious economic situation, became more sensitized to the importance of trade policy and federal–provincial relations had evolved to something called 'intra-state federalism,' where provincial interests were very much a factor to be considered in any trade policy formation. By the end of the Tokyo round of the GATT negotiations, the provinces were very much involved in trade discussions and their participation was regularized through specific mechanisms. The provinces began to establish their own offices abroad to protect their trade interests – a development that certainly challenged the notion of a federal monopoly on trade. By the late 1970s and early 1980s a new era of federal-provincial suspicion and disharmony, illustrated by Western Canada's outrage over federal energy policies and Quebec's focus on sovereignty, needed to be addressed. Brian Mulroney attempted to do so by way of the Regina Accord, which came out of the 1986 First Ministers' Conference, and was designed to provide a forum to consult and cooperate with the provinces on broad economic objectives, particularly free trade. The provinces quickly came to see this attempt at reconciliation as 'ironclad' and insisted on full participation in future trade negotiations. As the forces of continentalism become more obvious, federal consultation with the provinces over trade policy formation became even more entrenched, in effect changing the very nature of federalism.

Canadians have re-engaged with the debate on federalism, especially as it relates to globalization, and how globalization is changing the nature of the debate. As Janice Stein has pointed out, 'This debate is taking place in a very heated way in the county. It's probably more heated than it's been in a decade right now.'[49] Where that will leave Canadian federalism, and more specifically, the development and implementation of trade agreements negotiated with foreign countries, is anyone's guess. One thing is certain: the comfortable and watertight world of feder-

al jurisdiction over the country's foreign economic policy has passed
forever.

NOTES

1 James Rosenau, *Along the Domestic-Foreign Frontier: Exploring Governance
   in a Turbulent World* (Cambridge: Cambridge University Press, 1997), as
   quoted in Hamish Telford, 'Expanding the Partnership: The Proposed
   Council of the Federation and the Challenge of Globalization,' Institute of
   Intergovernmental Relations and Institute for Research on Public Policy,
   2003 1 at http://www.queensu.ca/iigr/working/archive/feden.html
2 However, see Douglas Brown, 'The Evolving Role of the Provinces in
   Canada–US Trade Relations,' in *States and Provinces in the International
   Economy*, ed. Douglas Brown and Earl Fry (Kingston, ON: Institute of
   Intergovernmental Relations, 1993), 107. Here, as Brown points out, the
   provinces have been potentially engaged in multilateral trade policy since
   1947. As a GATT signatory, Canada was bound by the federal state clause,
   article XXIV (12), which stated, 'Each contracting party shall take such
   reasonable measures as may be available to it to ensure observance of the
   provisions of this Agreement by the regional and local governments and
   authorities within its territory.'
3 Kim Richard Nossal, *The Politics of Canadian Foreign Policy* (Toronto: Prentice
   Hall, 1989), 258. He goes on to write, 'Nor, importantly, did the BNA Act
   deny the provinces the possibility of an international role.' See also Michael
   Whittington and Richard Van Loon, *Canadian Government and Politics:
   Institutions and Processes* (Toronto: McGraw-Hill Ryerson, 1996), 207. The
   authors note the wholesale attack on the POGG clause by the JCPC over fifty
   years, and how 'federal trade and commerce power was construed so as
   not to interfere with the provinces' power under 93(13).' Moreover, in what
   Whittington and Van Loon correctly call 'the [wild] imagination of Viscount
   Haldane in the Board of Commerce case and the Snider case,' the JCPC ruled
   that section 91(2) had to be taken as containing merely ancillary powers.
4 The JCPC was not technically a court at all. It was made up of judges who
   were appointed to the Queen's (or King's) Privy Council in the United
   Kingdom and who were mandated to advise the sovereign on the disposition of appeals from the common-law courts. Because the BNA Act was a
   British statute, the JCPC had to ensure that the laws passed by the provincial and federal governments were consistent with its provisions. See
   Whittington and Van Loon, *Canadian Government and Politics*, 203.

 5 Telford, 'Expanding the Partnership,' 3. To the contrary, the Fathers endorsed John A. Macdonald's concept, which he called subordinate federalism, in which the provinces would have been little more than glorified municipalities.

 6 See Ian Robinson, 'Trade Policy, Globalization, and the Future of Canadian Federalism,' in *New Trends in Canadian Federalism*, ed. Francois Rocher and Miriam Smith (Peterborough, ON: Broadview, 1995), 243. As Robinson points out, the federal government's exclusive right to make international treaties could undermine the federal principle if it acquired the right to legislate in an exclusively provincial area by signing a treaty. Given that, 'it could unilaterally make profound changes in the division of powers without formally amending the constitution or even consulting with the provinces' (243).

 7 The rounds over these twenty-five years were: Geneva, 1947; Annecy, 1949; Torquay, 1950–1; Dillon, 1963; Kennedy, 1964–7.

 8 Bora Laskin, *Canadian Constitutional Law: Cases, Text, and Notes on Distribution of Legislative Power* (Toronto: Carswell, 1960), 112.

 9 Ibid., 27.

10 Peter Hogg, *Constitutional Law* (Toronto: Carswell, 1985), 242.

11 See, for example, Stephen Clarkson, *Uncle Sam and Us: Globalization, Neoconservatism, and the Canadian State* (Toronto: University of Toronto Press, 2002), 267. As well, see Zagros Madjd-Sadjadi, 'Subnational Sabotage or National Paramountcy? Examining the Dynamics of Subnational Acceptance of International Agreements' (paper presented at the Southern Association for Canadian Studies, Atlanta, October 2004). Madjd-Sadjadi notes that a number of countries' constitutions contain provisions.

12 Telford, 'Expanding the Partnership,' 5.

13 Francois Rocher and Richard Nimijean, 'Global Economic Restructuring and the Evolution of Canadian Federalism and Constitutionalism,' in *New Trends in Canadian Federalism*, 215.

14 Donald J. Savoie, *Governing from the Centre: The Concentration of Political Power in Canadian Politics* (Toronto: University of Toronto Press, 1999), 107.

15 'Confederation in Danger,' *Sunday Morning Magazine*, CBC Radio, 1 December 1963. As the report noted, 'One theme that ran through much of the discussion was that there was not enough consultation between the federal and provincial governments.' This complaint would become louder over the next decade. It was also a landmark meeting because it was the first federal Liberal–Quebec Liberal meeting since the inception of the Quiet Revolution in 1960.

16 Canada, *Federal-Provincial Conference 1963*, Ottawa, 26–29 November 1963, 5.

17 Ibid., 10.
18 Raj Ahluwalia, 'The End of an Era,' 18 February 2001, CBC-TV, http://
    archives.cbc.ca/IDC-1-73-326-1718/politics_economy/auto_pact/clip9.
    As Denis DesRosiers, an automobile analyst, noted in 1992, the Auto Pact
    'was precedent-setting at the time, and to this date, it still probably the
    most precedent-setting, most unique, bilateral trade agreement negoti-
    ated anywhere in the world by far.' 'Building Block of an Economy,' *CBC
    Newsmagazine*, 17 January 1992, http://archives.cbc.ca/IDCC-1-73-326-
    1729/politics_economy/auto_pact/.
19 See Brown, 'The Evolving Role of the Provinces,' 103.
20 By 1965, Ontario had followed suit, creating a federal-provincial and inter-
    provincial affairs secretariat, and a full ministry in 1978, which would be
    responsible for relations with municipal, provincial, and federal govern-
    ments. In 1981, the ministry became responsible for interprovincial and
    federal relations only. As well, during the 1970s, Alberta, British Columbia,
    Manitoba, Newfoundland, Nova Scotia, Saskatchewan, and Yukon had
    established some mechanism for coordinating intergovernmental relations.
21 Ronald L. Watts, 'Managing Interdependence in a Federal Political Sys-
    tem,' in *The Art of the State: Governance in a World Without Frontiers*, ed. Tho-
    mas J. Courchene and Donald J. Savoie (Montreal: Institute for Research on
    Public Policy, 2003), 138.
22 Brown, 'The Evolving Role of the Provinces,' 104.
23 Ibid., 108.
24 A.E. Blanchette, ed., *Canadian Foreign Policy, 1966–1976: Selected Speeches
    and Documents* (Ottawa: Institute of Canadian Studies, 1980), 302.
25 Elliot J. Feldman and Lily Gardner Feldman, 'Canada,' in *Federalism and In-
    ternational Relations: The Role of Subnational Units*, ed. Hans J. Michelmann
    and Panayotis Soldatos (Oxford: Clarendon, 1990), 176.
26 In 1980, provincial governments were, from west to east by political affilia-
    tion, BC – Social Credit; AB – Conservative; SK – NDP; MB – Conservative;
    ON – Conservative; QC – Parti Québecois; NB – Conservative; NS – Con-
    servative; PEI – Conservative; NF – Conservative.
27 Increasingly, the federal government could ill afford to ignore the prov-
    inces. The NEP was key to understanding the decline of Liberal for-
    tunes in Western Canada as well as the suspicion with which the federal
    government came to viewed by most other governments. Barbara Frum,
    interviewing Senator Bud Olsen, the Liberal point man on the NEP file,
    suggested, then asked, if it was 'not about money – it's really about power.
    When Mr Trudeau invites Alberta to take him to court [over the consti-
    tutionality of the NEP], doesn't that imply that Mr Trudeau knows or

believes that a court will always find that the federal power has more authority?' Barbara Frum, 'Trudeau Slaps on Taxes with NEP,' *As It Happens*, CBC, 31 October 1980, http://archives.cbc.ca/IDC-1-73-378-2140/politics_economy/alberta_oil/. As Whittingdon and Van Loon have pointed out, that was generally the case. See Whittington and Van Loon, *Canadian Government and Politics*, 216.

28 'Opening Statement at the First Ministers' Conference on the Rights of Aboriginal Peoples, April 2–3, 1985,' http://www.collectionscanada.ca/primeministers/h4-4021-e.html

29 That said, the prime minister also let it be known that in any conflict between federal and provincial governments in the free trade negotiations, the former would prevail. As has been pointed out, however, prime ministers are on shakier ground when dealing with their own Cabinet or caucus: 'Premiers are not his political equals, but they shape the discussions at [intergovernmental conferences] and advance whatever position they wish, even when it is in sharp opposition to the prime minister's position' (Savoie, *Governing from the Centre*, 105). Whether prime ministerial opposition would be sufficient is debatable.

30 British Columbia, *Debates*, 1985 Legislative Session: 3rd Session, 33rd Parliament, p. 2291.

31 Michael Hart, with Bill Dymond and Colin Robertson, *Decision at Midnight: Inside the Canada-US Free Trade Negotiations* (Vancouver: UBC Press, 1994), 138.

32 Douglas Brown, 'The Evolving Role of Provinces in Canada–United States Trade Relations,' in *States and Provinces in the International Economy*, ed. Brown and Fry, 112.

33 Feldman and Feldman, 'Canada,' 198.

34 L. Ian MacDonald, *From Bourassa to Bourassa: Wilderness to Restoration* (Montreal and Kingston: McGill-Queen's University Press, 2003), 290. The federal government also established the Sectoral Advisory Groups on International Trade as a consultative channel for industry, which also provided input for Quebec Premier Robert Bourassa through the business community. Further, while the Free Trade Agreement was being negotiated, the Mulroney Tories had also (apparently) come to an agreement – the ill-fated Meech Lake Accord of June 1997 – with Quebec. That also played into its support for the FTA.

35 Feldman and Feldman, 'Canada,' 198.

36 Wendy Mesley, 'Canada Fights for Auto Pact,' *The National*, CBC, 22 June 1987, http://archives.cbc.ca/IDC-1-73-326-1717/politics_economy/auto_pact/clip7. Emphasis added.

37 Brown, 'Evolving Role,' 125.

38 Hart, *Decision at Midnight*, 227.

39 Michael Hart, *A North American Free Trade Agreement: The Strategic Implications for Canada* (Montreal: The Institute for Research on Public Policy, 1990), 135.

40 Russ Kuykendall, 'Six Trade Corridors to the US: The Lifeblood of Canada's Economy,' *Policy Options* (July/August 2006): 49.

41 Thomas Courchene, 'The Changing Nature of Quebec–Canada Relations: From the 1980 Referendum to the Summit of the Canadas,' Institute for Research on Public Policy, 14 September 2004, http://www.irpp.org/fasttrak/index.htm.

42 Ibid., 14.

43 'Softwood Lumber Dispute,' 23 August 2006, CBC News Online, http://www.cbc.ca/news/background/softwood_lumber/.
    The deal included provisions for
    • import duties of $4 billion that the United States had charged Canadian companies since 2002 to be returned, with the United States to keep $1 billion
    • a seven-year term, with a possible two-year extension
    • a ban on the United States from launching new trade actions
    • restrictions on Canadian exports to kick in if prices fall too far
    • neutral trade arbitrators to provide final and binding settlements of disputes
    In any event, much of this became academic as a rising Canadian dollar throughout 2007 and 2008 decimated the Canadian softwood lumber industry, pricing its products out of the U.S. market and resulting in the layoff of thousands of forest industry workers.

44 *The World at Six*, CBC Radio, 31 July 2006.

45 Pt. 1, chap. 8, 'Canada,' http://www.meti.go.jp/english/report. Emphasis added. The Japanese actually have a relatively sophisticated understanding of the forces in play within Canadian federalism.

46 Douglas Brown, 'Getting Things Done in the Federation: Do We Need New Rules for an Old Game?' Institute of Intergovernmental Relations and the Institute for Research on Public Policy, October 2003, http://www.queensu.ca/iigr/working/archive/feden.html

47 Telford, 'Expanding the Partnership,' 5.

48 Margaret Kopala, 'Alberta-BC Trade Pact a Tectonic Shift,' *Ottawa Citizen*, 29 July 2006, B7.

49 'The Future of Canadian Federalism,' *Ottawa Citizen*, 2 June 2006, http://www.canada.com/ottawacitizen/news/story.html?id=c143e0b8-9886-4078-a8db-d911012c36d5&k=31447.

9 Implementing the 'Innovation' Strategy: Post-secondary Education in the Chrétien Years

PAUL AXELROD

Over the course of its mandate, the government led by Jean Chrétien (1993–2003) first neglected and then embraced Canada's university sector. The period began with dramatic cuts to social spending, including higher education, and concluded with a flurry of initiatives designed to draw universities into a national economic development strategy. In an era of globalization, university-based research, in particular, was identified by the federal government as a critical instrument in the cultivation and sustenance of a 'knowledge society.' The commitment to this cause so impressed *Globe and Mail* columnist Jeffrey Simpson that he urged his readers to 'think R&D ... don't think Gomery' when assessing 'Chrétien's legacy.'[1]

How extensive and significant was the Chrétien government's support for higher education? This chapter sets the discussion of this question in historical context, tracks pertinent policy initiatives through the 1990s, and assesses their consequence with respect to the state of post-secondary education in Canada.

Constitutionally, post-secondary education falls within provincial jurisdiction, but throughout Canada's history, the federal government has, in selected areas, participated actively in the university and college sectors. In 1916 it created a body that led to the formation of the National Research Council, regulated university admission policies during the Second World War, financially supported veterans who attended university after the war, provided direct grants to universities beginning in 1951, established the Canada Council in 1957, funded the expansion of colleges and technical education in the 1960s, and initiated, with provincial collaboration, the Canada Student Loans Program in 1964.

Through the Federal-Provincial Fiscal Arrangements Act of 1967, the federal government replaced direct grants to universities with the transfer of cash and tax points to the provinces, which were intended to cover half the (continuously increasing) costs of post-secondary education. This scheme was replaced in 1977 by Established Programs Financing through which the federal government capped its contributions to higher education, medicare, and hospital insurance below the 50 per cent level, while gradually removing conditions on the provinces on their disbursement of these funds. Subsequently, the proportion of post-secondary and health costs covered by the federal government declined, which arguably was the precise purpose of the policy change. In 1985, the new Progressive Conservative Party finance minister, Michael Wilson, imposed a permanent cap on these cash transfers to the provinces.[2] A further cap followed in 1989, and in the 1990 federal budget, EPF payments were frozen at the 1989–90 level.[3]

Notwithstanding these efforts to limit the growth and volume of transfer payments to the provinces, the federal government, in the pre-Chrétien years, did signal its continuing interest in university-based research. In the wake of two major studies, one co-sponsored by the Science Council of Canada and the Canada Council and headed by John B. Macdonald, former president of the University of British Columbia, and the other undertaken by the Senate led by Maurice Lamontagne, Ottawa reconfigured its approach to the coordination of research policy by creating the Ministry of State for Science and Technology (MOSST) in 1971. The federal granting councils were restructured in 1977 in the form of the Natural Sciences and Engineering Research Council (NSERC) and the Social Sciences and Humanities Research Council (SSHRC). The Medical Research Council comprised the third component of the 'tri-council' research structure, and the Canada Council's role was confined to the allocation of funds for the fine and performing arts.[4]

Because of its perceived role in generating economic development, research continued to be the focus of federal initiatives in post-secondary education, particularly in science and technology. MOSST, started by the Liberal government of Pierre Trudeau, was absorbed into the new Department of Industry established under the Mulroney Conservatives. The latter introduced a matching grants program in 1986 that linked growth in granting counsels' support to their success in attracting matching funds from industry – a program whose effectiveness in securing private sector support was subsequently questioned by the Senate committee on national finances.[5]

The most significant post-secondary education policy initiative of the Mulroney era was the establishment in 1988 of the Networks of Centres of Excellence Program. Its purpose was to develop 'a web of national research networks – "research institutes without walls," anchored in academic settings – that in partnership with the private sector would target and develop practical and commercial applications.'[6] It forged collaborations among universities, industry, government, and not-for-profit organizations intended to explore 'issues of national significance such as respiratory health, telecommunications and space research.'[7] This program, eventually comprising some thirty networks, was permanently established in 1997 by the Chrétien government.[8]

Thus, a number of historical precedents pre-dated federal spending on post-secondary education in the Chrétien years, notwithstanding the constitutional questions that such initiatives invariably raised. How, indeed, can Ottawa's incursion into the field of post-secondary education, an area of provincial responsibility, be explained? The authority of the federal government to become so engaged has been found by legal scholars and the Courts to reside in the use of the federal spending power. 'Simply put, the federal government may spend the money that it collects under its power of taxation as it pleases. As long as it does not legislate directly in relation to matters within the provincial jurisdictions defined by sections 91 to 95 of the Constitution Act of 1867, the federal government may use its spending power and that power will not be found unconstitutional.'[9]

Despite the apparent clarity of this legal principle, the use of the federal spending power has frequently been a contested practice, not unlike experiences in other federal systems.[10] The Constitution Act (originally, the British North America Act) was designed in an era when government revenues and program spending, both federally and provincially, were limited and scarcely expected to grow on the scale experienced over the course of the following century. To address social needs in such areas as health, welfare, and education, federal and provincial government activity expanded tremendously through allocation processes that involved consensus, conflict, stalemate, and/or negotiation. Political and economic exigencies frequently affected decision-making outcomes. Impoverished at the end of the Second World War, provincial governments largely welcomed federal funding support for post-war veterans, and the direct per-capita grants to universities that followed in the 1950s. However, the government of Quebec, fiercely determined to guard its constitutional jurisdiction, opposed direct federal funding of post-secondary education. It subsequently secured the right to opt out of such shared-cost programs, while receiving income tax abatement equivalent to what would have been garnered through the per capita funding formula.[11]

Other provinces have, at times, joined Quebec in its objection to federal 'unilateralism' and to the terms imposed and conditions required through which Ottawa has employed its spending power in areas of provincial responsibility. Critical observers point, as well, to the problem of overlapping federal-provincial bureaucracies and to the ad hoc policy development and inefficient allocation of resources that often characterize such programs.[12]

On the other hand, some defend the flexible and creative policy making that has been a feature of Canadian federalism. The federal spending power enables Ottawa to support economically challenged regions of the country through equalization payments, and provides provinces with the means to shape social programs (within limits) in ways that are similar but not identical.[13] The 1999 Agreement on a Framework to Improve the Social Union for Canada (SUFA), signed by the federal government and all provinces and territories but Quebec, recognized Ottawa's right to spend in areas of provincial responsibility, facilitated greater collaboration between the federal and provincial governments in policy making, and secured the right of 'dissenting' provinces to opt out of particular programs so long as they 'reinvest' the money they receive from Ottawa 'in a similar or related policy area.'[14] Hailed as a breakthrough in federal–provincial relations, SUFA did not, in fact, end 'unilateralism' in federal policy making in the areas of health care, welfare, and post-secondary education. Nor was a commitment to review the agreement after its third year of operation fulfilled. As Brooke Jeffrey observed two years after the departure of Jean Chrétien, 'there is little evidence that such re-evaluation is taking place. Nor has any progress been made on a dispute resolution mechanism.'[15]

In his study of the 'spending power in federal systems,' Ronald L. Watts concludes that, its imperfections notwithstanding, the federal spending power is a rational and essential instrument of nation building and policy making.

> While complete disentanglement and independent jurisdiction of different orders of government may have a seductive appeal as a way of ensuring the federal principle that neither order of government should be subordinate to the other, in practice it has proven simply impossible to divide functions in federations into watertight compartments, particularly in the

realm of revenues and expenditures. This has made necessary in virtually all contemporary federations an acceptance of interdependence and interpretation of the functions of different levels of government, but with quite different approaches to collaboration between federal and provincial/state governments. For Canada this suggests that trying to confine the activities of the federal and provincial governments to separate, watertight compartments would in the long run be self-defeating, but also that processes involving genuine intergovernmental partnership in areas of overlap, including certain uses of the federal spending power, would be helpful.[16]

The Chrétien government assumed power in 1993 amid growing concern about the financial status of post-secondary education, including the future of support for research. That the country also faced a monumental debt burden did not augur well for universities or for the rest of the public sector. The Established Programs Financing system was, by now, a source of deep dissatisfaction for both the federal government and the universities. The former transferred funds to the provinces, largely unconditionally, and 'received no credit on campus or in the general public' for so doing, while the latter had no guarantee that the federal transfers would be spent on higher education, the costs of which were growing significantly in the wake of continuously expanding enrolments. Furthermore, in government support for research, Canada was falling further behind the United States where university lobbying for increased resources, evidently, had been more successful.[17]

The financial challenges intensified with the 1995 federal budget, which focused on reducing the deficit by cutting spending throughout the public sector, including transfer payments to the provinces. Through a process, referred to officially (and somewhat euphemistically) as 'program review,' the areas of social assistance, health, and post-secondary education incurred a major loss of income as a result of the cuts. Former University of Toronto president Robert Prichard contended that 'this was arguably the lowest point in the fifty-year history of federal support for post-secondary education and research.'[18]

In 1996, a new block grant system, the Canadian Social Transfer (CST), subsequently renamed the Canadian Health and Social Transfer (CHST), replaced the EPF scheme, enabling the federal government to contain its spending on provincially run programs. In total, some $6 billion was removed from the areas covered by the CHST, including post-secondary education. The provinces obtained more autonomy in the allocation of these funds, and virtually exclusive control over welfare policy, but the price was heavy – a significant reduction of resources.

Political tensions increased as the federal deficit turned into a surplus in 1997, while the provinces' financial burdens were largely unrelieved.[19]

But the accumulation of a federal budgetary surplus now opened the door to new program initiatives, and post-secondary education was high on the priority list. Over the course of the 1990s, the uncertain place of Canada in an increasingly globalized economy, and the under-performance of Canadian industry, particularly in comparison to the United States, were strikingly evident. 'By 1996, federal R&D investment in Canada had fallen to pre-1990 levels and the momentum of Canada's R&D enterprise expansion had been lost.'[20] Backed by a series of discussion and policy papers that stressed these themes, and receptive to intensive lobbying by the Association of Universities and Colleges of Canada, Prime Minister Chrétien and Finance Minister Paul Martin agreed that the government should forge an 'innovation' strategy, and that research and development should be pivotal elements in such a plan. Robert Giroux, former president of AUCC, recalled that the offices of the prime minister and the minister of finance were 'on the same wavelength' on this matter, and that the prime minister's senior policy advisor, Eddie Goldenberg, played a particularly significant role in promoting this agenda. The government was persuaded that improving and sustaining the 'quality of human resources' through investment in the country's 'intellectual infrastructure' were vital to the enhancement of Canada's global economic role.[21]

Robert Prichard identified 1997 as the year in which a 'new paradigm' shaped federal policy in higher education.

> The concerns of the new global economy took centre stage: Canada's disappointing record of productivity growth compared to the United States, Canada's relative under-investment in research and development, the loss of highly visible personnel to the United States, the growing importance of intellectual capital and intellectual property, and the growing pressures of the "knowledge economy" all demanded attention. These concerns led to a new policy consensus: that the pre-eminent federal concern with respect to higher education should be research and innovation and that major new investments were required if Canada were to compete successfully in the global economy. And beginning with the federal budget in February 1997, the government committed significant new resources to support this agenda.[22]

As noted earlier, a centrepiece of this strategy was the extension and renewal of the Networks of Centres of Excellence program, described in one study as the most 'dramatic change in Canadian science policy since the National Research Council was established in 1916.'[23] Situated within Industry Canada, the NCE sought to break down the 'walls' between industry and universities, to stimulate applied research, and to 'make scientific research more commercial.'[24] This was reflected in the re-working of NCE granting criteria, which heightened the importance of 'value-added' commercial relevance and reduced the assessed weight of 'scientific excellence' – a modification that had the effect of diminishing support for fundamental scientific research within NCE-funded programs, and signalled the federal government's interest in steering the direction of, as well as supporting, new research. 'The program's biggest achievement, according to one program officer, has been to establish "a market orientation in academic researchers and a pre-disposition for collaborating with the private sector."'[25] The program helped achieve another long-standing objective: it provided visibility to federal post-secondary educational policy initiatives.[26]

Indeed, this was true of several other important new programs, including the Canada Foundation for Innovation, which also featured prominently in the 1997 federal budget; it received an allocation of $800 million – increased to $1 billion in 1999, and then to $3.6 billion by 2003–4.[27] The funds were to be awarded on a competitive basis to universities deemed to have the most strategic and economically promising research programs. The foundation would cover 40 per cent of the approved projects' infrastructure costs, with the remaining 60 per cent provided by universities and their partners. Collaboration among some combination of universities, colleges, provincial governments, hospitals, private industry, and the voluntary sector was, therefore, required.[28]

A controversial aspect of the CFI program, with respect to federal-provincial dynamics, was the effect it had on 'leveraging' funds for research from provincial governments. Few projects could be sustained without provincial support, so that in order to secure badly needed federal resources, provinces were pressured into spending on a program they did not create and whose criteria they did not control. To address the particular challenge of Atlantic Canada, which found it especially difficult to raise matching grants required by the CFI, the federal government (in 2001) established the Atlantic Innovation Fund with a $300 million annual budget to be used to support research infrastructure and to facilitate the participation of Atlantic universities in the CFI program.[29]

Quebec's initial response to the CFI program was dramatically hostile. The minister of education, Pauline Marois, threatened to withhold provincial support, by an equivalent amount, from any university that accepted CFI funding. She complained not only about the operating costs that the province would endure in sustaining CFI projects, but, more significantly, about this latest intervention by the federal government into an area of provincial jurisdiction. She demanded that Ottawa assign Quebec's share of CFI funding directly to the provincial government, which would allocate the funds according to the province's own research priorities.[30] Federal Industry Minister John Manley responded in kind, condemning Quebec's 'stupid policy' as a throwback 'to the dark Duplessis years.' The government was threatening to 'deprive Quebec researchers' of the ability to do 'innovative work in the province.' Furthermore, he claimed that the support of research was historically a federal responsibility, and that the CFI was, in any event, an independent agency at arm's length from the federal government; thus the program did not violate provincial constitutional prerogatives.[31]

Rejecting CFI funding would have proved very costly to the Quebec academic community, and within one week of the eruption of the dispute, the province had adopted a more conciliatory stance. Intergovermental Affairs Minister Jacques Brassard publicly proposed a compromise that would become the basis for a formal agreement between the federal and Quebec governments in March 1998. In order to ensure that funded research projects were 'aligned with provincial priorities,' the Quebec government would review university research proposals and submit the approved list to the CFI for funding.[32] This arrangement, unique to the province of Quebec, remains in place today.

On the heels of the CFI strategy came the inauguration in 2000 of the unprecedented Canada Research Chairs Program. University presidents Martha Piper (University of British Columbia) and Robert LaCroix (Université de Montréal) were especially influential in the promotion of this initiative.[33] Designed to lure scholars back to Canada and to keep emerging academic 'stars' from leaving the country, the program provided funding for up to two thousand prestigious research chairs at Canadian universities. Tier I chairs, intended for senior scholars with distinguished records, were to be allocated $200,000 annually, while Tier II chairs, for especially promising academics, were provided with $100,000. These resources would generally cover salary and benefits. Universities would then, on behalf of the chairs, apply to the CFI for research support. Allocated to universities largely on the basis of their success in securing funding from the three federal granting councils, the awards have gone disproportionately to those in the medical and applied sciences over those in the humanities and social sciences

– a reflection of the relative scarcity of granting council research funds in the latter areas.[34]

If investment in science and technology became an important federal priority in the Chrétien years, so too did the fields of medicine and health. Public funding for medical research, steered primarily through the Medical Research Council, had declined steadily between 1989 and 1995, and in response, the research community reinvented itself and secured new funding commitments from the federal government.

Under the leadership of Dr. Henry Friesen, the Medical Research Council proffered a more robust notion of research that would now explicitly include health as well as medicine and that, potentially, would draw together different disciplines within and beyond the medical and scientific communities.[35] Such work was intended to extend the country's knowledge frontiers, strengthen Canada's position internationally in health research, inform policy, and, ideally, contribute to improving the state of Canadians' health. Friesen launched the Canadian Medical Discoveries Fund, a venture capital fund designed to commercialize medical research. His vision and initiatives resonated within the academic and policy communities. 'Finance Minister Paul Martin cited the Fund as an example of why government should invest in medical research.'[36]

These strategies culminated in the dissolution of the Medical Research Council and the creation, in 2000, of the Canadian Institutes for Health Research. Headed by Dr. Allan Bernstein, the CIHR was divided into thirteen virtual institutes, each focused on a different health area. 'CIHR was able to combine strategic, targeted initiatives through its Institutes, with core individual investigator-based discovery programs,' and between 2001–2 and 2003–4, CIHR increased its funding from $399 million to $576 million, substantially enhancing its profile and activities.[37]

Genome Canada, another science-based foundation, began in 2000 with a $160 million federal grant intended to develop and implement a national strategy for geonomics and proteomics (genetics) research, with an additional mandate to 'support projects that study and analyse the ethical, environmental, economic, legal and social issues related to this research.'[38] Its research has focused on health, agriculture, environment, forestry, and the fisheries.

The commercialization of university research, particularly in the applied sciences, emerged as a high priority in the Chrétien years. Reporting in March 1999, the Expert Panel on the Commercialization of University Research, which had been appointed by the federal Ministry of Industry Science and Technology, recommended that commercialization be made a fourth fundamental objective of academic life, alongside teaching, scholarship, and service, and that academics who produce marketable and profitable research be promoted and tenured especially quickly. The panel sought to ensure the commercialization of intellectual property by obligating all recipients of federal grants to turn their research results over to the university, which would then be expected to find investors to market their 'discoveries.' In the wake of major opposition from faculty associations and from many Canadian research scientists who would have been expected to participate in the scheme, these proposals were shelved.[39]

The issue, however, remained pertinent in policy circles. Recognizing that universities needed to persuade government of their critical economic importance in order to secure increased funding for research, the Association of Universities and Colleges of Canada promoted a commercialization agenda, both among its member institutions and in the halls of Parliament. It reported in 2001 on the growth of intellectual property assets in Canadian universities, which, by 1999, exceeded $22 million. AUCC estimated that university research and knowledge transfer contributed $50 billion to the Canadian economy in 2004, which was attributed, in part, to the spin-off of federal initiatives such as the NCE program. AUCC was careful – more careful than the Expert Panel had been – to defend fundamental principles of academic freedom, but it knew that the key to enhancing public funding was demonstrating the direct and indirect importance of universities to the knowledge economy.[40]

Policy makers in government were especially conscious of the 'productivity gap' between Canada and the United States, the latter of which appeared able to generate more wealth out of its public and private investments. Historically overly dependent on the exploitation of natural resources, and confronted currently by the shift of manufacturing activity from North America to the developing world, Canada required greater investment in 'innovation' (that is, in the kind of knowledge-based research in which universities were engaged) in order to forge and sustain a prosperous economy. This, in any event, was the case made by AUCC to the offices of the prime minister, the finance minister, and the ministry of industry Canada.[41]

In particular, AUCC lobbyists, with support from the Humanities and Social Federation of Canada, argued that universities would be continuously stifled, and Canada would remain incapable of closing the productivity gap with the United States, without the federal government's commitment to funding the 'indirect costs' of research. In order to undertake and sustain funded research, Canadian institutions, traditionally, had to provide infrastructure, computing services, and administrative and related requirements, which tri-council grants did not cover. Federally supported research agencies in the United States, by contrast, had been supporting the indirect costs of research for decades. If Canadian universities were to secure similar assistance, they could, in all likelihood, speed up the process of commercialization and contribute more effectively to economic growth. AUCC argued, furthermore, that such federal spending was constitutionally justifiable in light of the long history of Ottawa's involvement in research funding. Politically, this was a difficult case to make; AUCC President Giroux understood that the issue of indirect costs, though of great importance to the university research community, had little cachet on the hustings.[42]

Fortunately, the government was persuaded, and in 2001 it allocated $200 million in indirect funding to post-secondary institutions, which rose to $240 million by 2004. In turn, Allan Rock, the minister of industry Canada, required universities, in the interests of accountability, to report publicly on research outcomes, including commercialization success stories. This was a key element of a 'Framework of Agreed Principles on Federally Funded University Research,' which the Association of Universities and Colleges of Canada, on behalf of Canada's post-secondary institutions, signed with the federal government following a National Summit on Innovation and Learning in November 2002. The universities committed to 'tripling commercialization performance' and 'doubling their research and development activities' between 1999 and 2010, which, ideally, would enable Canada to become one of the 'top five countries in terms of R&D and commercialization outputs.'[43] In *Momentum: The 2005 Report on University Research and Knowledge Transfer*, AUCC claimed that universities were on 'target' to meet these goals. The *Momentum* report also provided numerous examples of innovative research in science, technology, health, and social science underway in Canadian universities, all of which was designed to demonstrate that federal government support for the direct and indirect costs of research was paying off.[44]

Notwithstanding such welcomed initiatives, which included the creation of the Trudeau Foundation Fellowships,[45] the Social Sciences and Humanities Research Council struggled continuously to meet its constituency's research needs. By 1996–7, SSHRC was able to fund just

5 per cent of the graduate students and 15 per cent of the faculty that it represented, and its budget was one-quarter that of the Natural Sciences and Engineering Research Council, which provided funding to 20 per cent of its student and 60 per cent of its faculty constituencies.[46] The situation improved in 1998 when the federally funded research agencies received an increase of $150 million, which had the effect of restoring SSHRC's funding to its 1994 levels. Even with this significant step, the resources allocated to SSHRC were simply not keeping pace with the research needs of a growing population of professors and graduate students. Comprising 55 per cent of the Canadian academic community (in 2002), SSHRC received only 12 per cent of the federal funds allocated for research and development, and the proportion of Standard Research Grant applications approved for funding, but not funded, because of insufficient resources, actually increased from 22 to 29 per cent between 1998 and 2002.[47]

SSHRC's disadvantage could be explained, in part, by the fact that research in the humanities and social sciences was less saleable to politicians and the public than 'cutting edge' work in science, technology, and health, which appeared to be more relevant to the needs of ordinary citizens. Some opposition members in Parliament and the media ritualistically mocked esoteric projects that received SSHRC funding,[48] and politicians who spoke favourably about the value of government investment in research virtually always ignored the humanities and social sciences while highlighting the areas of employment, trade, science, and technology as key drivers of the 'knowledge economy.'[49]

In response to these political and financial challenges, Marc Renaud, the president of the Social Sciences and Humanities Research Council, spearheaded a 'transformation' designed to heighten the profile, demonstrate the importance, increase the influence, and enhance the resources of the organization. SSHRC initiated a dialogue within the academic community to mobilize support for this mission, and it proposed to transform itself from a 'Granting Council' to a 'Knowledge Council' whose value to Canadian society, ideally, would be better illustrated, recognized, and rewarded than in the past. The national dialogue provoked lively and critical responses in universities, each of which appointed a delegate who was asked to convene campus consultations and to attend a national meeting in 2004 on the proposed transformation.[50] In the fall of 2005, SSHRC produced a new strategic plan.[51] But the (involuntary) departure of Marc Renaud from the presidency of SSHRC, and the 2006 election defeat of the Liberal government, which until then had been the object of a sustained SSHRC lobbying campaign, raised questions not only about SSHRC's prospects for more funding but about the commitment of the new government to the 'innovation' agenda itself.

A most unusual component of this agenda was the proposed establishment of the Canadian Learning Institute. The 2002 Speech from the Throne described it as an arm's length body that would 'work with Canadians, provinces, sector councils, labour organizations and learning institutions to create the skills and learning architecture that Canada needs,' including 'building our knowledge and reporting to Canadians about what is working and what is not.' As a type of informational clearing house, the institute would report on learning outcomes, recommend best practices, and disseminate pertinent information to those engaged in learning and skills development. Notably, it promised to 'respect jurisdiction, co-ordinate information and not duplicate any existing activities by government or third party organizations.'[52]

After considerable delay, the institute emerged in 2004 as the Canadian Council on Learning, which defined itself as a 'catalyst for life long learning across Canada.' Committed to promoting applied research and 'knowledge exchange,' and supported by an $85 million budget over five years, the council proceeded to establish five regionally dispersed 'knowledge centres' on the themes of Aboriginal Learning, Adult Learning, Early Childhood Learning, Health and Learning, and Work and Learning.[53] Universities competed with each other and with community-based learning agencies for CCL grants. Though playing no direct role in determining the council's specific priorities, the federal government intended, through this initiative, to steer academic research into projects that would contribute, in measurable ways, to the improvement of education and training throughout the country.

The 'knowledge economy' required not only enhanced opportunities and high-quality facilities for researchers, but better access to postsecondary education for promising students from all income groups, particularly in light of growing university tuition fees and student indebtedness, both of which had more than doubled over the course of the 1990s.[54] In response, the Chrétien government established the Canada Millennium Scholarship Foundation, which received a $2.5 billion endowment designed to last for ten years. Because it was 'conceived in obvious haste,' there was some confusion as to whether the program's primary purpose was to support the top students (the goal of most 'scholarship' plans), facilitate access, and/or diminish student debt.[55]

Indeed, within the government itself, this plan, perceived as one of Prime Minister Chrétien's 'legacy' initiatives, was reportedly the source of a pointed debate between those who favoured a needs-based and others who supported a merit-based system. Concerned about the growing problem of student debt, Human Resources Minister Pierre Pettigrew ultimately opted – as did the program itself – for a mainly needs-based allocation, an approach that duplicated that of the long-standing Canada Student Loans Plan.[56] In 2000, the first Millennium Scholarship Foundation bursaries, worth $3,000 each, were provided to 90,000 students with demonstrable financial needs. The program also allocated 930 merit-based entrance awards to high-performing high school graduates.

Behind the scenes, the foundation faced a number of challenges. While poorer provinces treated the fund as 'manna from heaven,' enabling them to provide low-income students with grants rather than loans only, in those provinces, such as Quebec and Ontario, where grants or subsidy programs were already available, questions emerged about how the Millennium bursaries would be allocated. Would they simply displace current provincial funding? The foundation negotiated distinctive arrangements with each province designed to ensure that Millennium funds would be appropriately spent. In the Quebec case, explained Norman Riddell, Millennium Foundation CEO and president, 'in return for the Foundation paying $70 million of bursaries that would otherwise have been paid by the province, the province undertook to provide $35 million to universities and colleges in order to moderate the growth of ancillary fees and $35 million (or more if required) to reduce the threshold (by 25 per cent) above which loans for all students receiving assistance from Quebec would be converted to grants.'[57]

A different plan was developed for Ontario, which had a program limiting student borrowing to $7,000 for a two-term academic year and $10,500 for a three-term year; debts above that level would be paid down by the government. But a Millennium Fund grant potentially reduced a student's eligibility for both loans and the debt-reduction entitlement. 'In its agreement with the Foundation, Ontario undertook to reinvest any savings in student financial assistance,' and ultimately did so by providing additional resources to Millennium Fund recipients, and by increasing its commitment to 'merit-based' assistance for Ontario students.[58]

In more recent years, the foundation has employed a new approach in its dealings with the provinces. It has allocated funds according to each province's share of Canada's population, and 'invited' provincial governments to 'build a program with the Foundation' that pursues general objectives such as improving the participation of low-income Canadians in post-secondary education. Through this 'mediated transfer,' Ottawa uses its spending power to provide funds through the vehicle of an independent foundation, which has created slightly different programs from one province to another. Were the federal government to run the program directly, it would be under greater pressure, constitutionally, to deliver a student assistance program that 'treats all Canadians in the same way, no matter where they live.'[59] Questions remained about the Millennium Foundation's effectiveness in improving access to post-secondary education for low-income students and/or reducing the burden of student debt, though its full impact could be determined only by sustained study over an extended period.[60] The foundation itself has regularly published data pointing to its growing significance in the world of student assistance. By 2005 it had distributed $1.7 billion in bursaries, and almost $48.7 million in merit-based scholarships.[61] In the meantime, through its varied agreements with the provinces, the Millennium program exemplified, by result, if not by original design, a form of 'asymmetric federalism.'[62]

Two other significant government initiatives spoke to the issues of funding and access for students. The Canada Graduate Scholarship Program, announced in the 2003 federal budget, would allocate, when fully implemented, more than $100 million annually for the support of 2,000 master's and 2,000 doctoral students. The former were to receive $17,000 annual awards, and the latter $35,000. Unlike the federally supported research programs, this plan assigned funds to the granting councils according to the proportion of students by academic field, so that those in the humanities and social sciences received 60 per cent of the awards, versus 30 per cent for those in science and engineering, and 10 per cent for those in health and medicine.[63]

The federal government sought to encourage private support for post-secondary education by making changes to the longstanding, but little-used, Registered Educational Savings Plan, which enabled families to create a tax-sheltered investment fund for their children's educational future. The 1996 and 1997 budgets provided enhancements to the scheme, permitting investors, for example, to transfer RESP funds to Registered Retirement Savings Plans (RRSP). In 1998, the government augmented this program with the introduction of the Canadian Education Savings Grant, which enabled families to top up their annual RESP contributions by an additional 20 per cent. Those who contributed the maximum of $2,000 per child per year would receive a $400 grant from the federal government. These changes significantly increased participation in the program, but it appeared to be of greatest benefit to middle- and upper-income earners, that is, to those who were actually in a position to set aside annual financial contributions for prospective higher educational costs.[64]

Piecemeal enhancement programs, designed in part to address such concerns, followed over the next several years. These included the Canada Study Grant, which provided special financial assistance to low-income students with children. In 2004, the federal government established the Canada Learning Bond, which was intended to 'help modest-income families start saving early for their child's education after high school.' Families (with children born since 1 January 2004) receiving the National Child Benefit Supplement (those with net incomes under $36,000 annually) were entitled to an additional $2,000 grant to be deposited over a fifteen-year period into their RESPs. With accumulated interest, the fund could grow to a total of $3,000.[65]

In adopting such 'student assistance' measures, including the Millennium Scholarship program, the federal government rejected the advice it had received from a number of political and academic quarters to implement an 'Income Contingency Repayment Financing Plan.' Schemes based on this model require students to pay substantially higher tuition fees and then repay student loans, or be forgiven a portion of such obligations, in accordance with their post-university or -college employment income. Proponents of this approach, which included former Human Resources Development minister Lloyd Axworthy pointed to the examples of Australia, New Zealand, and England where versions of the ICRFP had been implemented during the 1980s and 1990s.[66] Instead, for this and a variety of other post-secondary educational programs, the Chrétien government opted for a patchwork of high-profile policies that allowed it simultaneously to claim credit for implementing a bold, research-based 'innovation' agenda expected to fuel the Canada economy, boosting the cause of higher education, supporting educational opportunities for the poor, and serving the financial interests of the middle classes. The jurisdictional challenges that these initiatives might provoke seemed a small price to pay for the perceived political advantages they promised.

The post-secondary educational programs introduced by the federal government during the second half of the Chrétien years injected new resources and renewed enthusiasm into the world of higher education – a welcome contrast to the gloom created by the dramatic funding cuts of the first half-decade. The 'innovation strategy' was generally well received by university spokespersons – though beneficiaries of government largesse, for all intents and purposes, were politically obligated to publicly praise their benefactors, irrespective of any private concerns they may have had about the government's actions. There were many historical precedents for federal engagement in the funding of research, so programs such as the Canada Foundation for Innovation and the Networks of Centres of Excellence elicited relatively little opposition on constitutional grounds – the initial Quebec opposition to the CFI announcement notwithstanding.

While some individual academics lamented the resurgence of 'unilateral' decision making in areas of provincial jurisdiction, provincial governments themselves, and certainly the universities they oversaw, as in the past, were more diffident, because the federal programs added to the institutions' revenues.[67] The desperate need for new resources, in light of the funding cuts in the early 1990s, and in the wake of a relentless and growing demand for higher education in Canada, should not be underestimated. Indeed, provincial support for, and justification of, federal initiatives in post-secondary education could be found in a 2002 report, entitled *Working Together*, issued by the Council of Ministers of Education in Canada. The ministers called 'on the federal government to provide new flexible financial support, through mechanisms already in place by fully restoring the Canada Health and Social Transfer (CHST), a portion of which supports post-secondary learning, or through alternative mechanisms agreed to bilaterally with provinces and territories in order to meet their capacity needs.'[68]

Indeed, most of the new funding built upon established programs or was channelled through existing agencies, such as NSERC, CIHR, and SSHRC. The most controversial of these initiatives, the Millennium Scholarship Foundation program, muted criticism from the provinces, including Quebec, once its operations were integrated with provincially administered student assistance plans.[69]

Political dynamics aside, the challenges facing post-secondary education remained significant, even in the wake of the era of the 'new paradigm,' adopted in 1997. By all measures, the federal resources assigned to health care far outstripped those provided to post-secondary education – a trend that was likely to continue.[70] Universities faced daunting challenges, too, in infrastructural and faculty renewal. It was estimated in 2000 that deferred maintenance of universities totalled $3.6 billion, and that over the course of the ensuing decade, Canada would require twenty-five thousand to thirty thousand new professors.[71] It was unclear, at the end of the Liberal government's most recent tenure, whether the resources required to meet these basic needs would be available – from federal *or* provincial governments.

Finally, the federal government, like its provincial counterparts, perceived post-secondary education primarily, if not exclusively, as a vehicle for fostering economic growth. As Polster notes, university research was considered, potentially, 'a key force of innovation in the global knowledge-based economy ... designed to move the university beyond its role of a mere supporter of wealth creation toward a new role as co-producer of an economic revolution.'[72] This left professors and students in the humanities and social sciences (who constituted the majority of the academic population in Canada) in an especially vulnerable position. Support for research in these fields lagged, and politicians' enthusiasm for 'curiosity-based' or foundational scholarship, even in the 'knowledge society,' was scarcely visible. SSHRC itself reported to the Department of Industry Canada, a potent symbol of how narrowly the federal government perceived the purposes of university-based research. The federal policy changes also contributed significantly to the 'marketization' of higher education by increasingly requiring universities to find private-sector partners in order to qualify for major research grants, especially in 'strategic science.'[73] The election of a new Conservative government in January 2006 officially closed one chapter of an event-filled and turbulent period in post-secondary education, and in all likelihood, opened another.

NOTES

1 Jeffrey Simpson, 'Chrétien's Legacy: Don't Think Gomery, Think R&D,' *Globe and Mail*, 4 November 2005.
2 David M. Cameron, 'The Federal Perspective,' in *Higher Education in Canada: Different Systems, Different Perspectives*, ed. Glen A. Jones (New York: Garland, 1997), 18–21.
3 Gérald Bernier and David Irwin, 'Fiscal Federalism: The Politics of Intergovernmental Transfers,' in *New Trends in Canadian Federalism*, ed. François Rocher and Miriam Smith (Peterborough, ON: Broadview, 1995), 277.

4 David M. Cameron, 'Post-secondary Education Research: Whither Canadian Federalism?' in *Taking Public Universities Seriously*, ed. Frank Iacobucci
   and Carolyn Tuohy (Toronto: University of Toronto Press, 2005), 279; Donald Fisher, *The Social Sciences in Canada: 50 Years of National Activity by the
   Social Science Federation of Canada* (Waterloo, ON: Wilfrid Laurier University Press, 1991), 67–80.

5 Cameron, 'Post-secondary Education Research,' 280.

6 Janet Atkinson-Grosjean, *Public Science, Private Interests: Culture and Commerce in Canada's Networks of Centres of Excellence* (Toronto: University of
   Toronto Press, 2006), xiii.

7 Association of Universities and Colleges of Canada (AUCC), *Momentum:
   The 2005 Report on University Research and Knowledge Transfer* (Ottawa:
   AUCC, 2005), 8.

8 For a list of previous and current NCE projects, see http://www.nce.gc.ca/
   nets_e.htm.

9 Robert B. Asselin, 'The Canadian Social Union: Questions about the Division of Powers and Fiscal Federalism,' Political and Social Affairs Divisions, Library of Parliament, Parliamentary Information and Research
   Service, 18 January 2001, 6. http://www.parl.gc.ca/information/library/
   PRBpubs/prb0031-e.htm.

10 Ronald L. Watts, *The Spending Power in Federal Systems: A Comparative Study*
    (Kingston: Queen's University Institute of Intergovernmental Relations,
    1999), chap. 2–4.

11 Ibid., 2.

12 David A. Wolfe, 'Innovation and Research Funding: The Role of Govern-
    ment Support,' in *Taking Public Universities Seriously*, 330–2.

13 Jennifer Smith, *The Case for Asymmetry in Canadian Federalism*, Asymmetry
    Series, IIGR (Kingston: School of Policy Studies, Queen's University [6],
    2005).

14 Michael Howlett, 'Federalism and Public Policy,' in *Canadian Politics*, ed.
    James Bickerton and Alain-G. Gagnon (Peterborough, ON: Broadview,
    1999), 530–1. See also Asselin, 'The Canadian Social Union,' 7; edito-
    rial, 'How the Conservatives Will Approach Quebec,' *Globe and Mail*, 26
    January 2006; Brooke Jeffrey, 'From Collaborative Federalism to the New
    Unilateralism: Implications for the Welfare State,' in *Continuing and Change
    in Canadian Politics: Essays in Honour of David E. Smith*, Hans J. Michelmann
    and Christine de Clercy (Toronto: University of Toronto Press), 130–3.

15 Jeffrey, 'From Collaborative Federalism to the New Unilateralism,' 133.

16 Watts, *The Spending Power in Federal Systems*, 63–4.

17 J. Robert S. Prichard, 'Federal Support for Higher Education and Research

in Canada: The New Paradigm' (Killam Annual Lecture, Killam Trusts, Winnipeg, November 2000), 15.

18 Ibid., 17–18.

19 Howlett, 'Federalism and Public Policy,' 530–1.

20 AUCC, *Momentum*, 8. See also Jeffrey, 'From Collaborative Federalism to the New Unilateralism,' 136–7.

21 Interview with Robert Giroux, 12 April 2006.

22 Prichard, 'Federal Support for Higher Education and Research in Canada,' 20.

23 Atkinson-Grosjean, *Public Science, Private Interests*, xiii.

24 Donald Fisher, Janet Atkinson-Grosjean, and Dawn House, 'Changes in Academy/Industry/State Relations in Canada: The Creation and Development of the Networks of Centres of Excellence,' *Minerva* 39 (2001): 300.

25 Cited in Atkinson-Grosjean. *Public Science, Private Interests*, 61.

26 AUCC, *Momentum*, 8.

27 Cameron, 'Post-secondary Education Research,' 282.

28 Claire Polster, 'A Break from the Past: Impacts and Implications of the Canada Foundation on Innovation and the Canada Research Chairs Initiative,' *Canadian Review of Sociology and Anthropology* 39, no. 3 (2002): 275–99.

29 Atlantic Canada Opportunities Agency, 'Evaluations,' http://www.acoa.ca/e/library/audit/marchevaluation2004.shtml.

30 Elizabeth Thompson, 'Don't Take Federal Funds, Quebec Warns Universities,' *Gazette*, 9 December 1997, A8.

31 Terrence Wills, 'Blocking Federal Money Is Stupid', *Gazette*, 10 December 1997, AI, A8; Hugette Young, 'Manley dénonce le "chantage" de Marois et Rochon,' *Le Devoir*, 17 December 1997, A7.

32 Elizabeth Thompson, 'Quebec Relents on Federal Fund,' *Gazette*, 17 December 1997, A12; interview with Christian Sylvain, 29 November 2005.

33 Interview with Robert Giroux, 12 April 2006. See also Graham Fraser, 'University Research Is Not an Ivory-Tower Endeavour,' *Toronto Star*, 7 November 2004. He reports on a conversation between Robert LaCroix and Prime Minister Chrétien, which evidently helped secure support for the Canada Research Chairs Program.

34 See discussion below.

35 Prichard, 'Federal Support for Higher Education and Research in Canada,' 22. Jean Chrétien's brother, Michel Chrétien, a well-known chemist, is said to have been especially important in persuading the prime minister of the value of scientific – particularly medical – research. See Ann McIlroy, 'Brothers Link Worlds of Science and Politics: Michel Chrétien Has Been Influential in Shaping the PM's Legacy of Revitalizing University Research,' *Globe and Mail*, 19 May 2003.

36 Calvin R. Stiller, 'Contribution of Higher Education to Research and Innovation: Balancing the "Social Contract" of Universities with Their Drive for Scholarly Excellence,' in *Creating Knowledge: Strengthening Nations; The Changing Role of Higher Education*, ed. Glen A. Jones, Patricia L. McCarney, and Michael L. Skolnik (Toronto: University of Toronto Press, 2005), 270.

37 John R.G. Challis, Jose Sigourin, Judith Chadwick, and Michelle Broderick, 'The University Research Environment,' in *Taking Public Universities Seriously*, 363.

38 AUCC, *Momentum*, 9.

39 Paul Axelrod, *Values in Conflict: The University, the Marketplace and the Trials of Liberal Education* (Montreal and Kingston: McGill-Queen's University Press, 2002), 101; Peter Calami, 'Profit Spin-off Is Planned,' *Toronto Star*, 10 March 2000.

40 AUCC, 'University Research and Knowledge Transfer Add $50 Billion to Economy,' news release, 24 October 2005, http://www.aucc.ca/publications/media/2005/10_24_e.html.

41 Interview, Robert Giroux, 12 April 2006.

42 Ibid.; interview, Christian Sylvain, 29 November 2005.

43 AUCC, *Momentum*, 30–1. The 'Innovation Strategy' was articulated in two papers: 'Knowledge Matters: Skills and Learning for Canadians' (Ottawa: HRDC, 2002), and 'Achieving Excellence: Investing in People, Knowledge and Opportunities' (Ottawa: Industry Canada, 2002). See http://www. innovationstrategy.gc.ca. See also Jane Stewart, 'Remarks by the Honourable Jane Stewart, Minister of Human Resources Development Canada for News Conference to Announce Knowledge Matters: Skills and Learning for Canadians,' at Toromont Caterpillar Ltd, Kanata, ON, 12 February 2002, where she formally announced the Innovation Strategy. http://www. hrsdc.gc.ca/en/cs/comm/speeches/hrdc/2002/index02e-shtml.

44 For a critical discussion of the Innovation Agenda, see Shirley Neuman, 'Creating Knowledge, Strengthening Nations: The Role of Research and Education in Humanities and Social Sciences in Government Agendas for Innovation,' in *Creating Knowledge, Strengthening Nations: The Changing Role of Higher Education*, Glen A. Jones, Patricia L. McCarney, and Michael Skolnik, 227–45 (Toronto: University of Toronto Press, 2005).

45 This foundation, established in the name of the former prime minister, was awarded a $125 million endowment for the 'creation of a truly world-class program for advanced studies in the humanities.' See Allan Rock, minister of Industry Canada, 'Speaking Notes' in the House of Commons on the Pierre Elliott Trudeau Foundation Fellowships, 20 February 2002, http://www.ic.gc.ca/epic/site/icl.nsf/en/016zle.html.

46 Michel Groulx, 'Marc Renaud: Restoring the Value of Humanities Research,' *University Affairs* (February 1998): 14–15.
47 Janet E. Halliwell, SSHRC executive vice-president, 'Notes for a Statement to the House Standing Committee on Finance,' 28 May 2002; Social Sciences and Humanities Research Council, 'Post-secondary Education, the Social Sciences and Humanities, and the Innovation Agenda,' 10 July 2002.
48 See Randy Boswell, 'Intelligent Design Not Smart Enough for Science,' *Windsor Star*, 17 April 2006; Terry O'Neill, 'Some Ideas Are Ignored for a Reason,' *Western Standard*, 12 December 2005. See also Anne Marie Owens, 'Social Sciences' Serious Image Problem,' *National Post*, 20 May 2006, A1, A10.
49 For example, see the speeches in Parliament of government members defending the 1996 and 1997 budgets: Andy Mitchell, Leonard Hopkins, and Marlene Caterall, 18 March 1996; George Pound, 18 March 1997.
50 Marc Renaud, 'From Granting Council to Knowledge Council: Renewing the Social Sciences and Humanities in Canada' (paper presented to the Government Caucus on Post-secondary Education, 17 September 2003); Social Sciences and Humanities Research Council (SSHRC), *From Granting Council to Knowledge Council: Reviewing the Social Sciences and Humanities in Canada; Report on the Consultations* (Ottawa: SSHRC, January 2005).
51 SSHRC, Knowledge Council, *SSHRC: 2006–2011* (Ottawa: SSHRC, August 2005).
52 Canadian Learning Institute, 'Backgrounder,' 19 November 2002, http://www.sdc.gc.ca/en/cs/comm/news/2002/021119back.shtml.
53 See the Canadian Council on Learning website: http://www.ccl-cca.ca/ccl.
54 Stephen Bell and Glen A. Jones, 'Paying for a University Education: A Comparison of Public and Private Study Costs in Canada, Australia and Selected European Countries,' in *Preparing for Post-secondary Education: New Roles for Governments and Families*, ed. Robert Sweet and Paul Anisef (Montreal and Kingston: McGill-Queen's University Press, 2005), 93–5.
55 David M. Cameron, 'Post-secondary Education Research: Whither Canadian Federalism?' in *Taking Public Universities Seriously*, 283.
56 Edward Greenspon, '$3 Billion for Your Thoughts: Plans for (Jean) Chrétien's Millennium Scholarship Fund Ballooning, Government Sources Say,' *Globe and Mail*, 5 December 1997.
57 Interview with Norman Riddell, 16 December 2005.
58 Ibid.
59 Ibid.
60 Robert Sweet and Paul Anisef, 'Changing Partnerships: Families, Schools, and Governments,' in *Preparing for Post-secondary Education*, 4–5. An early

assessment, whose criticisms of the foundation's performance were cited widely in the press, was written by Harvey Lazar, ed., *Canadian Millennium Scholarship Foundation: Evaluation of the Foundation's Performance, 1998–2002* (Kingston: Institute of Intergovernmental Relations, Queen's University, 2003); Sarah Schmidt, 'Scholarship Fund Failed, Report Says: Chrétien Legacy Project,' *National Post*, 6 November 2003; Léo Charbonneau, 'Foundation's Effect on Access Questionable, Says Review,' *University Affairs*, January 2004, http://www.universityaffairs.ca/issues/2004/jan/news_4.html; Nelson Wyatt, 'Millennium Scholarship Administrators Deny in Montreal That It's a Failure,' CP Wire, 6 November 2003.

61 See http://www.millenniumscholarships.ca/en/map.asp. The foundation's publications included Sean Junor and Alexander Usher, *The Price of Knowledge: Access and Student Finance in Canada*, which was first published in 2002, and in a revised edition in 2004. In its 2008 budget, the Conservative government under Prime Minister Stephen Harper announced 'its intention not to renew the Canada Millennium Scholarship Foundation' after the expiration of the foundation's initial mandate at the end of 2009. See http://www.millenniumscholarships.ca/en/index.asp.

62 See for example, 'Memorandum of Understanding between the Canada Millennium Scholarship Foundation and the Province of British Columbia,' 25 February 2005; 'Agreement between the Canada Millennium Scholarship Foundation and Her Majesty the Queen in Right of Ontario, as Represented by the Minister of Training, Colleges and Universities,' 9 May 2005, typescripts, Canada Millennium Foundation Office Files, Ottawa. I am grateful to Norman Riddell for providing me with this material.

63 Donald Fisher, 'An Unprecedented Opportunity to Contribute to Progress in the 21st Century: The Future of Higher Education in Canada,' Brief to the House of Commons Standing Committee on Finance (Ottawa: Canadian Federation of the Humanities and Social Sciences, 27 October 2005).

64 Stephen Bell and Paul Anisef, 'Accessibility and Student Debt: The Shift from Public to Private Support in Canada,' in *Preparing for Post-Secondary Education*, 77.

65 Human Resources and Social Development Canada, 'Canada Learning Bond,' http://www.hrsdc.gc.ca/en/learning/education_savings/public/clb.shtml. See also Ellen Roseman, 'Learning Bond Sets Course for Low-Income Families, *Toronto Star*, 24 March 2004.

66 For an account of the rejection of Axworthy's proposal, see Edward Greenspon and Anthony Wilson-Smith, *Double Vision: The Inside Story of the Liberals in Power* (Toronto: Doubleday, 1996), 229; and David M. Cameron, 'The Federal Perspective,' in *Higher Education in Canada: Different Systems,*

254   Paul Axelrod

Different Perspectives, ed. Glen A. Jones, 9–29 (New York: Garland, 1997).
On the virtues of the ICRFP, see Benjamin Alarie and David Duff, 'An
Income-Contingent Financial Program for Ontario,' 554–596; and Ross
Finnie, 'Student Financial Aid: The Roles of Loans and Grants,' 476–597;
both in *Taking Public Universities Seriously*.

67 See, for example, the following communiqué: AUCC, 'Canada Foundation
for Innovation: Compatible Priorities,' 2 December 1997.

68 Provincial-Territorial Labour Market Ministers Council of Ministers of
Education, 'Working Together to Strengthen Learning and Labour Market
Training' (Council of Ministers of Education, Canada, July 2002), 6, http://
www.cmec.ca/publications/educlabour.en.pdf.

69 Criticism, however, did come from Sheila Fraser, the auditor general,
who claimed that the fifteen federally established foundations, including
the Millennium Scholarship Foundation and the Canada Foundation for
Innovation (the two largest of these entities) were insufficiently account-
able for the $9 billion of public funds they had received since 1997. The
'government has recorded these transfers as expenses although most of
the funds remain in the foundations' bank accounts and investments ac-
cumulating interest.' The Standing Senate Committee on National Finance,
news release, 22 February 2005. The auditor general had expressed similar
concerns in 2002. See Canada, Office of the Auditor General, *Report to
the House of Commons* (Ottawa: Public Works and Government Services
Canada, 2002), chap. 1. For the government's defence of the administration and operation of the foundations, see 'Accountability of Foundations,'
http://www.fin.gc.ca/toce/2005/accfound-e.html.

70 Donald Fisher et al., *Canadian Federal Policy and Postsecondary Education*
(Vancouver: Centre for Policy Studies in Higher Education and Training,
University of British Columbia Alliance for International Higher Education
Policy Studies, 2006), 48.

71 AUCC, 'University Funding,' November 2000, http://www.aucc.ca/
publications/reports/2000/election/funding_e.html.

72 Claire Polster, 'A Break from the Past: Impacts and Implications of the
Canada Foundation for Innovation and the Canada Research Chairs Initiative,' *Canadian Review of Sociology and Anthropology* 39, no. 3 (2002): 275–99.

73 See Atkinson-Grosjean, *Public Science, Private Interest*, for an extensive analysis of this process. See also Paul Axelrod, *Values in Conflict: Universities,
the Marketplace, and the Trials of Liberal Education* (Montreal and Kingston:
McGill-Queen's University Press, 2002).

10 The Unrealized Benefits of Canada's Unfederal Judicial System

PETER H. RUSSELL

When one thinks about the judiciary and Canadian federalism, the subject that immediately comes to mind is judicial interpretation of the constitution and its influence on the federal division of legislative powers. This is the focus of John Saywell's seminal work on the Judicial Committee of the Privy Council, and of nearly all other writing on the judicial aspects of Canadian federalism. In this essay I will explore another dimension of the judicial side of the Canadian federation that has attracted much less scholarly or political interest: the structure of Canada's court system. The main point of the story I have to tell is about the unplanned and unfulfilled benefits of a federation with a court structure designed for a unitary state.

Constitutional Foundations

The Fathers of Confederation expended little effort in designing the judicial system of Canada. Essentially they simply took the system that they already had as British colonists and adapted it to a federal system of governance. As with their treatment of parliamentary government, the constitution they framed has little to say about the judicial institutions of the federation they were founding.

The only section of Canada's founding constitution, the British North America Act, that makes any reference to specific courts is section 96, which states that the governor general of Canada 'shall appoint the judges of the Superior, District and County Courts in each province.'[1] These were the courts that were already functioning in the 'common law provinces': New Brunswick, Nova Scotia, and Ontario. A superior court based in the provincial capital with its judges going on circuit to hear the most serious cases was supplemented by locally based district or county courts. Quebec was a little bit different: instead of district or county courts, it had a decentralized superior court.

Like Parliament, the founding fathers simply accepted superior courts as part of Canada's English constitutional inheritance, and saw no need to spell out their essential nature. In the English judicial system that had evolved over many centuries the superior court was not an institution to which judges were assigned but consisted of the judges themselves exercising an inherent jurisdiction.[2] The superior court judges' authority, as 'royal judges,' originated with recognition of their authority by the Crown in the twelfth and thirteenth centuries. Over the ensuring centuries superior court judges simply asserted an inherent jurisdiction to hear and decide criminal and civil cases of all kinds, including, in the course of time, claims against the Crown itself. As John Saywell's *The Lawmakers* reminds us, it is this inherent jurisdiction that the provincial superior court judges were exercising when they accepted cases challenging the constitutionality of legislation in the Canadian federation's earliest years.[3] Although the jurisdiction of superior court judges in Canada as in England is inherent and was not created by Parliament, it can be and has been reduced by legislation. This has been done in both countries so that cases deemed to be less serious may be assigned to 'inferior courts.'[4]

County and district courts – the other courts specifically mentioned in the Constitution – are examples of 'inferior courts.' These courts were an Upper Canadian colonial invention, established by Governor Simcoe in 1794, primarily to provide a judicial service to merchants in frontier towns who found it inconvenient to wait for the infrequent visit of a superior court judge from the capital to settle legal disputes involving modest amounts of money. County courts were not established in England until 1846. After Confederation, these 'inferior courts' continued to operate in the common law provinces, their name depending on whether a province's regional administration was set up on a county or district basis.

The superior courts of the provinces were meant to be the keystone institutions of the new country's judicial structure. The judiciary of both the 'inferior' county and district courts and the superior courts of the provinces would be appointed by the federal government and their salaries would be fixed and provided by the federal Parliament. But it is only the superior court judiciary whose tenure is constitutionally secured. Section 99 of the Constitution states that 'Judges of the Superior

Courts shall hold office during good behaviour, but shall be removable by the Governor General on Address of the Senate and House of Commons.'[5] This language is modelled on the Act of Settlement of 1701, the charter of judicial independence in the United Kingdom.

It is a mistake to consider the courts recognized in section 96 – the superior courts as well as the county and district courts – as either federal or provincial institutions. They are both; they are hybrid institutions, partly federal and partly provincial. Their judges are appointed, paid, and removed by the federal government, while the courts themselves are organized, managed, and supported by provincial governments. Section 92 (14) of the Constitution gives the provincial legislature exclusive jurisdiction over 'The Administration of Justice in the Province, including the Constitution, Maintenance, and Organization of Provincial Courts, both of Civil and Criminal Jurisdiction.' This meant that the provinces would be responsible for organizing, housing, and administering its superior courts and its county or district courts, while the federal government would be responsible for appointing, removing, and paying the judges of these courts.

Thus Canada was to have a court system more akin to that of a unitary state than a federal state. By way of contrast, the judicial structure of the American federation has developed along the lines of a dual court system. In the United States, each state has its own system of courts presided over by its own state-appointed judiciary. Alongside these state courts, the federal government has developed an extensive system of trial and appeal courts to hear a broad range of federal law matters as well as diversity suits – that is, suits between citizens from different states. Canada's system of provincial courts with federally appointed judges removed grounds for fearing parochial justice for citizens who find themselves going to court outside their home province. Hence, there was no pressure to set up a parallel system of federal courts for 'diversity suits.' For a federation with more than its share of regional cleavages, the integrated nature of its foundational courts should be considered a blessing.

It would be nice to report that this advantage of the judicature provisions in the Canadian Constitution was the product of the founding fathers' visionary statecraft. But there is no evidence of any deep thinking about Canada's judicial system in the deliberations that produced the 1867 Constitution. The explanation of section 96 comes down basically to the assumption of the leaders of the Confederation project that the leading judges of the new nation would be centrally appointed as

they were in Great Britain. This assumption was fortified by an interest in keeping plum appointments to judicial office in their own hands
– hands that would soon be on the levers of power in Ottawa.[6] Some
justified this arrangement by expressing fear of the parochial politics
that might influence judicial appointments if left in the hands of provincial politicians.[7] The idea that federal politicians would rise above
party politics in discharging their responsibility of appointing judges,
to put it kindly, has an ironic ring today.

Though the section 96 courts were the only courts specifically mentioned in Canada's founding Constitution, other sections contained the
seeds of other courts. Unlike the courts recognized in section 96, these
other courts would be either purely provincial or purely federal. The
constitutional seed with the greatest potential was section 92 (14) with
its carte blanche mandate to provincial governments to constitute, maintain, and organize provincial courts of civil and criminal jurisdiction.
Besides giving the provinces legislative jurisdiction and administrative
responsibility over the superior, county, and district courts, section 92
(14) gave the provinces power to create other provincial courts, and for
these additional provincial courts, provincial governments would have
the responsibility of providing the judiciary. At the time of Confederation these entirely provincial courts dealt with minor criminal and civil
matters, and instead of having a professional, legally trained judiciary,
drew on the English tradition of lay justices of the peace. This rudimentary form of local lay justice would evolve into an extensive system of
provincial courts that, in a quantitative sense, became the major trial
court system in the country.

The other judicial seed, which proved to be much less fertile, is section 101 of the Constitution. Section 101 empowers the federal Parliament to establish, if and when it wishes, 'a General Court of Appeal
for Canada,' and then adds, almost as an afterthought, that Parliament
can also establish 'any Additional Courts for the Better Administration
of the Laws of Canada.' The first part of section 101 provided the constitutional authority for the creation of the Supreme Court of Canada.
It was not until 1875, eight years after Confederation, that Parliament
exercised its power to create the Supreme Court of Canada as a general
court of appeal for Canada – but not Canada's highest court of appeal.
That function would continue to be served, right up until 1949, by the
highest court in the British Empire, the Judicial Committee of the Privy
Council. At the time of Confederation and for a long time thereafter, appeal rights were severely limited, and there were no courts specializing

in appeals under the Supreme Court of Canada. Appeals below the Supreme Court were handled by judges of the provincial superior courts, hearing appeals from judges of their own court or reviewing decisions of 'inferior courts.'[8] Eventually, as the country became more litigious, all of the provinces established courts of appeal as their highest courts. These provincial courts of appeal were in effect emanations of their superior courts, with their judges appointed and paid by Ottawa.

The second part of section 101 – the bit about 'Additional Courts for the Better Administration of the Laws of Canada' – had the potential of establishing a separate tier of federal courts specializing in federal legal matters, analogous to the American system. Though there is evidence that John A. Macdonald was intending to make considerable use of this branch of section 101,[9] his plans met a great deal of provincial opposition, and it was used only to give supreme court justices some exchequer court jurisdiction. Out of that grew the eight-judge Exchequer Court of Canada. In 1971, the exchequer court was absorbed into the Federal Court of Canada, and although it has a significantly larger jurisdiction than the exchequer court – especially in matters of federal administrative law and immigration law – it is much smaller and more specialized than its US counterpart.[10] So, while a dual court system developed in Canada, it was not a system of federal and provincial courts, but a two-tier system of provincial trial courts, one with a federally appointed and remunerated judiciary, the other with a provincially appointed and remunerated judiciary.

Evolution of the Trial Court System

Since Confederation, the trial court system has evolved in a manner unforeseen by the founding fathers. The ever-increasing demands for court services generated by the urbanization and industrialization of the country were met mostly at the lowest level of the provincial court system, where responsibility for appointing and paying the judiciary rests entirely with the provinces. In the field of criminal justice most of the expanding caseloads were taken over by salaried magistrates, who replaced the benches of local gentry serving as justices of the peace. These increases in the criminal justice responsibilities of the lowest provincial courts were brought about by the federal Parliament in its periodic amendments of sections of the Criminal Code that designate the courts for trying various classes of criminal cases. Again, it would be nice to report that there was some intelligent plan behind the continuous expansion of the provincial magistrates' criminal jurisdiction, but one searches the federal Hansard in vain for any considered discussion of the merits of giving the lowest provincial courts such a major role in the administration of criminal justice. One has the impression that this was simply a cheap way for the federal government to off-load the growing costs of criminal justice to the provinces.

The provinces, in turn, for a very long time off-loaded the responsibility of managing and staffing magistrates courts to municipalities. The result was a not a pretty picture: a poorly qualified, mostly lay judiciary, operating inefficiently in shoddy surroundings and often closely associated with the police, had become the workhorse of Canada's criminal justice system, the portal through which every case that entered the system was processed. The picture was a little different in Quebec, where the province had converted its Court of Sessions of the Peace into a professional single-judge court that tried the criminal cases that in common law Canada were heard in county or district courts. But Quebec also had magistrates and municipal courts for less serious criminal cases. In the civil area it was also the purely provincial courts that provided the new kinds of judicial service required for handling family and consumer disputes. With the advance of the welfare state, the provinces established family and youth court services in a variety of institutional forms. It was also the provincially appointed judiciary that assumed most of the responsibility for trying civil suits involving small amounts of money.

In the 1960s and 1970s, in a wave of reform that I have referred to as 'the judicialization of the magistracy,'[11] the provinces transformed local magistrates courts into centralized systems of provincial courts. The provincial courts were staffed by a legally trained judiciary whose professional qualifications soon came to equal those of the federally appointed section 96 judiciary. The provincial court judiciary also came to enjoy security of tenure and judicial independence on a par with the federally appointed provincial judiciary. This upgrading of the professional qualifications and terms of office of provincial court judges was accompanied by further expansion of their jurisdiction. In the criminal justice area, the federal Parliament kept increasing the serious indictable offences for which trial before a provincial court judge was an option, and increasingly this option was chosen by defendants. By the end of the twentieth century, 98 per cent of the adult criminal court caseload in Canada was being resolved in the provincial courts. Provincial courts were also responsible for virtually all criminal justice relating to young offenders, and all family court adjudication, save the issuing of divorce decrees and related property matters that remain attached to the superior courts. Similarly, for civil suits, the monetary limit of the provincial courts' so-called small claims jurisdiction continued to creep upwards, eventually reaching $70,000 in Quebec.

While provincial courts were emerging as a major system of trial courts, the second level of trial courts provided for in the Constitution – the county and district courts – were fading away. In an age of modern transportation and communication, it no longer made sense to maintain a locally based county or district court judiciary with a jurisdiction just slightly less than that of a capital-based, itinerant superior court judiciary. Lawyers in cities like Calgary, Hamilton, and Ottawa were insisting on having their own resident superior court judiciary. Still, it took nearly twenty years – 1973 to 1992 – for the merger of the county and district courts into superior courts to be completed and it was accomplished not without a good deal of political skirmishing along the way.

A crucial consequence of the integrated nature of Canada's section 96 courts is that changes in them require joint action by federal and provincial authorities. While it is provincial governments and legislatures that must introduce and implement any legislation that restructures these courts, for these changes to come into effect, the federal government and Parliament must make the appropriate changes in the number of judges and provide for their remuneration. In 1969, when British Columbia made the first request to eliminate county and district courts and 'elevate' the judges of these courts to its superior court,[12] the federal government refused to cooperate. No public reason was offered for turning down BC's request. It would seem unlikely that federal reluctance stemmed from the modest increase in judicial salaries it would have to pay. A more plausible explanation is that superior court judges who were opposed to the merger had the ear of federal ministers. Certainly, the heart of opposition to merger came from the superior court judiciary. The crux of their concern was that such an enlargement of their numbers that a merger entailed would undermine the collegiality essential to maintaining the high quality of their work.[13] In the end, the practical arguments of provincial attorneys general about the inefficiencies of maintaining what in effect had become a three-tiered system of trial courts prevailed, and by 1992 the county and district courts had disappeared from the Canadian judicial scene.

The Canadian judicial system had evolved in ways unforeseen by the Fathers of Confederation. Most of Canada's adjudicative services were now provided by a two-tier system. But the two tiers were not the two levels of courts – superior and county or district courts – recognized in the founding constitution. The superior courts of the provinces with their federally appointed judiciary remained as the highest general jurisdiction courts, but under them there was now a much more extensive system of provincial courts staffed by a provincially appointed judiciary. In law these provincial courts were considered to be 'inferior courts,' even though the qualifications of their judges had become comparable to those of the superior court judiciary, and their adjudicative responsibilities had expanded to cover the bulk of criminal justice as well as civil matters of great social concern. By this time the same dualism was established in Yukon and the Northwest Territories, where residential territorial courts mirrored the provincial courts[14] and visiting justices from the provinces' superior courts provided higher court services.

Once the provincially appointed judiciary had acquired professional qualifications and adjudicative responsibilities commensurate with those of the federally appointed provincial judiciary, it became difficult to defend the distinction between the two groups of provincial judges as one between 'inferior court' judges and 'superior court' judges. The stage was now set for a struggle to unify Canada's trial courts.

Emergence of the Court Unification Issue

Initially it was legal academics and law reformers who questioned maintaining a two-tier system of trial courts. It did not seem to make any sense, for instance, to authorize a judge of the provincial court to conduct a judge-alone trial that could send a person to prison for life but to insist that only a federally appointed superior court judge could conduct a jury trial. Martin Friedland in a 1968 report written for the Ouimet Commission on Corrections recommended eliminating the distinction between inferior and superior judges and that 'all judicial officers should have concurrent jurisdiction to try all offences, with or without a jury, in a court perhaps called the criminal court for the particular province.'[15] In 1973, Darrel Roberts, in a report written for the Law Commission of Canada, came to the same conclusion as Friedland. 'Our whole criminal process,' wrote Roberts, 'is debased by the system of various grades of courts, when its most important court is looked upon as inferior and subordinate.'[16] Two years later, the Law Reform Commission published a country-wide study of family law litigation that highlighted the pernicious effects of divided jurisdiction between superior courts and ('inferior') family courts for the handling of family-related disputes.[17] For example, while only superior courts could issue divorce decrees and the settlement of family property, disputes arising from the enforcement of settlements would come before a family court judge, who had no power to adjust the settlement ordered by the higher court. Maintaining and coordinating two separate tiers of trial courts was adding considerably to the cost of administering justice within the province and was increasingly seen as an impediment to modernizing judicial administration.[18]

It is not surprising, then, that provincial governments soon joined the academics and law reformers in questioning the two-tier system. Besides the extra cost and inconvenience of the two-tier system, federal control over appointment of the senior provincial judiciary did not sit well with provincial governments in an era when 'province-building' had become a major force in the politics of the federation. Nowhere was this more evident than in Quebec, where the justice minister (in a federalist government), Jerome Choquette, issued a ringing denunciation of section 96 of the Constitution.[19] In the constitutional negotiations of 1978–9 the provinces pressed to have section 96 amended so that all aspects of family law could be dealt with by provincially appointed judges,[20] and in 1980 they raised the ante, with nine of the ten provinces calling for the termination of section 96 so that the provinces would have the power to appoint the judges of all provincial courts.[21]

The provinces' constitutional assault on section 96 came to nought as Pierre Trudeau was able to resist the provinces' agenda for constitutional reform and push through his own nation-building agenda. Not only were the provinces being rebuffed at the political level, but also in the judicial arena supreme court decisions were throwing up additional roadblocks to their court reform projects. In a series of cases in the early 1980s, the court used an expansive interpretation of the federal appointing power in section 96 to restrict provincial legislative power over the administration of justice in the province. A residential tenancy commission could not decide landlord and tenant disputes;[22] a professions tribunal could not hear appeals from professional discipline committees;[23] a provincial family court could deal with custody of children but not occupancy of the family home.[24] A core of inherent jurisdiction must be preserved for federally appointed superior court judges, otherwise, reasoned Justice Brian Dickson, 'what was conceived as a strong constitutional base of national unity, through a unitary judicial system, would be gravely undermined.'[25]

The climax came in 1983 when New Brunswick, one of several provinces seeking to unify criminal jurisdiction in a single court, persuaded the federal government to join it in asking the supreme court whether the federal Criminal Code could be amended so that a court staffed by provincially appointed judges could hear all criminal cases. The question was answered in the negative through an unsigned 'opinion of the Court,' which held that section 96 limited not only provincial jurisdiction over the administration of justice but federal legislative power as well. Here it was the protection of independence, which section 99 affords only superior court judges, that was the key rationale of the decision.

The *McEvoy* decision did not deflect provincial attorneys general from their efforts to establish a unified criminal court. By 1990 all of the provinces supported the principle of a unified provincial criminal court. But now these efforts assumed that the only way to do this constitutionally was to have provincially appointed judges 'elevated' to the superior court. A province that took this path to unification would have to hand over its judicial appointment responsibilities to Ottawa. Such a transfer of appointing power would be unattractive at any time, but it was doubly problematic in a context that found the provinces reforming their system of appointing provincial court judges much more thoroughly than the federal government was reforming its system of appointing superior court judges. While the provinces and territories were establishing true merit systems through the use of independent nominating committees or councils, the federal process of appointing section 96 judges remained mired in political patronage.[26]

While progress towards unifying criminal trial jurisdiction stalled in the 1990s, some progress was made in unifying family court jurisdiction, beginning with PEI and a few cities in the 1970s, and then spreading to other provinces, until there was some family court unification in every province except British Columbia and Quebec. These family court unification projects were achieved by the federal government making appointments to a special family law division of the provincial superior court. This approach to court unification caused tensions and political friction. It stalled in Ontario because of the superior court's resistance to the rigid specialization it introduces into the superior court, which has a long tradition of being a court of general jurisdiction. Provinces that had well-developed, highly professional, provincial family courts working in close collaboration with a network of social agencies were not about to scrap these institutions. This certainly has had much to do with the reluctance of British Columbia to become involved in family court unification at the superior court level. As for Quebec, packing up its own family and youth court and handing this jurisdiction over to Ottawa-appointed judges was unthinkable. By 1988, Quebec had consolidated its provincial courts and administrative tribunals into the Court of Quebec.[27] Any further unification of that province's courts would be done through the Court of Quebec structure.

By the end of the century, efforts to sort out the proper roles for the federally appointed and provincially appointed judiciaries had reached an unsatisfactory point. Provincial court judiciaries with qualifications at least commensurate with those of the superior court jurisdiction and adjudicative responsibilities of a very serious kind (particularly in the field of criminal justice) had outgrown their original status as 'inferior court' judges. In a seminal article published in 2000, Noel Lyon and Gerald Seniuk posed the question, 'If the Provincial Court is neither functionally an *inferior* nor constitutionally a *superior* court, then in which of these two categories should it belong?'[28] Lyon and Seniuk proposed that the time had come to address this question through a dialogue among 'the various groups responsible for maintaining confidence in the administration of justice.'[29] This proposal led to organizing the Conference on the Trial Courts of the Future, in Saskatoon in May 2002.

The conference was the first ever held in Canada 'on the evolving role of trial courts and how they serve the needs of Canadians, and to consider options and constraints for structural reform.'[30] The attendees included lawyers and citizens who use the courts, justice department officials from both levels of government, court administrators, provincial justice ministers, legal and social science academics, journalists, persons experienced in mediation and other forms of alternative dispute resolution, and judges, lots of them, from both the provincial and superior courts. It was, without a doubt, a gathering whose composition met the organizers' objective of bringing together a comprehensive assembly of persons to dialogue about the future of the country's trial courts – the judicial institutions in which Canadians are most likely to experience the administration of justice.

At the Saskatoon conference much of the discussion focused on the possibility of overcoming jurisdictional fragmentation and moving towards a system in which the responsibilities of the provincial and superior courts are based on functional considerations rather than on an outdated hierarchy of status.[31] At the time of the conference, Canada's first fully unified trial court, the Nunavut Court of Justice, had been in operation for more than two years.[32] It was clear that in designing a judicial system of this new territory it simply made no sense to have a two-tiered trial court. It was also clear that in Nunavut, locally based justices of the peace, many if not all of whom would be Inuit, would perform ancillary judicial services under the direction of Nunavut's superior court. Similarly, justices of the peace and Indigenous peace-keepers were an important feature of the House of Justice model an integrated judicial service presented by Saskatchewan's Chief Judge Gerry Seniuk and Professor John Borrows.[33] The House of Justice judiciary would be federally appointed superior court judges selected by federal-provincial nominating committees, an idea put forward many years earlier by Professor William Lederman.[34] Giving provincial representatives a strong role in selecting superior court judges was also central to the presentation of David Hancock, Alberta's minister of justice, who committed himself to working for the unification of trial courts in his province.[35] The presentation by Quebec Chief Judge Huguette St Louis, however, left no doubt that the completion of trial court integration in Quebec would be through expanding the jurisdiction of judges appointed by the province.[36]

The possibility of giving provincially appointed judges full criminal jurisdiction received some encouragement at the conference. In a carefully researched paper, Professor Patrick Healy advanced the view that the Supreme Court's 1983 *McEvoy* decision may no longer be good law.[37] The rationale of the court's decision limiting the jurisdiction of provincially appointed judges was that only federally appointed superior court judges enjoyed judicial independence. But since then, the Supreme Court itself in several decisions had recognized that the provincially appointed judiciary enjoys full constitutionally protected judicial independence. If Healy was correct, the federal Parliament could now fill the few gaps that existed in the criminal jurisdiction of provincial courts. Were Parliament to do this, it would most likely do so on a basis that left federally appointed judges a concurrent jurisdiction to try the most serious cases.

The Saskatoon conference also benefited from reports on trial court integration in England and the United States. For many years there has been a movement in both countries towards simplifying and integrating judicial structures. Two leading scholars and practitioners of court restructuring, Professor Ian Scott from England and Professor Clark Kelso of California, reported on these developments. Scott laid out the broad theoretical case for trial court integration.[38] Instead of trying to match a hierarchy of courts to a pyramid of cases, it makes much more sense to have a single institution whose judiciary can deliver a diverse range of adjudicative services. Though England has retained its different ranks of judges – high court judges ('officers'), circuit and district judges ('other ranks') and magistrates ('volunteers or reservists') – they are all centrally appointed and increasingly subject to a single system of court administration. Clark showed how the trial courts of the largest US state, California, had evolved over several decades from a highly fragmented two-tier system into a totally unified state-wide trial court performing the full range of judicial services in communities throughout the state.[39] The key political factor in this story was that unification, in its final stages, was led by the highest level, superior court judges.

The Roads Ahead

Unlike in Canada, court restructuring in England and within US states does not have to deal with the complexities of a federal state. That is the benefit of the US dual court system: each state is free to develop its own judicial system. This is not so in Canada, where the highest level of provincial judiciary is federally appointed and paid.

This difficulty that has its root in section 96 of the Constitution would be better handled if that lovely but scarce political commodity, cooperative federalism, were applied to the management of the judicial system. But alas, over the years there has been precious little cooperative federalism in this field. Even though its actions have a vital bearing on provincial courts, the federal government has never displayed any interest in or capacity for being a thoughtful and informed policy-making partner with the provinces in this area. This situation is unlikely to change until there is a strong political champion of judicial reform at the federal level.

This is not likely to happen under the Harper Conservative government. Harper's first justice minister, Vic Toews, was a former provincial attorney general (of Manitoba) who, as his party's justice critic, attacked the extent to which political patronage influences federal judicial appointments. In opposition he was receptive to the proposals of a special Justice Committee subcommittee to reform the federal system of appointing judges by strengthening the role of the advisory committees in that process.[40] The advisory committees in place since 1988 have included provincial appointees but have functioned simply as screening committees advising the government on whether candidates are 'highly qualified,' 'qualified,' or 'not qualified.' This left the government free to pass over candidates on the A list (i.e., persons considered highly qualified) to appoint political friends from the B list (i.e., persons considered merely qualified). It would not have been a big or, it seemed, an uncongenial step for Mr Toews to eliminate the B list and ask the advisory committees to supply him with short lists of the persons the committees considered most highly qualified for judicial service. Instead, Mr Toews did exactly the opposite and eliminated the A list! So now the government receives long lists of qualified candidates, undifferentiated into those who are outstanding and those who are not. To make matters worse, he and Mr Harper insisted that conservative-minded persons, in particular police officers, should be added to the committees.[41]

Reform of the federal judicial appointing system that turned federal-provincial advisory committees into real nominating bodies would make it much easier for provinces to merge their provincial courts into their superior courts. That option likely remains attractive to New Brunswick and smaller provinces that like the idea of Ottawa being responsible for remunerating the provincial judiciary. But Canada being Canada, a symmetrical federal outcome is not to be expected. Some provinces will not be induced – either by off-loading salary costs to Ottawa or by sharing in judicial selection – to have all their trial court judges federally appointed. That is clear in the case of Quebec. British Columbia and Alberta (despite its former attorney general's views) will also be reluctant to move in that direction. In Ontario, while strengthening the provincial role in judicial selection might facilitate more family court unification at the superior court level, its superior court judges' strong resistance to court unification is likely to bar any wholesale unification of the province's trial courts. However, in provinces that retain two-tier trial court systems, many, if not most, of the practical benefits of a more integrated court system can be realized by following the English model and bringing the management of the courts under a single administration. It is encouraging to note that Ontario's superior court judges support this kind of administrative integration.[42]

The federally appointed superior court judiciary in diverse ways will continue to be an integral part of the administration of justice in Canada's provinces and territories. For Canadians who care about the strength and integrity of their federation, it is to be hoped that the judicature sections of our founding Constitution will not be used to preserve a dysfunctional and illogical two-tier system of provincial trial courts. To reap the potential benefits of the integrated system that the Founding Fathers unwittingly bequeathed to the country will require some exceptional political and judicial leadership at both the federal and provincial levels.

NOTES

1 In 1982 the original Constitution was renamed *The Constitution Act, 1982*.
2 See John P. Dawson, *The Oracles of the Law* (Ann Arbor: University of Michigan Law School, 1968).
3 John T. Saywell, *The Lawmakers: Judicial Power and the Shaping of Canadian Federalism* (Toronto: University of Toronto Press, 2002), chap. 2.
4 On the colonial court system in Canada, see Bora Laskin, *The British Tradition in Canadian Law* (London: Stevens, 1969); and Peter H. Russell, *The Judiciary in Canada: The Third Branch of Government* (Toronto: McGraw-Hill/ Ryerson, 1987).
5 In 1960, section 99 was amended to provide for the mandatory retirement of Superior Court judges at age seventy-five.
6 See, for instance, the speech of John Rose, *Parliamentary Debates on the Subject of the Confederation of the British North American Provinces*, 1865, 387.
7 This is a key point in the speech of Hector Langevin, who gave the only sustained defence of federal control over the appointment of provincial judges. Ibid., 387–8.
8 For an account of the development of provincial courts of appeal, see Peter H. Russell, *The Judiciary in Canada: The Third Branch of Government* (Toronto: McGraw-Hill Ryerson, 1987), chap. 12.
9 See, Peter H. Russell, *The Supreme Court of Canada as a Bilingual and Bicultural Institution* (Ottawa: Queen's Printer, 1969), 5.
10 See Ian Bushnell, *The Federal Court of Canada: A History, 1875–1992* (Toronto: University of Toronto Press, 1997).
11 Russell, *The Judiciary in Canada*, 208–10.
12 In BC, this court is called the Supreme Court of British Columbia, even though the British Columbia Court of Appeals is the province's highest court.
13 For a discussion of the debate over merger of the section 96 courts, see Russell, *The Judiciary in Canada*, 268–73.
14 Except that the Territorial Courts had to be established by federal legislation because the federal Parliament has a plenary legislative authority over the territories.

15 Martin Friedland, 'The Provincial Court and the Criminal Law, *Criminal Law Quarterly* 48 (2004): 19. In this article Martin revisits his report to the Ouimet Commission and his 1968 article, 'Magistrates' Courts: Functioning and Facilities,' *Criminal Law Quarterly* 11 (1968): 52–74.
16 Quoted in Russell, *The Judiciary in Canada*, 216.
17 Law Reform Commission of Canada, *Working Paper No. 1, The Family Court* (Ottawa: Ministry of Supply and Services, 1975).
18 See Perry S. Millar and Carl Baar, *Judicial Administration in Canada* (Montreal and Kingston: McGill-Queen's University Press, 1981), chap. 3.
19 Jerome Choquette, *Justice Today* (Quebec: Gouvernement de Quebec, 1975).
20 Roy Romanow, John Whyte, and Howard Leeson, *Canada Not Withstanding: The Making of the Constitution 1976–1982* (Toronto: Carswell/Methuen, 1984), 39.
21 Russell, *The Judiciary in Canada*, 55.
22 *Re Residential Tenancies Act*, (1981) 1 S.C.R. 714.
23 *Crevier v. A.G. Quebec*, (1981) 2 S.C.R. 230.
24 *B.C. Family Relations Act Reference*, (1982) 1 S.C.R. 62.
25 *Re Residential Tenancies Act*, at 723.
26 See Peter H. Russell and Jacob S. Zeigel, 'Federal Judicial Appointments: An Appraisal of the First Mulroney Government's Appointments,' *University of Toronto Law Journal* 41 (1991): 4–37.
27 Huguette St-Louis, 'Reform of the Trial Courts on Quebec,' in *Canada's Trial Courts: One Tier or Two?* ed. Peter H. Russell (Toronto: University of Toronto Press, 2007), 123–33.
28 Gerald T.G. Seniuk and Noel Lyon, 'The Supreme Court of Canada and the Provincial Court of Canada,' *Canadian Bar Review* 79 (2000): 80.
29 Ibid.
30 Lorne Calvert, 'A Message from the Premier of Saskatchewan,' Trial Court of the Future Proceedings, Saskatoon, 2002.
31 A number of the papers presented at the conference are included in Russell, ed., *Canada's Trial Courts: Two Tiers or One?* Much of the material in this chapter is based on my introduction and conclusion, 3–34, 265–82.
32 Nora Sanders, 'Trial Court Unification in Nunavut,' in *Canada's Trial Courts: Two Tiers or One?* 144–51.
33 Gerald Seniuk and John Borrows, 'The House of Justice: A Single Trial Court,' in *Canada's Trial Courts: One Tier or Two?* 163–80.
34 W.R. Lederman, 'Current Proposals for Reform of the Supreme Court of Canada,' *Canadian Bar Review* 57 (1979): 687.
35 David Hancock, 'Reforming Alberta's Trial Courts,' in *Canada's Trial Courts: Two Tiers or One?* 152–62.

36 Huguette St Louis, 'Reform of Trial Courts in Quebec,' in *Canada's Trial Courts: Two Tiers or One?* 123–33.

37 'Constitutional Limitations upon the Allocation of Trial Jurisdiction to the Superior and Provincial Courts in Criminal Matters,' in *Canada's Trial Courts: Two Tiers or Two?* 85–122. A fuller version of this paper can be found in *Criminal Law Quarterly* 48 (2004): 31–76.

38 Ian Scott, 'Trial Court Integration in England,' in *Canada's Trial Courts: Two Tiers or One?* 234–64.

39 Clark Kelso, 'The Dynamics of Trial Court Unification in California,' in *Canada's Trial Courts: Two Tiers?* 217–33.

40 House of Commons, 'Process for Appointment to the Federal Judiciary: Interim Report of the Standing Committee on Justice, Human Rights, Public Safety and Emergency Preparedness,' Ottawa, November 2005.

41 Peter H. Russell, 'An Error of Judgment,' *Globe & Mail*, 7 February 2007, A21.

42 See 'Report of the Ontario Superior Court of Justice,' in *Canada's Trial Courts: Two Tiers or One?*

Epilogue: Celebrating Jack

J.L. GRANATSTEIN

I first met Jack Saywell in September 1961 and promptly had him investigated by the Royal Canadian Mounted Police. As a graduate the previous May from the Royal Military College, I was on leave without pay from the Army to do a master of arts in history at the University of Toronto. One of my four courses was Saywell's political history seminar. What was I to write on? I had no idea, so I asked Saywell, who said that no one had looked at the Communist Party in the Second World War and the way it had jumped up and down, backwards and forwards, to follow Moscow's directives. Ever obedient, I saluted and agreed.

Within a week I had visited the Party headquarters on Cecil Street and begun the process of securing access to the pre-war and wartime files they still had. Then it suddenly occurred to me that I was a lieutenant, and it might not be a good idea to work on a subject that put me in constant proximity to Moscow's Canadian legions. It was 1961, after all, and the Cold War was at its most bitter. So I telephoned the intelligence officer at the Army's Central Command Headquarters in Oakville and, after a day or two, was told to call a certain officer of the RCMP in Toronto. 'Who gave you my name?' were the first words from the RCMP sergeant's mouth. I explained, he grumped, but then he promised to call me back.

Meanwhile I continued my reading for Saywell and my other courses. I waited on the Mounties' callback and, when it came a few days later, the sergeant told me the Party had checked me out – heaven help me if the Communists thought I was clean! – and so had the RCMP. The Mounties had also investigated Saywell and decided that he, too, was OK, not a 'pinko' like so many of those professors at the University of Toronto. As far as the Mounties were concerned, I could do the paper –

but I had to be debriefed after every visit to Cecil Street. Ouch. This was simply not on for a student struggling to keep up with a heavy load. I at once told the sergeant I was going to change my research topic.

The next day I went to see Saywell, told him what had happened, and apologized. No problem, he said, it wasn't the first time he had been investigated by the RCMP. Then I asked if I might switch topic. Could he suggest something else? He offered the Conservative Party in the Second World War, and I agreed. I have always been grateful to the Mounties, who indirectly kept me from being locked into the sectarian historical ghetto of the left, and grateful to Jack for steering me to a centrist political party, albeit one that has made paranoid politics its specialty then and since.

It is difficult not to overstate the impact Saywell made on me and my colleagues in his graduate class. He was young, just thirty-two in 1961, he radiated charisma, and he seemed to be hugely busy doing radio and television, writing articles and books, and delivering speeches. There was much gossip about his active social life in the pubs where we drank. And yet, despite his hectic professional and private schedule, he seemed to be available to see his students, never in a rush, and full of ideas, almost always good ones. His seminar too was superb. I had good historical training at RMC from some first-rate teachers, but I had never been in a seminar like Saywell's, where everyone did the reading, where ideas crackled, and where he led us to the endpoint he wanted each class to reach. I found it hugely stimulating and, if truth be told, very intimidating. He was the best teacher I had had and, for someone who had originally wanted to work on American history, he made the history of Canada seem fascinating.

But what I remember most about that graduate school year was that in April, Saywell took the class for a boozy lunch at Chez Paree, a good French restaurant on Bloor Street. This was where my family had gone for (infrequent) special occasions, so I was impressed right off the bat. Jack didn't blanch at the bill, and he talked to us as if we were friends, colleagues, co-workers. No other professor had done such a thing, and I swore that if I ever ended up teaching in a university, I would try to emulate Saywell's actions (in this respect, if not all!).

A few years later, I was on yet another leave without pay from the Army, doing my doctoral work at Duke University and, for some now unknowable reason, heading up the Graduate Students' Historical Society. We invited Saywell, who had only recently left Toronto to go to York University to become the dean of arts and science, to give a talk and flew him to Durham, North Carolina. I had publicized his subject as 'A Funny Thing Happened on the Way to Confederation,' but, as Jack told me in no uncertain terms, he had said 'the Centennial,' not 'Confederation,' which in 1964 or 1965 made logical sense, given that he wanted to speak about the rising political unrest in Quebec. No matter: none of the American students knew the difference between Confederation and the Centennial, and he was a big hit with his fluent, funny, pointed remarks. My wife Elaine still remembers that Saywell was to come for dinner at our apartment but, the post-lecture drinking never-ending, by the time we arrived the meal was completely spoiled. (I now know that Jack only likes well-done, indeed burnt, meat!)

In early 1966, still in the Army and posted at the Historical Section in Ottawa, I accepted a job at York. Edgar McInnis was chair of the History Department, but I had never met him and went through no interview process, so the job offer came from the dean, John Tupper Saywell. There was a tough negotiation on salary: his offer was for $7,800 but I insisted on $8,000, which the dean grudgingly conceded. By the time the contract came to me, the floor for assistant professors had been raised to $8,500. Ah, Jack, teaching the young sprats a hard lesson at the outset.

I received my PhD in June, left the military in July, and spent the next three decades teaching and writing at the Glendon campus at first and then, from 1968 on, at York's main campus. Part of the job always was watching Saywell – with admiration, fascination, amusement, and occasionally just a touch of horror.

John Saywell was born in Weyburn, Saskatchewan, on 3 April 1929, and lived at Mossbank, southwest of Regina. His father, who had served in the infantry during some of the Canadian Corps' heaviest fighting in France and Flanders, was a schoolteacher there. His mother, Vera Sayles, had taught during the Great War when male teachers were scarce. The family's genealogy could be traced – as Jack did in an exhaustive history written for his children and grandchildren – back some five hundred years to England and the Channel Islands, and there were links to both Major-General Sir Isaac Brock and Sir Charles Tupper.

The Saywells moved to the Lake Cowichan area of Vancouver Island in 1937, and it was there Jack and his younger brother were raised. He was a fine athlete, playing basketball and baseball, pitching his team to the provincial championship round three years in a row, a violinist, and a first-class student. During the Second World War, his father commanded No. 20 Company of the Pacific Coast Militia Rangers (PCMR), an army reserve scouting force, and Jack hung around the unit and also went on training exercises with a conscript battalion stationed in the area. He recalls accompanying PCMR soldiers who found what may have been Japanese camps hidden away in the interior (almost certainly his memory is embellishing the story) and has recollections of Japanese balloon-bombs set free in late 1944 and early 1945 on the prevailing winds and aimed at North America (this, at least, is true). His view of the war in the Pacific remained notably realistic.[1]

Jack went down-island to Victoria College, not yet a university, for two years, then to the University of British Columbia, from which he received his BA in history and political science in 1950. He thought of applying for entry to the Department of External Affairs, but Professor Fred Soward, likely impressed that Saywell had already published two articles in the *British Columbia Historical Quarterly*, persuaded him to stay at UBC to do an MA. He wrote his thesis on Canada and sanctions from the origins of the League of Nations to the Italo-Ethiopian War and, despite being challenged during his oral by S. Mack Eastman, who objected to his strong criticism of France's role, he did well. Encouraged to apply for graduate fellowships in the United States, he received offers from a number of good schools, including Brown and Northwestern, but he decided to accept an offer from Harvard University in 1951, considering it the leading institution in the world. Harvard offered him its best award, tuition, and a stipend sufficient to cover his rent; his father, though a poorly paid principal, offered to help, but that assistance was unneeded, even though Jack had married Pat Knudsen in 1950. She worked in Boston until they had their first child, Lynn, in 1952; they had three children in all before separating in 1968.

At Harvard, Saywell worked on modern British history, European expansion, and medieval Britain. There was no Canadian history taught at Harvard and, indeed, he recalls, there was almost not much Canadian history of consequence yet written. Saywell passed his general examinations in April 1953, earning David Owen's comment that his oral was a 'top-flight performance.' His dissertation, directed by Owen, was on 'The Office of Lieutenant-Governor.' Funded by New York's Social Science Research Council, Saywell's dissertation research took him to the Public Archives of Canada for long stretches, and there he met and became close friends with H. Blair Neatby. There were not many academic historians working in the Archives (then or later!), and the two friends collaborated on a 1956 article in the *Canadian Historical Review*, 'Chapleau and the Conservative Party in Quebec,' that won the University of Western Ontario prize for best article. Saywell's dissertation, mined for several articles, was accepted without the necessity of an oral defence in 1956 (and won Harvard's John Jay Prize) and published the next year to excellent reviews. This was political-constitutional history, the usual boring stuff, as present-day social historians would say, but in 1957 it was fresh and new and notable for the high quality of its prose.

Saywell took a job as a lecturer in history at the University of Toronto in 1954 at a salary of $2,400. Soon after he was offered a Social Science Research Council fellowship that would have paid half his salary and provided funding for research, but the department chair, Donald Creighton, would not permit him to accept. That upset Jack, but it did not stop him from taking on the editorship of the *Canadian Historical Review* in 1957, the year he became an associate professor, in an effort to liven up the journal by broadening its range of articles and reviews. He also began writing high school texts. The first, *The British Epic*, appeared in 1959, and he began a long collaboration with history teacher John Ricker, still his closest friend.[2] Together, and frequently with others in collaboration, they wrote a half-dozen more texts that educated a generation of Canadians. The royalties were always at least equal to his salary and frequently much greater, and Saywell began to buy art (Riopelle, Ferron, Town, Ronald, Bloore, Teitelbaum, Brittain, and Humphrey were among his favourites), drive a sports car, and live a very comfortable life. In 1960, as well, Saywell persuaded the University of Toronto Press to begin publishing a modern version of the *Canadian Annual Review*, and he would remain as editor for two decades and get two books on Quebec and Canada (1971 and 1977) out of his *CAR* work. In 1960, as well, the Champlain Society published his edited volume, *The Canadian Life of Lady Aberdeen*, a book whose superb introduction forced a reinterpretation of the politics of the 1890s.

At roughly the same time, Saywell was getting heavily involved with the media, fast becoming one of Canada's most recognized public intellectuals. He dressed well and spoke fluently and intelligently and, with either a cigarette or a pipe in hand, his face, wreathed in smoke, seemed to be everywhere. While he did write press articles and commentary on current politics, Saywell primarily established himself as a television historian. With Eric Koch and Vincent Tovell, he began to work on historical dramas for CBC Television. The first was a study of Lord Durham's Canada in three parts, with Jack appearing on-screen as an analyst. Then in 1962, he wrote most of another dramatization on the failed American attempt to take Canada in 1775 and one on the War of

1812. The technique employed was 'I was there,' with Saywell being the 'I' and explaining the background and consequences of the situations portrayed. As if that was not enough, in 1961, he travelled the country interviewing politicians and others for a four-part series 'Portrait of the Thirties' that ran on CBC. Focusing on premiers Mitch Hepburn, Maurice Duplessis, and 'Bible Bill' Aberhart, the interviews and photograph and archival research would be useful when he wrote his biography of Hepburn thirty years later.

A few years on, Saywell did another series of TV programs on post-Confederation Canada, deliberately giving the historical material a contemporary focus. The same problems still persisted, he said, like regionalism, provincial self-interests, economic nationalism, and the question of American investment. The events and the characters on, say, the provincial conference of 1887 came to the screen through correspondents' reports from the field, not simply talking heads.

But what made Jack Saywell truly well known was the CBC public affairs program *The Way It Is*, where he was, as one writer described him, from 1967 to 1969 'the gentle host and, occasionally, the incisive interviewer ... the best-known and least-cloistered young university professor in the country.' The program, on air on Sunday nights, was must viewing for its coverage of public affairs, but many felt Saywell was underemployed as host. His 'tame use,' writer Margaret Penman tartly observed, 'is rather like using a Ferrari to deliver groceries.'[3] His university commitments limited his availability to the program to one day a week, not enough to let him do much more than be the public face of the program.

Those university commitments, and his university, had changed by the time he was a regular on *The Way It Is*. While he enjoyed teaching undergraduate and graduate students, loved research, and liked the university life, Saywell and other younger faculty at Toronto's History Department found Creighton's iron rule oppressive and irksome. He, J.M.S. Careless, and Jim Conacher used to complain that future chairs had to be elected by the faculty or at least after consultations, but Careless nonetheless accepted an appointment to succeed Creighton from Simcoe Hall, the administration's offices at the University of Toronto. Toronto's rigid curriculum also bothered Saywell, and he bemoaned the long meetings that squabbled over petty details instead of focusing on broad curricular questions.

Thus when the new York University began operations in 1960, first in a building at the University of Toronto and then at the Glendon campus at Bayview and Lawrence avenues, Saywell was very interested. When Murray Ross, the president, approached him in 1962 about coming to the new institution, Saywell was receptive. He was offered an associate professorship in history in 1963 with the promise that he would become a full professor and dean of arts and science the next year. It was the challenge of building a new university that attracted him, the chance to do education differently – better – than the University of Toronto.

At York, Saywell's task was to create the university. Everywhere institutions of higher education were expanding rapidly or being created. In Canada, there were the new campuses of the Université de Québec, Brock, Laurentian, Waterloo, Lakehead, Regina, Calgary, Simon Fraser, and others. All were seeking faculty, desperately trying to recruit in Canada, Britain, and the United States. Canada's graduate schools were small, and there were few PhDs available. Canadians might be repatriated from the United States or United Kingdom, but only the bravest wanted to leave established universities to risk a career at new and untried institutions.

But somehow Saywell tackled his tasks. He knew there simply were not enough Canadians to take the jobs, and he knew that someone, as he put it, 'had to teach the kids.' This would get him into difficulty when the Canadianization movement, sparked by Carleton University poet Robin Mathews, swept the country, but essentially Saywell was right: someone had to teach the kids. Mathews, in Jack's unchanging view, preferred unqualified Canadian instructors to well-qualified others. That made no sense.

Saywell did extraordinarily well in recruiting, finding leading scientists and others of high promise to establish York's science departments. He created a Faculty of Education that soon set the standard for the country and a Faculty of Fine Arts that became prominent almost from its creation. He revolutionized language teaching by turning it away from the teaching of foreign literatures by professors who couldn't speak the language. He also created fine Political Science and Psychology departments at York's big, main campus in Downsview in the far northwest of Toronto.

How did he do it? First, there was Saywell's superb judgment of academic worth and his ability to gauge 'promise,' often all there was to go on with newly minted PhDs. But Saywell's York also recruited in high style, many hiring committees meeting candidates at expensive restaurants in Toronto's Yorkville district. I recall one committee wining and dining a prospect (I think it was Gabriel Kolko) and, at the end of the

meal, Saywell ordering a Louis XIII cognac, even in the early 1970s cost-
ing $15 an ounce. Jack was 'a longtime stand-up drinker,' as one writer
said of him, but he usually preferred good wines or Scotch and didn't
like cognac. He was showing off here, but the rest of the committee all
said in unison, 'the same, please.' There were also heavily embroidered
stories, surely made up of whole cloth, of Jack and Willard Piepenburg,
his able associate dean, chartering aircraft to pursue candidates or of
Jack taking a whole floor at the Bayshore Inn in Vancouver so he could
recruit (and party) at the Learned Societies' meetings. It was an era
very different from the abstemious and politically correct present, but
it worked. York found the faculty it needed, and surprisingly many became academic stars.

His greatest achievement – this is a Festschrift for a historian, after
all – was the History Department which, like everything at York, had
three separate wings – York main, Glendon College, and Atkinson College for part-time students. Historians could also be found in the Social
Sciences and Humanities divisions, and York's gaggle of historians was
huge – and extraordinarily capable. Saywell recruited distinguished
scholars such as John Bosher, Ramsay Cook, Gabriel Kolko, and Jerome Chen, and hired young academics by the score: Chris Armstrong,
Peter Oliver, Viv Nelles, Michiel Horn, Tim LeGoff, Paul Lovejoy, Irv-
ing Abella, and Michael Kater, to name only a few; many had been his
students at Toronto. These and many others often proved to be superb
scholars, and York History by the end of the 1970s was simply the best
in the country. Those at 'the National University,' the University of Toronto, did not always agree, but they were wrong.

Jack had been approached to run for public office in the mid-1960s,
but he had refused. 'You have to give up your privacy,' he said once.
(His father had run for the Liberals on Vancouver Island in 1965, so he
knew whereof he spoke.) In 1968, however, he and Ramsay Cook were
instrumental in organizing academics and others to urge Pierre Elliott
Trudeau to run for Liberal leader. Saywell himself wrote the introduction to Trudeau's *Federalism and the French Canadians*, which appeared
before the Liberal convention and helped to bolster Trudeau's academic credentials with party delegates. Most had not read the book – and
many who had didn't agree – but that mattered little. Trudeau won and
would reshape Canada over the next decade and a half. In 1974, the
prime minister asked Saywell to run, but the negotiations, in the end,
went nowhere.

If there was a new regime in Ottawa, there would soon be change in

Downsview. By 1969, Murray Ross was coming to the end of his time as York University's president. Saywell was interested in the job, but he had opponents on the Board of Governors who were concerned that his flamboyant personal life was unsuited to the job of a university president. The Board's candidate of choice was James Gillies, the dean of the Faculty of Administrative Studies, and Saywell ran to stop him. He succeeded, and the choice ultimately fell on Queen's University economist David Slater in 1970. Within a very few years, Slater fell victim to the growing financial crisis that threatened to ruin the university. A difficult, confused struggle resulted, Saywell much involved in trying to right the sinking ship. The Board finally selected H. Ian Macdonald, the deputy treasurer of Ontario, as the university's president in 1974.

By this time, Saywell had left the dean's post and gone to Kenya. York had operated a continuing project in that East African nation in cooperation with the Canadian International Development Agency and, unless Saywell had been willing to take it over, CIDA intended to pull the plug. For the next five years, Jack spent at least half his time in Kenya, setting up shop in the Department of Finance in Nairobi with a group of experts devoted to analysing capital projects proposed by donor states. The other half of the program was sending young Kenyans to York for training and then to put them back into ministries in Nairobi. Saywell fired some foreign experts, hired others, and ensured that at York both mentors and a real academic program greeted the visiting Kenyans. The project's overall success was probably limited, but other universities and agencies sought Saywell's advice and assistance when they saw what he was doing.

Saywell probably had a greater and longer-lasting impact in Japan, where he went as a Canadian Studies professor in 1979. Although his predecessor, York historian Viv Nelles, had lived in Tsukuba, well outside Tokyo, Saywell insisted that the Department of External Affairs find him an apartment in the capital. In return, he worked closely with the embassy, speaking across Japan, trying to impose academic and research standards on grants controlled by the Japanese Association for Canadian Studies, and forging close links with Todai and Meiji University, Japan's preeminent academic institutions. His book, *How Are We Governed*, and his pamphlet, *Past and Present*, basic texts on Canadian politics and life, were translated into Japanese (and several other languages) and widely used. After his two years in Tokyo, Saywell returned to Japan at least once a year into the mid-1980s, and he worked as an adviser to Ontario's agent-general there as well.

His African and Japanese stints introduced him to different art forms. Jack was fascinated by African art and brought large quantities to Toronto and set up the Makonde Gallery on Lowther Avenue. It was not a success. He never tried to set up a gallery to sell Japanese art, but he did amass a good, small collection of *shunga*, the wonderful erotic block prints.

Between his African and Japanese stints, Jack had met Suzanne Firth at a Toronto party. A teacher of English as a Second Language and an adjunct professor in York's Faculty of Education, she accompanied him to Japan in 1979 and they married in Toronto in 1983. They live in Toronto's Danforth area.

After his work in Japan was concluded, Saywell was ready to go back to writing history. Research and writing is hard at the best of times; it is particularly difficult after years away from it. Few academic administrators seem able to resume their scholarly work, and certainly Jack struggled as he began to write a biography of Mitch Hepburn, the Ontario Liberal premier from 1934 to 1942.

Adding to his difficulties with Hepburn was that Saywell became graduate director in the History Department at York in 1987, a post he held until his retirement in 1999. He did this job superbly, engaging the students, helping them find the money they needed to finish their studies, and presiding over the comprehensive and oral examinations – and the subsequent parties. Saywell instituted an annual faculty-student softball game – which resulted in his breaking his arm in his last appearance as the faculty's ace pitcher – and he and Diane Jenner, his exceptionally able administrative assistant, were vital in giving the program its esprit. *Field of Pain*, the movie version of one of the softball games, should be suppressed!

But there was no doubt that this administrative post delayed Saywell's research and writing on Hepburn. Part of the difficulty was simply his historical rustiness, as I remember from reading some of Saywell's early drafts. He had acquired a computer early in the 1980s and taught himself to write on it. His typing skills were negligible (Saywell is the only person I have ever met whose typing is even worse than his illegible handwriting, and I regularly get emails from him signed 'Kack'). That made his life difficult enough, but for some inexplicable reason, he also decided that he did not need references in his first drafts. This meant that eventually he had to go back to insert his notes into the text, a Herculean chore that must have added at least six months to his labours. Moreover, his drafts were enormous (the published book, much trimmed, was still well over six hundred pages long) and over-researched. Hepburn had been a bean and onion farmer in the St Thomas area, for example, and one of Saywell's early drafts had some twenty pages on the history of the bean in southwestern Ontario. I was impressed at the depth of the research, but I have teased him unmercifully about his bean history ever since. As a Mackenzie King admirer, I also believed that Jack was too harsh on a prime minister who had to cope with Hepburn's erratic ways; even so, the biography did paint Hepburn as a reckless and destructive creature, a man who squandered his undoubted talents and left Ontario Liberalism in utter ruination for almost a half-century.

'Just Call Me Mitch': The Life of Mitchell F. Hepburn was published in 1991 and won the Floyd Chalmers Award for Ontario History. The reviews were glowing, and Jack proved again that he could still write as well as any historian in the nation. Former Ontario NDP leader Donald C. MacDonald called the biography 'superb,' and Sid Noel of the University of Western Ontario, while complaining that the tangled history of Ontario Hydro went on too long, commented gleefully on Hepburn's 'legendary appetite for liquor and women and the fast life' and noted that one of his mistresses called him 'Uncle Dudley.' Trust Jack to note that kind of detail.

By the 1990s, Saywell was teaching a graduate course on Canadian constitutional history. This was not a popular subject in the York History Department, its faculty and students increasingly focused on social history of the gender and cultural varieties. But Saywell drew good students and, as his interest in his subject increased, he set out to write a big book on the way judicial power had shaped – or, in Jack's uncommonly well-informed view, distorted – Canadian federalism. This was a massive project, forcing him to secure access to hitherto unused judicial records in Ottawa and to track down the papers and records of justices on the Judicial Committee of the Privy Council in Britain. As his research progressed, he became even more convinced that judicial philosophies and prejudices had shaped the way the law lords interpreted the British North America Act in place, one reviewer said, 'of a profound or searching comprehension of the BNA Act or the context of its creation.'[4] To Saywell, the JCPC interpretations were idiosyncratic and problematical in the way they stripped residual powers from the federal government and offered the provinces a sweeping interpretation of property and civil rights. Bluntly, forcefully, and with the stylistic grace that was always his hallmark, Saywell argued against the

JCPC's literalist interpretations and for the BNA Act as it was intended to be. His book, *The Lawmakers: Judicial Power and the Shaping of Canadian Federalism*, published in 2002 when Jack turned seventy-three, was undoubtedly his best and most significant historical work. It won the J.W. Dafoe Prize and was shortlisted for the Shaugnessy Cohen Prize for Political Writing.

By the time *The Lawmakers* appeared on the shelves, Saywell had retired from York University. The university had made him a university professor in 1980, and on his departure in 1998 York created a lecture series and the John Saywell Forest on campus in his honour. The lectures ran once only and, as Saywell says darkly, he expects the forest, never formally dedicated, soon will be paved over for use as a parking lot.

In other words, Saywell's extraordinary role in developing York University, in shaping its faculties and hiring the key members of its professoriate, is now being forgotten. In part this is inevitable, a consequence of the passage of time. But Jack Saywell deserves to be remembered and celebrated. He was a great teacher, a fine scholar, and a superb, charismatic administrator. Without his efforts, countless students would not have learned as much about their nation's history. Without him, York University could never have become what was for a time a path-breaking institution.

Now, Saywell has completed a memoir/history of his time as dean of the Faulty of Arts and Sciences. Others, Murray Ross for one, have written about this era. Saywell's account, a historian's researched account published by the University of Toronto Press in May 2008 as *Someone to Teach Them: York and the Great University Explosion*, tells the story from his unique perspective. At least I know what really happened in those years when I was a junior faculty member and the foundations were being laid for 'the house that Jack built.'

NOTES

1 While he was at the University of Toronto, Saywell and other professors met with a delegation of visiting Japanese. 'Their job was to sell Japan,' he said to a reporter writing a profile of him. 'I got impatient with a kind of gloss being put on the Second World War by some of the Japanese envoys. I said, "Are we talking about the same war?" I asked my colleagues, "How can you guys sit there and nod your heads? This was a deliberate war of

aggression with the worst atrocities." They found me indiscreet.' Margaret
Penman, 'This Is the Way It REALLY Is with John Saywell,' Toronto *Star
Weekly*, 8 June 1968.
2 Ricker told a journalist he had first met Saywell at a publisher's office to
talk about a Grade 9 text. 'Saywell was his usual offensive self. He said the
plans drawn up were awful. We fought through the meeting. He struck me
as an arrogant, offensive, discourteous little twerp. But I did think that what
he was saying ... was right.' Penman, *'This Is the Way.'*
3 Penman, 'This Is the Way.'
4 Jonathan Swaiger, review of *The Lawmakers: Judicial Power and the Shaping of
Canadian Federalism*, in *Canadian Historical Review* 85, no. 1 (2004): 119.

Contributors

Dimitry Anastakis is an associate professor of history at Trent University.

Paul Axelrod is professor and dean of education at York University.

Michael Behiels is professor of history and university research chair at the University of Ottawa.

R. Blake Brown is an assistant professor in the Department of History at St Mary's University.

P.E. Bryden is associate professor of history at the University of Victoria.

J.L. Granatstein is professor emeritus, York University, and former director and CEO of the Canadian War Museum.

T. Stephen Henderson is an assistant professor, Department of History, Acadia University.

Mark Kuhlberg teaches history at Laurentian University.

Bruce Muirhead is professor of history at University of Waterloo.

Richard A. Rajala is an associate professor of history at the University of Victoria.

Peter H. Russell is professor emeritus, Department of Political Science, University of Toronto.

Index

298   Index